THE
CASE
FOR A
CREATOR

Resources by Lee Strobel

The Case for Christ
The Case for Christ audio
The Case for Christ—Student Edition (with Jane Vogel)
The Case for Easter
The Case for Faith
The Case for Faith audio
The Case for Faith—Student Edition (with Jane Vogel)
God's Outrageous Claims
Inside the Mind of Unchurched Harry and Mary
Surviving a Spiritual Mismatch in Marriage (with Leslie Strobel)
Surviving a Spiritual Mismatch in Marriage audio
What Jesus Would Say

THE
CASE
FOR A
CREATOR

A Journalist Investigates Scientific
Evidence That Points Toward God

LEE STROBEL

ZONDERVAN™

GRAND RAPIDS, MICHIGAN 49530 USA

WILLOW

Willow Creek Resources

ZONDERVAN™

The Case for a Creator
Copyright © 2004 by Lee Strobel

This title is also available as a Zondervan ebook product.

This title is also available as a Zondervan audio product.

Requests for information should be addressed to:

Zondervan, *Grand Rapids, Michigan 49530*

ISBN 0-310-24144-8 (hardcover)

All Scripture quotations, unless otherwise indicated, are taken from the *Holy Bible: New International Version*®. NIV®. Copyright © 1973, 1978, 1984 by International Bible Society. Used by permission of Zondervan. All rights reserved.

The website addresses recommended throughout this book are offered as a resource to you. These websites are not intended in any way to be or imply an endorsement on the part of Zondervan, nor do we vouch for their content for the life of this book.

Interior design by Michelle Espinoza

Printed in the United States of America

CONTENTS

1

WHITE-COATED SCIENTISTS VERSUS BLACK-ROBED PREACHERS

The deadline was looming for the "Green Streak," the afternoon edition of the *Chicago Tribune*, and the frenzied atmosphere in the newsroom was carbonated with activity. Teletypes clattered behind Plexiglas partitions. Copy boys darted from desk to desk. Reporters hunched over their typewriters in intense concentration. Editors barked into telephones. On the wall, a huge clock counted down the minutes.

A copy boy hustled into the cavernous room and tossed three copies of the *Chicago Daily News*, hot off the presses, onto the middle of the city desk. Assistant city editors lunged at them and hungrily scanned the front page to see if the competition had beaten them on anything. One of them let out a grunt. In one motion, he ripped out an article and then pivoted, waving it in the face of a reporter who had made the mistake of hovering too closely.

"Recover this!" he demanded. Without looking at it, the reporter grabbed the scrap and headed for his desk to quickly make some phone calls so he could produce a similar story.

Reporters at City Hall, the Criminal Courts Building, the State of Illinois Building, and Police Headquarters were phoning assistant city editors to "dope" their stories. Once the reporters had provided a quick capsule of the situation, the assistants would cover their phone with a hand and ask their boss, the city editor, for a decision on how the article should be handled.

"The cops were chasing a car and it hit a bus," one of them called over to the city editor. "Five injured, none seriously."

"School bus?"

"City bus."

The city editor frowned. "Gimme a four-head," came the order—code for a three-paragraph story.

"Four head," the assistant repeated into the phone. He pushed a button to connect the reporter to a rewrite man, who would take down details on a typewriter and then craft the item in a matter of minutes.

The year was 1974. I was a rookie, just three months out of the University of Missouri's school of journalism. I had worked on smaller newspapers since I was fourteen, but this was the big leagues. I was already addicted to the adrenaline.

On that particular day, though, I felt more like a spectator than a participant. I strolled over to the city desk and unceremoniously dropped my story into the "in" basket. It was a meager offering—a one-paragraph "brief" about two pipe bombs exploding in the south suburbs. The item was destined for section three, page ten, in a journalistic trash heap called "metropolitan briefs." However, my fortunes were about to change.

Standing outside his glass-walled office, the assistant managing editor caught my attention. "C'mere," he called.

I walked over. "What's up?"

"Look at this," he said as he handed me a piece of wire copy. He didn't wait for me to read it before he started filling me in.

"Crazy stuff in West Virginia," he said. "People getting shot at, schools getting bombed—all because some hillbillies are mad about the textbooks being used in the schools."

"You're kidding," I said. "Good story."

My eyes scanned the brief Associated Press report. I quickly noticed that pastors were denouncing textbooks as being "anti-God" and that rallies were being held in churches. My stereotypes clicked in.

"Christians, huh?" I said. "So much for loving their neighbors. And not being judgmental."

He motioned for me to follow him over to a safe along the wall. He twirled the dial and opened it, reaching in to grab two packets of twenty-dollar bills.

"Get out to West Virginia and check it out," he said as he handed me the six hundred dollars of expense money. "Give me a story for the bulldog." He was referring to the first edition of next Sunday's paper. That didn't give me much time. It was already noon on Monday.

I started to walk away, but the editor grabbed my arm. "Look—be careful," he said.

I was oblivious. "What do you mean?"

He gestured toward the AP story I was clutching. "These hillbillies hate reporters," he said. "They've already beaten up two of them. Things are volatile. Be smart."

I couldn't tell if the emotional surge I felt was fear or exhilaration. In the end, it didn't really matter. I knew I had to do whatever it would take to get the story. But the irony wasn't lost on me: these people were followers of the guy who said, "Blessed are the peacemakers," and yet I was being warned to keep on guard to avoid getting roughed up.

"*Christians* . . . ," I muttered under my breath. Hadn't they heard, as one skeptic famously put it, that modern science had already dissolved Christianity in a vat of nitric acid?[1]

IS DARWIN RESPONSIBLE?

From the gleaming office buildings in downtown Charleston to the dreary backwood hamlets in surrounding Kanawha County, the situation was tense when I arrived the next day and began poking around for a story. Many parents were keeping their kids out of school; coal miners had walked off the job in wildcat strikes, threatening to cripple the local economy; empty school buses were being shot at; firebombs had been lobbed at some vacant classrooms; picketers were marching with signs saying, "Even Hillbillies Have Constitutional Rights." Violence had left two people seriously injured. Intimidation and threats were rampant.

The wire services could handle the day-to-day breaking developments in the crisis; I planned to write an overview article that explained the dynamics of the controversy. Working from my hotel room, I called for appointments with key figures in the conflict and then drove in my rental car from homes to restaurants to schools to offices in order to interview them. I quickly found that just mentioning the word "textbook" to anybody in these parts would instantly release a flood of vehement opinion as thick as the lush trees that carpet the Appalachian hillsides.

"The books bought for our school children would teach them to lose their love of God, to honor draft dodgers and revolutionaries, and to lose their respect for their parents," insisted the intense, dark-haired wife of a Baptist minister as I interviewed her on the front porch of her house. As a recently elected school board member, she was leading the charge against the textbooks.

A community activist was just as opinionated in the other direction. "For the first time," she told me, "these textbooks reflect real Americanism, and I think it's exciting. Americanism, to me, is listening to all kinds of voices, not just white, Anglo-Saxon Protestants."

The school superintendent, who had resigned at the height of the controversy, only shook his head in disdain when I asked him what he thought. "People around here are going flaky," he sighed. "Both poles are wrong."

Meanwhile, ninety-six thousand copies of three hundred different textbooks had been temporarily removed from classrooms and stored in cardboard cartons at a warehouse west of Charleston. They included Scott Foresman Co.'s *Galaxy* series; McDougal, Littel Co.'s *Man* series; Allyn & Bacon Inc.'s *Breakthrough* series; and such classics as *The Lord of the Flies*, *Of Human Bondage*, *Moby Dick*, *The Old Man and the Sea*, *Animal Farm*, and Plato's *Republic*.

What were people so angry about? Many said they were outraged at the "situational ethics" propounded in some of the books. One textbook included the story of a child cheating a merchant out of a penny. Students were asked, "Most people think that cheating is wrong. Do you think there is ever a time when it might be right? Tell when it is. Tell why you think it is right." Parents seized on this as undermining the Christian values they were attempting to inculcate into their children.

"We're trying to get our kids to do the right thing," the parent of an elementary student told me in obvious frustration. "Then these books come along and say that sometimes the wrong thing is the right thing. We just don't believe in that! The Ten Commandments are the Ten Commandments."

But there was also an undercurrent of something else: an inchoate fear of the future, of change, of new ideas, of cultural transformation. I could sense a simmering frustration in people over how modernity was eroding the foundation of their faith. "Many of the protesters," wrote the *Charleston Gazette*, "are demonstrating against a changing world."

This underlying concern was crystallized for me in a conversation with a local businessman over hamburgers at a Charleston diner. When I asked him why he was so enraged over the textbooks, he reached into his pocket and took out a newspaper clipping about the textbook imbroglio.

"Listen to what *Dynamics of Language* tells our kids," he said as he quoted an excerpt from the textbook: "Read the theory of divine origin and the story of the Tower of Babel as told in Genesis. Be prepared to explain one or more ways these stories could be interpreted."

He tossed the well-worn clipping on the table in disgust. "The *theory* of divine origin!" he declared. "The Word of God is *not* a theory. Take God out of creation and what's left? Evolution? Scientists want to teach our kids that divine origin is just a theory that stupid people believe but that evolution is a scientific fact. Well, it's not. And that's at the bottom of this."

I cocked my head. "Are you saying Charles Darwin is responsible for all of this?"

"Let me put it this way," he said. "If Darwin's right, we're just sophisticated monkeys. The Bible is wrong. There is no God. And without God, there's no right or wrong. We can just make up our morals as we go. The basis for all we believe is destroyed. And that's why this country is headed to hell in a handbasket. Is Darwin responsible? I'll say this: people have to choose between science and faith, between evolution and the Bible, between the Ten Commandments and make-'em-up-as-you-go ethics. We've made our choice—and we're not budging."

He took a swig of beer. "Have you seen the teacher's manual?" he asked. I shook my head. "It says students should compare the Bible story of Daniel in the Lion's Den to that myth about a lion. You know which one I'm talking about?"

"Androcles and the Lion?" I asked, referring to the Aesop fable about an escaped slave who removed a thorn from the paw of a lion he encountered in the woods. Later, the recaptured slave was to be eaten by a lion for the entertainment of the crowd at the Roman Coliseum, but it turned out to be the same lion he had befriended. Instead of eating him, the lion gently licked his hand, which impressed the emperor so much that the slave was set free.

"Yeah, that's the one," the businessman said as he wagged a french fry at me. "What does it tell our kids when they're supposed to compare that to the Bible? That the Bible is just a bunch of fairy tales? That it's all a myth? That you can interpret the Bible any way you darn well please, even if it rips the guts out of what it really says? We've got to put our foot down. I'm not going to let a bunch of eggheads destroy the faith of my children."

I felt like I was finally getting down to the root of the controversy. I scribbled down his words as well as I could. Part of me, though, wanted to debate him.

Didn't he know that evolution *is* a proven fact? Didn't he realize that in an age of science and technology that it's simply irrational to believe the ancient myths about God creating the world and shaping human beings in his own image? Did he really want his children clinging desperately to religious pap that is so clearly disproved by modern cosmology, astronomy, zoology, comparative anatomy, geology, paleontology, biology, genetics, and anthropology?

I was tempted to say, "Hey, what *is* the difference between Daniel in the Lion's Den and Androcles and the Lion? They're *both* fairy tales!" But I wasn't there to get into an argument. I was there to report the story—and what a bizarre story it was!

In the last part of the twentieth century, in an era when we had split the atom and put people on the moon and found fossils that prove evolution beyond all doubt, a bunch of religious zealots were tying a county into knots because they couldn't let go of religious folklore. It simply defied all reason.

I thought for a moment. "One more question," I said. "Do you ever have any doubts?"

He waved his hand as if to draw my attention to the universe. "Look at the world," he said. "God's fingerprints are all over it. I'm absolutely sure of that. How else do you explain nature and human beings? And God has told us how to live. If we ignore him—well, then the whole world's in for a whole lot of trouble."

I reached for the check. "Thanks for your opinions," I told him.

STANDING TRIAL IN WEST VIRGINIA

All of this was good stuff for my story, but I needed more. The leaders I had interviewed had all denounced the violence as being the unfortunate actions of a few hotheads. But to tell the whole story, I needed to see the underbelly of the controversy. I wanted to tap into the rage of those who chose violence over debate. My opportunity quickly came.

A rally, I heard, was being planned for Friday night over in the isolated, heavily wooded community of Campbell's Creek. Angry parents were expected to gather and vote on whether to continue to keep their kids out of school. Tempers were at a boiling point, and the word was that reporters were not welcome. It seemed that folks were incensed over the way some big newspapers had caricatured them as know-nothing hillbillies, so this was intended to be a private gathering of the faithful, where they could freely speak their minds.

This was my chance. I decided to infiltrate the rally to get an unvarnished look at what was really going on. At the time, it seemed like a good idea.

I rendezvoused with Charlie, a top-notch photojournalist dispatched by the *Tribune* to capture the textbook war on film. We decided that we would sneak into the rural school where hundreds of agitated protesters were expected to pack the bleachers. I'd scribble my notes surreptitiously; Charlie would see whether he could snap a few discreet photos. We figured if we could just blend into the crowd, we'd get away with it.

We figured wrong.

Our shiny new rental car stood in sharp contrast with the dusty pick-up trucks and well-used cars that were hastily left at all angles on the gravel parking lot. We tried to be as inconspicuous as possible as we walked nonchalantly beside the stragglers who were streaming toward the gymnasium. Charlie kept his Nikons hidden beneath his waist-length denim jacket, but there was no way he could conceal his long black hair.

At first, I thought we'd gotten away with it. We flowed with the crowd through a side door of the gym. Inside, the noise was deafening. Two large bleachers were packed with animated and agitated people who all seemed to be talking at once. Someone was setting up a small speaker on the floor of the gym. Charlie and I were milling around with people who were standing by the door, unable to find a seat. Nobody seemed to be paying any attention to us.

A beefy man in a white short-sleeve shirt and dark, narrow tie took the handheld microphone and blew into it to see if it was working. "Let me have your attention," he shouted over the din. "Let's get started."

People began to settle down. But as they did, I got the uncomfortable feeling that a lot of eyes were starting to bore in on us. "Wait a minute," the guy at the microphone said. "We've got some intruders here!" With that, he turned and glared at Charlie and me. People around us pivoted to confront the two of us. The room fell silent.

"C'mon out here!" the man demanded, gesturing for both of us to come onto the gym floor. "Who are you? You're not welcome here!"

With that, the crowd erupted into catcalls and jeers. Unsure what to do, Charlie and I stepped hesitantly toward the man with the microphone. It seemed like all of the anger in the room was suddenly focused on the two of us.

My first thought was that I didn't like becoming part of the story. My second thought was that this mob was going to throw us out of the place—and we were going to get roughed up along the way. My third thought was that nothing in journalism school had prepared me for this.

"What should we do with these two boys?" the man asked, baiting the crowd. Now the folks were really riled! I felt like I was being put on trial. When I used to hear the phrase *my knees were shaking*, I thought it was just a figure of speech. But my knees *were* shaking!

"Let's get rid of them!" he declared.

The door was blocked. There was nowhere to run. But just as some men were surging forward to grab us, a part-time truck driver, part-time preacher stepped up and wrested away the microphone. He raised his hand to stop them.

"Hold on!" he shouted. "Just a minute! Settle down!" Obviously, he was someone the crowd respected. The noise subsided. "Now listen to me," he continued. "I've seen this reporter around town the last few days, interviewing both sides of this thing. I think he wants to tell the story like it is. I think he wants to be fair. I say we give him a chance. I say we let him stay!"

The crowd was uncertain. There was some grumbling. The preacher turned toward me. "You're gonna be fair, aren't you?" he asked.

I nodded as reassuringly as I could.

The preacher turned to the crowd. "How else are we going to get our story out?" he asked. "Let's welcome these fellas and trust they're gonna do the right thing!"

That seemed to convince them. The mood quickly shifted. In fact, some people started applauding. Instead of throwing us out, someone ushered us to seats in the front row of the bleachers. Charlie took out his cameras and began snapping pictures. I took out my notebook and pen.

"WE'LL WIN—ONE WAY OR THE OTHER"

The preacher took control of the meeting. He turned to the crowd and held aloft a book titled *Facts about VD*. "This is gonna turn your stomachs, but this is the kind of book your children are reading!" he shouted in his Mayberry accent.

There were gasps. "Get those books out of the schools!" someone shouted. "Get 'em out!" several others echoed as if they were saying "amen" at a revival meeting.

The preacher began to pace back and forth, perspiration rings expanding on his white shirt, as he waved the book. "Y'all have got to force yourselves to look at these books so you can really understand what the issue is all about!" he declared. "Your children may be reading these books. This is not the way to teach our kids about sex—divorced from morality, divorced from God. And that's why we've got to continue keeping our kids out of school for another week to boycott these filthy, un-American, anti-religious books."

That catapulted the crowd into a clapping frenzy. Money poured into the Kentucky Fried Chicken buckets being passed around for donations to fight the battle.

The rally continued in that vein for another half an hour or so. At one point, the preacher's words were reminiscent of the businessman's comments earlier in the week. "We're not evolved from slime," he declared defiantly. "We're created in the image of God Almighty. And he's given us the best textbook in the world to tell us how to live!" The folks roared their approval.

"The only victory we'll accept is a total victory," he declared. "We'll win—one way or the other."

When he raised the issue of whether the school boycott should be continued through the coming week, the resounding response was yes. The goal of the rally accomplished, he issued a quick "God bless y'all," and the meeting was over.

Now I had all the color I needed for my story. I hustled back to my hotel and banged out a piece for Sunday's paper, which appeared on the front page under the headline, "Textbook Battle Rages in Bible Belt County." I followed that with an in-depth article that also ran on the front page the next day.[2]

Settling back into my seat as I flew back to Chicago, I reflected on the experience and concluded that I had fulfilled my promise to the preacher: I had been fair to both sides. My articles were balanced and responsible. But, frankly, it had been difficult.

Inside that gymnasium Friday night, I felt like I had stared unadorned Christianity in the face—and saw it for the dinosaur it was.

Why couldn't these people get their heads out of the sand and admit the obvious: science had put their God out of a job! White-coated scientists of the modern world had trumped the black-robed priests of medieval times. Darwin's theory of evolution—no, the absolute *fact* of evolution—meant that there is no universal morality decreed by a deity, only culturally conditioned values that vary from place to place and situation to situation.

I knew intuitively what prominent evolutionary biologist and historian William Provine of Cornell University would spell out explicitly in a debate years later. If Darwinism is true, he said, then there are five inescapable conclusions:

there's no evidence for God

there's no life after death

there's no absolute foundation for right and wrong

there's no ultimate meaning for life

people don't really have free will[3]

To me, the controversy in West Virginia was a symbolic last gasp of an archaic belief system hurtling toward oblivion. As more and more young people are taught the ironclad evidence for evolution, as they understand the impossibility of miracles, as they see how science is on the path to ultimately explaining everything in the universe, then belief in an invisible God, in angels and demons, in a long-ago rabbi who walked on water and multiplied fish and bread and returned from the dead, will fade into a fringe superstition confined only to dreary backwoods hamlets like Campbell's Creek, West Virginia.

As far as I was concerned, that day couldn't come soon enough.

2

THE IMAGES OF
EVOLUTION

*The problem is to get [people] to reject irrational and super-
natural explanations of the world, the demons that exist only
in their imaginations, and to accept a social and intellectual
apparatus, Science, as the only begetter of truth.*

Harvard geneticist Richard Lewontin[1]

*Science ... has become identified with a philosophy known as
materialism or scientific naturalism. This philosophy insists
that nature is all there is, or at least the only thing about which
we can have any knowledge. It follows that nature had to do
its own creating, and that the means of creation must not have
included any role for God.*

Evolution critic Phillip E. Johnson[2]

Rewind history to 1966. The big hit on the radio was Paul McCart-
ney crooning "Michelle." On a television show called *I Spy*, Bill
Cosby was becoming the first African-American to share the lead in
a dramatic series. Bread was nineteen cents a loaf; a new Ford Fair-
lane cost $1,600.

As a fourteen-year-old freshman at Prospect High School in north-
west suburban Chicago, I was sitting in a third-floor science classroom overlooking the asphalt parking lot, second row from the window,
third seat from the front, when I first heard the liberating information
that propelled me toward a life of atheism.

I already liked this introductory biology class. It fit well with my
logical way of looking at the world, an approach that was already tug-
ging me toward the evidence-oriented fields of journalism and law. I
was incurably curious, always after answers, constantly trying to figure out how things worked.

As a youngster, my parents once gave me an electric train for
Christmas. A short time later my dad discovered me in the garage,

repeatedly hurling the locomotive against the concrete floor in a futile attempt to crack it open. I didn't understand why he was so upset. All I was doing, I meekly explained, was trying to figure out what made it work.

That's why I liked science. Here the teacher actually encouraged me to cut open a frog to find out how it functioned. Science gave me an excuse to ask all the "why" questions that plagued me, to try genetic experiments by breeding fruit flies, and to peer inside plants to learn about how they reproduced. To me, science represented the empirical, the trustworthy, the hard facts, the experimentally proven. I tended to dismiss everything else as being mere opinion, conjecture, superstition—and mindless faith.

I would have resonated with what philosopher J. P. Moreland wrote years later, when he said that for many people the term *scientific* meant something was "good, rational, and modern," whereas something not scientific was old-fashioned and not worth the belief of thinking people.[3]

My trust in science had been shaped by growing up in post-Sputnik America, where science and technology had been exalted as holding the keys to the survival of our country. The Eisenhower administration had exhorted young people to pursue careers in science so America could catch up with—and surpass—our enemy, the Soviets, who had stunned the world in 1957 by launching the world's first artificial satellite into an elliptical orbit around Earth.

Later, as our nation began unraveling in the 1960s, when social conventions were being turned upside down, when relativism and situational ethics were starting to create a quicksand of morality, when one tradition after another was being upended, I saw science as remaining steady—a foundation, an anchor, always rock-solid in its methodology while at the same time constantly moving forward in a reflection of the American can-do spirit.

Put a man on the moon? Nobody doubted we would do it. New technology, from transistors to Teflon, kept making life in America better and better. Could a cure for cancer be far off?

It was no accident that my admiration for scientific thinking was developing at the same time that my confidence in God was waning. In Sunday school and confirmation classes during my junior high school years, my "why" questions weren't always welcomed. While many of the other students seemed to automatically accept the truth of the

Bible, I needed reasons for trusting it. But more often than not, my quest for answers was rebuffed. Instead, I was required to read, memorize, and regurgitate Bible verses and the writings of Martin Luther and other seemingly irrelevant theologians from the distant past.

Who cared what these long-dead zealots believed? I had no use for the "soft" issues of faith and spirituality; rather, I was gravitating toward the "hard" facts of science. As Eugenie Scott of the National Center for Science Education observed, "You can't put an omnipotent deity in a test tube."[4] If there wasn't any scientific or rational evidence for believing in such an entity, then I wasn't interested.

That's when, on that pivotal day in biology class in 1966, I began to learn about scientific discoveries that, to borrow the words of British zoologist Richard Dawkins, "made it possible to be an intellectually fulfilled atheist."[5]

THE IMAGES OF EVOLUTION

I tend to be a visual thinker. Images stick in my mind for long periods of time. When I think back to those days as a high school student, what I learned in the classroom and through my eager consumption of outside books can be summed up in a series of pictures.

Image #1: The Tubes, Flasks, and Electrodes of the Stanley Miller Experiment

This was the most powerful picture of all—the laboratory apparatus that Stanley Miller, then a graduate student at the University of Chicago, used in 1953 to artificially produce the building blocks of life. By reproducing the atmosphere of the primitive earth and then shooting electric sparks through it to simulate lightning, Miller managed to produce a red goo containing amino acids.

The moment I first learned of Miller's success, my mind flashed to the logical implication: if the origin of life can be explained solely through natural processes, then God was out of a job! After all, there was no need for a deity if living organisms could emerge by themselves out of the primordial soup and then develop naturally over the eons into more and more complex creatures—a scenario that was illustrated by the next image of evolution.

Image #2: Darwin's "Tree of Life"

The first time I read Charles Darwin's *The Origin of Species*, I was struck that there was only one illustration: a sketch in which he depicted the development of life as a tree, starting with an ancient ancestor at the bottom and then blossoming upward into limbs, branches, and twigs as life evolved with increasing diversity and complexity.

As a recent textbook explained, Darwinism teaches that all life forms are "related through descent from some unknown prototype that lived in the remote past."[6]

It seemed obvious to me that there's such a phenomenon as micro-evolution, or variation within different kinds of animals. I could see this illustrated in my own neighborhood, where we had dozens of different varieties of dogs. But I was captivated by the more ambitious claim of macroevolution—that natural selection acting on random variation can explain how primitive cells morphed over long periods of time into every species of creatures, including human beings. In other words, fish were transformed into amphibians, amphibians into reptiles, and reptiles into birds and mammals, with humans having the same ancestor as apes.

So while Miller seemed to establish that life could have arisen spontaneously in the chemical oceans of long-ago Earth, Darwin's theory accounted for how so many millions of species of organisms could slowly and gradually develop over huge expanses of time. Then came further confirmation of our common ancestry, illustrated by the next image.

Image #3: Ernst Haeckel's Drawings of Embryos

German biologist Ernst Haeckel, whose sketches of embryos could be found in virtually every evolution book I studied, provided even more evidence for all of life having the same ancient progenitor. By juxtaposing drawings of an embryonic fish, salamander, tortoise, chick, hog, calf, rabbit, and human, Haeckel graphically established that they all appeared strikingly similar in their earliest stages of development. It was only later that they became distinctly different.

As my eyes scanned the top row of Haeckel's drawings, representing the early stage of embryonic development, I was stunned by how these vertebrates—which would eventually grow to become so radically different from each other—were virtually indistinguishable.

Who could tell them apart? The human embryo could just as easily have been any one of the others. Obviously, Darwin was right when he said "we ought to frankly admit" universal common ancestry. And certainly the inexorable progression toward ever-increasing complexity could be seen in the next image.

Image #4: The Missing Link

The fossil is so astounding that one paleontologist called it "a holy relic of the past that has become a powerful symbol of the evolutionary process itself."[7] It's the most famous fossil in the world: the *archaeopteryx*, or "ancient wing," a creature dating back 150 million years. With the wings, feathers, and wishbone of a bird, but with a lizard-like tail and claws on its wings, it was hailed as the missing link between reptiles and modern birds.

One look at a picture of that fossil chased away any misgivings about whether the fossil record supported Darwin's theory. Here was a half-bird, half-reptile—I needed to look no further to believe that paleontology backed up Darwin. Indeed, the *archaeopteryx*, having been discovered in Germany immediately after *The Origin of Species* was published, "helped enormously to establish the credibility of Darwinism and to discredit skeptics," Johnson said.[8]

These images were just the beginning of my education in evolution. By the time I had completed my study of the topic, I was thoroughly convinced that Darwin had explained away any need for God. And that's a phenomenon I have seen over and over again.

I've lost count of the number of spiritual skeptics who have told me that their seeds of doubt were planted in high school or college when they studied Darwinism. When I read in 2002 about an Eagle Scout being booted from his troop for refusing to pledge reverence to God, I wasn't surprise to find out he "has been an atheist since studying evolution in the ninth grade."[9]

As Oxford evolutionist Dawkins said: "The more you understand the significance of evolution, the more you are pushed away from an agnostic position and towards atheism."[10]

DARWIN VERSUS GOD

Not everyone, however, believes that Darwinian evolutionary theory and God are incompatible. There are some scientists and theologians who see no conflict between believing in the doctrines of Darwin and the doctrines of Christianity.

Nobel-winning biologist Christian de Duve insisted there's "no sense in which atheism is enforced or established by science,"[11] while biology professor Kenneth R. Miller of Brown University declared that evolution "is not anti-God."[12] Philosopher Michael Ruse, himself an ardent naturalist, answered the question, "Can a Darwinian be a Christian?" by declaring, "Absolutely!" In his view, "No sound argument has been mounted showing that Darwinism implies atheism."[13]

Biologist Jean Pond, who formerly taught at Whitworth College, proudly describes herself as "a scientist, an evolutionist, a great admirer of Charles Darwin, and a Christian."[14] She elaborated by saying: "Believing that evolution occurred—that humans and all other living things are related as part of creation's giant family tree, that it is possible that the first cell arose by the natural processes of chemical evolution—neither requires nor even promotes an atheistic worldview."[15]

Personally, however, I couldn't understand how the Darwinism I was taught left any meaningful role for God. I was told that the evolutionary process was by definition *undirected*—and to me, that automatically ruled out a supernatural deity who was pulling the strings behind the scene.

One recent textbook was very clear about this: "By coupling undirected, purposeless variation to the blind, uncaring process of natural selection, Darwin made theological or spiritual explanations of life processes superfluous."[16] Other textbooks affirm that evolution is "random and undirected" and "without either plan or purpose" and that "Darwin gave biology a sound scientific basis by attributing the diversity of life to natural causes rather than supernatural creation."[17]

If this is how scientists define Darwinism, then it seemed to me that God has been given his walking papers. To try to somehow salvage an obscure role for him appears pointless, which Cornell's William Provine readily concedes: "A widespread theological view now exists saying that God started off the world, props it up and works through laws of nature, very subtly, so subtly that its action is undetectable," he said. "But that kind of God is effectively no different to my mind than atheism."[18]

Certainly Christians would say that God is not a hidden and uninvolved deity who thoroughly conceals his activity, but rather that he has intervened in the world so much that the Bible says his qualities "have been clearly seen . . . from what has been made."[19] Cambridge-educated philosopher of science Stephen C. Meyer, director of the Center for Science and Culture at the Discovery Institute in Seattle, put it this way:

Many evolutionary biologists admit that science cannot categorically exclude the possibility that some kind of deity still might exist. Nor can they deny the possibility of a divine designer who so masks his creative activity in apparently natural processes as to escape scientific detection. Yet for most scientific materialists such an undetectable entity hardly seems worthy of consideration.[20]

Even so, Meyer stressed that "contemporary Darwinism does not envision a God-guided process of evolutionary change."[21] He cites a famous observation by the late evolutionary biologist George Gaylord Simpson that Darwinism teaches "man is the result of a purposeless and natural process that did not have him in mind."[22] The ramifications are unmistakable, according to Meyer: "To say that God guides an inherently unguided natural process, or that God designed a natural mechanism as a substitute for his design, is clearly contradictory."[23]

Nancy Pearcey, who has written extensively on science and faith, insists that "you can have God *or* natural selection, but not both."[24] She pointed out that Darwin himself recognized that the presence of an omnipotent deity would actually undermine his theory. "If we admit God into the process, Darwin argued, then God would ensure that only 'the right variations occurred . . . and natural selection would be superfluous.'"[25]

Law professor Phillip Johnson, author of the breakthrough critique of evolution *Darwin On Trial*, agrees that "the whole point of Darwinism is to show that there is no need for a supernatural creator, because nature can do the creating by itself."[26]

In fact, many of the evolutionists who have felt the sting of Johnson's criticism nevertheless find themselves in agreement with him on this particular matter. For example, evolutionary biologist Ernst Mayr emphasized that "the real core of Darwinism" is natural selection, which "permits the explanation of adaption . . . by natural means, instead of by divine intervention."[27]

Another leading evolutionist, Francisco Ayala, who was ordained a Dominican priest prior to his science career and yet refused in a recent interview to confirm whether he still believes in God,[28] said Darwin's "greatest accomplishment" was to show that "living beings can be explained as the result of a natural process, natural selection, without any need to resort to a Creator or other external agent."[29]

When an attorney asked the outspoken Provine whether there is "an intellectually honest Christian evolutionist position ... or do we simply have to check our brains at the church house door," Provine's answer was straightforward: "You indeed have to check your brains."[30] Apparently to him, the term "Christian evolutionist" is oxymoronic.

Pulitzer Prize–winning sociobiologist Edward O. Wilson was adamant on this issue. "If humankind evolved by Darwinian natural selection," he said, "genetic chance and environmental necessity, *not God*, made the species."[31] No ambiguity there.

Characteristically, *Time* magazine summed up the matter succinctly: "Charles Darwin didn't want to murder God, as he once put it. But he did."[32]

DARWIN'S UNIVERSAL ACID

I wasn't aware of these kind of observations when I was a student. I just knew intuitively that the theories of Darwin gave me an intellectual basis to reject the mythology of Christianity that my parents had tried to foist on me through my younger years.

At one point, I remember reading the *World Book Encyclopedia* that my parents had given me as a birthday present to answer the "why" questions with which I was always tormenting them. Reading selectively from the entry on evolution served to reinforce my sense that Christianity and Darwinism are incompatible.

"In the Bible, God is held to be the Creator, the Sustainer, and the Ultimate End of all things," the encyclopedia said. "Many Christians believe that it is impossible to reconcile this conviction with the idea that evolutionary development has been brought about by natural forces present in organic life."[33]

Everything fell into place for me. My assessment was that you didn't need a Creator if life can emerge unassisted from the primordial slime of the primitive earth, and you don't need God to create human beings in his image if we are merely the product of the impersonal forces of natural selection. In short, you don't need the Bible if you've got *The Origin of Species*.

I was experiencing on a personal level what philosopher Daniel Dennett has observed: Darwinism is a "universal acid" that "eats through just about every traditional concept and leaves in its wake a revolutionized worldview."[34]

My worldview was being revolutionized, all right, yet in my youthful optimism I wasn't ready to examine some of the disheartening implications of my new philosophy. I conveniently ignored the grim picture painted by British atheist Bertrand Russell, who wrote about how science had presented us with a world that was "purposeless" and "void of meaning."[35] He said:

> That man is the product of causes which had no prevision of the end they were achieving; that his origin, his growth, his hopes and fears, his loves and beliefs are but the outcome of accidental collocations of atoms; that no fire, no heroism, no intensity of thought and feeling, can preserve an individual life beyond the grave; that all the labors of the ages, all the devotion, all the inspiration, all the noonday brightness of human genius are destined to extinction ... that the whole temple of man's achievement must inevitably be buried—all these things, if not quite beyond dispute, are yet so nearly certain, that no philosophy which rejects them can hope to stand. Only within the scaffolding of these truths, only on the firm foundation of unyielding despair, can the soul's habitation henceforth be safely built.[36]

Rather than facing this "unyielding despair" that's implicit in a world without God, I reveled in my newly achieved freedom from God's moral strictures. For me, living without God meant living one hundred percent for myself. Freed from someday being held accountable for my actions, I felt unleashed to pursue personal happiness and pleasure at all costs.

The sexual revolution of the '60s and '70s was starting to dawn, and I was liberated to indulge as much as I wanted, without having to look over my shoulder at God's disapproving gaze. As a journalist, I was unshackled to compete without always having to abide by those pesky rules of ethics and morality. I would let nothing, and certainly nobody, stand between me and my ambitions.

Who cared if scientific materialism taught that there is nothing other than matter and therefore no person could possibly survive the grave? I was too young to trifle with the implications of that; instead, I pursued the kind of immortality I could attain by leaving my mark as a successful journalist, whose investigations and articles would spur new legislation and social reform. As for the finality of death—

well, I had plenty of time to ponder that later. There was too much living to do in the meantime.

So the seeds of my atheism were sown as a youngster when religious authorities seemed unwilling or unable to help me get answers to my questions about God. My disbelief flowered after discovering that Darwinism displaces the need for a deity. And my atheism came to full bloom when I studied Jesus in college and was told that no science-minded person could possibly believe what the New Testament says about him.

According to members of the left-wing Jesus Seminar, the same impulse that had given rise to experimental science, "which sought to put all knowledge to the test of close and repeated observation," also prompted their efforts to finally distinguish "the factual from the fictional" in Jesus' life. They concluded that in "this scientific age," modern thinkers can no longer believe that Jesus did or said much of what the Bible claims. As they put it:

> The Christ of creed and dogma, who had been firmly in place in the Middle Ages, can no longer command the assent of those who have seen the heavens through Galileo's telescope. The old deities and demons were swept from the skies by that remarkable glass. Copernicus, Kepler, and Galileo have dismantled the mythological abodes of the gods and Satan, and bequeathed us secular heavens.[37]

By the time I was halfway through college, my atheistic attitudes were so entrenched that I was becoming more and more impatient toward people of mindless faith, like those protesters I would later encounter in West Virginia. I couldn't fathom their stubborn reluctance to subject their outmoded beliefs to that "universal acid" of modern scientific thought.

I felt smugly arrogant toward them. Let them remain slaves to their wishful thinking about a heavenly home and to the straightjacket morality of their imaginary God. As for me, I would dispassionately follow the conclusions of the scientists and historians whose logical and consistent research has reduced the world to material processes only.

THE INVESTIGATION BEGINS

If I had stopped asking questions, that's where I would have remained. But with my background in journalism and law, the demanding of answers was woven into my nature. So five years after my adventure in West Virginia, when my wife Leslie announced that she had decided to become a follower of Jesus, it was understandable that the first words I uttered would be in the form of an inquiry.

It wasn't asked politely. Instead, it was spewed in a venomous and accusatory tone: *"What has gotten into you?"* I simply couldn't comprehend how such a rational person could buy into an irrational religious concoction of wishful thinking, make-believe, mythology, and legend.

In the ensuing months, however, as Leslie's character began to change, as her values underwent a transformation, as she became a more loving and caring and authentic person, I began asking the same question, only this time in a softer and more sincere tone of genuine wonderment: *"What has gotten into you?"* Something—or, as she would claim, Someone—was undeniably changing her for the better.

Clearly, I needed to investigate what was going on. And so I began asking more questions—a lot of them—about faith, God, and the Bible. I was determined to go wherever the answers would take me— even though, frankly, I wasn't quite prepared back then for where I would ultimately end up.

This multifaceted spiritual investigation lasted nearly two years. In my previous book, *The Case for Christ*, which retraced and expanded upon this journey, I discussed the answers I received from thirteen leading experts about the historical evidence for Jesus of Nazareth.[38] In my subsequent book, *The Case for Faith*, I pursued answers to the "Big Eight" questions about Christianity—the kind of issues that began troubling me even as a youngster but that nobody had been willing to answer.[39]

In those earlier books, however, I barely touched upon another important dimension to my investigation. Because science had played such an instrumental role in propelling me toward atheism, I also devoted a lot of time to posing questions about what the latest research says about God. With an open mind, I began asking:

- Are science and faith doomed to always be at war? Was I right to think that a science-minded individual must necessarily eschew religious beliefs? Or is there a fundamentally different way to view the relationship between the spiritual and the scientific?

- Does the latest scientific evidence tend to point toward or away from the existence of God?
- Are those images of evolution that spurred me to atheism still valid in light of the most recent discoveries in science?

When I first began exploring these issues in the early 1980s, I found that there was a sufficient amount of evidence to guide me to a confident conclusion. Much has changed since then, however. Science is always pressing relentlessly forward, and a lot more data and many more discoveries have been poured into the reservoir of scientific knowledge during the past twenty years.

All of which has prompted me to ask a new question: does this deeper and richer pool of contemporary scientific research contradict or affirm the conclusions I reached so many years ago? Put another way, in which direction—toward Darwin or God—is the current arrow of science now pointing?

"Science," said two-time Nobel Prize winner Linus Pauling, "is the search for the truth."[40] And that's what I decided to embark upon—a new journey of discovery that would both broaden and update the original investigation I conducted into science more than two decades ago.

My approach would be to cross-examine authorities in various scientific disciplines about the most current findings in their fields. In selecting these experts, I sought doctorate-level professors who have unquestioned expertise, are able to communicate in accessible language, and who refuse to limit themselves only to the politically correct world of naturalism or materialism. After all, it wouldn't make sense to rule out any hypothesis at the outset. I wanted the freedom to pursue *all* possibilities.

I would stand in the shoes of the skeptic, reading all sides of each topic and posing the toughest objections that have been raised. More importantly, I would ask the experts the kind of questions that personally plagued me when I was an atheist. In fact, perhaps these are the very same issues that have proven to be sticking points in your own spiritual journey. Maybe you too have wondered whether belief in a supernatural God is consistent with what science has uncovered about the natural world.

If so, I hope you'll join me in my investigation. Strip away your preconceptions as much as possible and keep an open mind as you eavesdrop on my conversations with these fascinating scientists and science-trained philosophers. At the end you can decide for yourself whether their answers and explanations stand up to scrutiny.

Let me caution you, though, that getting beyond our prejudices can be difficult. At least, it was for me. I once had a lot of motivation to stay on the atheistic path. I didn't want there to be a God who would hold me responsible for my immoral lifestyle. As the legal-affairs editor at the most powerful newspaper in the Midwest, I was used to pushing people around, not humbly submitting myself to some invisible spiritual authority.

I was trained not only to ask questions, however, but to go wherever the answers would take me. And I trust you have the same attitude. I hope you'll be willing to challenge what you may have been taught in a classroom some time back—information that might have been eclipsed by more recent discoveries.

Scientists themselves will tell you that this is entirely appropriate. "All scientific knowledge," said no less an authority than the National Academy of Sciences, "is, in principle, subject to change as new evidence becomes available."[41]

What does this new evidence show? Be prepared to be amazed— *even dazzled*—by the startling new narrative that science has been busy writing over the past few decades.

"The Old Story of Science is scientific materialism," wrote theoretical physicist George Stanciu and science philosopher Robert Augros. "It holds that only matter exists and that all things are explicable in terms of matter alone."[42] But, they said, in recent years "science has undergone a series of dramatic revolutions" that have "transformed the modern conception of man and his place in the world."[43]

This astounding "New Story of Science"—with its surprising plot twists and intriguing characters—unfolds in the coming pages, starting with an interview that rewrites the books that first led me into atheism.

DOUBTS ABOUT
DARWINISM

No educated person any longer questions the validity of the so-called theory of evolution, which we now know to be a simple fact.

Evolutionary biologist Ernst Mayr[1]

Scientists who utterly reject evolution may be one of our fastest-growing controversial minorities. . . . Many of the scientists supporting this position hold impressive credentials in science.

Larry Hatfield in *Science Digest*[2]

There were one hundred of them—biologists, chemists, zoologists, physicists, anthropologists, molecular and cell biologists, bioengineers, organic chemists, geologists, astrophysicists, and other scientists. Their doctorates came from such prestigious universities as Cambridge, Stanford, Cornell, Yale, Rutgers, Chicago, Princeton, Purdue, Duke, Michigan, Syracuse, Temple, and Berkeley.

They included professors from Yale Graduate School, the Massachusetts Institute of Technology, Tulane, Rice, Emory, George Mason, Lehigh, and the Universities of California, Washington, Texas, Florida, North Carolina, Wisconsin, Ohio, Colorado, Nebraska, Missouri, Iowa, Georgia, New Mexico, Utah, Pennsylvania, and elsewhere.

Among them was the director of the Center for Computational Quantum Chemistry and scientists at the Plasma Physics Lab at Princeton, the National Museum of Natural History at the Smithsonian Institute, the Los Alamos National Laboratory, and the Lawrence Livermore Laboratories.

And they wanted the world to know one thing: *they are skeptical.*

After spokespersons for the Public Broadcasting System's seven-part television series *Evolution* asserted that "all known scientific evidence supports [Darwinian] evolution" as does "virtually every reputable scientist in the world," these professors, laboratory researchers, and other scientists published a two-page advertisement in a national magazine under the banner: "A Scientific Dissent From Darwinism."

Their statement was direct and defiant. "We are skeptical of claims for the ability of random mutation and natural selection to account for the complexity of life," they said. "Careful examination of the evidence for Darwinian theory should be encouraged."[3]

These were not narrow-minded fundamentalists, backwoods West Virginia protesters, or rabid religious fanatics—just respected, world-class scientists like Nobel nominee Henry F. Schaefer, the third most-cited chemist in the world; James Tour of Rice University's Center for Nanoscale Science and Technology; and Fred Figworth, professor of cellular and molecular physiology at Yale Graduate School.

Together, despite the specter of professional persecution, they broached the politically incorrect opinion that the emperor of evolution has no clothes.

As a high school and university student studying evolution, I was never told that there were credible scientists who harbored significant skepticism toward Darwinian theory. I had been under the impression that it was only know-nothing pastors who objected to evolution on the grounds that it contradicted the Bible's claims. I wasn't aware that, according to historian Peter Bowler, substantive scientific critiques of natural selection started so early that by 1900 "its opponents were convinced it would never recover."[4]

Viewers of the popular 2001 PBS series weren't told that, either. In fact, its one-sided depiction of evolution spurred a backlash from many scientists. A detailed, 151-page critique claimed it "failed to present accurately and fairly the scientific problems with the evidence for Darwinian evolution" and even systematically ignored "disagreements among evolutionary biologists themselves."[5]

In my quest to determine if contemporary science points toward or away from God, I knew I had to first examine the claims of evolution in order to conclude once and for all whether Darwinism creates a reasonable foundation for atheism. That's because if the materialism of Darwinian evolution is a fact, then the atheistic conclusions I reached as a student might still be valid. Only after resolving this issue could I move ahead to assessing whether there is persuasive affirmative evidence for a Creator.

So I decided to return, in effect, to my days as a student by reexamining those images of evolution—the Miller experiment, Darwin's tree of life, Haeckel's embryos, and the *archaeopteryx* missing link—

which had convinced me that undirected and purposeless evolutionary processes accounted for the origin and complexity of life.

Those symbols are hardly outdated. In fact, to this day those very same icons are still featured in many biology textbooks and are being seared into the minds of students around the country. But are they accurate in what they convey? What do they *really* tell us about the trustworthiness of Darwinism?

I was thinking about this late one night while I was hunched over my computer keyboard, surfing the Internet for airline tickets. Leslie strolled into my office and peered over my shoulder.

"Where are you headed?" she asked.

"Seattle," I replied. I swiveled in my chair to face her. "There's a scientist up there who can make sense of those images of evolution that influenced me. I think I can relate to him."

"What do you mean?"

"Well," I said, "he studied evolution as a college student—and guess what happened?"

Leslie looked puzzled. "What?" she asked.

"He became an atheist."

INTERVIEW #1: JONATHAN WELLS, PHD, PHD

Science classes weren't heavily steeped in Darwinism when Jonathan Wells was a high school student in the late 1950s, but when he began studying geology at Princeton University, he found that everything was viewed through evolutionary lenses. Though he had grown up in the Presbyterian church, by the time Wells was halfway through college he considered himself to be an atheist.

"Was your atheism influenced by the Darwinian paradigm?" I asked.

"Oh, absolutely," he said. "The evolutionary story simply replaced the religious imagery I had grown up with. I didn't need the spiritual anymore—except this vague, Gandhian, search-for-truth feeling I had."

I was sitting with Wells in an office at the Discovery Institute, located on the fourth floor of an obscure office building in downtown Seattle. Wells serves as a senior fellow with the Institute's Center for Science and Culture, an organization that neatly blends his dual passions for both hard science and the issue of science's influence on the broader society.

His undergraduate degree from the University of California at Berkeley was in geology and physics, with a minor in biology. At Yale Graduate School, where he earned a doctorate in religious studies, Wells specialized in the nineteenth-century controversies surrounding Darwin. His book, *Charles Hodge's Critique of Darwinism*, was published in 1988.[6]

In 1994, Wells received a doctorate in molecular and cell biology from Berkeley, where he focused primarily on vertebrate embryology and evolution. He later worked at Berkeley as a post-doctorate research biologist. Wells has written on the scientific and cultural aspects of evolution in such journals as *Origins & Design*, *The Scientist*, *Touchstone*, *The American Biology Teacher*, and *Rhetoric and Public Affairs*, while his technical articles—with such scintillating titles as "Microtubule-mediated transport of organelles and localization of beta-catenin to the future dorsal side of Xenopus eggs"—have appeared in *Proceedings of the National Academy of Sciences USA*, *Development*, and *BioSystems*.

An inveterate iconoclast, Wells doesn't shy away from controversy. After a two-year stint in the Army, he became an antiwar activist at Berkeley and ended up doing jail time for refusing to go to Vietnam as a reservist. While later living a Thoreau-like existence in a remote California cabin, he became enthralled by the grandeur of creation and gained new confidence that God was behind it. His spiritual interest rejuvenated, Wells explored numerous religious alternatives, visiting gurus, preachers, and swamis.[7]

I hadn't come to Seattle, however, to seek spiritual wisdom from Wells. Instead, I sought him out because of his scientific expertise— and because he authored a book whose title intrigued me the moment I first saw it.

Icons of Evolution, which was published in 2000, takes a clear-headed, scientific look at the very same visual images that had convinced me of the truth of Darwinian evolution. The Miller experiment, Darwin's tree of life, Haeckel's embryos, the *archaeopteryx* missing link—they were all there, along with several other symbols of evolution. The book's subtitle especially piqued my curiosity: *Why Much of What We Teach about Evolution Is Wrong*.[8]

Here was my chance to put these images—and the broader question of Darwinism's overall reliability—to the test. I eased into a comfortable chair that squarely faced the bearded and bespectacled Wells, who was sitting behind a wooden desk. He was casually dressed in a striped, short-sleeve shirt. While soft-spoken and mild-mannered as we chatted informally before our interview, he would quickly become animated as we began delving into his hot-button topic of evolutionary theory.

I flipped through my yellow legal pad to find a fresh page and took a pen in hand. More than thirty-five years after these icons of evolution led me on a journey into naturalism and atheism, I was anxious to get the real story.[9]

INVESTIGATING THE ICONS

Starting at the beginning, I briefly recounted for Wells how the four images of evolution had influenced my slide into atheism. In a subtle expression of empathy, he would nod almost imperceptibly as I talked, as if to reassure me that he understood what I had gone through. At the conclusion of my story, I gestured toward a copy of his book that was on the desk.

"You included all four of those symbols in your book, along with several others," I said, "and you called them 'icons of evolution.' Why did you use that term?"

Wells leaned forward, putting his elbows on the desk. "Because if you ask almost any scientist to describe the evidence for Darwinism, time after time they give these same examples," he said. "They're in our textbooks. They're what we teach our students. For many scientists, they *are* the evidence for evolution."

"What are the other icons?"

"In addition to the four that influenced you, there is the similarity of bone structures in a bat's wing, a porpoise's flipper, a horse's leg, and a human hand. This is touted as evidence of their origin in a common ancestor. Then there are the pictures in textbooks of peppered moths on tree trunks, showing how camouflage and predatory birds result in natural selection. Of course, there are Darwin's finches—the Galapagos Island birds that are also used to support natural selection. Probably the most famous icon, though, is the drawing we see parodied in so many cartoons—the march of ape-like creatures as they slowly evolve into human beings, which suggests that we're merely animals that evolved by purposeless natural causes."

I paused for a moment while I took some notes. "Before we go any further," I said, "let's get our definitions straight. When some people say 'evolution,' they mean merely that there has been change over time. But that's not an accurate description, is it?"

"Absolutely not," Wells replied. "If that's all there was to Darwinism, then there wouldn't be any controversy, because we all agree there has been biological change over time. Others define evolution as just being 'descent with modification.' But again, everyone agrees that all organisms within a single species are related through descent with modification. This occurs in the ordinary course of biological reproduction.

"Darwinism claims much more than that—it's the theory that *all* living creatures are modified descendents of a common ancestor that lived long ago. You and I, for example, are descendants of ape-like ancestors—in fact, we share a common ancestor with fruit flies. Darwinism claims that every new species that has ever appeared can be explained by descent with modification. Neo-Darwinism claims these modifications are the result of natural selection acting on random genetic mutations."[10]

"If these icons are the illustrations most cited as evidence of evolution, then I can see why they're important," I said. "What did you find as you examined them one by one?"

Wells didn't hesitate. "That they're either false or misleading," he replied.

"False or misleading?" I echoed. "Wait a second—are you saying my science teacher was lying to me? That's a pretty outrageous charge!"

Wells shook his head. "No, I'm not saying that. He probably believed in the icons too. I'm sure he wasn't even aware of the way they misrepresent the evidence. But the end result is the same— much of what science teachers have been telling students is simply wrong. A lot of what you personally were told about the icons, for instance, is probably false."

I considered the implications for a moment. "Okay, let me follow your logic," I said. "If these icons are cited by scientists so often because they're among the best evidence for Darwinism—"

"—And if they're either false or misleading," he said, picking up my thought, "then what does that tell us about evolutionary theory? That's the point. The question I'm raising is whether all of this is really science—or is it actually a kind of mythology?"

That's the very question I wanted to pursue. I decided that my approach would be to ask Wells for the straight story on each of the icons that especially influenced me. I started with the one that had the biggest impact: the picture of the tubes, flasks, and electrodes of Stanley Miller's 1953 experiment in which he shot electricity through an atmosphere like the one on the primitive earth, creating amino acids—the building blocks of life.

The clear implication—that life could be created naturalistically, without the intervention of a Creator—had been largely responsible for untethering me from my need for God.

IMAGE #1: THE MILLER EXPERIMENT

Obviously, the significance of Miller's experiment—which to this day is still featured in many biology textbooks—hinges on whether he used an atmosphere that accurately simulated the environment of the early earth. At the time, Miller was relying heavily on the atmospheric theories of his doctoral advisor, Nobel laureate Harold Urey.

"What's the best scientific assessment today?" I asked Wells. "Did Miller use the correct atmosphere or not?"

Wells leaned back in his chair. "Well, nobody knows for sure what the early atmosphere was like, but the consensus is that the atmosphere was not at all like the one Miller used," he began.

"Miller chose a hydrogen-rich mixture of methane, ammonia, and water vapor, which was consistent with what many scientists thought back then. But scientists don't believe that anymore. As a geophysicist with the Carnegie Institution said in the 1960s, 'What is the evidence for a primitive methane-ammonia atmosphere on earth? The answer is that there is *no* evidence for it, but much against it.'[11]

"By the mid-1970s, Belgian biochemist Marcel Florkin was declaring that the concept behind Miller's theory of the early atmosphere 'has been abandoned.'[12] Two of the leading origin-of-life researchers, Klaus Dose and Sidney Fox, confirmed that Miller had used the wrong gas mixture.[13] And *Science* magazine said in 1995 that experts now dismiss Miller's experiment because 'the early atmosphere looked nothing like the Miller-Urey simulation.'"[14]

I asked, "What's the current thinking of scientists concerning the gas content of the early earth?"

"The best hypothesis now is that there was very little hydrogen in the atmosphere because it would have escaped into space. Instead, the atmosphere probably consisted of carbon dioxide, nitrogen, and water vapor," Wells said. "So my gripe is that textbooks still present the Miller experiment as though it reflected the earth's early environment, when most geochemists since the 1960s would say it was totally unlike Miller's."

I asked the next logical question: "What happens if you replay the experiment using an accurate atmosphere?"

"I'll tell you this: you do not get amino acids, that's for sure," he replied. "Some textbooks fudge by saying, well, even if you use a realistic atmosphere, you still get organic molecules, as if that solves the problem."

Actually, that sounded promising. "*Organic* molecules?" I said. "I'm not a biochemist, but couldn't those be precursors to life?"

Wells recoiled. "That's what they sound like, but do you know what they are? Formaldehyde! Cyanide!" he declared, his voice rising for emphasis. "They may be organic molecules, but in my lab at Berkeley you couldn't even have a capped bottle of formaldehyde in the room, because the stuff is so toxic. You open the bottle and it fries proteins all over the place, just from the fumes. It kills embryos. The idea that using a realistic atmosphere gets you the first step in the origin of life is just laughable.

"Now, it's true that a good organic chemist can turn formaldehyde and cyanide into biological molecules. But to suggest that formaldehyde and cyanide give you the right substrate for the origin of life," he said, breaking into a chuckle, "Well, it's just a joke."

He let the point sink in before delivering the clincher. "Do you know what you get?" he asked. "Embalming fluid!"

PUTTING HUMPTY-DUMPTY TOGETHER

The march of science has clearly left Miller's experiment in the dust, even if some textbooks haven't yet noticed. But I wanted to press on and test other scenarios.

"Let's say that a scientist someday actually manages to produce amino acids from a realistic atmosphere of the early earth," I began. I could see Wells was ready to interrupt, so I preempted him: "Look, I understand it's not chemically possible, but let's say it was. Or let's say amino acids came to earth in a comet or some other way. My question is this: how far would that be from creating a living cell?"

"Oh," he said as he pounced on the question, "*Very* far. *Incredibly* far. That would be the first step in an extremely complicated process. You would have to get the right number of the right kinds of amino acids to link up to create a protein molecule—and that would still be a long way from a living cell. Then you'd need dozens of protein molecules, again in the right sequence, to create a living cell. The odds against this are astonishing. The gap between nonliving chemicals and even the most primitive living organism is absolutely tremendous."

I needed a visual picture to help me understand this. "Can you give me an illustration?" I asked.

"Let me describe it this way," he said. "Put a sterile, balanced salt solution in a test tube. Then put in a single living cell and poke a hole in it so that its contents leak into the solution. Now the test tube has all the molecules you would need to create a living cell, right? You would already have accomplished far more than what the Miller experiment ever could—you've got all the components you need for life."

I nodded. "That's right."

"The problem is you can't make a living cell," he said. "There's not even any point in trying. It would be like a physicist doing an experiment to see if he can get a rock to fall upwards all the way to the moon. No biologist in his right mind would think you can take a test tube with those molecules and turn them into a living cell."

"In other words," I said, "if you want to create life, on top of the challenge of somehow generating the cellular components out of nonliving chemicals, you would have an even bigger problem in trying to put the ingredients together in the right way."

"Exactly! In my illustration, the cell is dead, and you can't put Humpty-Dumpty back together again. So even if you could accomplish the thousands of steps between the amino acids in the Miller tar—which probably didn't exist in the real world anyway—and the components you need for a living cell—all the enzymes, the DNA, and so forth—you're still immeasurably far from life."

"But," I protested, "the first cell was probably a lot more primitive than even the simplest single-cell organism today."

"Granted," he said. "But my point remains the same—the problem of assembling the right parts in the right way at the right time and at the right place, while keeping out the wrong material, is simply insurmountable. Frankly, the idea that we're on the verge of explaining the origin of life naturalistically is just silly to me."

"There's no theory, then, that can account for how life could have naturally come together by itself without any direction or guidance?"

Wells stroked his salt-and-pepper beard. "The word 'theory' is very slippery," he replied. "I can make up a story, but it would be unsupported at every crucial step by any experimental evidence worth counting. I'm an experimentalist at heart. I'd want to see some evidence—and it's just not there.

"For instance, one popular theory was that RNA, a close relative of DNA, could have been a molecular cradle from which early cells developed. This 'RNA world' hypothesis was heralded as a great possibility for a while. But nobody could demonstrate how RNA could have formed before living cells were around to make it, or how it could have survived under the conditions on the early earth.

"Gerald Joyce, a biochemist at the Scripps Research Institute, ruled out the RNA-first theory very colorfully by saying, 'You have to build straw man upon straw man to get to the point where RNA is a viable first biomolecule.'[15]

"In short," declared Wells, "it was a dead end—as all other theories have been."

" . . . AND HENCE A MIRACLE"

In hindsight, my materialistic philosophy had been built on a foundation that history has subsequently dismantled piece by piece. Miller's experiment, once a great ally to my atheism, has been reduced to a mere scientific curiosity.

"What is the significance of his experiment today?" I asked Wells.

"To me, it has virtually no scientific significance," he replied. "It's historically interesting, because it convinced a lot of people through the years—yourself included—that life could have arisen spontaneously, a point which I believe is false. Does it have a place in a science textbook? Maybe as a footnote."

"But it's more than a footnote in most texts, right?"

"Unfortunately, yes," he said. "It's prominently featured in current textbooks, often with pictures. The most generous thing I can say is that it's misleading. It's wrong to even give the impression that science has empirically shown how life could have originated. Now, they may have a disclaimer buried in the text, saying the earth's atmosphere may not have been what Miller thought it was. But then they say that if a realistic environment is used, you still get organic molecules. To me, that's just as misleading."

I thought about a student who encounters the Miller experiment today. Would he gloss over in his mind the complexities of creating life? Would he understand the nuances of the Miller story, or would he hear the term "organic molecules" and conclude that scientists are on the verge of resolving the problem of how nonliving chemicals somehow became living cells? Would a young person looking for an excuse to escape the accountability of God cling to the false conclusion that the origin-of-life problem is only a minor obstacle in the relentless march of evolutionary theory?

"Why do you think the Miller experiment is still published in textbooks?" I asked.

Wells shrugged. "It's becoming clearer and clearer to me that this is materialistic philosophy masquerading as empirical science. The attitude is that life *had* to have developed this way because there's no other materialistic explanation. And if you try to invoke another explanation—for instance, intelligent design—then the evolutionists claim you're not a scientist."

Wells's explanation was consistent with another interview I had conducted with origin-of-life expert Walter Bradley, a former professor at Texas A&M University, who co-authored the landmark 1984 book *The Mystery of Life's Origin*.[16]

I questioned Bradley about the various theories advanced by scientists for how the first living cell could have been naturalistically generated—including random chance, chemical affinity, self-ordering tendencies, seeding from space, deep-sea ocean vents, and using clay to encourage prebiotic chemicals to assemble—and he demonstrated that not one of them can withstand scientific scrutiny.[17]

Many other scientists have reached that same conclusion. "Science doesn't have the slightest idea how life began," journalist Gregg Easterbrook wrote about the origin-of-life field. "No generally accepted theory exists, and the steps leading from a barren primordial world to the fragile chemistry of life seem imponderable."[18]

Bradley not only shares that view, but he said that the mind-boggling difficulties in bridging the yawning gap between nonlife and life mean that there may very well be no potential of ever finding a theory for how life could have arisen spontaneously. That's why he's convinced that the "absolutely overwhelming evidence" points toward an intelligence behind life's creation.

In fact, he said: "I think people who believe that life emerged naturalistically need to have a great deal more faith than people who reasonably infer that there's an Intelligent Designer."[19]

Even those who look askance at religious faith have been forced to conclude that the odds against the spontaneous creation of life are so absurdly high that there must be more to the creation story than mere materialistic processes. They can't help but invoke the only word that seems to realistically account for it all: *miracle*. It's a label many scientists are loathe to use but which the circumstances seem to demand.

For instance, one of the country's leading science journalists, John Horgan, who identifies himself as a "lapsed Catholic," conceded in 2002 that scientists have no idea how the universe was created or "how inanimate matter on our little planet coalesced into living creatures." Then came that word: "Science, you might say, has discovered that our existence is infinitely improbable, and hence a miracle."[20]

Even biochemist and spiritual skeptic Francis Crick, who shared the Nobel Prize for discovering the molecular structure of DNA, cautiously invoked the word a few years ago. "An honest man, armed with all the knowledge available to us now, could only state that in some sense, the origin of life appears at the moment to be almost a miracle, so many are the conditions which would have had to have been satisfied to get it going," he said.[21]

Others are more adamant. "If there isn't a natural explanation and there doesn't seem to be the potential of finding one, then I believe it's appropriate to look at a supernatural explanation," said Bradley. "I think that's the most reasonable inference based on the evidence."[22]

IMAGE #2: DARWIN'S TREE OF LIFE

It was time to advance to the next image of evolution. One of the most recognizable icons is the drawing Darwin sketched for *The Origin of Species* to illustrate his theory that all living creatures had a common ancestor and that natural selection drove the eventual development of the countless organisms we see in the modern world. To me, his sketch of the evolutionary tree encapsulated why Darwinian evolution was so compelling: it seemed to explain everything in natural history. The question, though, is whether the tree represents reality.

"We now have more than a century of fossil discoveries since Darwin drew his picture," I said to Wells. "Has this evolutionary tree held up?"

"Absolutely not," came his quick reply. "As an illustration of the fossil record, the Tree of Life is a dismal failure. But it *is* a good representation of Darwin's theory.

"You see, he believed that if a population was exposed to one set of conditions, and another part of the population experienced other conditions, then natural selection could modify the two populations in different ways. Over time, one species could produce several varieties, and if these varieties continued to diverge, they would eventually become separate species. That's why his drawing was in the pattern of a branching tree.

"A key aspect of his theory was that natural selection would act, in his own words, 'slowly by accumulating slight, successive, favorable variations' and that 'no great or sudden modifications' were possible."

I didn't want to miss the significance of what Wells was claiming. "You're saying that the tree of life illustrates Darwin's ideas but that his theory is not supported by the physical evidence scientists have found in fossils?"

"That's right," he continued. "In fact, Darwin knew the fossil record failed to support his tree. He acknowledged that major groups of animals—he calls them divisions, now they're called phyla—appear suddenly in the fossil record.[23] That's not what his theory predicts.

"His theory predicts a long history of gradual divergence from a common ancestor, with the differences slowly becoming bigger and bigger until you get the major differences we have now. The fossil evidence, even in his day, showed the opposite: the rapid appearance of phylum-level differences in what's called the 'Cambrian explosion.'

"Darwin believed that future fossil discoveries would vindicate his theory—but that hasn't happened. Actually, fossil discoveries over the last hundred and fifty years have turned his tree upside down by showing the Cambrian explosion was even more abrupt and extensive than scientists once thought."

That begged for further explanation. "Elaborate on the Cambrian explosion," I said.

"The Cambrian was a geological period that we think began a little more than 540 million years ago. The Cambrian explosion has been called the 'Biological Big Bang' because it gave rise to the sudden appearance of most of the major animal phyla that are still alive today, as well as some that are now extinct," Wells said.

"Here's what the record shows: there were some jellyfish, sponges, and worms prior to the Cambrian, although there's no evidence to support Darwin's theory of a long history of gradual divergence.

"Then at the beginning of the Cambrian—*boom!*—all of a sudden, we see representatives of the arthropods, modern representatives of which are insects, crabs, and the like; echinoderms, which include modern starfish and sea urchins; chordates, which include modern vertebrates; and so forth. Mammals came later, but the chordates—the major group to which they belong—were right there at the beginning of the Cambrian.

"This is absolutely contrary to Darwin's Tree of Life. These animals, which are so fundamentally different in their body plans, appear fully developed, all of a sudden, in what paleontologists have called the single most spectacular phenomenon of the fossil record."

Spectacular, indeed. It was staggering! But I was having trouble thinking in vast geological terms, where words like "sudden" and "abrupt" have meanings quite different from how we might use them in everyday conversation. I needed more clarity.

"How suddenly did these animals come onto the scene?" I asked Wells. "Put it into context for me."

"Okay," he said. His eyes swept the room, looking for a suitable illustration. Finding none, he turned to me and asked: "Are you a football fan?"

I felt trapped. I didn't want to admit that I've followed the hapless Chicago Bears ever since I was a teenager.[24] After all, my credibility was at stake! So I kept my answer vague: "Uh, yeah, I like the game."

"Okay," he said, "imagine yourself on one goal line of a football field. That line represents the first fossil, a microscopic, single-celled organism. Now start marching down the field. You pass the twenty-yard line, the forty-yard line, you pass midfield, and you're approaching the other goal line. All you've seen this entire time are these microscopic, single-celled organisms.

"You come to the sixteen-yard line on the far end of the field, and now you see these sponges and maybe some jellyfish and worms. Then—*boom!*—in the space of a single stride, all these other forms of animals suddenly appear. As one evolutionary scientist said, the major animal groups 'appear in the fossil record as Athena did from the head of Zeus—full blown and raring to go.'[25]

"Now, nobody can call that a branching tree! Some paleontologists, even though they may think Darwin's overall theory is correct, call it a lawn rather than a tree, because you have these separate blades of grass sprouting up. One paleontologist in China says it actually stands Darwin's tree on its head, because the major groups of animals—instead of coming last, at the top of the tree—come first, when animals make their first appearance.

"Either way, the result is the same: the Cambrian explosion has uprooted Darwin's tree."

THE HYPOTHESIS FAILS

There seemed, however, to be an easy comeback. "Maybe," I said, "Darwin was right after all—the fossil record is still incomplete. Who knows how natural history might be rewritten next week by a discovery that will be made in a fossil dig somewhere? Or perhaps," I speculated, "the organisms that existed prior to the Biological Big Bang were too small or their bodies were too soft to have left any trace in the fossil record."

Having raised those objections, I sat back in my chair. "Frankly, you can't prove otherwise," I said, my words almost a taunt.

Wells yielded a little. "As a scientist," he conceded, "I have to leave open the possibility that next year someone will discover a fossil bed in the Congo or somewhere that will suddenly fill in the gaps."

I nodded at his admission. However, he wasn't finished.

"But I sure don't think that's likely," he added. "It hasn't happened after all this time, and millions of fossils have already been dug up. There are certainly enough good sedimentary rocks from before the Cambrian era to have preserved ancestors if there were any. I have to agree with two experts in the field who said that the Cambrian explosion is 'too big to be masked by flaws in the fossil record.'[26]

"As for the pre-Cambrian fossils being too tiny or soft to be preserved—well, we have microfossils of bacteria in rocks dating back more than three billion years. And there have been soft-bodied organisms from before the Cambrian that have been found in Australia. In fact, scientists have found soft-bodied animals in the Cambrian explosion itself. So I don't think that's a very good explanation, either. Today evolutionists are turning to molecular evidence to try to show there was a common ancestor prior to the Cambrian."

"How does that work?" I asked.

"Not very well," he quipped. "But here's the process: you can't get molecular evidence from the fossils themselves; all of it comes from living organisms. You take a molecule that's basic to life—say, ribosomal RNA—and you examine it in a starfish, and then you study its equivalent in a snail, a worm, and a frog. You're looking for similarities. If you compare this one molecule across different categories of animal body plans and find similarities, and if you make the assumption that they came from a common ancestor, then you can construct a theoretical evolutionary tree.

"But there are too many problems with this. If you compare this molecular tree with a tree based on anatomy, you get a different tree. You can examine another molecule and come up with another tree altogether. In fact, if you give one molecule to two different laboratories, you can get two different trees. There's no consistency, including with the dating. It's all over the board. Based on all this, I think it's reasonable for me, as a scientist, to say that maybe we should question our assumption that this common ancestor exists."

Wells stopped for a moment. He apparently felt some elaboration was in order. "Of course, descent from a common ancestor is true at some levels," he continued. "Nobody denies that. For example, we can trace generations of fruit flies to a common ancestor. Within a single species, common ancestry has been observed directly. And it's possible that all the cats—tigers, lions, and so on—descended from a common ancestor. While that's not a fact, it might be a reasonable inference based on interbreeding.

"So as we go up these different levels in the taxonomic hierarchy—species, genus, family, order, class—common ancestry is certainly true at the species level, but is it true at higher levels? It becomes an increasingly uncertain inference the higher we go in the taxonomic hierarchy. When you get to the level of phyla, the major animal groups, it's a very, very shaky hypothesis. In fact, I would say it's disconfirmed. The evidence just doesn't support it."

The facts were compelling. Nobody can claim that Darwin's tree is an accurate description of what the fossil record has produced. Protestations from Darwinists aside, the evidence has failed to substantiate the predictions that Darwin made. Yet when I encountered the drawing as a student, I walked away with the conclusion that it illustrated the success of his revolutionary ideas.

"Is the drawing still featured in textbooks today?" I asked.

"Not only is it included in the textbooks, but it's called a fact," Wells replied, sounding genuinely astonished. "I don't mind that it's shown; I think it's a good illustration of an interesting theory. What I mind is when textbooks call it a fact that all animals share a common ancestor. Well, it's *not* a fact!" he declared, his voice punctuating his point.

"If you consider all of the evidence, Darwin's tree is false as a description of the history of life. I'll even go further than that: it's not even a good hypothesis at this point."

IMAGE #3: HAECKEL'S EMBRYOS

Like every young student of evolution, Wells had seen Ernst Haeckel's comparative drawings of embryos, often described as among the best evidence for Darwinism. But it wasn't until Wells was working on his doctorate in vertebrate embryology that he saw the sketches for what they really were.

Haeckel's most renowned images depict the embryos of a fish, salamander, tortoise, chicken, hog, calf, rabbit, and human side-by-side at three stages of development. The illustrations support Darwin's assertion that the striking similarities between early embryos is "by far the strongest single class of facts" in favor of his theory that all organisms share a universal ancestor.

I was mesmerized by the nineteenth-century drawings when I first encountered them as a student. As I carefully compared the embryos at their earliest stage, looking back and forth from one to the other, I could see they were virtually indistinguishable. I searched my mind, but I couldn't think of any logical explanation for this phenomenon other than a common ancestor. My verdict was swift: Darwin prevails.

The real explanation, as it turns out, would have been far too bizarre for me to have even considered at the time.

"When you saw these drawings," I said to Wells, "did you have the same reaction that I did—that this was strong evidence for Darwinism?"

"Yes, I did, the first time I looked at them," Wells answered. "It wasn't until I was doing my graduate work that I began to compare actual photographs of embryos to what Haeckel had drawn."

"And what did you find?"

"I was stunned!" he said, his eyes widening. "They didn't fit. There was a big discrepancy. It was really hard to believe."

As he described what had happened, I slowly shook my head in amazement at the implications of what he was saying. "I sort of rationalized by saying, well, textbooks tend to oversimplify things," he continued. "But over time it bothered me more and more."

I was hungry for details. "What was it specifically that bothered you?" I asked.

"There are three problems with these drawings," he said. "The first is that the similarities in the early stages were faked."

He leveled the accusation without emotion in his voice, but nevertheless it was a stunning charge. "Faked?" I repeated. "Are you sure?" It seemed inconceivable that the books I had relied upon as a student could have so blatantly misled me.

"You can call them fudged, distorted, misleading, but the bottom line is that they were faked," he replied. "Apparently in some cases Haeckel actually used the same woodcut to print embryos from different classes because he was so confident of his theory that he figured he didn't have to draw them separately. In other cases he doctored the drawings to make them look more similar than they really are. At any rate, his drawings misrepresent the embryos."

"That's amazing!" I said. "How long has this been known?"

"They were first exposed in the late 1860s, when his colleagues accused him of fraud."

I cocked my head. "Wait a minute—I saw these drawings in books that I studied when I was a student in the 1960s and '70s— more than a hundred years later. How is that possible?"

"It's worse than that!" he declared. "They're *still* being used, even in upper-division textbooks on evolutionary biology. In fact, I analyzed and graded ten recent textbooks on how accurately they dealt with this topic. I had to give eight of them an F. Two others did only slightly better; I gave them a D."

Anger was brewing inside of me. I had bought into Darwinism— and subsequently atheism—partially on the basis of drawings that scientists had known for a century were doctored. "This is really hard to believe," I said. "Doesn't it make you mad?"

"Of course it does, because I was raised on this stuff too. I was misled," he said. "There was no excuse for it. When some biologists exposed this in an article a few years ago, the evolutionist Stephen Jay Gould of Harvard complained that this was nothing new. He had known about it for twenty years! It was no secret to the experts.

"But then why was it still in textbooks? Even Gould said textbook writers should be ashamed of the way the drawings had been mindlessly recycled for over a century. At least he was honest enough to call it what it was: 'the academic equivalent of murder.'"27

THE SINS OF HAECKEL

Wells's first disclosure about Haeckel's embryos was a stunner, but he had said there were a total of three problems with the drawings. I couldn't wait to hear him address the others. "What are the other two problems?" I asked.

"The minor problem is that Haeckel cherry-picked his examples," Wells explained. "He only shows a few of the seven vertebrate classes. For example, his most famous rendition has eight columns. Four are mammals, but they're all placental mammals. There are two other kinds of mammals that he didn't show, which are different. The remaining four classes he showed—reptiles, birds, amphibians, and fish—happen to be more similar than the ones he omitted. He used a salamander to represent amphibians instead of a frog, which looks very different. So he stacked the deck by picking representatives that came closest to fitting his idea—and then he went further by faking the similarities."

That sounded like a pretty serious breach of scientific protocol to me. "If that's the minor problem," I said sarcastically, "then what's the major one?"

Wells moved to the edge of his chair; clearly, this was tapping into his passion area. "To me, as an embryologist, the most dramatic problem is that what Haeckel claimed is the early stage of development is nothing of the sort. It's actually the midpoint of development," he explained. "If you go back to the earlier stages, the embryos look far more different from each other. But he deliberately omits the earlier stages altogether."

I didn't immediately catch the full significance of this. "Why is that important?"

"Remember Darwin claimed that because the embryos are most similar in their early stages, this is evidence of common ancestry. He thought that the early stage showed what the common ancestor looked like—sort of like a fish.

"But embryologists talk about the 'developmental hourglass,' which refers to the shape of an hourglass, with its width representing the measure of difference. You see, vertebrate embryos start out looking very different in the early cell division stages. The cell divisions in a mammal, for example, are radically different from those in any of the other classes. There's no possible way you could mix them up. In fact, it's extremely different within classes. The patterns are all over the place.

"Then at the midpoint—which is what Haeckel claimed in his drawings was the early stage—the embryos become more similar, though nowhere near as much as Haeckel claimed. Then they become very different again."

What a devastating critique! Haeckel's drawings, which had been published countless times over more than a century, had failed on three levels. I couldn't help but ask Wells: "If they're so misleading, then why did scientists continue to publish them for generation after generation of students?"

"One explanation that's often given," he replied, "is that although the drawings are false, they teach a concept that's basically true. Well, this is *not* true. Biologists know that embryos are *not* most similar in their earliest stages."

With that, Wells picked up his book from the desk and flipped to the chapter on Haeckel. "Yet listen to this: one textbook shows Haeckel's drawings and says, 'Early developmental stages of animals whose adult forms appear radically different are often surprisingly similar.' One 1999 textbook has a slightly redrawn version of Haeckel's work and tells students, 'Notice that the early embryonic stages of these vertebrates bear a striking resemblance to each other.'

"Another textbook accompanies its drawings with the statement: 'The early embryos of vertebrates strongly resemble one another.' Another says flatly: 'One fact of embryology that pushed Darwin toward the idea of evolution is that the early embryos of most vertebrates closely resemble one another.'"[28]

Wells snapped the book shut. "As I said, it's just false that embryos are most similar in their earliest development. Of course, some Darwinists try to get around Haeckel's problems by changing their tune. They use evolutionary theory to try to explain why the differences in the embryos are there. They can get quite elaborate," he said.

"But that's doing the same thing that the theory-savers were doing with the Cambrian explosion. What was supposed to be primary evidence for Darwin's theory—the fossil or embryo evidence—turns out to be false, so they immediately say, well, we know the theory's true, so let's use the theory to explain why the evidence doesn't fit.

"But then, *where's the evidence for the theory?*" he demanded, sounding both frustrated and perturbed. "That's what I'd like to know. Why should I accept the theory as being true at all?"

THE TRUTH ABOUT GILLS

Wells's explanation made me feel foolish for ever having believed the embryo drawings I had seen as a student, much less the previous two icons that Wells had already deconstructed. I felt a little like the victim of a con game, blaming myself for being so uncritical and naive in accepting what evolution textbooks and biology teachers had told me.

But Haekel's drawings weren't the only evidence I had been taught about universal ancestry. I also had been told a fascinating fact that helped convince me that our progenitors dwelled in the ocean: all human embryos, so my teachers said, go through a stage in which they actually develop gill-like structures on their necks.

The encyclopedia I consulted as a youngster declared unequivocally that "the fetuses of mammals at one stage have gill slits which resemble those of fish," which to me was dramatic confirmation of our aquatic ancestry.[29] In 1996, *Life* magazine described how human embryos grow "something very much like gills," which is "some of the most compelling evidence of evolution."[30] Even some contemporary biology textbooks assert that human embryos have "gill pouches" or "gill slits."[31]

This colorful tidbit stayed with me from the first time I heard it. "Aren't gills strong evidence that our ancestors lived in the ocean?" I asked Wells.

He sighed. Apparently, I was not the first person to raise this issue with him. "Yes, that's the standard argument, but—here," he said, gesturing toward me, "Look down toward your navel for a moment." Feeling a little awkward, I bowed my head. "Now, feel your neck," he said. "There are ridges in the skin, right?" I nodded.

"Well, if you look at an embryo, it's doubled over. It has ridges in the neck. I'm not saying they're only skin folds; they're more complicated than that. But it's just an anatomical feature that grows out of the fact that this is how vertebrate embryos develop.

"Let me be clear: they're *not* gills!" he stressed. "Even fish don't have gills at that stage. In humans, the ridges become one thing; in fish, they become gills. They're not even gill slits. To call them gill-like structures is merely reading evolutionary theory back into the evidence. They're never gill-like except in the superficial sense that they're lines in the neck area. As British embryologist Lewis Wolpert said, the resemblance is only illusory.[32]

"It's interesting how these misconceptions continue to thrive," he went on. "Evolutionists used to teach that famous phrase 'ontogeny recapitulates phylogeny,' which is a fancy way of saying that embryos repeat their evolutionary history by passing through the adult forms of their ancestors as they develop.

"But this theory has been widely dismissed for many decades, because it's empirically false. Even so, there are aspects of it that still come up. And 'gill slits' would be a prime example of that."

WING, FLIPPER, LEG, HAND

Earlier in our interview, Wells had brought up another category of evidence for universal ancestry: homology in vertebrate limbs. I remember as a student seeing the drawings depicting the similar bone structures in a bat's wing, a porpoise's flipper, a horse's leg, and a human's hand. I was told that even though these limbs have been adapted for different uses, their underlying similarity—or "homology"—is proof that they all share a common ancestor.

Wells had briefly mentioned this phenomenon at the outset of our interview. "Isn't homology good evidence for Darwinism?" I asked.

"Actually, these homologies were described and named by Darwin's predecessors—and they were *not* evolutionists," he replied. "Richard Owen, who was the most famous anatomist of Darwin's time, said they pointed toward a common archetype or design, not toward descent with modification."

"But," I protested, "the similarities are there—you can't deny that."

"Yes, but the explanation can go either way: design or descent with modification. How do we determine which is true? Listen—similarity alone doesn't tell us. Look at Berra's Blunder."

He threw out that comment assuming I would know what he was referring to. Although the term sounded vaguely familiar, I couldn't pinpoint what it meant. "Berra's Blunder?" I asked. "What's that?"

"Phillip Johnson coined that term based on a book that was written by a biologist named Tim Berra in 1990. Berra compared the fossil record to a series of automobile models, saying that if you compare a 1953 and 1954 Corvette side by side, and then a 1954 and 1955 Corvette and so on, then it becomes obvious that there has been descent with modification. He said this is what paleontologists do with fossils, 'and the evidence is so solid and comprehensive that it cannot be denied by reasonable people.'[33]

"Far from demonstrating his point, the illustration shows that a designer could have been involved," Wells said. "These successive models of the Corvette are based on plans drawn up by engineers, so there's intelligence at work to guide and implement the process. If you wanted to demonstrate that the similar features resulted from a Darwinian process, you would have to show that once you somehow got an automobile, the natural forces of rust, wind, water, and gravity would turn one model into its successor.

"The point I want to make is this: quite unintentionally, Berra had illustrated the fact that merely having a succession of similar forms does not provide its own explanation. A mechanism is needed. With the Corvette, that mechanism is human manufacturing."

"What mechanism is proposed for Darwinism?" I asked.

"One is called 'common developmental pathways,' which means if you have two different animals with homologous features and you trace them back to the embryo, they would come from similar cells and processes. This happens to be mostly untrue.

"I mentioned frogs earlier. There are some frogs that develop like frogs and other frogs that develop like birds, but they all look pretty much the same when they come out the other end. They're frogs. So the developmental pathway explanation is false—I don't know anybody who studies development and takes it seriously.

"A more common explanation nowadays is that the homologies come from similar genes. In other words, the reason two features are homologous in two different animals would be that they're programmed by similar genes in the embryo. But it turns out this doesn't work very well, either. We know some cases where you have similar features that come from different genes, but we have lots and lots of cases where we have similar genes that give rise to very different features.

"I'll give you an example: eyes. There's a gene that's similar in mice, octopuses, and fruit flies. If you look at a mouse eye and an octopus eye, there's a superficial similarity, which is odd because nobody thinks their common ancestor had an eye like that. What's more striking is if you look at a fruit fly's eye—a compound eye with multiple facets—it's totally different. Yet all three of these eyes depend on the same or very similar gene.

"In fact, it's so similar that you can put the mouse gene into a fruit fly that's missing that gene and you can get the fruit fly to develop its eyes as it normally would. The genes are that similar. So neither the developmental pathway explanation nor the similar gene explanation really accounts for homology."

I asked, "What's the answer, then?"

Wells shrugged. "Frankly, it remains a mystery. If you read the literature on homology, the experts know it's a mystery. They may not give up Darwinism, but they know they haven't solved the problem. To me, if you haven't solved the problem of a mechanism, then you haven't distinguished between common descent and common design. It could be either one. The evidence isn't pointing one way or the other.

"I think students deserve to know that scientists haven't resolved this problem. Instead, some textbooks simply define homology as similarity due to common ancestry. So the theory becomes true by definition. What the textbook is saying is that similarity due to common ancestry is due to common ancestry. And *that's* circular reasoning."

HUMAN GENES, APE GENES

Since Wells had brought up genetics, I was reminded of another question I wanted to raise with him about the theory of common descent. "What about recent genetic studies that show humans and apes share ninety-eight or ninety-nine percent of their genes?" I asked. "Isn't that evidence that we share a common ancestor?"

"If you assume, as neo-Darwinism does, that we are products of our genes, then you're saying that the dramatic differences between us and chimpanzees are due to two percent of our genes," he replied. "The problem is that the so-called body-building genes are in the ninety-eight percent. The two percent of genes that are different are really rather trivial genes that have little to do with anatomy. So the supposed similarity of human and chimpanzee DNA is a problem for neo-Darwinism right there.

"Second, it's not surprising that when you look at two organisms that are similar anatomically, you often find they're similar genetically. Not always; there's a striking discordance with some organisms. But does this prove common ancestry?"

He shook his head as he answered his own question: "No, it's just as compatible with common design as it is with common ancestry. A designer might very well decide to use common building materials to create different organisms, just as builders use the same materials—steel girders, rivets, and so forth—to build different bridges that end up looking very dissimilar from one another."

As I mentally wrestled with this concept, I stood to stretch my legs. Walking over to the window, I looked down at cars backed up along the busy street and people hustling down the sidewalks on either side. A rudimentary illustration popped into my mind.

"Let me see if I understand you. If I were to chemically analyze that street and sidewalk," I said, pointing out the window, "I'd find they would be identical or very similar. They'd both be made of concrete. But that wouldn't mean that they shared a common ancestor—say, a path for a golf cart—that got wider and more substantial over millions of years. A better explanation would be that there was a common designer who decided to use basically the same materials to construct similar, but functionally different, structures."

Wells thought about my example for a moment. "Essentially, that's right," he said. "It sounds ridiculous to suggest a golf path could evolve into a sidewalk and street, but it's not any more outlandish than some of the claims for biological evolution. The important point is that similarity by itself doesn't distinguish between design and Darwinism."

We had strayed from Haeckel's embryos, but the issues were the same: is there persuasive evidence through embryology or homology that all living creatures evolved over time from an ancient progenitor? I concluded that Darwin was wrong: examining embryos of different creatures in their early stages does not yield support for his theory. And the undeniable similarities between some vertebrate limbs certainly doesn't distinguish between design or descent as a cause. Once again, the persuasive power of the evolutionary icons had been deflated.

I glanced at my watch; if I were to catch my plane back to Los Angeles, I would need to turn to the last of the four evolutionary images from my days as a student: the awe-inspiring fossil of a prehistoric creature that once effectively silenced many of Darwin's critics.

IMAGE #4: THE *ARCHAEOPTERYX* MISSING LINK

When Darwin's *The Origin of Species* was published in 1859, he conceded that "the most obvious and gravest objection which can be urged against my theory" was that the fossil record failed to back up his evolutionary hypothesis.

"Why," he asked, "if species have descended from other species by insensibly fine gradations, do we not everywhere see innumerable transitional forms?" He attributed the problem to the fossil record being incomplete and predicted that future discoveries would vindicate his theory.

As if on cue, two years later scientists unearthed the *archaeopteryx* (pronounced ar-key-OPT-er-icks) in a German quarry. Darwin's supporters were thrilled—surely this missing link between reptiles and modern birds, unveiled so promptly after the appearance of Darwin's book, would just be the first of many future fossil discoveries that would validate Darwin's claims.

Like many people, including the scientist who "actually fell upon his knees in awe" when he first glimpsed the *archaeopteryx* at the National History Museum in England,[34] I was enthralled by the dramatic pictures of the prehistoric creature. I was under the impression that it was featured in my books on evolution because it is just one example of many transitional links that have been found. But I was wrong.

Since that time I have come to learn that the fossil record has utterly let Darwin down. Michael Denton, in his book *Evolution: A Theory in Crisis*, summarized the bleak situation this way:

> ... [T]he universal experience of paleontology ... [is that] while the rocks have continually yielded new and exciting and even bizarre forms of life ... what they have never yielded is any of Darwin's myriads of transitional forms. Despite the tremendous increase in geological activity in every corner of the globe and despite the discovery of many strange and hitherto unknown forms, the infinitude of connecting links has still not been discovered and the fossil record is about as discontinuous as it was when Darwin was writing the *Origin*. The intermediates have remained as elusive as ever and their absence remains, a century later, one of the most striking characteristics of the fossil record.[35]

As a result, said Denton, the fossil record "provides a tremendous challenge to the notion of organic evolution."[36] But what about the *archaeopteryx*? The fossils of this magnificent creature, its detailed image pressed into fine-grained limestone, still seemed to stand in stark contrast to this trend.

"Doesn't *archaeopteryx* fill the gap between reptiles and modern birds?" I asked Wells.

"There are several problems with that," came his reply. "Does it show Darwinian evolution? Well, no, for the same reason that the Corvettes don't illustrate Darwinian evolution. We would need more than an intermediate form to show that; we would need to know how you get from one to the other.

"The question is, do you get from a reptile to a bird—which is an astonishingly huge step—by some totally natural process or does this require the intervention of a designer? An *archaeopteryx*, as beautiful as it is, doesn't show us one way or the other. Besides, we see strange animals around today, like the duck-billed platypus, which nobody considers transitional but which has characteristics of different classes."

"But the *archaeopteryx* is a half-bird, half-reptile, right?"

"No, not even close," he insisted. "It's a bird with modern feathers, and birds are very different from reptiles in many important ways—their breeding system, their bone structure, their lungs, their distribution of weight and muscles. It's a bird, that's clear—not part bird and part reptile.

"But there are more interesting parts to the *archaeopteryx* story," he added. "The main one comes from a branch of evolutionary theory called *cladistics*. This takes Darwinian theory to the extreme. Cladists define homology, or physical similarities, as being due to common ancestry. Then they say, well, the main way we can group animals in the evolutionary tree is through homologies, which is already a bit of a circular argument. When they go back into the fossil record, they assume birds came from reptiles by descent, and they look for reptiles that are more bird-like in their skeletal structure."

"Where do they find them?" I asked.

Wells smiled. "That's the fascinating part," he said. "It turns out they find them millions of years after *archaeopteryx*! So here we have *archaeopteryx*, which is undeniably a bird, and yet the fossils that look most like the reptilian ancestors of birds occur tens of millions of years *later* in the fossil record. The missing link is still missing! Now evolutionists are stuck looking for another theoretical ancestor to try to fill the gaps, but it hasn't been found."

"So the *archaeopteryx* is not an ancestor of modern birds?"

"Not at all. Paleontologists pretty much agree on that. There are too many structural differences. Larry Martin, a paleontologist from the University of Kansas, said clearly in 1985 that the *archaeopteryx* is not an ancestor of any modern birds; instead, it's a member of a totally extinct group of birds."[37]

So much for the power of *archaeopteryx* to authenticate Darwin's claims. Even ardent evolutionist Pierre Lecomte du Nouy agrees:

> We are not even authorized to consider the exceptional case of the *archaeopteryx* as a true link. By link, we mean a necessary stage of transition between classes such as reptiles and birds, or between smaller groups. An animal displaying characters belonging to two different groups cannot be treated as a true link as long as the intermediary stages have not been found, and as long as the mechanisms of transition remain unknown.[38]

Yet even if *archaeopteryx* had turned out to be a transitional creature, it would have been but a whisper of protest to the fossil record's deafening roar against classical Darwinism.

"If we are testing Darwinism rather than merely looking for a confirming example or two," Phillip Johnson said, "then a single good candidate for ancestor status is not enough to save a theory that posits a worldwide history of continual evolutionary transformation."[39]

FRAUDS AND TURKEYS

Paleontologists, however, have been on a frenzy to try to locate an actual reptilian ancestor for birds. Driven by an all-consuming commitment to evolutionary theory, their zeal has resulted in some recent embarrassments for science. Wells was more than willing to regale me with some examples.

"A few years ago the National Geographic Society announced that a fossil had been purchased at an Arizona mineral show that turned out to be 'the missing link between terrestrial dinosaurs and birds that could actually fly,'" he said. "It certainly looked that way. They called it the *archaeoraptor*, and it had the tail of a dinosaur and the forelimbs of a bird. *National Geographic* magazine published an article in 1999 that said there's now evidence that feathered dinosaurs were ancestors of the first bird."

"That sounds pretty convincing," I said.

"Well, the problem was that it was a fake!" Wells said. "A Chinese paleontologist proved that someone had glued a dinosaur tail to a primitive bird. He created it to resemble just what the scientists had been looking for. There was a firestorm of criticism—the curator of birds at the Smithsonian charged that the Society had become aligned with 'zealous scientists' who were 'highly biased proselytizers of the faith' that birds evolved from dinosaurs."

Then Wells made a blanket statement that struck me at the time as being too cynical. "Fakes are coming out of these fossil beds all the time," he said, "because the fossil dealers know there's big money in it."

I remained skeptical about that charge until I subsequently read an interview with ornithologist Alan Feduccia, an evolutionary biologist at the University of North Carolina at Chapel Hill. When a reporter for *Discover* magazine raised the *archaeoraptor* fraud, Feduccia said:

> *Archaeoraptor* is just the tip of the iceberg. There are scores of fake fossils out there, and they have cast a dark shadow over the whole field. When you go to these fossil shows, it's difficult to tell which ones are faked and which ones are not. I have heard there is a fake-fossil factory in northeast China, in Liaoning Province, near the deposits where many of these recent alleged feathered dinosaurs were found.[40]

Asked what would motivate such fraud, Fedducia replied: "Money. The Chinese fossil trade has become a big business. These fossil forgeries have been sold on the black market for years now, for huge sums of money. Anyone who can produce a good fake stands to profit."[41]

Other outlandish incidents occurred at about the same time the *archaeoraptor* fraud was coming to light. Wells was attending a conference in Florida, where the star of the show was a fossil called *bambiraptor*, a chicken-sized dinosaur with supposedly bird-like characteristics.

"Again, paleontologists called it the missing link," Wells told me. "And, sure enough, the reconstructed animal on display had feathers or feather-like structures on it. The problem was that no feathers were ever found with the fossil! But because scientists said they *should* be there, they were added. And the dinosaur looked even more like a bird because the guy who did the reconstruction used the same artificial eyes that taxidermists put in stuffed eagles." While there was a brief disclaimer, he added, it was rather cryptically written.

"Then a group of molecular biologists at the conference reported finding bird DNA in dinosaur bones that were sixty-five million years old. Now, that would be pretty exciting! They suggested that this was genetic evidence that birds are closely related to dinosaurs.

"The problem is that the bones from which the DNA was supposedly extracted are from a branch of dinosaurs that had nothing to do with bird ancestry. Furthermore, the DNA they found was not ninety or ninety-nine percent similar to birds—it was *one-hundred-percent* turkey DNA! Even chickens don't have DNA that's one hundred percent similar to turkey DNA. Only turkeys have one-hundred-percent turkey DNA.

"So these people said they found turkey DNA in a dinosaur bone—and it actually got published in *Science* magazine! This is just incredible to me! The headline in the magazine said with a straight face: 'Dinos and Turkeys: Connected by DNA?'"

That last story begged the next question: "How in the world do you explain how the turkey DNA got in there?"

Shaking his head, Wells said, "Maybe somebody dropped a turkey sandwich in the dig or there was lab contamination. If I had reported something like this in my grad student research, I would have been laughed out of the room. They would have told me, 'Go do the test again—it's contaminated.'

"But for goodness sake, this was taken seriously enough to publish it in *Science*! Even the scientist who reported the finding admitted he was 'quite skeptical' of his own work at this point—and yet people were willing to seize on it to support their belief in Darwinian theory."[42]

THE LEGEND OF JAVA MAN

I couldn't end my conversation without touching on one more icon related to the fossil evidence: the pictures I've seen from time to time of a parade of ape-like creatures that morph into modern human beings. In fact, this illustration is emblazoned across the cover of a 1998 edition of *The Origin of Species*.[43] For many, this "ultimate icon" is not just a theory, but an established fact.

"If you go back far enough," legendary newscaster Walter Cronkite intoned in a documentary on evolution, "we and the chimps share a common ancestor. My father's father's father's father, going back maybe a half-million generations—about five million years ago—was an ape."[44]

That kind of certainty about human evolution was engendered in me as a youngster, when I would devour my *World Book Encyclopedia*. One of my favorite entries was "Prehistoric Man," where I would linger for hours, fascinated by the part-ape, part-human nicknamed "Java man." Apparently, I wasn't the only member of this missing link's fan club. Said the author of a book on paleoanthropology:

> Java man is like an old friend. We learned about him in grade school. . . . In fact, the vast majority of people who believe in human evolution were probably first sold on it by this convincing salesman. Not only is he the best-known human fossil, he is one of the only human fossils most people know.[45]

World Book's two-page spread highlighted a parade of prehistoric men. Second in line was a lifelike bust of Java man from the American Museum of Natural History, accompanied by an outline showing his profile. With his sloping forehead, heavy brow, jutting jaw, receding chin and bemused expression, he was exactly what a blend of ape and man should look like. For me, studying his face and looking into his eyes helped cement the reality of human evolution.

The encyclopedia confidently described how Dutch scientist Eugene Dubois, excavating on an Indonesian Island in 1891 and 1892, "dug some bones from a riverbank." Java man, which he dated back half a million years, "represents a stage in the development of modern man from a smaller-brained ancestor."[46] He was, according to Dubois, *the* missing link between apes and humans.[47]

And I believed it all. I was blithely ignorant, however, of the full Java man story. "What is not so well known is that Java man consists of nothing more than a skullcap, a femur (thigh bone), three teeth, and a great deal of imagination," one author would later write.[48] In other words, the lifelike depiction of Java man, which had so gripped me when I was young, was little more than speculation fueled by evolutionary expectations of what he *should* have looked like if Darwinism were true.

As a youngster beginning to form my opinions about human evolution, I wasn't aware of what I have more recently discovered: that Dubois' shoddy excavation would have disqualified the fossil from consideration by today's standards. Or that the femur apparently didn't really belong with the skullcap. Or that the skull cap, according to prominent Cambridge University anatomist Sir Arthur Keith, was distinctly human and reflected a brain capacity well within the range of humans living today.[49] Or that a 342-page scientific report from a fact-finding expedition of nineteen evolutionists demolished Dubois' claims and concluded that Java man played no part in human evolution.[50]

In short, Java man was not an ape-man as I had been led to believe, but he was "a true member of the human family."[51] This was a fact apparently lost on *Time* magazine, which as recently as 1994 treated Java man as a legitimate evolutionary ancestor.[52]

THE NARRATIVE OF HUMAN EVOLUTION

Wells listened intently as I described to him how my exposure to misinformation about Java man had paved the way for my eventual wholehearted embrace of Darwinian evolution. The factors that contributed to that debacle, he pointed out, are still quite relevant.

"One of the major problems with paleoanthropology is that compared to all the fossils we have, only a minuscule number are believed to be of creatures ancestral to humans," Wells said. "Often, it's just skull fragments or teeth.

"So this gives a lot of elasticity in reconstructing the specimens to fit evolutionary theory. For example, when *National Geographic* hired four artists to reconstruct a female figure from seven fossil bones found in Kenya, they came up with quite different interpretations. One looked like a modern African-American woman; another like a werewolf; another had a heavy, gorilla-like brow; and another had a missing forehead and jaws that looked a bit like a beaked dinosaur.

"Of course, this lack of fossil evidence also makes it virtually impossible to reconstruct supposed relationships between ancestors and descendents. One anthropologist likened the task to trying to reconstruct the plot of *War and Peace* by using just thirteen random pages from the book."[53]

Wells reached over again to pick up *Icons of Evolution.* "I thought Henry Gee, the chief science writer for *Nature*, was quite candid in talking about this issue in 1999," Wells said as he searched for the right page. "Gee wrote, 'The intervals of time that separate fossils are so huge that we cannot say anything definite about their possible connection through ancestry and descent.'

"He called each fossil 'an isolated point, with no knowable connection to any other given fossil, and all float around in an overwhelming sea of gaps.' In fact, he said that all the fossil evidence for human evolution 'between ten and five million years ago—several thousand generations of living creatures—can be fitted into a small box.'

"Consequently, he concluded that the conventional picture of human evolution is 'a completely human invention created after the fact, shaped to accord with human prejudices.' Then he said quite bluntly: 'To take a line of fossils and claim that they represent a lineage is not a scientific hypothesis that can be tested, but an assertion that carries the same validity as a bedtime story—amusing, perhaps even instructive, but not scientific.'"[54]

Wells put down the book. "In other words, you're not going to reconstruct human evolutionary history just based on examining the few fossils we have," he continued. "The only reason anyone thinks the evidence supports human evolution is because Darwinism is assumed to be true on other grounds. If it is, then it makes perfect sense to extrapolate that to human history, which is what Darwin did in his book *The Descent of Man*.

"But what if the other evidence for Darwinism is faulty—which, in fact, it is? You and I didn't even go into the major flaws with a whole host of other evolution icons that are used to teach students today. There's no shortage of books debunking Darwin. And without any compelling evidence for Darwinism in these areas, the whole question of human evolution is up for grabs.

"Instead, Darwinists assume the story of human life is an evolutionary one, and then they plug the fossils into a preexisting narrative where they seem to fit. The narrative can take several forms depending on one's biases. As one anthropologist said, the process is 'both political and subjective' to the point where he suggested that 'paleoanthropology has the form but not the substance of a science.'[55]

"In fact, a paleoanthropologist named Misia Landau wrote a book in which she talked about the similarities between the story of human evolution and old-fashioned folk tales. She concluded that many classic texts in the field were 'determined as much by traditional narrative frameworks as by material evidence' and that these themes 'far exceed what can be inferred from the study of fossils alone.'"[56]

I took a few moments to soak in what Wells had said. He was right—certainly Java man's fall from grace is instructive. It highlights how many people, including myself, became adherents of Darwinism through fossils or other evidence that later discoveries have either undermined or disproved. But the damage has already been done in many cases—the student, unaware of these subsequent findings, has already graduated into full-fledged naturalism.

As I leaf back through my time-worn copies of the *World Book* from my childhood, I can now see how faulty science and Darwinian presuppositions forced my former friend Java man into an evolutionary parade that's based much more on imagination than reality. Unfortunately, he's not the only example of that phenomenon, which is rife to the point of rendering the record of supposed human evolution totally untrustworthy.

"There is no encompassing theory of [human] evolution," conceded Berkeley evolutionary biologist F. Clark Howell. "Alas, there never really has been."[57]

OUTDATED, DISTORTED, FAKE, FAILURE

At the end of our discussion about the fossil record, I reflected back on the four images that had paved the way for my descent into atheism. I could only shake my head.

I was left with an origin-of-life experiment whose results have been rendered meaningless; a Tree of Life that had been uprooted by the Biological Big Bang of the Cambrian explosion; doctored embryo drawings that don't reflect reality; and a fossil record that stubbornly refuses to yield the transitional forms crucial to evolutionary theory. Doubts piled on doubts.

Are these icons the sole evidence for Darwinism? Of course not. But their fate is illustrative of what happens time after time when macroevolution is put under the microscope of scrutiny. As I continued to investigate the scientific and philosophical underpinnings of evolutionary theory, in a long-standing probe that goes far beyond my encounter with Wells, I kept getting the same kind of results. No wonder a hundred scientists signed a public dissent from Darwinism.

Yet every time an icon of evolution is discredited, Darwinists claim with religious zeal that it was never really the whole story in the first place and insist that new findings really do buttress macroevolution. New narratives are created; new stories are told. The theory of evolution, now unsupported by the original icon, is never questioned; instead, it's used afresh to justify a redesigned model.

For instance, several years ago Gould and a colleague proposed a new hypothesis, called "punctuated equilibrium," in a desperate bid to explain away the fossil gaps. They suggested that radically new species somehow managed to develop rapidly among isolated populations, conveniently leaving behind no fossils to document the process. When these new creatures rejoined the larger, central populations, this resulted in the preserving of fossils that suggested the sudden appearance of new species. This model has been roundly criticized, and rightly so, for creating far more questions than answers.[58] In the end, Darwinism has remained a philosophy still in search of convincing empirical data to back it up.

Similarly, neo-Darwinists have proudly displayed four-winged fruit flies as evidence that small genetic changes can yield major physiological differences in organisms. As Wells reveals in his book, however, these fruit flies must be carefully bred from three artificially maintained mutant strains—an exceedingly unlikely circumstance in nature.

What's more, the males have difficulty mating, and because the extra wings are nonfunctional, these mutant flies are seriously handicapped. "As evidence for evolution," he said, "the four-winged fruit fly is no better than a two-headed calf in a circus sideshow."[59]

Once again, closer investigation revealed that even the latest icons cannot buttress the sagging credibility of evolutionary theory. As for me, I finally came to the point where I realized that I just didn't have enough faith to maintain my belief in Darwinism. The evidence, in my estimation, was simply unable to support its grandest and most sweeping claims.

THE CRY OF "DESIGN!"

Before I packed my belongings and grabbed a cab for the airport, I wanted to ask Wells a few closing questions about the overall case for Darwinian evolution. "After years of studying this," I said, "when you take the most current scientific evidence into consideration, what is your conclusion about Darwin's theory?"

Wells's answer began as soon as the words left my mouth. "My conclusion is that the case for Darwinian evolution is bankrupt," he said firmly. "The evidence for Darwinism is not only grossly inadequate, it's systematically distorted. I'm convinced that sometime in the not-too-distant future—I don't know, maybe twenty or thirty years from now—people will look back in amazement and say, 'How could anyone have believed this?' Darwinism is merely materialistic philosophy masquerading as science, and people are recognizing it for what it is.

"Now, having said that," he continued, "I still see room for some evolutionary processes in limited instances. But saying evolution works in some cases is far from showing that it accounts for everything."

I asked, "If macroevolution has failed to prove itself to be a viable theory, then where do you believe the evidence of science is pointing?"

There was no equivocation in Wells's voice. Speaking with conviction, he said: "I believe science is pointing strongly toward design. To me, as a scientist, the development of an embryo cries out, 'Design!' The Cambrian explosion—the sudden appearance of complex life, with no evidence of ancestors—is more consistent with design than evolution. Homology, in my opinion, is more compatible with design. The origin of life certainly cries out for a designer. None of these things make as much sense from a Darwinian perspective as they do from a design perspective."

"Let me get this straight," I said. "You're not merely saying that the evidence for evolution is weak and therefore there must be an intelligent designer. You're suggesting there is also affirmative evidence for a designer."

"I am," he relied. "However, the two are connected, because one of the main functions of Darwinian theory is to try to make design unnecessary. This is what you experienced as you became an atheist. This is what I experienced. So showing that the arguments for evolution are weak certainly opens the door to design.

"And then," he said, "when you analyze all of the most current affirmative evidence from cosmology, physics, astronomy, biology, and so forth—well, I think you'll discover that the positive case for an intelligent designer becomes absolutely compelling."

I stood and shook Wells' hand. "That," I said, "is what I'm going to find out."

SCIENCE VERSUS FAITH

The plane ride through the black velvet sky over the Pacific Coast was exceptionally smooth that evening, and I closed my eyes as I reclined my seat as far as it would go. I felt satisfied by my interview with Wells and was anxious to determine whether the most up-to-date scientific evidence supports the existence of the intelligent designer he had talked about. Still, though, some pesky questions continued to bother me.

I remained troubled by the intersection of science and faith. I needed to resolve whether these two domains are destined to be at war with each other, as some people claim. Can a scientific person legitimately entertain the idea of the supernatural? How much can empirical data tell us about the divine? Should scientists merely stick to their test tubes and let the theologians ponder God? Should pastors be allowed to poke their nose into the research laboratory? Can science and faith ever really be partners in pursuit of the ultimate answers of life?

I knew I needed to get some answers to those questions before I could go any further. I pulled the blanket up to my neck and decided to get some sleep. Tomorrow, I'd be planning another journey.

FOR FURTHER EVIDENCE
More Resources on This Topic

Denton, Michael. *Evolution: A Theory in Crisis*. Bethesda, Md.: Adler & Adler, 1986.

Hanegraaff, Hank. *The Face that Demonstrates the Farce of Evolution*. Nashville: Word, 1998.

Johnson, Phillip. *Darwin on Trial*. Downers Grove, Ill.: Inter-Varsity Press, second edition, 1993.

Wells, Jonathan. *Icons of Evolution*. Washington, D.C.: Regnery, 2000.

WHERE SCIENCE MEETS FAITH

I am all in favor of a dialogue between science and religion, but not a constructive dialogue. One of the great achievements of science has been, if not to make it impossible for an intelligent person to be religious, then at least to make it possible for them not to be religious. We should not retreat from this accomplishment.

Physicist Steven Weinberg,[1]

Science and religion ... are friends, not foes, in the common quest for knowledge. Some people may find this surprising, for there's a feeling throughout our society that religious belief is outmoded, or downright impossible, in a scientific age. I don't agree. In fact, I'd go so far as to say that if people in this so-called "scientific age" knew a bit more about science than many of them actually do, they'd find it easier to share my view.

Physicist and theologian John Polkinghorne[2]

Allan Rex Sandage, the greatest observational cosmologist in the world—who has deciphered the secrets of the stars, plumbed the mysteries of quasars, revealed the age of globular clusters, pinpointed the distances of remote galaxies, and quantified the universe's expansion through his work at the Mount Wilson and Palomar observatories—prepared to step onto the platform at a conference in Dallas.

Few scientists are as widely respected as this one-time protégé to legendary astronomer Edwin Hubble. Sandage has been showered with prestigious honors from the American Astronomical Society, the Swiss Physical Society, the Royal Astronomical Society, and the Swedish Academy of Sciences, receiving astronomy's equivalent of the Nobel Prize. The *New York Times* dubbed him the "Grand Old Man of Cosmology."

As he approached the stage at this 1985 conference on science and religion, there seemed to be little doubt where he would sit. The discussion would be about the origin of the universe, and the panel would be divided among those scientists who believed in God and those who didn't, with each viewpoint having its own side of the stage.

Many of the attendees probably knew that the ethnically Jewish Sandage had been a virtual atheist even as a child. Many others undoubtedly believed that a scientist of his stature must surely be skeptical about God. As *Newsweek* put it, "The more deeply scientists see into the secrets of the universe, you'd expect, the more God would fade away from their hearts and minds."[3] So Sandage's seat among the doubters was a given.

Then the unexpected happened. Sandage set the room abuzz by turning and taking a chair among the theists. Even more dazzling, in the context of a talk about the Big Bang and its philosophical implications, he disclosed publicly that he had decided to become a Christian at age fifty.

The Big Bang, he told the rapt audience, was a supernatural event that cannot be explained within the realm of physics as we know it. Science had taken us to the First Event, but it can't take us further to the First Cause. The sudden emergence of matter, space, time, and energy pointed to the need for some kind of transcendence.

"It was my science that drove me to the conclusion that the world is much more complicated than can be explained by science," he would later tell a reporter. "It was only through the supernatural that I can understand the mystery of existence."[4]

Sitting among the Dallas crowd that day, astounded by what he was hearing from Sandage, was a young geophysicist who had dropped by the conference almost by accident. Stephen Meyer had become a Christian through a philosophical quest for the meaning of life, but he hadn't really explored the issue of whether science could provide evidential support for his faith.

Now here was not only Sandage but also prominent Harvard astrophysicist Owen Gingerich concluding that the Big Bang seemed to fit best into a theistic worldview. Later came a session on the origin of life, featuring Dean Kenyon, a biophysicist from San Francisco State University, who had co-authored an influential book asserting that the emergence of life might have been "biochemically predestined," because of an inherent attraction between amino acids.[5] This seemed to be the most promising explanation for the conundrum of how the first living cell could somehow self-assemble from nonliving matter.

To Meyer's surprise, Kenyon stepped to the podium and actually repudiated the conclusions of his own book, declaring that he had come to the point where he was critical of all naturalistic theories of origins. Due to the immense molecular complexity of the cell and the information-bearing properties of DNA, Kenyon now believed that the best evidence pointed toward a designer of life.

Instead of science and religion being at odds, Meyer heard specialists at the highest levels of achievement who said they were theists—not in spite of the scientific evidence but because of it. As Sandage would say, "Many scientists are now driven to faith by their very work."[6]

Meyer was intrigued. It seemed to him that the theists had the intellectual initiative in each of the three issues discussed at the conference—the origin of the universe, the origin of life, and the nature of human consciousness. Even skeptics on the panels conceded the shortcomings of naturalistic explanations. Their main response was only to challenge the theists to provide "scientific answers" instead of merely invoking the idea of intelligent design.

That objection didn't make much sense to Meyer. "Maybe the world *looks* designed," he mused, "because it really *is* designed!"

As he walked away from the conference, Meyer was brimming with excitement over what he had experienced. Despite his background in science, he simply had been unaware of the powerful scientific findings that were supporting belief in God. All of this, he decided, was worth a much more thorough investigation.

He didn't know it at the time, but his life's mission had just crystallized.

INTERVIEW #2: STEPHEN C. MEYER, PHD

Already having earned degrees in physics and geology, Meyer went on to receive his master's degree in the history and philosophy of science at prestigious Cambridge University in England, where he focused on the history of molecular biology, the history of physics, and evolutionary theory. He then obtained his doctorate from Cambridge, where his dissertation analyzed the scientific and methodological issues in origin-of-life biology—a field he first got excited about when he heard Kenyon speak at the Dallas conference.

In the past fifteen years, Meyer has become one of the most knowledgeable and compelling voices in the burgeoning Intelligent

Design movement. He has contributed to numerous books—including *Darwinism, Design and Public Education; Mere Creation: Science, Faith and Intelligent Design*; *Signs of Intelligence: Understanding Intelligent Design*; *Science and Christianity: Four Views*; *The Creation Hypothesis: Scientific Evidence for an Intelligent Creator*; *Science and Evidence for Design in the Universe*; *The History of Science and Religion in the Western Tradition*; *Of Pandas and People: The Central Question of Biological Origins*; *Darwinism: Science or Philosophy*; and *Facets of Faith and Science*, and is currently finishing books on DNA and the Cambrian explosion.

He has spoken at symposia at Cambridge, Oxford, Yale, Baylor, the University of Texas, and elsewhere; debated skeptics, including Michael Shermer, editor of *The Skeptical Inquirer*; written for magazines ranging from *Origins and Design* (where he's an associate editor) to *The Journal of Interdisciplinary Studies* to *National Review*; appeared in the *Wall Street Journal, Washington Times, Chicago Tribune*, and a host of other newspapers; and faced off with Darwinists on National Public Radio, PBS, and network television.

When I flew into snowy Spokane, Washington, to interview Meyer at Whitworth College, where he was an associate professor of philosophy, I wasn't aware that he was in the midst of telling his colleagues that he would be leaving soon to become director and senior fellow at the Center for Science and Culture at the Discovery Institute in Seattle. His impending departure was a poignant time for Meyer, since he had spent more than a decade as one of the most popular professors at the school.

To steal some time alone, we commandeered a nondescript off-campus office, where decorating was an apparent afterthought, and sat down in facing chairs for what would turn out to be virtually an entire day of animated, rapid-fire conversation. In fact, the full transcript of our discussion would top a whopping thirty thousand words—a small book in itself!

At one point, Meyer said, "I was once tested for hyperactivity as a kid. Can you imagine?" Yes, I could. Dressed in a dark blue suit, patterned tie, woolly gray socks, and brown Doc Martin shoes, the lanky Meyer was crackling with energy, speaking enthusiastically in quick bursts of words. His wispy brown hair spilled down onto his forehead, giving him a youthful appearance, but his eyebrows were furrowed in intensity.

His students sometimes faulted him for an absentminded professor's lack of classroom organization, but he made up for it with his infectious passion and disarming sincerity. When he answered my questions, it was in a thorough, systematic, and structured way, almost as if he were reading off invisible note cards. He came off as being brilliant, articulate, and driven.

After swapping some personal stories, we zeroed in on the issue of science and faith. His perspective, not surprisingly, was vastly different from the one I had when I began studying Darwinism in school.

"A ROBUST CASE FOR THEISM"

"We live in a technological culture where many people believe science trumps all other forms of knowledge," I said to Meyer. "For example, philosopher J. P. Moreland described meeting an engineer who was completing his doctorate in physics. 'According to him,' Moreland said, 'only science is rational; only science achieves truth. Everything else is mere belief and opinion. He went on to say that if something cannot be quantified or tested by the scientific method . . . it cannot be true or rational.'[7] Harvard geneticist Richard Lewontin claimed science is 'the only begetter of truth.'[8] Do you agree with those perspectives?"

"No, I don't," came Meyer's reply. "Ironically, to say that science is the only begetter of truth is self-contradicting, because that statement in itself cannot be tested by the scientific method. It's a self-defeating philosophical assumption.

"Beyond that," he continued, "while I certainly respect science, I don't believe scientific knowledge necessarily takes precedence over other things that we know. For instance, Moreland has argued that there are some things we know more certainly through introspection than we know from the sciences. I know I have free will on the basis of my introspection, and no studies in the social sciences will convince me otherwise."

He motioned toward a light switch on the wall. "I know I can turn that switch on, and I refute those who say I was determined thus," he said, leaning over to turn on the light. "In addition, history can tell us much, even though we can't test it by repeated experiment.

"Now, there's no question that science does teach us many important things about the natural world. But the real question is, 'Do these things point to anything beyond themselves?' I think the answer is yes. Science teaches us many true things, and some of those true things point toward God."

I quickly interrupted. "On the contrary," I said, "when I learned about Darwinism as a student, I was convinced that science and faith were at odds—and that science definitely had the edge in the credibility department. What would you say to someone who believes that science and Christianity are destined to be at war?"

"Well, that's certainly one way that people have conceptualized the relationship between science and faith," he said. "Some claim science and faith are fundamentally at odds. Others have said science and faith represent two separate and distinct realms that don't and can't interact with each other.

"However, I personally take a third approach, which is that scientific evidence actually supports theistic belief. In fact, across a wide range of the sciences, evidence has come to light in the last fifty years which, taken together, provides a robust case for theism. Only theism can provide an intellectually satisfying causal explanation for all of this evidence."

"For instance?"

"For instance," he continued, "if it's true there's a beginning to the universe, as modern cosmologists now agree, then this implies a cause that transcends the universe. If the laws of physics are fine-tuned to permit life, as contemporary physicists are discovering, then perhaps there's a designer who fine-tuned them. If there's information in the cell, as molecular biology shows, then this suggests intelligent design. To get life going in the first place would have required biological information; the implications point beyond the material realm to a prior intelligent cause.

"Those are just three examples," he concluded. "And that's just the beginning."

THE PROBLEM WITH NOMA

"Isn't it dangerous to mix science and faith that way?" I asked. "A lot of scientists follow the lead of the late Stephen Jay Gould in saying that science and faith occupy distinctly different 'magisteria' or domains.

"He called this philosophy NOMA, which is short for 'non-overlapping magisteria.' He said: 'The net of science covers the empirical universe . . . [while] the net of religion extends over questions of moral meaning and value.'[9] What's wrong with having that kind of strong dividing line between the hard facts of science and the soft faith of religion?"

"I think NOMA is partially true," Meyer said—a concession that surprised me a bit. "There are domains of science that are metaphysically neutral. They answer questions like: 'How many elements are in the periodic table?' Or 'What is the mathematical equation that describes gravitational attraction?' Or 'How does nature ordinarily behave under a given set of conditions?' Questions of this sort don't affect big worldview issues one way or the other. Some people use Galileo's old aphorism—'Science tells you how the heavens go, and the Bible tells you how to go to heaven.'"

I jumped in. "That sounds trite, but it does make some sense."

"Of course," he said. "There is a sense in which science and religion do have different objects of interest and focus, like the nature of the Trinity on one hand, and what are the elementary particles present at the Big Bang on the other hand.

"However, there are other scientific questions that bear directly on the great worldview issues. For instance, the question of origins. If fully naturalistic models are correct, then theism becomes an unnecessary hypothesis. It's in these instances where science and metaphysics intersect—where worldview questions are at stake—that it's impossible to impose the NOMA principle. That's because what science discovers will inevitably have implications for these larger worldview questions. The only real way to keep the two separate is to subtract from the claims of one or the other.

"You see, NOMA says science is the realm of facts, and religion is the realm of morality and faith. The essential problem is that biblical religion makes very specific claims about facts. It makes claims about the universe having a beginning, about God playing a role in creation, about humans having a certain kind of nature, and about historical events that are purported to have happened in time and space.

"Let's just take the historic Christian creed: 'I believe in God the Father almighty, maker of heaven and earth: And in Jesus Christ his only son, our Lord; who was conceived by the Holy Spirit, born of the Virgin Mary, suffered under Pontius Pilate, was crucified, dead, and buried; the third day he rose again from the dead.'

"Well, Pontius Pilate is situated historically in Palestine in the first century. A claim is made that Jesus of Nazareth lived at the same time. An assertion is made that he rose from the dead. God is called the Creator of heaven and earth. You see, it's inherent to the Christian faith to make claims about the real world. According to the Bible, God has revealed himself in time and space, and so Christianity—for good or ill—is going to intersect some of the factual claims of history and science. There's either going to be conflict or agreement.

"To make NOMA work, its advocates have to water down science or faith, or both. Certainly Gould did—he said religion is just a matter of ethical teaching, comfort, or metaphysical beliefs about meaning. But Christianity certainly claims to be more than that."

This particular statement about Gould seemed vague. I wanted to pin him down by demanding specifics. "Could you give me one concrete example of how Gould watered down Christianity to make NOMA work?" I asked.

"Sure," he said. "In his book *Rocks of Ages*, Gould reduces the appearance of the resurrected Jesus to doubting Thomas to being merely 'a moral tale.'[10] This was necessary for Gould to do under the rules of NOMA because all of Jesus' post-resurrection appearances come from a religious document—the Bible—and NOMA says religion must confine its claims to matters of morality and values. But the Bible clearly portrays Jesus' appearances as being actual historical events. Christianity hinges on the conviction that they really occurred.

"NOMA may try to exclude this possibility by restricting religion to mere matters of morality, but the writers of the Bible did not see fit to limit their claims about God to the nonfactual domain that NOMA has allocated to religion. Now, there might be some religions that can fit comfortably with NOMA. But biblical Christianity—because it's built not just on faith, but on facts—simply cannot."

Law professor Phillip Johnson also has been strongly critical of the NOMA concept. "Stephen Jay Gould condescendingly offers to allow religious people to express their subjective opinions about morals, provided they don't interfere with the authority of scientists to determine the 'facts'—one of the facts being that God is merely a comforting myth," he said.[11]

"So," I said to Meyer in summing up, "while much of science and biblical religion are concerned with different things, they clearly do have some overlapping territory."

"Precisely. And when that happens, either they agree or disagree. The judgment of nineteenth-century historians, who were writing mainly out of an Enlightenment framework, was that where they did overlap, they invariably disagreed—and of the two domains, science was a more warranted system of belief. They believed conflict would continually grow between science and biblical religion."

"What do *you* believe?" I asked.

"My judgment is quite different," he said. "I believe that the testimony of science *supports* theism. While there will always be points of tension or unresolved conflict, the major developments in science in the past five decades have been running in a strongly theistic direction."

He paused momentarily, then punched his conclusion: "Science, *done right*, points toward God."

CREATIO EX NIHILO

Meyer's perspective couldn't be more different from the one I had when I was studying evolution in school. I had concluded that the persuasive naturalistic theories of Darwin eliminated any need for God. Meyer, however, was convinced that science and faith are pointing toward the same truth. I decided to press him for more details.

"Could you list, say, half a dozen examples of how you believe science points toward theism?" I asked.

Meyer settled deeper into his chair. "I would start," he said, "with the new cosmology—the Big Bang theory and its accompanying theoretical underpinning in general relativity. These two theories now point to a definite beginning of the universe. The fact that most scientists now believe that energy, matter, space, and time had a beginning is profoundly antimaterialistic.

"You can invoke neither time nor space nor matter nor energy nor the laws of nature to explain the origin of the universe. General relativity points to the need for a cause that transcends those domains. And theism affirms the existence of such an entity—namely, God.

"In short," he added, "naturalism is on hard times in cosmology; the deeper you get into it, the harder it is to get rid of the God hypothesis. Taken together, the Big Bang and general relativity provide a scientific description of what Christians call *creatio ex nihilo*—creation out of nothing. As Nobel Prize–winner Arno Penzias said about the Big Bang, 'The best data we have are exactly what I would have predicted had I nothing to go on but the first five books of Moses, the Psalms and the Bible as a whole.'"[12]

Meyer waited, apparently to see if I had any further questions, but I motioned for him to continue with his examples.

"The second category of evidence would be for 'anthropic fine-tuning.' This means the fundamental laws and parameters of physics have precise numerical values that could have been otherwise. That is, there's no fundamental reason why these values have to be the way they are. Yet all of these laws and constants conspire in a mathematically incredible way to make life in the universe possible."

I asked him for an example. "Take the expansion rate of the universe, which is fine-tuned to one part in a trillion trillion trillion trillion trillion," he said. "That is, if it were changed by one part in either direction—a little faster, a little slower—we could not have a universe that would be capable of supporting life.

"As Sir Fred Hoyle commented, 'A commonsense interpretation of the facts suggests that a superintellect has monkeyed with physics, as well as chemistry and biology, and that there are no blind forces worth speaking about in nature.'[13]

"Well, maybe this looks fine-tuned because there actually is a fine-tuner. In the opinion of physicist Paul Davies, 'The impression of design is overwhelming.'[14] And I thoroughly agree. This is powerful evidence for intelligent design.

"The third example of science pointing toward God is the origin of life and the origin of information necessary to bring life into existence," he continued. "Life at its root requires information, which is stored in DNA and protein molecules.

"Richard Dawkins of Oxford said that 'the machine code of the genes is uncannily computer-like.'[15] If you reflect on that, you realize that computers run on software programs that are produced by intelligent engineers. Every experience we have about information—whether it's a computer code, hieroglyphic inscription, a book, or a cave painting—points toward intelligence. The same is true about the information inside every cell in every living creature."

"Isn't that just an argument from ignorance?" I asked. "Scientists may not currently be able to find any explanation for how life began, but that doesn't necessarily point toward a supernatural conclusion."

"This is *not* an argument from ignorance," Meyer insisted. "We're not inferring design just because the naturalistic evolutionary theories all fail to explain information. We infer design because all those theories fail *and* we know of another causal entity that is capable of producing information—namely, intelligence. Personally, I find this to be a very strong argument indeed."

AN ENSEMBLE OF EVIDENCE

Continuing on to the fourth example, Meyer said, "Then there's the evidence for design in molecular machines that defy explanation by Darwinian natural selection. These integrative, complex systems in biological organisms—which microbiologist Michael Behe calls 'irreducibly complex'—include signal transduction circuits, sophisticated motors, and all kinds of biological circuitry."

"What's the argument based on this?" I asked.

"You see, these biological machines need all of their various parts in order to function. But how could you ever build such a system by a Darwinian process of natural selection acting on random variations? Natural selection only preserves things that perform a function—in other words, which help the organism survive to the next generation. That's survival of the fittest.

"The problem with irreducibly complex systems is that they perform no function until all the parts are present and working together in close coordination with one another. So natural selection cannot help you build such systems; it can only preserve them once they've been built. And it's virtually impossible for evolution to take such a huge leap by mere chance to create the whole system at once.

"Of course, this forces the question: how did the biochemical machine arise? Behe says maybe these biological systems look designed because they really *were* designed. After all, whenever we see irreducibly complex systems and we know how they arose, invariably a designer was the cause."

"How strong of an argument do you think that is?" I asked.

"I think it's very strong," he replied with a smile. "And you see that in the weak objections that are proposed by Darwinists. And again, that's just one more example. The next one would be the Cambrian explosion, which is yet another striking piece of evidence for design in the history of life."

I told him that in a previous interview Jonathan Wells had already explained the basics of Biology's Big Bang. "He talked about it primarily in terms of being an argument against Darwinism," I said.

"Indeed, it is," Meyer replied. "You have between twenty and thirty-five completely novel body plans that come online in the Cambrian. You have a huge jump in complexity, it's sudden, and you have no transitional intermediates.

"But this is also affirmative evidence for design, because in our experience information invariably is the result of conscious activity. Here we have the geologically sudden infusion of a massive amount of new biological information needed to create these body plans, far beyond what any Darwinian mechanism can produce. Darwinism simply can't account for it; design is a better explanation.

"Think about how suddenly these new body plans emerged. As one paleontologist said, 'What I want to know from my biology friends is just how fast does this evolution have to happen before they stop calling it evolution?' Darwin said nature takes no sudden leaps. Yet here's a huge leap—which is what intelligent agents cause. Consequently, the Cambrian explosion provides not just a negative case against Darwinian evolution, but also a compelling positive argument for design."

"All right," I said, "I asked for half a dozen examples. What would be the sixth?"

Meyer thought for a moment. "I'd say human consciousness certainly supports a theistic view of human nature," he said. "Judaism and Christianity clearly teach that we are more than just matter—we're not a 'computer made of meat,' in the words of Marvin Minsky, but we're made in God's image.

"We have the capacity for self-reflection, for representational art, for language, for creativity. Science can't account for this kind of consciousness merely from the interaction of physical matter in the brain. Where did it come from? Again, I think theism provides the best explanation."

Meyer scooted to the edge of his chair. "So what we have here," he said, wrapping up his impromptu presentation in a tone of urgency, "is an ensemble of half a dozen evidences that point to a transcendent, intelligent cause. This is mind-boggling stuff! Scientists in the nineteenth century weren't aware of these things when they said naturalism accounts for everything. Thanks to the discoveries of the last five decades, we know a lot more today."

"Based on the evidence you've mentioned," I said, "how do you complete the case for God?"

"First, theism, with its concept of a transcendent Creator, provides a more causally adequate explanation of the Big Bang than a naturalistic explanation can offer," he said. "The cause of the universe must transcend matter, space, and time, which were brought into existence with the Big Bang. The Judeo-Christian God has precisely this attribute of transcendence. Yet naturalism, by definition, denies the existence of any entity beyond the closed system of nature.

"The fine-tuning of the physical laws and constants of the universe and the precise configuration of its initial conditions, dating back to the very origin of the universe itself, suggest the need for a cause that's intelligent. Theism affirms the existence of an entity that's not only transcendent but intelligent as well—namely, God. Thus, theism can explain both Big Bang cosmology and the anthropic fine-tuning.

"Pantheism can't explain the origin of the universe, because pantheists believe in an impersonal god that's coextensive with the physical universe. Such a god can't bring the universe into being from nothing, since such a god doesn't exist independently of the physical universe. If initially the physical universe didn't exist, then the pantheistic god wouldn't have existed either. If it didn't exist, it couldn't cause the universe to exist."

"What about deism?" I interjected, referring to the belief that God created the world but has since let it run on its own. "Can't deism account for the origin of the universe too?"

"Yes, I'll provide that caveat—deism can do the same," he acknowledged. "But I believe the existence of design subsequent to the Big Bang undermines deism as an adequate explanation.

"You see, deism can't explain the evidence of discrete acts of design or creation after the universe was created. The deistic god never intervenes in nature, yet we're seeing evidence of intelligent design in the history of life. For example, the high information content in the cell provides compelling evidence for an act of intelligent design of the first life, long after the beginning of the universe.

"Taken together, what we know today gives us heightened confidence—*from science*—that God exists. The weight of the evidence is very, very impressive—in fact, in my opinion it's sufficiently conclusive to say that theism provides the best explanation for the ensemble of scientific evidence we've been discussing.

"Science and faith are not at war. When scientific evidence and biblical teaching are correctly interpreted, they can and do support each other. I'd say to anyone who doubts that: investigate the evidence yourself."

Meyer's whirlwind tour was exhilarating. At first blush, the cumulative case for God, built point by point from the discoveries of science, seemed staggering. Of course, I had a whole slew of follow-up questions, some of which I intended to pose to Meyer, and others I would save for the experts I planned to interview in each of the categories of evidence Meyer had mentioned. I decided to begin with the issue of just how much evidence for God is needed to establish the case for a Creator.

THE GOD HYPOTHESIS

In the legal arena, different courtrooms have different standards of proof. In criminal cases, the prosecutor must prove the defendant guilty beyond a reasonable doubt. In most civil cases, the plaintiff must prevail by a considerably lesser standard, called a preponderance of the evidence. In some civil cases, there's even a third level of proof situated between the other two: clear and convincing evidence.[16]

When I asked Meyer what standard of proof he considered appropriate in the theological realm, he gave me an interesting history lesson on the topic of evidence for God. I decided to sit back and let him talk, reserving my follow-up questions for the end.

"One extreme is to deny that there is any evidential basis for Christian belief and instead to say that all we need is faith," Meyer began. "That's known as 'fideism.' This came out of the Enlightenment, with the perceived failure of certain theistic proofs for the existence of God.

"In particular, French philosopher René Descartes offered some pretty sloppy proofs to try to establish with absolute certainty that God exists. He used what are called 'deductive proofs,' where you have major and minor premises, and if these premises can be shown to be true and the logic of the argument is correct, then the conclusion follows with certainty. For example, 'All men are mortal, Socrates is a man, therefore Socrates is mortal.' Descartes set the bar unrealistically high—that is, using his proofs to try to create ironclad certainty that God exists—and he couldn't clear it. You can't absolutely prove—or disprove—the existence of God.

"As a result, the opinion developed that arguments for God's existence don't work and that therefore there's no rational basis for faith. Then Darwin, by showing that the appearance of design could be explained through natural mechanisms without an actual designer, contributed to the conviction that there was no rational or evidential basis for believing in God.

"In light of that, religious believers had a choice: reject faith, because it has no rational foundation, or reject the idea that you need a rational foundation for faith. The ones who remained believers took the latter, by saying, 'I believe, I just don't have or need a rational basis for doing so.' They would then adopt strategies that would compartmentalize faith and reason, which led to the conclusion that faith and science occupy two different realms.

"But there's a third option, which involves making a persuasive case for faith without using deductive proofs. Mathematician William Dembski and I wrote an article in 1998, articulating a model of reasoning that we think can be used to support theistic belief. It's called 'inference to the best explanation.'

"This is a form of practical reasoning that we use in life all the time. It says if we want to explain a phenomenon or event, we consider a whole range of hypotheses and infer to the one which, if true, would provide the best explanation. In other words, we do an exhaustive analysis of the possible explanations and keep adding information until only one explanation is left that can explain the whole range of data.

"The way you discriminate between the competing hypotheses is to look at their explanatory power. Often, more than one hypothesis can explain the same piece of evidence. For instance, as we just agreed, deism and theism can both explain the beginning of the universe. Okay, fine. But if you keep looking at the data, you find that only theism can explain the evidence for design in biology after the origin of the universe. And so theism has superior explanatory power.

"We reach conclusions with a high degree of confidence using this form of reasoning in our everyday life. This is what detectives do. This is what lawyers do in courts of law. Scientists use this approach. This model can enable us to achieve a high degree of practical certainty.

"And when we look at the evidence I've mentioned from cosmology, physics, biology, and human consciousness, we find that theism has amazing explanatory scope and power. The existence of God explains this broad range of evidence more simply, adequately, and comprehensively than any other worldview, including its main competitors, naturalism or pantheism. And the discovery of corroborating or supportive evidence is accelerating.

"In 1992, the historian of science Frederic Burnham said the God hypothesis 'is now a more respectable hypothesis than at any time in the last one hundred years.'[17] I'd go even further. More than just being 'respectable,' I'd say that the God hypothesis is forceful enough to warrant a verdict that he's alive and well."

THE MOTIVES OF SCIENTISTS

Several questions popped into my mind as I listened to Meyer's analysis. "I gave you the opportunity to offer six strands of scientific evidence for theism, and I'll be following up with specific objections when I explore them in-depth with other experts," I said. "But I don't want to leave without posing at least four overall challenges to you."

As he listened, Meyer removed his gold-rimmed glasses and started cleaning them with a handkerchief. He looked up at me and said, "That sounds fair. Go ahead. What's your first question?"

I glanced down at my notes before speaking. "If the scientific evidence for theism is so compelling," I began, "then why don't more scientists believe in God? A study in 1966 showed that sixty percent of scientists either disbelieve or were doubtful about God, and the percentage goes up if you look at the most elite scientists."[18]

Meyer pursed his lips as he reflected on the question. "Initially, I'd say that it takes time for new discoveries to percolate and for their implications to be fully considered, and some of the best evidence for theism is very new," he said. "Scientists who are focused on one particular field may not be aware of discoveries in other fields that point toward theism.

"Also, the materialistic worldview has exercised dominance on intellectual life in western culture for a hundred and fifty years. It has become the default worldview in science, philosophy, and academia in general. It's presupposed. Some people who dissent from it have experienced intense hostility and sometimes persecution. That could discourage others from exploring this area or speaking out favorably toward it."

This point reminded me of a quote by Sandage, who once told a reporter that the scientific community is so scornful of faith that "there is a reluctance to reveal yourself as a believer, the opprobrium is so severe."[19]

"Finally," continued Meyer, "within the scientific culture there are belief systems that are philosophically very questionable. For instance, many believe that science must only allow naturalistic explanations, which excludes from consideration the design hypothesis. Many scientists put blinders on, refusing to acknowledge that evidence, and a kind of 'group think' develops."

His answer sounded plausible, but it prompted a second line of inquiry. "There's a flip side to that issue," I said. "Skeptic Michael Shermer said almost all the people he sees in the Intelligent Design movement are Christians.[20] Doesn't that undermine the legitimacy of their science? Maybe they're only looking for what they want to find and aren't open to naturalistic explanations that might be sufficient."

This challenge seemed to push a button with Meyer. "Every scientist has a motive," he said firmly, "but motives are irrelevant to assessing the validity of scientific theories, a case in court, or an argument in philosophy. You have to respond to the evidence or argument that's being offered, regardless of who offers it or why. If every person in the Intelligent Design movement were a fundamentalist who attends Baptist Bible Church, it wouldn't matter. Their arguments have to be weighed on their own merits."

"But is this an exclusively Christian movement?" I asked.

"No, it's not," he replied. "There are scientists who are proponents of intelligent design who are agnostic or Jewish, but I still don't think that's relevant. The vast majority of people who advocate Darwinism are naturalists or materialists, so you could play the motive-mongering game either way.

"Besides, look at it this way: if a scientist becomes persuaded by the evidence that theism is true and thus becomes a follower of God, should he or she then be disqualified from doing science in that area? Of course not. I say let's get beyond this side issue and let the evidence speak for itself. Is design the best explanation or not?"

"That leads to the third question," I said. "If scientists do allow the possibility of the miraculous as an explanation, then doesn't that foreclose further investigation? Biologist Kenneth Miller has suggested that inferring the existence of an intelligent designer would result in a scientific dead-end.[21] Why continue to explore an area scientifically once you've thrown up your hands and said, 'God did this'?"

Meyer immediately fired back. "I think the shoe is exactly on the other foot," he said.

"How so?"

"Let's take the issue of origins, for example," he said. "The question that's asked is, 'How did the cell arise on earth?' If you say, 'We're only going to let you consider answers that involve materialistic processes,' then that shuts down inquiry, because one of the possible causal explanations for the origin of life is that intelligence could have played a role."

"So," I said, "you believe that ruling out the possibility of intelligent design stifles intellectual and scientific inquiry."

"That's exactly right," he replied. "And I've seen it happen far too often."

I pointed at him. "You want to change the rules of the game, don't you?" I said, my tone suggesting I had just caught him with his hand in the cookie jar.

"In a sense, yes," he conceded. "I don't think it's right to invoke a self-serving rule that says only naturalistic explanations can be considered by science. Let's have a new period in the history of science where we have methodological rules that actually foster the unfettered seeking of truth. Scientists should be allowed to follow the evidence wherever it leads—even if it leads to a conclusion that makes some people uncomfortable."

SEEING EYE TO EYE

My fourth objection concerned a topic called "disteleology," which refers to apparent poor design in the biological and physical world. "To adopt the explanation of design, we are forced to attribute a host of flaws and imperfections to the Designer," Miller wrote.[22] The implication is that an imperfect design disproves the existence of a perfect God.

One example Miller cited is the vertebrate eye. "We would have to wonder why an intelligent designer placed the neural wiring of the retina on the side facing the incoming light," he wrote. "This arrangement scatters the light, making our vision less detailed than it might be, and even produces a blind spot at the point that the wiring is pulled through the light-sensitive retina to produce the optic nerve that carries visual images to the brain."[23]

Other Darwinists, including Oxford's Richard Dawkins, also have decried the eye's poor structure, with George Williams going so far as to declare it "stupidly" designed because "the retina is upside down."[24]

This seemed to be a compelling counter-argument to intelligent design. "If there is a designer," I said to Meyer, "doesn't the botched eye design prove he's not really intelligent?"

He pounced on the issue. "There's an important physiological reason as to why the retina has to be inverted in the eye," he said. "Within the overall design of the system, it's a tradeoff that allows the eye to process the vast amount of oxygen it needs in vertebrates. Yes, this creates a slight blind spot, but that's not a problem because people have two eyes and the two blind spots don't overlap. Actually, the eye is an incredible design."

With that, Meyer stood and walked to the other side of the room, where his briefcase was leaning against a desk. He rifled through some papers and finally withdrew a photocopy of an article.

"In fact," he said as he handed it to me, "biologist George Ayoub wrote this piece to refute the claim that the eye was badly created." I glanced at the technical article, in which Ayoub, a professor whose expertise is the cellular physiology of the retina, concludes:

> The vertebrate retina provides an excellent example of functional—though non-intuitive—design. The design of the retina is responsible for its high acuity and sensitivity. It is simply untrue that the retina is demonstrably suboptimal, nor is it easy to conceive how it might be modified without significantly decreasing its function.[25]

Feeling a little chagrined, I put down the article. "Okay," I conceded, "maybe that's not a good example of disteleology, but there are a lot of others."

Meyer interrupted. "Don't move on too quickly," he said. "There's a good lesson here. People make a lot of claims about bad biological design, but sometimes the entire picture is changed when you hear the rest of the story. For instance, people claim a design is bad because they look at only one parameter and claim it could have been better designed. However, engineers know all designs require optimizing a whole suite of parameters, and so tradeoffs are inevitable to create the best overall result."

That was a mouthful that demanded elaboration. "Give me an example," I said.

He gestured toward the Apple computer in the open briefcase at my feet. "One illustration that's sometimes given is a laptop," he said.

"You could look at the screen and say, 'Bad design; it should have been bigger.' You could look at the memory and say, 'Bad design; should have had a larger capacity.' You could look at the keyboard and say, 'Bad design; should have been easier to use.'

"But the engineer isn't supposed to be creating the *best* screen, the *best* memory, and the *best* keyboard—he's supposed to be producing the best computer he can given certain size, weight, price, and portability requirements. Could the screen be bigger? Yes, but then portability suffers. Could the computer have more memory? Sure, but then the cost goes too high.

"So there are inevitable tradeoffs and compromises. Each individual part might be criticized for being suboptimal, but that's not the issue. The real issue is how well the overall laptop functions. That's how good engineering works—and that explains some of the examples of supposed disteleology that are raised."

While that made sense, it didn't answer everything. "You'll have to admit that there are other illustrations of disteleology that are more difficult to explain away," I said.

"I don't deny that," he relied. "Some are just silly. Others are more thoughtful and serious, and they require effort to think through. For instance, Gould claimed the panda's thumb looks jerry-rigged and not designed. Well, experts on the panda say it's a pretty efficient way of scraping the bark off bamboo. In the absence of a standard of good design, which Gould can't provide, it's really hard to say whether it's good or bad. It seems to perform its function exceedingly well.

"Other illustrations of disteleology get into issues of theodicy, or reconciling belief in God and natural evil. For example, what about viruses and bacteria that harm people? Did God create those? Natural theologians in the nineteenth century believed that if a perfect God created the world, then it would be perfect, so they were ill-equipped to deal with Darwin's disteleological arguments.

"However, from a biblical point of view, there isn't an expectation that nature would be perfect. The Bible says there has been decay or deterioration because evil entered the world and disrupted the original design. We're not given all of the specifics on how this happened, but the biblical book of Romans affirms the natural world is groaning for its redemption, because something has gone wrong with the original creation.[26] Based on the biblical account, we would expect to see both evidence of design in nature as well as evidence of deterioration or decay—which we do."

It was time to move on, but I glanced down at the laptop computer in my briefcase. I had to admit that Meyer's basic explanations about disteleology did make a lot of sense.

ROADMAP TO THE FUTURE

As we wrapped up our conversation, I felt a little like Meyer did when he attended the Dallas conference in 1985: enthused about the affirmative scientific case for God. So far, the evidence from the telescope to the microscope was pointing powerfully in the direction of a Creator—a circumstance I never would have dreamed possible back in my days as a student. I was left with an urgent desire to continue my investigation.

Still, I also was experiencing an underlying skepticism. Would the case for a Creator hold up when it was scrutinized more carefully and when I could cross-examine experts with all of the questions that plagued me? What fascinating new details would be supplied by those who have spent years studying the various categories of evidence that Meyer had described? Would his case emerge strengthened, weakened, or destroyed?

As a legal affairs journalist, I had seen a lot of trials where the prosecutor provided a persuasive overview of the evidence during his opening statement to the jury. But the judge always instructs the jury that the prosecutor's words aren't evidence. They're merely a road map to help them process the subsequent testimony by witnesses.

In a sense, this is what Meyer had provided for me: an outline of the scientific evidence for theism. Now was the time for me to put experts in cosmology, physics, astronomy, microbiology, biological information, and consciousness to the test and see whether the case is as strong as Meyer claimed. My plan was to start at the literal beginning—the origin of the universe, which occurred in an explosion of energy so incomprehensibly powerful that its echo, in effect, is still being heard billions of years later.

I couldn't wait to get started!

THE WRY SMILE OF GOD

I didn't want to leave, however, without taking a few moments to ponder my impressions of Meyer. I especially liked his endearing blend of a professor's academic depth combined with an advocate's savvy and an enthusiast's winsome earnestness. But while we had talked a lot about science, a bit about philosophy, and a little about theology, I realized we hadn't delved into Meyer's personal reflections. His journey from scientist to intelligent design advocate was fascinating to me, and I was curious about the state of Stephen Meyer's spiritual life.

"Over the years as you've studied the scientific evidence that supports theism, how has this affected your faith?" I asked.

"It has strengthened it, no question," he replied. "The trend is definitely toward more discoveries that point toward God, and that excites me. More and more people are going to find themselves open to God as a result of new findings that make theistic belief the best explanation for the evidence of nature."

He stopped at that. It was a safe answer, but I could tell he was weighing whether he should risk more. I sensed he was the kind of person who would be more comfortable extolling the virtues of microbiology than opening up about something as personal as his own relationship with God. But as I sat quietly and listened, he was about to prove me wrong.

"One thing I haven't told you about my spiritual journey," he continued, "is that for a two-year period in my life, I was very attracted to Nietzsche's version of existentialism. Nietzsche had a different objection than the ones we've been talking about. He asked, *Why should God rule and I serve?* This resonated with me. Why should a condition of my happiness be submission to the will of God? I sensed I couldn't be happy without him; I knew my bad lifestyle only brought misery. So I ended up literally shaking my fist at God in a wheat field in Washington state.

"My point is that the intellectual rebellion the apostle Paul talks about is very true in my own life. Even in my Christian thinking today, I find a tendency to slide back into what Paul refers to as the natural mind. And here's what the scientific evidence for God does for me: it realigns me. It helps me recognize that despite my natural tendency toward self-focus and self-absorption, I can't ignore what God has accomplished in this world to let everyone know that he is real, that he is the Creator, and that we need to get right with him.

"I see this not only in cosmology and physics and biology, but also in the historical revelation of the Bible, principally in the revelation of Jesus Christ himself. He is *so* compelling! Einstein thought so. Napoleon thought so. This Nazarene captivated their attention, and he continues to captivate mine.

"I remember thinking at one point that if the Jesus of the Bible weren't real, I would need to worship the person who created the character. Jesus is so beyond what I can comprehend! And the evidence for God in nature constantly challenges me to a deeper and fuller relationship with him. My study of the scientific evidence isn't separate from my life as a Christian; it's marbled throughout that experience.

"I remember when I first began teaching a college course on the evidence for God, I got flack from some people who claimed that these kinds of arguments can produce an idol of the mind or make science a god. I felt a little reticent for a while—but no longer. I've come to an even stronger conviction that this is evidence that God has used to reveal himself to us.

"I look at the stars in the night sky or reflect on the structure and information-bearing properties of the DNA molecule, and these are occasions for me to worship the Creator who brought them into existence. I think of the wry smile that might be on the lips of God as in the last few years all sorts of evidence for the reliability of the Bible and for his creation of the universe and life have come to light. I believe he has caused them to be unveiled in his providence and that he delights when we discover his fingerprints in the vastness of the universe, in the dusty relics of paleontology, and in the complexity of the cell.

"So exploring the scientific and historical evidence for God is not only a cognitive exercise, but it's an act of worship for me. It's a way of giving the Creator the credit and honor and glory that are due to him. To attribute creation to a mere natural process is a form of idolatry to which we're all prone. I don't judge my naturalistic colleagues for being prone to that. That's how I'm constituted as well. All of us have a tendency to minimize God, to think and behave as if we weren't really immersed in his creation and that we aren't ourselves the product of his unimaginable creative power.

"Looking at the evidence—in nature and in Scripture—reminds me over and over again of who he is. And it reminds me of who I am too—someone in need of him."

FOR FURTHER EVIDENCE
More Resources on This Topic

Dembski, William. *The Design Revolution: Answering the Toughest Questions about Intelligent Design.* Downer's Grove, Ill.: InterVarsity, 2004.

McGrath, Alister. *Glimpsing the Face of God*. Grand Rapids, Mich.: Eerdmans. 2002.

Meyer, Stephen C. "Evidence for Design in Physics and Biology." In *Science and Evidence for Design in the Universe*, eds. Michael J. Behe, William A. Dembski, and Stephen C. Meyer. San Francisco: Ignatius, 1999.

——. "Modern Science and the Return of the God Hypothesis." In *Science and Christianity: Four Views*, ed. Richard F. Carlson. Downer's Grove, Ill.: InterVarsity, 2000.

Moreland, J. P. *Christianity and the Nature of Science*. Grand Rapids, Mich.: Baker, 1989.

Witham, Larry. *By Design: Science and the Search for God*. San Francisco: Encounter, 2003.

5

THE EVIDENCE
OF COSMOLOGY:
BEGINNING WITH
A BANG

Set aside the many competing explanations of the Big Bang;
something made an entire cosmos out of nothing. It is this real-
ization—that something transcendent started it all—which
has hard-science types . . . using terms like 'miracle.'

Journalist Gregg Easterbrook[1]

Perhaps the best argument . . . that the Big Bang supports the-
ism is the obvious unease with which it is greeted by some athe-
ist physicists. At times this has led to scientific ideas . . . being
advanced with a tenacity which so exceeds their intrinsic worth
that one can only suspect the operation of psychological forces
lying very much deeper than the usual academic desire of a
theorist to support his or her theory.

Astrophysicist C. J. Isham[2]

My eyes scanned the magazines at the newsstand near my home.
A beautiful woman graced *Glamour*. Sleek, high-performance
cars streaked across the front of *Motor Trend*. And there on the cover
of *Discover* magazine, sitting by itself, unadorned, floating in a sea of
pure white background, was a simple red sphere. It was smaller than
a tennis ball, tinier than a Titleist—just three quarters of an inch in
diameter, not too much bigger than a marble.

As staggering as it seemed, it represented the actual size of the
entire universe when it was just an infinitesimal fraction of one second old. Cried out the headline: *Where Did Everything Come From?*[3]

Thousands of years ago, the Hebrews believed they had the
answer: "In the beginning God created the heavens and the earth,"

opens the Bible.[4] Everything began, they claimed, with the primordial *fiat lux*—the voice of God commanding light into existence.[5] But is that a simplistic superstition or a divinely inspired insight? What do the cosmologists—scientists who devote their lives to studying the origin of the universe—have to say about the issue?

It seemed to me that the beginning of everything was a good place to start my investigation into whether the affirmative evidence of science points toward or away from a Creator. At the time, I wasn't particularly interested in internal Christian debates over whether the world is young or old. The "when" wasn't as important to me as the "how"— how do scientific models and theories explain the origin of all?[6]

"In the beginning there was an explosion," explained Nobel Prize–winning physicist Steven Weinberg in his book *The First Three Minutes*. "Not an explosion like those familiar on Earth, starting from a definite center and spreading out to engulf more and more of the circumambient air, but an explosion which occurred simultaneously everywhere, filling all space from the beginning with every particle of matter rushing apart from every other particle."[7]

Within the tiniest split second, the temperature hit a hundred thousand million degrees Centigrade. "This is much hotter than in the center of even the hottest star, so hot, in fact, that none of the components of ordinary matter, molecules, or atoms, or even the nuclei of atoms, could have held together," he wrote.[8]

The matter rushing apart, he explained, consisted of such elementary particles as negatively charged electrons, positively charged positrons, and neutrinos, which lack both electrical charge and mass. Interestingly, there were also photons: "The universe," he said, "was filled with light."[9]

"In three minutes," wrote Bill Bryson in *A Short History of Nearly Everything*, "ninety-eight percent of all the matter there is or will ever be has been produced. We have a universe. It is a place of the most wondrous and gratifying possibility, and beautiful, too. And it was all done in about the time it takes to make a sandwich."[10]

The most intriguing question is what caused the universe to suddenly spring into existence. For Bryson and many others, its mere presence somehow seems to explain itself. In a chapter called "How to Build a Universe," he vaguely speculates on exotic theories about a "false vacuum," or "scalar field," or "vacuum energy"—some sort of "quality or thing" that may have "introduced a measure of instability into the nothingness that was" and thus sparked the Big Bang through which emerged the entire universe.

"It seems impossible that you could get something from nothing," he said, "but the fact that once there was nothing and now there is a universe is evident proof that you can."[11]

Yet could there be another explanation that better accounts for the evidence? Might the mysterious causation be divine? Maybe Edward Milne was right when he capped his mathematical treatise on relativity by saying: "As to the first cause of the Universe ... that is left for the reader to insert, but our picture is incomplete without Him."[12]

I knew this investigation would take me into the slippery world of theoretical physics, where it's sometimes difficult to discern between what's profoundly scholarly and what's just plain silly. That was well-illustrated in late 2002 when a debate broke out over a highly speculative theory from two French mathematical physicists (who happened to be twins) about what might have preceded the Big Bang.

As amazing—and amusing—as it seems, the scientific community couldn't figure out whether the brothers "are really geniuses with a new view of the moment before the universe began or simply earnest scientists who are in over their heads and spouting nonsense," said a *New York Times* article that featured the provocative headline: "Are They *a)* Geniuses or *b)* Jokers?"

While one professor found their work "intriguing," another dismissed it as "nutty." Yet another protested: "Scientifically, it's clearly more or less complete nonsense, but these days that doesn't much distinguish it from a lot of the rest of the literature." The journal that published a paper by the disputed scientists, who had both received their doctorates with the lowest passing grades, later repudiated it.[13]

Obviously, delving into the dawning of the universe—way back to the first 1/10 million trillion trillion trillionths of a second, which is the furthest back scientists believe they can peer—is going to require a certain degree of speculation. Theories abound. Conceded one prominent cosmologist from Stanford University: "These are very close to religious questions."[14]

As for myself, I wasn't interested in unsupported conjecture or armchair musings by pipe-puffing theorists. I wanted the hard facts of mathematics, the cold data of cosmology, and only the most reasonable inferences that can be drawn from them. And that's what sent me to

Georgia to visit the home of a widely published expert who has studied and debated these issues for decades.

INTERVIEW #3: WILLIAM LANE CRAIG, PHD, THD

As a college student who graduated in 1971, Bill Craig had been taught that various arguments for the existence of God were weak, outdated, and ultimately ineffective. And that's what he believed—until he happened upon philosopher Stuart C. Hackett's 1957 book, *The Resurrection of Theism.*[15]

This dense tome never burned up the best-seller list. In fact, the self-effacing Hackett commented years later that "the book fell stillborn from the press because of its heavy style and technical context."[16] Still, it absolutely stunned Craig.

Hackett is a brilliant thinker who took these theistic arguments seriously, rigorously defending them from every objection he could find or imagine. One argument in the book was that the universe must have had a beginning and, therefore, a Creator. Craig was so intrigued that he decided to use his doctoral studies under British theologian John Hick to come to a resolution in his own mind concerning the soundness of this argument. Would it really withstand scrutiny? Craig ended up writing his dissertation on the topic—an exercise that launched him into a lifetime of exploring cosmology.

Craig's books include a landmark debate with atheist Quentin Smith called *Theism, Atheism and Big Bang Cosmology*, published by Oxford University Press; *The* Kalam *Cosmological Argument*; *The Existence of God and the Beginning of the Universe*; *The Cosmological Argument from Plato to Leibniz*; and *Reasonable Faith*, as well as contributions on this and related topics to the books *Does God Exist?*; *Faith and Reason*; *A Companion to Philosophy of Religion*; *Questions of Time and Tense*; *Mere Creation*; *The History of Science and Religion in the Western Tradition*; *Naturalism: A Critical Appraisal*; and *God and Time*.

His articles on cosmological issues also have appeared in a wide range of scientific and philosophical journals, including *Astrophysics and Space Science*, *Nature*, *The British Journal for the Philosophy of Science*, *The Journal of Philosophy*, and *International Studies in the Philosophy of Science*.

A member of nine professional societies, including the American Philosophical Association, the Science and Religion Forum, the

American Scientific Affiliation, and the Philosophy of Time Society, Craig currently is a research professor at the Talbot School of Theology.

I hardly needed directions to Craig's suburban Atlanta home. In previous visits, I had interviewed him for *The Case for Christ* and *The Case for Faith*, both times walking away thoroughly impressed by his scholarly depth and disarming sincerity. He has an uncanny ability to communicate complex concepts in accessible and yet technically accurate language—a rare skill that I would certainly put to the test again with this challenging subject.

Craig answered the front door wearing a short-sleeved shirt, dark blue shorts, and brown moccasins. We descended a short flight of stairs to his office, where a soft, humid breeze wafted through a half-opened window. He sat behind his desk and leaned back in his chair, clasping his hands behind his head. I pulled up a chair and set up my tape recorder.

We were ready to investigate what Craig himself believes to be "one of the most plausible arguments for God's existence"[17]—an argument based on evidence that the universe is not eternal, but that it had a beginning in the Big Bang.

THE *KALAM* COSMOLOGICAL ARGUMENT

"You're a famous proponent of an argument for God's existence that's formally called the '*kalam* cosmological argument,'" I said in opening our conversation. "Before you define what that is, though, give me some background. What does *kalam* mean?"

"Let me describe the origins of the argument," he said. "In ancient Greece, Aristotle believed that God isn't the Creator of the universe but that he simply imbues order into it. In his view, both God and the universe are eternal. Of course, that contradicted the Hebrew notion that God created the world out of nothing. So Christians later sought to refute Aristotle. One prominent Christian philosopher on the topic was John Philoponus of Alexandria, Egypt, who lived in the fourth century. He argued that the universe had a beginning.

"When Islam took over North Africa, Muslim theologians picked up these arguments, because they also believed in creation. So while this tradition was lost to the Christian West, it began to be highly developed within Islamic medieval theology. One of the most famous Muslim proponents was al-Ghazali, who lived from 1058 to 1111.

"These arguments eventually got passed back into Latin-speaking Christendom through the mediation of Jewish thinkers, who lived side-by-side with Muslim theologians, particularly in Spain, which at that time had been conquered by the Muslims. They became hotly debated.

"Bonaventure, the Italian philosopher, supported the arguments in the thirteenth century; John Locke, the British philosopher, used them in the seventeenth century, though I don't know if he knew of their Islamic origins; and eventually they found their way to Immanuel Kant, the German philosopher, in the eighteenth century.

"Now, back to your question about the word *kalam*—it reflects the argument's Islamic origin. It's an Arabic word that means 'speech' or 'doctrine,' but it came to characterize the whole medieval movement of Islamic theology. That was called *kalam*—this highly academic theology of the Middle Ages, which later evaporated."

I spoke up. "Obviously, none of these early philosophers knew about any of the scientific evidence for the origin of the universe," I said. "How did they argue that the universe had a beginning?"

"They relied on philosophical and mathematical reasoning," he said. "However, when scientists in the last century began to discover hard data about the Big Bang, this provided a more empirical foundation."

"How do you frame the *kalam* argument?"

"As formulated by al-Ghazali, the argument has three simple steps: 'Whatever begins to exist has a cause. The universe began to exist. Therefore, the universe has a cause.' Then you can do a conceptual analysis of what it means to be a cause of the universe, and a striking number of divine attributes can be identified."

I decided to work my way through all three steps of al-Ghazali's nearly millennium-old argument, starting with a point that—surprisingly—has become more and more disputed in recent years.

STEP #1: WHATEVER BEGINS TO EXIST HAS A CAUSE

"When I first began to defend the *kalam* argument," Craig said, "I anticipated that its first premise—that whatever begins to exist has a cause—would be accepted by virtually everyone. I thought the second premise—that the universe began to exist—would be much more controversial. But the scientific evidence has accumulated to the extent that atheists are finding it difficult to deny that the universe had a beginning. So they've been forced to attack the first premise instead."

Craig shook his head. "To me, this is absolutely bewildering!" he declared, his voice rising in dismay. "It seems metaphysically necessary that anything which begins to exist *has* to have a cause that brings it into being. Things don't just pop into existence, uncaused, out of nothing. Yet the atheist Quentin Smith concluded our book on the topic by claiming that 'the most reasonable belief is that we came from nothing, by nothing, and for nothing.'[18] That sounds like a good conclusion to the Gettysburg Address of Atheism! It simply amazes me that anyone can think this is the most rational view.

"Generally, people who take this position don't try to prove the premise is false, because they can't do that. Instead, they fold their arms and play the skeptic by saying, 'You can't prove that's true.' They dial their degree of skepticism so high that nothing could possibly convince them."

"On the other hand," I interjected, "they have every right to play the skeptic. After all, the burden of proof should be on you to present affirmative evidence to establish this first premise."

Craig conceded my point with a nod. "Yes, but you shouldn't demand unreasonable standards of proof," he cautioned.

I asked, "What positive proof can you offer?"

"In the first place," he replied, "this first premise is intuitively obvious once you clearly grasp the concept of absolute nothingness. You see, the idea that things can come into being uncaused out of nothing is worse than magic. At least when a magician pulls a rabbit out of a hat, there's the magician and the hat!

"But in atheism, the universe just pops into being out of nothing, with absolutely no explanation at all. I think once people understand the concept of absolute nothingness, it's simply obvious to them that if something has a beginning, that it could not have popped into being out of nothing but must have a cause that brings it into existence."

Admittedly, that was difficult to dispute, but I needed something more substantial. "Can you offer anything harder than just intuition? What scientific evidence is there?"

"Well, we certainly have empirical evidence for the truth of this premise. This is a principle that is constantly confirmed and never falsified. We never see things coming into being uncaused out of nothing. Nobody worries that while he's away at work, say, a horse might pop into being, uncaused, out of nothing, in his living room, and be there defiling the carpet. We don't worry about those kinds of things, because they never happen.

"So this is a principle that is constantly verified by science. At least, Lee, you have to admit that we have better reason to think it's true than it's false. If you're presented with the principle and its denial, which way does the evidence point? Obviously, the premise is more plausible than its denial."

Still, my research had yielded at least one substantive objection to *kalam's* first premise. It emanates from the wacky world of quantum physics, where all kinds of strange, unexpected things happen at the subatomic level—a level, by the way, at which the entire universe existed in its very earliest stages, when electrons, protons, and neutrinos were bursting forth in the Big Bang. Maybe our commonplace understanding of cause-and-effect doesn't apply in this circus-mirror environment of "quantum weirdness," a place where, as science writer Timothy Ferris writes, "the logical foundations of classical science are violated."[19]

IS THE UNIVERSE A FREE LUNCH?

I pulled out the copy of the *Discover* magazine that I had been prompted to purchase after I had seen the marble-sized universe on its cover. I flipped it open and read the following to Craig:

> Quantum theory ... holds that a vacuum ... is subject to quantum uncertainties. This means that things can materialize out of the vacuum, although they tend to vanish back into it quickly.... Theoretically, anything—a dog, a house, a planet—can pop into existence by means of this quantum quirk, which physicists call a vacuum fluctuation. Probability, however, dictates that pairs of subatomic particles ... are by far the most likely creations and that they will last extremely briefly.... The spontaneous, persistent creation of something even as large as a molecule is profoundly unlikely. Nevertheless, in 1973 an assistant professor at Columbia University named Edward Tryon suggested that the entire universe might have come into existence this way.... The whole universe may be, to use [MIT physicist Alan] Guth's phrase, "a free lunch."[20]

I closed the magazine and tossed it on Craig's desk. "Maybe Tryon was right when he said, 'I offer the modest proposal that our universe is simply one of those things which happen from time to time.'"[21]

Craig was listening intently. "Okay, that's a good question," he replied. "These subatomic particles the article talks about are called 'virtual particles.' They are theoretical entities, and it's not even clear that they actually exist as opposed to being merely theoretical constructs.

"However, there's a much more important point to be made about this. You see, these particles, if they are real, do *not* come out of nothing. The quantum vacuum is not what most people envision when they think of a vacuum—that is, absolutely nothing. On the contrary, it's a sea of fluctuating energy, an arena of violent activity that has a rich physical structure and can be described by physical laws. These particles are thought to originate by fluctuations of the energy in the vacuum.

"So it's not an example of something coming into being out of nothing, or something coming into being without a cause. The quantum vacuum and the energy locked up in the vacuum are the cause of these particles. And then we have to ask, well, what is the origin of the whole quantum vacuum itself? Where does *it* come from?"

He let that question linger before continuing. "You've simply pushed back the issue of creation. Now you've got to account for how this very active ocean of fluctuating energy came into being. Do you see what I'm saying? If quantum physical laws operate within the domain described by quantum physics, you can't legitimately use quantum physics to explain the origin of that domain itself. You need something transcendent that's beyond that domain in order to explain how the entire domain came into being. Suddenly, we're back to the origins question."

Craig's answer satisfied me. In fact, there didn't seem to be any rational objection that could seriously jeopardize the initial assertion of the *kalam* argument. And it has been that way since the early philosophers began to use it centuries ago.

"Even the famous skeptic David Hume didn't deny the first premise," Craig noted. "Hume wrote in 1754, 'I never asserted so absurd a proposition as that anything might arise without a cause.'[22] It wasn't until the discovery of scientific confirmation for the beginning of the universe in the twentieth century that people began to say, well, maybe the universe just came from nothing.

"Nobody has defended such an absurd position historically," said Craig, "which, again, makes me inclined to think this is just a corner they're being backed into by the evidence for the beginning of the universe."

STEP #2: THE UNIVERSE HAD A BEGINNING

Turning to the second premise of the *kalam* argument, I said to Craig, "If we were sitting here a hundred years ago, the idea that the universe began to exist at a specific point in the past would have been very controversial, wouldn't it?"

"No question about it," replied Craig. "The assumption ever since the ancient Greeks has been that the material world is eternal. Christians have denied this on the basis of biblical revelation, but secular science always assumed the universe's eternality. Christians just had to say, well, even though the universe appears static, nevertheless it did have a beginning when God created it. So the discovery in the twentieth century that the universe is not an unchanging, eternal entity was a complete shock to secular minds. It was utterly unanticipated."

Still, I needed evidence. "How do we really know that the universe started at some point in the past?" I asked. "What proof is there?"

"Essentially," said Craig, "there are two pathways toward establishing it. One could be called either mathematical or philosophical, while the other is scientific. Let's begin with the mathematical argument, which, incidentally, picks up on the thinking of Philoponus and the medieval Islamic theologians I mentioned earlier."

THE PATHWAY OF MATHEMATICS

The early Christian and Muslim scholars, Craig explained, used mathematical reasoning to demonstrate that it was impossible to have an infinite past. Their conclusion, therefore, was that the universe's age must be finite—that is, it must have had a beginning.

"They pointed out that absurdities would result if you were to have an actually infinite number of things," he said. "Since an infinite past would involve an actually infinite number of events, then the past simply can't be infinite."

It took a moment for that statement to sink in. I have always been a reluctant student of mathematics, especially such esoteric permutations as transfinite arithmetic. Before we could venture into any mathematical complexities, I reached over and pushed the "pause" button on my tape recorder.

"Hold on a minute, Bill," I said. "If I'm going to track with you on this, you're going to have to give me some illustrations to clarify things."

Craig already had some in mind. "Okay, no problem," he replied. When I turned the recorder back on, he continued.

"Let's use an example involving marbles," he said. "Imagine I had an infinite number of marbles in my possession, and that I wanted to give you some. In fact, suppose I wanted to give you an infinite number of marbles. One way I could do that would be to give you the entire pile of marbles. In that case I would have zero marbles left for myself.

"However, another way to do it would be to give you all of the odd numbered marbles. Then I would still have an infinity left over for myself, and you would have an infinity too. You'd have just as many as I would—and, in fact, each of us would have just as many as I originally had before we divided into odd and even! Or another approach would be for me to give you all of the marbles numbered four and higher. That way, you would have an infinity of marbles, but I would have only three marbles left.

"What these illustrations demonstrate is that the notion of an actual infinite number of things leads to contradictory results. In the first case in which I gave you all the marbles, infinity minus infinity is zero; in the second case in which I gave you all the odd-numbered marbles, infinity minus infinity is infinity; and in the third case in which I gave you all the marbles numbered four and greater, infinity minus infinity is three. In each case, we have subtracted the identical number from the identical number, but we have come up with nonidentical results.

"For that reason, mathematicians are forbidden from doing subtraction and division in transfinite arithmetic, because this would lead to contradictions. You see, *the idea of an actual infinity is just conceptual*; it exists only in our minds. Working within certain rules, mathematicians can deal with infinite quantities and infinite numbers in the conceptual realm. However—and here's the point—*it's not descriptive of what can happen in the real world.*"

I was following Craig so far. "You're saying, then, that you couldn't have an infinite number of events in the past."

"Exactly, because you would run into similar paradoxes," he said. "Substitute 'past events' for 'marbles,' and you can see the absurdities that would result. So the universe can't have an infinite number of events in its past; it must have had a beginning.

"In fact, we can go further. Even if you could have an actual infinite number of things, you couldn't form such a collection by adding one member after another. That's because no matter how many you add, you can always add one more before you get to infinity. This is sometimes called the Impossibility of Traversing the Infinite.

"But if the past really were infinite, then that would mean we have managed to traverse an infinite past to arrive at today. It would be as if someone had managed to count down all of the negative numbers and to arrive at zero at the present moment. Such a task is intuitively nonsense. For that reason as well, we can conclude there must have been a beginning to the universe."

Still, I spotted an inconsistency that threatened to unravel Craig's argument. "If the idea of the universe being infinitely old leads to absurd conclusions, then what about the idea of God being infinitely old?" I asked. "Doesn't your reasoning also automatically rule out the idea of an eternal deity?"

"That depends," he said. "It rules out the concept of a God who has endured through an infinite past time. But that's not the classic idea of God. Time and space are creations of God that began at the Big Bang. If you go back beyond the beginning of time itself, there is simply eternity. By that, I mean eternity in the sense of timelessness. God, the eternal, is timeless in his being. God did not endure through an infinite amount of time up to the moment of creation; that would be absurd. God transcends time. He's beyond time. Once God creates the universe, he could enter time, but that's a different topic altogether."

I quickly reviewed in my mind what Craig had said so far, concluding that it was logically coherent. "How convincing do you think the mathematical pathway is?" I asked.

"Well, I'm convinced of it!" he replied with a chuckle. "In fact, this is such a good argument that even if I were living in the nineteenth century, when there was little scientific evidence for the beginning of the universe, I would still believe that the universe is finite in the past on the basis of these arguments. For me, the scientific evidence is merely confirmation of a conclusion already arrived at on the basis of philosophical reasoning."

THE PATHWAY OF SCIENCE

At this point, we turned the corner to begin discussing the scientific evidence for the universe being created in the Big Bang billions of years ago. "What discoveries began pointing scientists toward this model?" I asked.

"When Albert Einstein developed his general theory of relativity in 1915 and started applying it to the universe as a whole, he was shocked to discover it didn't allow for a static universe. According to his equations, the universe should either be exploding or imploding. In order to make the universe static, he had to fudge his equations by putting in a factor that would hold the universe steady.

"In the 1920s, the Russian mathematician Alexander Friedman and the Belgium astronomer George Lemaître were able to develop models based on Einstein's theory. They predicted the universe was expanding. Of course, this meant that if you went backward in time, the universe would go back to a single origin before which it didn't exist. Astronomer Fred Hoyle derisively called this the Big Bang— and the name stuck!

"Starting in the 1920s, scientists began to find empirical evidence that supported these purely mathematical models. For instance, in 1929, the American astronomer Edwin Hubble discovered that the light coming to us from distant galaxies appears to be redder than it should be, and that this is a universal feature of galaxies in all parts of the sky. Hubble explained this red shift as being due to the fact that the galaxies are moving away from us. He concluded that the universe is literally flying apart at enormous velocities. Hubble's astronomical observations were the first empirical confirmation of the predictions by Friedman and Lemaître.

"Then in the 1940s, George Gamow predicted that if the Big Bang really happened, then the background temperature of the universe should be just a few degrees above absolute zero. He said this would be a relic from a very early stage of the universe. Sure enough, in 1965, two scientists accidentally discovered the universe's background radiation—and it was only about 3.7 degrees above absolute zero. There's no explanation for this apart from the fact that it is a vestige of a very early and a very dense state of the universe, which was predicted by the Big Bang model.

"The third main piece of evidence for the Big Bang is the origin of light elements. Heavy elements, like carbon and iron, are synthesized in the interior of stars and then exploded through supernovae into space. But the very, very light elements, like deuterium and helium, cannot have been synthesized in the interior of stars, because you would need an even more powerful furnace to create them. These elements must have been forged in the furnace of the Big Bang itself at temperatures that were billions of degrees. There's no other explanation.

"So predictions about the Big Bang have been consistently verified by scientific data. Moreover, they have been corroborated by the failure of every attempt to falsify them by alternative models. Unquestionably, the Big Bang model has impressive scientific credentials."

"And that," I observed, "has surprised a lot of people."

"It was an absolute shock!" he declared. "Up to this time, it was taken for granted that the universe as a whole was a static, eternally existing object."

I knew, however, that there have been more recent refinements of the standard Big Bang model. "Most scientists would add inflation theory to the description of how the universe got started," I said. "How has that changed the way we look at the Big Bang?"

"Yes, inflation is a wrinkle that most theorists would add," he acknowledged. He paused for a moment, then added: "Personally, though, I think the reasons for it are a bit suspect."

That took me aback. "Why is that?"

"You see, the Big Bang was not a chaotic, disorderly event. Instead, it appears to have been fine-tuned for the existence of intelligent life with a complexity and precision that literally defies human comprehension. In other words, the universe we see today—and our very existence—depends upon a set of highly special initial conditions. This phenomenon is strong evidence that the Big Bang was not an accident, but that it was designed. Theorists who are uncomfortable about this want to avoid the problem by trying to explain how you can get a universe like ours without these special initial conditions. Inflation is one attempt to do this."

I had read about inflation theory in several books and articles, but I asked Craig to describe it so that we were working from a common definition.

"Inflation says that in the very, very early history of the universe, the universe underwent a period of super-rapid, or 'inflationary,' expansion. Then it settled down to the more leisurely expansion we observe today. This inflationary expansion supposedly avoids the problem of the initial conditions of the universe by blowing them out beyond the range of what we can observe. So in a sense, inflation isn't something that is motivated by the scientific evidence; it's motivated by a desire to avoid these special initial conditions that are present in the standard model.

"And inflation itself has been plagued with problems. There are probably fifty different inflationary models. Nobody knows which, if any, is correct. There isn't any empirical test that proves inflation has occurred. So even though most theorists accept inflation today, I'm rather suspicious of the whole thing, because it appears to be motivated by a philosophical bias."

I stopped to analyze Craig's comments. As I thought about inflationary theory, I didn't understand how it would erode anyone's confidence in the overall Big Bang model. "Since this inflationary period supposedly happened a microsecond *after* the Big Bang occurred," I said, "then it really doesn't affect the question of the origin of the universe."

"That's right," Craig replied. "Prior to inflation, the universe still shrinks back to a singularity."

I put up my hand to stop him. "A *what?*"

"A singularity," he repeated. "That's the state at which the space-time curvature, along with temperature, density, and pressure, becomes infinite. It's the beginning point. It's the point at which the Big Bang occurred."

I nodded to acknowledge the clarification. "Okay," I said. "Then how would you assess the health of the Big Bang model today?"

"It's the standard paradigm of contemporary cosmology," he answered. "I would say that its broad framework is very securely established as a scientific fact. Stephen Hawking has said, 'Almost everyone now believes that the universe, and time itself, had a beginning at the Big Bang.'"[23]

By this point in our discussion, Craig had provided compelling facts to support the two premises of the *kalam* argument. All that remained was its conclusion—and the absolutely staggering implications that logically flow from it.

STEP #3: THEREFORE, THE UNIVERSE HAS A CAUSE

In arguing for the existence of God, thirteenth-century Christian philosopher Thomas Aquinas always presupposed Aristotle's view that the universe is eternal. On the basis of that difficult assumption, he then sought to prove that God exists. Why did he take this approach? Because, Aquinas said, if he were to start with the premise that the universe had a beginning, then his task would be too easy! Obviously, if there was a beginning, *something* had to bring the universe into existence.

But now, modern astrophysics and astronomy have dropped into the lap of Christians precisely the premise that, according to Aquinas, makes God's existence virtually undeniable.

Craig offered that story to punch his next point. "Given that whatever begins to exist has a cause and that the universe began to exist, there *must* be some sort of transcendent cause for the origin of the universe," Craig told me.

"Even atheist Kai Nielsen said, 'Suppose you suddenly hear a loud bang . . . and you ask me, 'What made that bang?' and I reply, 'Nothing, it just happened.' You would not accept that.'[24] He's right, of course. And if a cause is needed for a small bang like that, then it's needed for the Big Bang as well. This is an inescapable conclusion— and it's a stunning confirmation of the millennia-old Judeo-Christian doctrine of creation out of nothing."

At the time an agnostic, American astronomer Robert Jastrow was forced to concede that although details may differ, "the essential element in the astronomical and biblical accounts of Genesis is the same; the chain of events leading to man commenced suddenly and sharply, at a definite moment in time, in a flash of light and energy."[25]

But although logic dictates that a cause sparked the Big Bang, I wondered how much logic can also tell us about its identity. "What specifically can you deduce about this cause?" I asked Craig.

"There are several qualities we can identify," he replied. "A cause of space and time must be an uncaused, beginningless, timeless, spaceless, immaterial, personal being endowed with freedom of will and enormous power," he said. "And that is a core concept of God."

"Hold on, hold on!" I insisted. "Many atheists see a fatal inconsistency. They don't see how you can say the Creator could be 'uncaused.' For instance, atheist George Smith says, 'If *everything* must have a cause, how did god become exempt?'[26] In *The Necessity of Atheism*, David Brooks says: 'If everything must have a cause, then the First Cause must be caused and therefore: Who made God? To say that this First Cause always existed is to deny the basic assumption of this theory.'[27] What would you say to them?"

Craig's eyebrows shot up. "Well, that just misses the point!" he exclaimed. "Obviously, they're not dealing with the first premise of the *kalam* argument, which is *not* that *everything* has a cause, but that *whatever begins to exist* has a cause. I don't know of any reputable philosopher who would say everything has a cause. So they're simply not dealing with a correct formulation of the *kalam* argument.

"And this is not special pleading in the case of God. After all, atheists have long maintained that the universe doesn't need a cause, because it's eternal. How can they possibly maintain that the universe can be eternal and uncaused, yet God cannot be timeless and uncaused?"

At that point, another objection popped into my mind. "Why does it have to be one Creator?" I asked. "Why couldn't multiple Creators have been involved?"

"My opinion," Craig answered, "is that Ockham's razor would shave away any additional creators."

"What's Ockham's razor?"

"It's a scientific principle that says we should not multiply causes beyond what's necessary to explain the effect. Since one Creator is sufficient to explain the effect, you would be unwarranted in going beyond the evidence to posit a plurality."

"That seems a little soft to me," I said.

"Well, it's a universally accepted principle of scientific methodology," he replied. "And besides, the *kalam* argument can't prove everything about the Creator. Nothing restricts us from looking at wider considerations. For instance, Jesus of Nazareth proclaimed the truth of monotheism, and he was vindicated by his resurrection from the dead, for which we have convincing historical evidence.[28] Consequently, we have good grounds for believing that what he said was true."

I conceded the point, but at the same time my mind began to fill with other objections concerning the identity of the universe's cause. Among the most troubling was whether the *kalam* argument can tell us if the Creator is personal, as Christians believe, or merely an impersonal force, as many New Age adherents maintain.

THE PERSONAL CREATOR

"You said earlier that there's evidence that the cause of the universe was personal," I said. "I don't see how this can be logically deduced. In fact, Smith has complained that arguments like yours cannot establish whether the first cause was, or is, alive or conscious—'and,' he says, 'an inanimate, unconscious god is of little use to theism.'[29] He has a point there, doesn't he?"

"No, I don't think so," said Craig. "One of the most remarkable features of the *kalam* argument is that it gives us more than just a transcendent cause of the universe. It also implies a personal Creator."

"How so?"

Craig leaned back into his chair. "There are two types of explanations—scientific and personal," he began, adopting a more professorial tone. "Scientific explanations explain a phenomenon in terms of certain initial conditions and natural laws, which explain how those initial conditions evolved to produce the phenomenon under consideration. By contrast, personal explanations explain things by means of an agent and that agent's volition or will."

I interrupted to ask Craig for an illustration. He obliged me by saying: "Imagine you walked into the kitchen and saw the kettle boiling on the stove. You ask, 'Why is the kettle boiling?' Your wife might say, 'Well, because the kinetic energy of the flame is conducted by the metal bottom of the kettle to the water, causing the water molecules to vibrate faster and faster until they're thrown off in the form of steam.' That would be a scientific explanation. Or she might say, 'I put it on to make a cup of tea.' That would be a personal explanation. Both are legitimate, but they explain the phenomenon in different ways."

So far, so good. "But how does this relate to cosmology?"

"You see, there cannot be a scientific explanation of the first state of the universe. Since it's the first state, it simply cannot be explained in terms of earlier initial conditions and natural laws leading up to it. So if there is an explanation of the first state of the universe, it *has* to be a personal explanation—that is, an agent who has volition to create it. That would be the first reason that the cause of the universe must be personal.

"A second reason is that because the cause of the universe transcends time and space, it cannot be a physical reality. Instead, it must be nonphysical or immaterial. Well, there are only two types of things that can be timeless and immaterial. One would be abstract objects, like numbers or mathematical entities. However, abstract objects can't cause anything to happen. The second kind of immaterial reality would be a mind. A mind can be a cause, and so it makes sense that the universe is the product of an unembodied mind that brought it into existence.

"Finally, let me give you an analogy that will help explain a third reason for why the first cause is personal. Water freezes at zero degrees Centigrade. If the temperature were below zero degrees from eternity past, then any water that was around would be frozen from eternity past. It would be impossible for the water to just begin to freeze a finite time ago. In other words, once the sufficient conditions were met—that is, the temperature was low enough—then the consequence would be that water would automatically freeze.

"So if the universe were just a mechanical consequence that would occur whenever sufficient conditions were met, and the sufficient conditions were met eternally, then it would exist from eternity past. The effect would be co-eternal with the cause.

"How do you explain, then, the origin of a finite universe from a timeless cause? I can only think of one explanation: that the cause of the universe is a personal agent who has freedom of will. He can create a new effect without any antecedent determining conditions. He could decide to say, 'Let there be light,' and the universe would spring into existence. I've never seen a good response to this argument on the part of any atheist."

Putting the issue a bit simpler, British physicist Edmund Whittaker made a similar observation in his book *The Beginning and End of the World*. He said, "There is no ground for supposing that matter and energy existed before and was suddenly galvanized into action. *For what could distinguish that moment from all other moments in eternity?* It is simpler to postulate creation *ex nihilo*—Divine will constituting Nature from nothingness."[30]

Craig had made a good case for the cause of the universe being personal, and yet he offered no evidence concerning whether the Creator is still living today. Perhaps the Creator put the universe into motion and then ceased to exist. Smith also makes this challenge, saying that an argument like Craig's is "capable only of demonstrating the existence of a mysterious first cause in the distant past. It does not establish the *present* existence of the first cause."[31]

This objection, though, didn't faze Craig. "It's certainly plausible that this being would still exist," he said, "because he transcends the universe and is therefore above the laws of nature, which he created. It therefore seems unlikely that anything in the laws of nature could extinguish him. And, of course, Christians believe this Creator has not remained silent but has revealed himself decisively in the person, ministry, and resurrection of Jesus of Nazareth, which shows that he's still around and still working in history.

"Again, the *kalam* argument can't prove *everything*, and that's fine. We're free to look around for other evidence that the Creator still exists. Let's see if he answers prayers, if he raised Jesus from the dead, if he revealed himself in the fulfillment of prophecy, and so forth. It seems that the burden of proof should be on the person claiming he did once exist, but he no longer does."

Even though that seemed to make sense, something inside of me was saying, *"Not so fast!"* The *kalam* argument was a little too cut-and-dried; Craig's evidence seemed a bit too airtight. Was his conclusion that a personal Creator was behind the Big Bang really warranted, or might there be a way to get around it?

There was too much at stake not to probe every reasonable possibility, including whether there's an explanation that would negate the need for an absolute beginning of the universe—and thus eliminate the Creator that the Big Bang implies.

ALTERNATIVES TO THE BIG BANG

Efforts to come up with alternatives to the standard Big Bang model have intensified in recent years. Many scientists are troubled by the fact that the beginning of the universe necessitates a Creator. Others are perturbed because the laws of physics can't account for the creation event.

Einstein admitted the idea of the expanding universe "irritates me"[32] (presumably, said one prominent scientist, "because of its theological implications").[33] British astronomer Arthur Eddington called it "repugnant." MIT's Phillip Morrison said, "I would like to reject it."[34] Jastrow said it was "distasteful to the scientific mind," adding:

> There is a kind of religion in science; it is the religion of a person who believes there is order and harmony in the Universe. Every event can be explained in a rational way as the product of some previous event; every effect must have its cause; there is no First Cause. . . . This religious faith of the scientist is violated by the discovery that the world had a beginning under conditions in which the known laws of physics are not valid, and as a product of forces or circumstances we cannot discover. When that happens, the scientist has lost control. If he really examined the implications, he would be traumatized.[35]

Has this attitude, I asked Craig, fueled efforts to circumvent the idea of the Big Bang?

"I believe it has. A good example is the Steady State theory proposed in 1948," he replied. "It said that the universe was expanding all right but claimed that as galaxies retreat from each other, new matter comes into being out of nothing and fills the void. So in contradiction to the First Law of Thermodynamics, which says that matter is neither created nor destroyed, the universe is supposedly being constantly replenished with new stuff."

The concept was intriguing if nothing else. "What was the evidence for it?" I asked.

"There was none!" Craig exclaimed. "It never secured a single piece of experimental verification. It was motivated purely by a desire to avoid the absolute beginning of the universe predicted by the Big Bang model—in fact, one of its originators, Sir Fred Hoyle, was quite overt about this. He was very up front about his desire to avoid the metaphysical and theological implications of the Big Bang by proposing a model that was eternal in the past."

I interrupted. "Wait a minute, Bill," I said. Recalling a comment by science philosopher Stephen C. Meyer in my earlier interview, I asked: "Wouldn't you agree that the motivations behind a theory are independent of its scientific worth?"

"Yes, yes, I'd agree with that," Craig replied. "In this case, though, there were no scientific data supporting it. It's a good illustration of how scientists are not mere thinking machines but are driven by philosophical and emotional factors as well."

Rather than try to second-guess the motivations of cosmologists, I decided to ask Craig about several alternatives to the standard Big Bang model that have gained currency through the years. Maybe one of them could succeed in toppling the theistic conclusion of the *kalam* argument.

EXPLORING SAGAN'S COSMOS

The first alternative I mentioned to Craig—the Oscillating Model of the universe—was popularized by astronomer Carl Sagan on his *Cosmos* television program. This theory eliminates the need for an absolute beginning of the universe by suggesting that the universe expands, then collapses, then expands again, and continues in this cycle indefinitely. Interestingly, Sagan even quoted from

Hindu scriptures to show how this is consistent with its cyclical themes. When I asked Craig about Sagan's theory, he said that, yes, he was quite familiar with it.

"That model was popular in the 1960s, particularly among Russian cosmologists," he said. "In 1968, when I was at the World Congress on Philosophy in Düsseldorf, I heard Soviet bloc cosmologists espousing this model, simply because of their commitment to dialectical materialism. They could not deny the eternality of matter because this was part of Marxist philosophy, and so, despite the evidence, they were holding out hope for the Oscillating Model."

"But," I interjected, "support for this model apparently hasn't waned. As recently as 2003, Bill Bryson, in his best-seller *A Short History of Nearly Everything*, said that 'one notion' among scientists is that 'we're just one of an eternal cycle of expanding and collapsing universes, like the bladder on an oxygen machine.'"[36]

"Well, several problems with the Oscillating Model have been well known for decades," he replied. "For one thing, it contradicts the known laws of physics. Theorems by Hawking and Penrose show that as long as the universe is governed by general relativity, the existence of an initial singularity—or beginning—is inevitable, and that it's impossible to pass through a singularity to a subsequent state. And there's no known physics that could reverse a contracting universe and suddenly make it bounce before it hits the singularity. The whole theory was simply a theoretical abstraction. Physics never supported it.

"Another problem is that in order for the universe to oscillate, it has to contract at some point. For this to happen, the universe would have to be dense enough to generate sufficient gravity that would eventually slow its expansion to a halt and then, with increasing rapidity, contract it into a big crunch. But estimates have consistently indicated that the universe is far below the density needed to contract, even when you include not only its luminous matter, but also all of the invisible dark matter as well.

"Recent tests, run by five different laboratories in 1998, calculated a ninety-five-percent certainty that the universe will not contract, but that it will expand forever. In fact, in a completely unexpected development, the studies indicated that the expansion is not decelerating, but it's actually accelerating. This really puts the nails in the coffin for the Oscillating Model.

"And one more problem: even if physics allowed the universe to contract, scientific studies have shown that entropy would be conserved from one cycle to the next. This would have the effect of each expansion getting bigger and bigger and bigger. Now, trace that backwards in time and what do you get? They get smaller and smaller and smaller, until you finally come to the smallest cycle—and then the beginning of the universe. So Joseph Silk, in his book *The Big Bang*, estimates that even if the universe were oscillating, it could not have gone through more than a hundred previous oscillations prior to today."[37]

All of this did, indeed, seem to doom this theory. "Sagan was an agnostic who liked to say that the universe 'is all there is, or ever was, or ever will be,'"[38] I said. "But you're saying that the evidence indicates—"

"—that the Oscillating Model itself implies the beginning of the universe which its proponents sought to avoid. That's right," Craig said.

"But," I pointed out, "permutations of his theory are being proposed even today." I removed a newspaper article from my briefcase and read the headline to Craig: *Princeton Physicist Offers Theory of Cyclic Universe.*[39]

"This cosmologist says the Big Bang is not the beginning of time but a bridge to a pre-existing era," I said. "He says the universe undergoes an endless sequence of cycles in which it contracts with a big crunch and reemerges in an expanding Big Bang, with trillions of years of evolution in between. He says mysterious 'dark energy' first pushes the universe apart at an accelerating rate, but then it changes its character and causes it to contract and then rebound in cycle after cycle."

Craig was familiar with the concept. "This model is based on a certain version of string theory, which is an alternative to the standard quark model of particle physics," he explained.

"The scenario postulates that our universe is a three-dimensional membrane in a five-dimensional space, and that there's another three-dimensional membrane which is in an eternal cycle of approaching our membrane and colliding with it. When this happens, it supposedly causes an expansion of our universe from the point of collision. Then our universe retreats and repeats the cycle again, and on and on.

"The idea is that this five-dimensional universe is eternal and beginningless. So you have a cyclic model of our universe that is expanding, but nevertheless this larger dimensional universe as a whole is eternal."

Though difficult to conceptualize, this idea had a certain amount of appeal. "What do you think of this model?" I asked.

"Well, this isn't even a model, it's just sort of a scenario, because it hasn't been developed. The equations for string theory haven't even all been stated yet, much less solved. So this is extremely speculative and uncertain. But let's consider it on its merits," he said.

"This cyclic scenario is plagued with problems. For one thing, it is inconsistent with the very string theory it's based on! Nobody has been able to solve that problem. Moreover, this is simply the five-dimensional equivalent of a three-dimensional oscillating universe. As such, it faces many of the same problems that the old oscillating model did.

"But more interesting is that in 2001, inflation theorist Alan Guth and two other physicists wrote an article on how inflation is not past eternal. They were able to generalize their results to show that they were also applicable to multidimensional models, like the one in this newspaper article. So it turns out that even the cyclical model in five dimensions has to have a beginning."

Craig sighed as he sat back in his chair. "It's amazing how this falls into a consistent pattern," he said. "Theories designed to avoid the beginning of the universe have either turned out to be untenable, like the Steady State theory, or else they imply the very beginning of the universe that their proponents have been desperately trying to avoid."

"So the future of this cyclic scenario is . . . what?"

"It will probably provide grist for further exploration," he said. "Still, another prominent inflation theorist, André Linde, said this concept has been very popular among journalists and very unpopular among cosmologists."

"Speaking of Linde," I said, "he proposed another theory, called chaotic inflation, that would eliminate the need for a beginning point."

"That's right," Craig said. "He speculated that maybe inflation—this rapid expansion of the universe—never really quits. He said maybe the universe expands like a balloon, and when it reaches a certain point, then inflation is spawned off of it and begins to expand,

and then something expands off of that. So you have inflation begetting inflation begetting inflation, and it goes on forever. The obvious question, then, is this: could inflation be eternal in the past? Could every inflationary domain be the creation of a prior domain so that the universe is an eternally inflating and self-reproducing entity?"

"Is that possible?"

"I'm afraid not. As I said earlier, a universe that is eternally inflating toward the future cannot be past eternal. Two prominent physicists demonstrated that as far back as 1994. There has to be a beginning at some point in the indefinite past. In Linde's response, he admitted they were correct."

I thought about another popular alternative: quantum models of the universe, like Edward Tryon's, which I mentioned earlier. There are several variations, but basically they claim that our universe is part of a bigger mother universe, which is made up of a quantum vacuum where fluctuations occur and turn into baby universes. Our universe is one of these offspring. While our universe is expanding, the bigger mother universe is infinite and eternal.

When I brought up this concept, though, Craig pointed out two fatal problems with it. "Remember we said earlier in our conversation that a quantum vacuum isn't nothing, but that it's a very active sea of fluctuating energy that itself demands an explanation for how it came into being," he said. "What accounts for its beginning? And second, there is a positive—that is, a non-zero—probability that a fluctuation would occur and a universe would be spawned at each and every point in this quantum vacuum.

"So if the mother universe were eternal, eventually a universe would have formed at each point. Think about that. Finally these universes would be running into each other or coalescing until the entire quantum vacuum in the mother universe would be filled with an infinitely old universe, which contradicts our observations. That's why this model hasn't survived."

HAWKING'S CHALLENGE

Most developments in cosmology live an obscure existence within the pages of arcane scientific journals, with only a few—often, the most outlandish ones—receiving even the briefest mention in the popular press. Luminaries in the field, such as Linde and Guth, are hardly household names. But when Stephen William Hawking speaks, the public listens.

A theoretical physicist who is currently the Lucasian Professor of Mathematics at Cambridge University, a post once held by Sir Isaac Newton, Hawking has become a science icon. He has sold millions of copies of *A Brief History of Time*, although *Business Week* once quipped that the book is "the least-read best-seller ever."[40] His celebrity status was validated when he achieved cartoon form on *The Simpsons* and played a cameo role on *Star Trek*, where he challenged a holographic Einstein to a game of chess.

Hawking, who uses a wheelchair for mobility and a synthesizer for speech due to a progressive neuromuscular disease, has been on a quest for the elusive Theory of Everything, which would unify general relativity with quantum theory. Along the way, he has proposed a quantum gravity model for the universe that he says eliminates the need for a singularity—that is, the Big Bang.

When actress Shirley MacLaine asked Hawking whether he believes God created the universe, he replied simply, "No."[41] He told the BBC: "We are such insignificant creatures on a minor planet of a very average star in the outer suburbs of one of a hundred thousand million galaxies. So it is difficult to believe in a God that would care about us or even notice our existence."[42]

In a chapter called "The Origin and Fate of the Universe" in *A Brief History of Time*, Hawking says: "So long as the universe had a beginning, we could suppose it had a creator. But if the universe is really completely self-contained, having no boundary or edge, it would have neither beginning nor end: it would simply be. What place, then, for a creator?"[43]

I broached Hawking's theory to Craig. "It sure sounds like he has finally managed to put God out of business," I said.

"Not quite," replied Craig.

When I asked him to explain why not, Craig pulled a piece of paper and pen out of his top drawer. "Let me draw you two pictures that will clarify what I mean," he said.

"The standard Big Bang theory can be represented by a cone," he said, drawing what looked like an empty sugar cone from Baskin-Robbins. "The point of the cone represents the beginning of the universe—the singularity where the Big Bang occurred. It's the beginning point, and it has a sharp edge to it.[44] The expansion of the universe, as it gets older and grows, is represented by the cone's overall expanding shape."

I nodded that I was tracking with him. Then he took a second sheet of paper and began drawing a picture of Hawking's theory. "Hawking's model is like a cone, too, except it doesn't come to a point." He drew a picture of what resembled a badminton birdie; instead of coming to a sharp point, the end of the cone was rounded.

"As you can see, there's no singularity. There's no sharp edge. If you were to start at the mouth of the cone and go backward in time," he said, his pencil tracing the long side of the cone, "you would not come back to a beginning point. You would simply follow the curve— and suddenly you would find yourself heading forward in time again."

This was consistent with the way Hawking's biographers envisioned his theory. They said it would be like walking northward until you reach the North Pole, and then suddenly, if you keep walking, you find yourself heading south.[45] "There is no beginning and no end— no boundaries," one writer explained. "The universe always was, always is, and always shall be."[46]

Craig put down his pencil. "Presto!" I exclaimed as I looked at his drawing. "No beginning, no singularity, no Big Bang—no need for God."

Craig grimaced. "Let's think about this for a minute before you come to that conclusion," he said.

THE WORLD OF IMAGINARY NUMBERS

"Has Hawking made a mistake?" I asked. The mere suggestion sounded impossible!

"I think he has made a philosophical error by thinking that having a beginning entails having a beginning point. And that's simply not the case," Craig replied.

He pointed toward his rendering of Hawking's model. "Granted, there isn't any singular point here, but notice this: the universe is still finite in its past. It still has a beginning in the sense that something has a finite past duration. In other words, pick an interval of time— say, a second, a minute, or a year. For any finite interval of time you pick, there are only a finite number of equal intervals prior to that time. And in that sense, Hawking's model has a beginning. Even he says that the universe has an origin out of nothing in the sense that there's absolutely nothing that comes before it.

"So this would be an example of a model that has a beginning but doesn't involve a singularity. That's what many scientists are trying to come up with, because the laws of physics would apply all the way back. They don't break down in a singularity. And that's more palatable to them."

Before I could ask another question, Craig added: "Now, I've been taking Hawking's model at face value, but it's also important to note that he is only able to achieve this rounding-off effect by substituting 'imaginary numbers' for real numbers in his equations."

"What are imaginary numbers?"

"They are multiples of the square root of negative one," he said. "In this model, they have the effect of turning time into a dimension of space. The problem is that when imaginary numbers are employed, they're just computational devices used to grease the equations and get the result the mathematician wants. That's fine, but when you want to get a real, physical result, you have to convert the imaginary numbers into real ones. But Hawking refuses to convert them. He just keeps everything in the imaginary realm."

"What happens if you convert the numbers into real ones?"

"*Presto*, the singularity reappears!" Craig said. "In fact, the singularity is really there the whole time; it's just hidden behind the device of so-called imaginary time. Hawking concedes this in a subsequent book he co-authored with Roger Penrose.[47] He said he doesn't pretend to be describing reality, because he says he doesn't know what reality is. So Hawking himself recognizes that this is not a realistic description of the universe or its origin; it's merely a mathematical way of modeling the beginning of the universe in such a manner that the singularity doesn't appear."

I was amazed! Even though Hawking's Internet site says his theory implies that the universe "was completely determined by the laws of science,"[48] even he wasn't able to successfully write God out of the picture.

"What's important to understand, Lee, is how reversed the situation is from, say, a hundred years ago," Craig continued. "Back then, Christians had to maintain by faith in the Bible that despite all appearances to the contrary, the universe was not eternal but was created out of nothing a finite time ago. Now, the situation is exactly the opposite.

"It is the atheist who has to maintain, by faith, despite all of the evidence to the contrary, that the universe did not have a beginning a finite time ago but is in some inexplicable way eternal after all. So the shoe is on the other foot. The Christian can stand confidently within biblical truth, knowing it's in line with mainstream astrophysics and cosmology. It's the atheist who feels very uncomfortable and marginalized today."

As I sat there in Craig's office, my mind could conjure up no rational scenario that could derail the inexorable logic of the *kalam* argument. The philosophical and scientific evidence of contemporary cosmology was pointing persuasively toward the conclusion that a personal Creator of the universe does exist. This was powerful stuff— and I still had a long way to go in my investigation.

I wondered, however, how a cosmologist or physicist might respond to Craig. As compelling as the *kalam* argument undeniably is, does it really have the potential to change the mind of a scientist? Or would it merely become fodder for more and more creative—or, as some might say, desperate—counter-arguments and objections? Christians often caution that a skeptic cannot be argued into the faith. Yet if someone were sincerely open-minded, could Craig's case be sufficient to prompt a personal verdict in favor of God?

I mused about this aloud to Craig. He thought for a moment and then launched into a fascinating story about a doctoral dissertation, a handmade booklet, and a changed life.

PHYSICAL LAWS, SPIRITUAL LAWS

While in Germany to pursue his second doctorate, Bill and his wife, Jan, were attending a convention of the Alexander von Humboldt Foundation, a prestigious German organization devoted to promoting international research cooperation between scholars. While chatting with various scientists, they met a prominent Eastern European physicist, who described for them how physics had destroyed her belief in God.

"She said that now when she looks at the world, all she sees is darkness without and darkness within," Craig recalled. "I remember how that struck me so forcefully. What a description of the modern world's predicament—utter meaninglessness and despair.

"Suddenly, Jan spoke up. 'You should read Bill's doctoral dissertation,' she said. 'He uses physics to prove the existence of God.'"

Craig's eyes got wide as he relived the scene. "My first thought was, 'Oh, no! What is this famous physicist going to say?' But she replied that, yes, she would be very interested in reading it.

"So we gave her a copy of my dissertation on the *kalam* cosmological argument—the very kind of material we've been discussing today, Lee. As she read it over the coming days, she started to get more and more excited. She told me, 'I know these people you're quoting! These are my colleagues!' Finally, she returned the dissertation to us and announced, 'I now believe in the existence of God. Thank you so much for restoring my faith in him.'

"We were thrilled! We said, 'Would you like to know him in a personal way?' She was a bit hesitant, but she said, 'Uh, of course.' So we asked her to meet us that night in the local restaurant.

"That afternoon Jan and I prepared a little handwritten version of the Four Spiritual Laws, which spell out how a person can become a follower of Jesus.[49] When we sat down with her at the meal that night, we opened the booklet and read the first sentence: 'Just as there are physical laws that govern the physical universe, so there are spiritual laws that govern your relationship with God.' And she said, 'Oh, physical laws! Spiritual laws! This is something I can understand! This is just for me!'

"Finally, we got to the point in the booklet that asks whether God is outside of your life or on the throne of your life. She clamped her hand over the booklet and said, 'Ah, this is so personal! I just can't answer at this time.' We said, 'That's all right. Let us just explain how you can receive Christ as your personal savior.' We described how she could pray to ask God to forgive her wrongdoing and to receive Jesus as her forgiver and leader. After that, we let her take the booklet home with her.

"Well, the next day when we saw her, her face was just radiant with joy! She told us she had gone home that night and there in her room had prayed to give her life to Christ. Then she took all her tranquilizers and booze and flushed them down the toilet!

"We gave her a copy of the New Testament and parted ways for several months. When we saw her later at another convention, we wondered what the status of her faith would be. But she had the same joy, the same radiance, and she greeted us with love and told us that her most precious possessions were her New Testament and her handmade Four Spiritual Laws."

Bill smiled. "You asked whether God can use cosmology to change the life of a scientist," he said. "Yes, I've seen it. I've seen it happen with all kinds of skeptics. Once I gave a talk at a college in

Canada on the *kalam* argument. Afterward a student said, 'I've been an agnostic all my life. I've never heard anything like this. I now believe that God exists! I can hardly wait to go share this with my brother, who's an atheist.'"

Craig glanced out the window as he pondered what else to say. Then he turned to me once more. "Certainly there have been earlier ages when the culture was more sympathetic toward Christianity," he said. "But I think it's indisputable that there has never been a time in history when the hard evidence of science was more confirmatory of belief in God than today."

I leaned over and punched the "stop" button on my recorder. I couldn't think of a better segue to my next interview. Now that Craig had made a powerful case for God as Creator of the universe, it was time to consider the laws and parameters of physics. Is there any credibility, I wondered, to the claim that they have been tuned to an incomprehensible precision in order to create a livable habitat for humankind?

FOR FURTHER EVIDENCE
More Resources on This Topic

Craig, William Lane. "Design and the Cosmological Argument." In *Mere Creation*, ed. William A. Dembski. Downer's Grove, Ill.: InterVarsity, 1998.

———. *Reasonable Faith*. Wheaton, Ill.: Crossway, revised edition, 1994.

———, and Quentin Smith. *Theism, Atheism and Big Bang Cosmology*. Oxford: Oxford University Press, 1993.

Moreland, J. P. and Kai Nielsen. *Does God Exist?* Amherst, N.Y.: Prometheus, 1993.

THE EVIDENCE OF PHYSICS: THE COSMOS ON A RAZOR'S EDGE

It is hard to resist the impression that the present structure of the universe, apparently so sensitive to minor alterations in numbers, has been rather carefully thought out. . . . The seemingly miraculous concurrence of these numerical values must remain the most compelling evidence for cosmic design.

Physicist Paul Davies[1]

Would it not be strange if a universe without purpose accidentally created humans who are so obsessed with purpose?

Sir John Templeton.[2]

He became a spiritual skeptic when he learned about Darwinism as a student. He worked for a while at a major Chicago newspaper and went to graduate school at an Ivy League university. Spurred by his wife's Christianity, he later began investigating the evidence for a Creator. With his mind opened by the facts, he ended up shedding his atheism and embracing God, eventually writing a book that recounted his intellectual journey to faith.

If that sounds like my story, it is[3]—but, coincidentally, it's also the story of Patrick Glynn, a former arms-control negotiator for the Reagan administration and currently the associate director of the George Washington University Institute for Communitarian Policy Studies in Washington, D.C.

Glynn first encountered evolutionary theory while a student in parochial school, immediately recognizing that it was incompatible with the Bible. "I stood up in class and told the poor nun as much," he recalled.

Convinced that reason was "the only path to truth," Glynn became a confirmed atheist by the time he received his doctorate from Harvard

University in the 1970s. "Darwin had demonstrated that it was not even necessary to posit a God to explain the origin of life," he said. "Life, and the human species itself, was the outcome of essentially random mechanisms operating over the eons."

After marrying a Christian and finding himself in frequent debates with her over spiritual matters, Glynn said his mind "became sufficiently open" so that he was willing to check out whether there was any rational evidence for the existence of God. He was hardly prepared for what he would learn:

> Gradually, I realized that in the twenty years since I opted for philosophical atheism, a vast, systematic literature had emerged that not only cast deep doubt on, but also, from any reasonable perspective, effectively refuted my atheistic outlook. . . . Today, it seems to me, there is no good reason for an intelligent person to embrace the illusion of atheism or agnosticism, to make the same intellectual mistakes I made.[4]

What evidence was responsible for this stunning spiritual turnaround? Among the most influential discoveries he encountered in his investigation was the so-called "anthropic principle." The term, derived from the Greek word *anthropos* for "man," was coined by Cambridge physicist Brandon Carter, who delivered a ground-breaking paper called "Large Number Coincidences and the Anthropic Principle in Cosmology" at a prestigious scientific conference in 1973.

The principle, as Glynn learned, essentially says that "all the seemingly arbitrary and unrelated constants in physics have one strange thing in common—these are precisely the values you need if you want to have a universe capable of producing life."[5]

In his subsequent book *God: The Evidence,* Glynn credits the absolutely incredible fine-tuning of the cosmos as being among the key reasons why he concluded that the universe must have been the handiwork of a master designer.

"As recently as twenty-five years ago, a reasonable person weighing the purely scientific evidence on the issue would likely have come down on the side of skepticism. That is no longer the case," he said. "Today the concrete data point strongly in the direction of the God hypothesis. It is the simplest and most obvious solution to the anthropic puzzle."[6]

THE *PRIMA FACIE* EVIDENCE

Alister McGrath, the erudite theologian who studied molecular biophysics at Oxford and wrote the ambitious three-volume series *A Scientific Theology*, has a penchant for penetrating to the core of complex issues. In the case of the anthropic principle, he managed to summarize the essential challenge in two succinct questions, which he posed with a dash of British understatement: "Is it a pure coincidence that the laws of nature are such that life is possible? Might this not be an important clue to the nature and destiny of humanity?"[7]

Those two questions formed my roadmap as I sought fresh answers concerning how and why physics so precariously balances life on a razor's edge. I already knew that an increasing number of scientists and philosophers have been following the clues to their own conclusions in recent decades, including "some who are innocent of any influence from a conventional religious agenda," in the words of physicist and theologian John Polkinghorne.[8]

"It is quite easy to understand why so many scientists have changed their minds in the past thirty years, agreeing that the universe cannot reasonably be explained as a cosmic accident," said Walter Bradley, coauthor of *The Mystery of Life's Origin*. "Evidence for an intelligent designer becomes more compelling the more we understand about our carefully crafted habitat."[9]

For instance, the once-skeptical Paul Davies, the former professor of theoretical physics at the University of Adelaide, is now convinced that there must be a purpose behind the universe.

"Through my scientific work I have come to believe more and more strongly that the physical universe is put together with an ingenuity so astonishing that I cannot accept it merely as a brute fact," he said in his book *The Mind of God*. "I cannot believe that our existence in this universe is a mere quirk of fate, an accident of history, an incidental blip in the great cosmic drama."[10]

Saying that "many scientists, when they admit their views, incline toward the teleological or design argument," cosmologist Edward Harrison has come to this conclusion: "The fine tuning of the universe provides *prima facie* evidence of deistic design."[11]

The eminent astrophysicist Sir Fred Hoyle put it this way: "I do not believe that any scientists who examined the evidence would fail to draw the inference that the laws of nuclear physics have been deliberately designed with regard to the consequences they produce inside stars."[12]

That observation, and others like it from Hoyle, prompted Harvard astronomy professor Owen Gingerich, senior astronomer at the Smithsonian Astrophysical Observatory, to comment: "Fred Hoyle and I differ on lots of questions, but on this we agree: a common sense and satisfying interpretation of our world suggests the designing hand of a superintelligence."[13]

Oxford-educated John Leslie, who catalogues many anthropic examples in his eye-opening 1989 book *Universes*, said he believes that if ours is the only universe—and there are no scientific data proving any others exist—then the fine tuning is "genuine evidence . . . that God is real."[14]

In their book *The New Story of Science*, Robert Augros and George Stanciu sum up the inferences of the amazing confluence of "coincidences" that make life possible in the cosmos. "A universe aiming at the production of man implies a mind directing it," they said. "Though man is not at the physical center of the universe, he appears to be at the center of its purpose."[15]

Those conclusions aside, I was looking for my own personal answers to the fundamental questions posed by McGrath. I wanted not only to explore the scientific evidence for the universe's precarious balancing act, but I also wanted to see if the anthropic principle could survive the challenge of a hypothesis which, according to some skeptics, may very well render it obsolete.

While studying the fine-tuning issue, I came across the writings of an articulate, physics-trained philosopher who has done his own original research on the issue. I especially liked his reputation—he was known as being careful and conservative in his calculations, unwilling to make judgments that exceed the bounds of the data. In short, just what I was looking for.

A few phone calls later, I was on a plane for Pennsylvania and a picturesque campus of redbrick buildings situated not far north of the Civil War battlefield of Gettysburg.

INTERVIEW #4: ROBIN COLLINS, PHD

As a seventh-grade student, Robin Collins sent away for several free booklets from the Atomic Energy Commission—and a love for physics was born. He went on to earn degrees in physics and mathematics at Washington State University (with a grade point average a scant 0.07 points shy of perfection) and then entered a doctoral program in physics at the University of Texas in Austin.

His other love was philosophy—in fact, it was his third major in college. This expertise came in handy while working on his doctorate in an office he shared with a group of graduate students that included an atheist and an agnostic. As for Collins, he had been a Christian since his last year of high school.

The four of them ended up sparring late into the night about philosophical and theological issues, which Collins found so stimulating that he decided to pursue a doctorate in philosophy at the University of Notre Dame. The legendary Alvin Plantinga, perhaps the best American philosopher of modern times, supervised Collins's dissertation.

It was a stray comment by Plantinga in class one day that first exposed Collins to the issue of the fine-tuning of the universe. Captivated by the concept, Collins delved deeply into the subject and soon found a perfect wedding between his expertise in physics and philosophy.

Not only did his training in physics equip him to understand the often-complex mathematical equations in the field—sometimes prompting him to politely correct the errors of more famous scholars—but his experience in philosophy aided him in formulating rigorous arguments from the evidence. Now, after years of research and analysis, he has emerged as one of the most informed and persuasive voices on the anthropic principle.

Collins has written about the topic for numerous books, including *God and Design: The Teleological Argument and Modern Science*; *The Rationality of Theism*; *God Matters: Readings in the Philosophy of Religion*; *Philosophy of Religion: A Reader and Guide*; and *Reason for the Hope Within*. Funded by a grant from the Pew Foundation, he's currently completing a book titled *The Well-Tempered Universe: God, Fine-Tuning, and the Laws of Nature*. In addition, he has spoken at numerous symposia and conferences at Yale, Concordia, Baylor, Stanford, and elsewhere, including a plenary address at the 2003 Russian-U.S. conference on *God and Physical Cosmology* held at Notre Dame.

After serving as a postdoctoral fellow at Northwestern University, Collins has spent the last decade doing research, writing, and teaching at Messiah College, where he is currently an associate professor of philosophy. That's where I connected with him on a warm Saturday afternoon.

Collins's office was so utterly dominated by stacks and shelves and piles and boxes and heaps of books that there was nowhere for us to sit, so we commandeered a conference room nearby. The room was awash in the afternoon sun, which streamed through a large window and created dancing pools of light on the carpet.

Collins removed his green sports coat and tossed it over a chair as we got ready to begin. He has curly, rusty-colored hair and a beard, and the lean physique of a runner (he jogs nearly ninety minutes a day for exercise and meditation). We sat across a plain table from each other, Collins sipping from a mug of his favorite beverage: a concoction of half black and half green tea.

I was anxious to begin. Collins once said that the facts concerning the universe's remarkable "just-so" conditions are widely regarded as "by far the most persuasive current argument for the existence of God"[16]—a statement that set a high standard. I pulled out my notebook and started by asking him to give me an overview of what the fine-tuning of the cosmos was all about.

THE IMPRESSION OF DESIGN

"When scientists talk about the fine-tuning of the universe," Collins said, "they're generally referring to the extraordinary balancing of the fundamental laws and parameters of physics and the initial conditions of the universe. Our minds can't comprehend the precision of some of them. The result is a universe that has just the right conditions to sustain life. The coincidences are simply too amazing to have been the result of happenstance—as Paul Davies said, 'the impression of design is overwhelming.'[17]

"I like to use the analogy of astronauts landing on Mars and finding an enclosed biosphere, sort of like the domed structure that was built in Arizona a few years ago. At the control panel they find that all the dials for its environment are set just right for life. The oxygen ratio is perfect; the temperature is seventy degrees; the humidity is fifty percent; there's a system for replenishing the air; there are systems for producing food, generating energy, and disposing of wastes. Each dial has a huge range of possible settings, and you can see if you were to adjust one or more of them just a little bit, the environment would go out of whack and life would be impossible. What conclusion would you draw from that?"

The answer was obvious. "That someone took great care in designing and building it," I said.

"That's right," he replied. "You'd conclude that this biosphere was not there by accident. Volcanoes didn't erupt and spew out the right compounds that just happened to assemble themselves into the biosphere. Some intelligent being had intentionally and carefully designed and prepared it to support living creatures. And that's an analogy for our universe.

"Over the past thirty years or so, scientists have discovered that just about everything about the basic structure of the universe is balanced on a razor's edge for life to exist. The coincidences are far too fantastic to attribute this to mere chance or to claim that it needs no explanation. The dials are set too precisely to have been a random accident. Somebody, as Fred Hoyle quipped, has been monkeying with the physics."[18]

This has to be among the most fascinating scientific discoveries of the century. "Who first noticed this?" I asked.

"Way back in the late 1950s, Hoyle talked about the precise process by which carbon and oxygen are produced in a certain ratio inside stars. If you tinker with the resonance states of carbon, you won't get the materials you need for building life. Incidentally, recent studies by the physicist Heinz Oberhummer and his colleagues show that just a one-percent change in the strong nuclear force would have a thirty- to a thousand-fold impact on the production of oxygen and carbon in stars. Since stars provide the carbon and oxygen needed for life on planets, if you throw that off balance, conditions in the universe would be much less optimal for the existence of life.

"Anyway—back to your question—most of the research and writing about the fine-tuning has taken place since the early 1980s. There have been hundreds of articles and books written on it from both a technical and popular perspective."

Physics can get very complicated very quickly. So when I asked Collins to describe one of his favorite examples, I was relieved that he chose one that's among the easier to envision.

"Let's talk about gravity," he said. "Imagine a ruler, or one of those old-fashioned linear radio dials, that goes all the way across the universe. It would be broken down into one-inch increments, which means there would be billions upon billions upon billions of inches.

"The entire dial represents the range of force strengths in nature, with gravity being the weakest force and the strong nuclear force that binds protons and neutrons together in the nuclei being the strongest, a whopping ten thousand billion billion billion billion times stronger than gravity.[19] The range of possible settings for the force of gravity can plausibly be taken to be at least as large as the total range of force strengths.

"Now, let's imagine that you want to move the dial from where it's currently set. Even if you were to move it by only one inch, the impact on life in the universe would be catastrophic."

"One inch compared to the whole universe?" I asked. "What kind of impact could that have?"

"That small adjustment of the dial would increase gravity by a *billion*-fold," he said.

"Whoa!" I said. "That sounds like a lot."

"Actually, it's not," he replied, "Relative to the entire radio dial—that is, the total range of force strengths in nature—it's extraordinarily small, just one part in ten thousand billion billion billion."

"Wow, that puts it into perspective," I said. "What would happen to life?"

"Animals anywhere near the size of human beings would be crushed," he said. "As astrophysicist Martin Rees said, 'In an imaginary strong gravity world, even insects would need thick legs to support them, and no animals could get much larger.'[20] In fact, a planet with a gravitational pull of a thousand times that of the Earth would have a diameter of only forty feet, which wouldn't be enough to sustain an ecosystem. Besides which, stars with lifetimes of more than a billion years—compared to ten billion years for our sun—couldn't exist if you increase gravity by just three thousand times.

"As you can see, compared to the total range of force strengths in nature, gravity has an incomprehensibly narrow range for life to exist. Of all the possible settings on the dial, from one side of the universe to the other, it happens to be situated in the exact right fraction of an inch to make our universe capable of sustaining life."

And gravity is just one parameter that scientists have studied. One expert said there are more than thirty separate physical or cosmological parameters that require precise calibration in order to produce a life-sustaining universe.[21]

As for Collins, he likes to focus on gravity and a handful of other examples that he has personally investigated and which he believes are sufficient by themselves to establish the case for a designer. I decided to ask Collins about another parameter—the so-called "cosmological constant"—a phenomenon so bewildering that it even boggles the mind of one of the world's most skeptical scientists.

THROWING DARTS AT AN ATOM

Nobel-winning physicist Steven Weinberg, an avowed atheist, has expressed amazement at the way the cosmological constant—the energy density of empty space—is "remarkably well adjusted in our favor."[22] The constant, which is part of Einstein's equation for General Relativity, could have had any value, positive or negative, "but from first principles one would guess that this constant should be very large," Weinberg said.

Fortunately, he added, it isn't:

> If large and positive, the cosmological constant would act as a repulsive force that increases with distance, a force that would prevent matter from clumping together in the early universe, the process that was the first step in forming galaxies and stars and planets and people. If large and negative, the cosmological constant would act as an attractive force increasing with distance, a force that would almost immediately reverse the expansion of the universe and cause it to recollapse.[23]

Either way, life loses—big time. But astonishingly, that's not what has happened.

"In fact," Weinberg said, "astronomical observations show that the cosmological constant is quite small, very much smaller than would have been guessed from first principles."[24]

When I asked Collins about this, he told me that the unexpected, counterintuitive, and stunningly precise setting of the cosmological constant "is widely regarded as the single greatest problem facing physics and cosmology today."

"How precise is it?" I asked.

Collins rolled his eyes. "Well, there's no way we can really comprehend it," he said. "The fine-tuning has conservatively been estimated to be at least one part in a hundred million billion billion billion billion billion. That would be a ten followed by fifty-three zeroes. That's inconceivably precise."

He was right—I couldn't imagine a figure like that. "Can you give me an illustration?" I asked.

"Put it this way," he said. "Let's say you were way out in space and were going to throw a dart at random toward the Earth. It would be like successfully hitting a bull's eye that's one trillionth of a trillionth of an inch in diameter. That's less than the size of one solitary atom."

Breathtaking was the word that came into my mind. *Staggering.* "No wonder scientists have been blown away by this," I said.

"I'll tell you what," Collins said, "in my opinion, if the cosmological constant were the only example of fine-tuning, and if there were no natural explanation for it, then this would be sufficient by itself to strongly establish design."

I had to agree. The way I saw it, if the universe were put on trial for a charge of having been designed, and the fine-tuning of the cosmological constant were the only evidence introduced by the prosecution, I would have to vote "guilty"—assuming there was no hidden naturalistic explanation. Statistically, this would be a far stronger case than even the DNA evidence that is used to establish guilt in many criminal trials today.

Collins continued. "Now, think about adding together the evidence for just the two factors I've discussed so far—the cosmological constant and the force of gravity," he said. "This would create an unimaginably stronger case. When you combine the two, the fine-tuning would be to a precision of one part in a hundred million trillion trillion trillion trillion trillion trillion. That would be the equivalent of one atom in the entire known universe!"

And Collins wasn't through. "There are other examples of fine-tuning," he said. "For instance, there's the difference in mass between neutrons and protons. Increase the mass of the neutron by about one part in seven hundred and nuclear fusion in stars would stop. There would be no energy source for life.

"And if the electromagnetic force were slightly stronger or weaker, life in the universe would be impossible. Or consider the strong nuclear force. Imagine decreasing it by fifty percent, which is tiny—one part in ten thousand billion billion billion billion, compared to the total range of force strengths."

"What would happen if you tinkered with it by that amount?"

"Since like charges repel, the strong nuclear force would be too weak to prevent the repulsive force between the positively charged protons in atomic nuclei from tearing apart all atoms except hydrogen," he said. "And regardless of what they may show on *Star Trek*, you can't have intelligent life forms built from hydrogen. It simply doesn't have enough stable complexity."

I knew Collins could go on and on, but I needed a way to visualize the implications of these increasingly abstract concepts. "Go back to your Martian biosphere illustration," I said.

"Okay," he replied. "Set aside the issue of how the biosphere got there in the first place. Let's say when you found it, there were twelve dials that controlled the conditions inside the dome. Each dial had an incredibly huge range of possible settings. When you departed, you left the dials at random and as a result no life was possible in the biosphere.

"Then you come back a year later. When you look at the dials, you're amazed to find that each one of them has been carefully calibrated to just the right setting so that life is flourishing in the dome. Twelve dials, twelve different factors—all optimally set for life.

"Do you know what the headline would be in the newspaper the next day? It would say: EXTRATERRESTRIAL LIFE EXISTS. We would take that as proof that an intelligent being had landed and set those dials precisely where they needed to be for life.

"And I'm saying that the dials for the fundamental properties of the universe have been set like that. In fact, the precision is far greater. This would be totally unexpected under the theory that random chance was responsible. However, it's not unexpected at all under the hypothesis that there is a Grand Designer."

READY, AIM, FIRE!

Few concepts stretch the mind as much as the fine-tuning of the universe. For example, Oxford physicist Roger Penrose said one parameter, the "original phase-space volume," required fine-tuning to an accuracy of one part in ten billion multiplied by itself one hundred and twenty three times. Penrose remarked that it would be impossible to even write down that number in full, since it would require more zeroes than the number of elementary particles in the entire universe! This showed, he said, "the precision needed to set the universe on its course."[25]

As *Discover* magazine marveled: "The universe is unlikely. Very unlikely. *Deeply, shockingly unlikely.*"[26]

In light of the infinitesimal odds of getting all the right dial settings for the constants of physics, the forces of nature, and other physical laws and principles necessary for life, it seems fruitless to try to explain away all of this fine-tuning as merely the product of random happenstance.

"As long as we're talking about probabilities, then theoretically you can't rule out the possibility—however remote—that this could occur by chance," Collins said.

"However, if I bet you a thousand dollars that I could flip a coin and get heads fifty times in a row, and then I proceeded to do it, you wouldn't accept that. You'd know that the odds against that are so improbable—about one chance in a million billion—that it's extraordinarily unlikely to happen. The fact that I was able to do it against such monumental odds would be strong evidence to you that the game had been rigged. And the same is true for the fine-tuning of the universe— before you'd conclude that random chance was responsible, you'd conclude that there is strong evidence that the universe was rigged. That is, designed.

"I'll give you another illustration," he continued. "Let's say I was hiking in the mountains and came across rocks arranged in a pattern that spelled out, WELCOME TO THE MOUNTAINS ROBIN COLLINS. One hypothesis would be that the rocks just happened to be arranged in that configuration, maybe as the result of an earthquake or rockslide. You can't totally rule that out. But an alternative hypothesis would be that my brother, who was visiting the mountains before me, arranged the rocks that way.

"Quite naturally, most people would accept the brother theory over the chance theory. Why? Because it strikes us as supremely improbable that the rocks would be arranged that way by chance, but not at all improbable that my brother would place them in that pattern. That's a quite reasonable assumption.

"In a similar way, it's supremely improbable that the fine-tuning of the universe could have occurred at random, but it's not at all improbable if it were the work of an intelligent designer. So it's quite reasonable to choose the design theory over the chance theory. We reason that way all the time. Were the defendant's fingerprints on the gun because of a chance formation of chemicals or because he touched the weapon? Jurors don't hesitate to confidently conclude that he touched the gun if the odds against chance are so astronomical."

While random chance was insufficient to explain away the anthropic "coincidences," perhaps there were other alternatives to the conclusion that the universe was the handiwork of a designer. It was time to put some of those to the test.

"What if there's some undiscovered principle that makes the universe the way it is?" I asked. "Maybe the elusive Theory of Everything that physicists have been seeking for so long will turn out to require the parameters of physics to have exactly the values they do."

Collins was unperturbed by the idea. "It wouldn't bother me a bit," he replied. "It simply moves the improbability of the fine-tuning up one level."

"What do you mean?"

"It would really be amazing if this Grand Unified Theory—out of the incredible range of possibilities—managed to force all the fine-tuning dials to where they just happened to create a life-sustaining universe," he said. "It would be like some predetermined law at the outset of the universe caused everything to fall into place so that when I came to the mountain, I saw a pattern of rocks spelling out WELCOME TO THE MOUNTAINS ROBIN COLLINS."

"So," I said, "this wouldn't destroy the argument for intelligent design?"

"Quite the opposite," he replied. "It would amplify it, because it would show that the designer was even more ingenious than we first thought. As difficult as it would be to fine-tune the universe by adjusting all of the individual dials, it would be even more difficult to create an underlying law of nature that then forced all the dials into those specific positions. All that would do would be to make me even more in awe of the Creator."

Some skeptics have attacked the fine-tuning argument from another direction, raising what has become known as the Weak Anthropic Principle. According to this idea, if the universe were not fine-tuned for life, then human beings wouldn't be around to observe it. Consequently, they contend that the fine-tuning requires no explanation.

"You have to admit, there's a certain intuitive appeal to that," I said to Collins.

"I think John Leslie had the best answer to that," he replied. "Suppose you were standing before a firing squad of fifty highly trained marksmen who were all aiming directly at your chest from a short distance away. You heard the order, 'Ready! Aim! Fire!' But you didn't feel anything. You remove your blindfold and see you're still very much alive. Not one bullet hit you.

"Now, you wouldn't allow the skeptic to simply dismiss the situation by saying, 'Oh well, if they had shot you, you wouldn't be here to comment on the situation.' No—the circumstances are still surprising and they would still demand an explanation. Did they conspire together to miss you? Was this a mock execution? And the same thing is true for the fine-tuning of the universe. It still demands an explanation. My assessment is that the best explanation is a designer."

Despite Collins's confidence, however, a more serious threat to the fine-tuning argument has been raised by some scientists in recent years. Many scientists would say that the so-called "many-universes hypothesis" looms as the most formidable challenge to the conclusion that the universe was crafted with artful precision by a transcendent designer. That, I decided, would be my next line of questioning.

THE METAPHYSICAL ESCAPE HATCH

Spiritual skeptic Martin Rees, who became a professor of astronomy at Cambridge when he was in his thirties and was named Astronomer Royal by Queen Elizabeth in 1995, could not ignore how the cosmic parameters are so incredibly choreographed to create a life-friendly universe. If the six numbers that underlie the fundamental physical properties of the universe were altered "even to the tiniest degree," he said, "there would be no stars, no complex elements, no life."[27]

Declared Rees: "The expansion speed, the material content of the universe, and the strengths of the basic forces, seem to have been a prerequisite for the emergence of the hospitable cosmic habitat in which we live."[28]

One author nicely encapsulated this example from Rees:

For the universe to exist as it does requires that hydrogen be converted to helium in a precise but comparatively stately manner—specifically, in a way that converts seven one-thousandths of its mass to energy. Lower that value very slightly—from 0.007 percent to 0.006 percent, say—and no transformation could take place: the universe would consist of hydrogen and nothing else. Raise the value very slightly—to 0.008 percent—and bonding would be so wildly prolific that the hydrogen would long since have been exhausted. In either case, with the slightest tweaking of the numbers the universe as we know and need it would not be here.[29]

When the other five numbers that represent "the deep forces that shape the universe" are taken into consideration, said Rees, the universe's structure becomes "unlikely to an absurd degree."[30]

Still, is Rees surprised by the universe's exquisitely precarious balancing act? *No.* Does he believe the fine-tuning points to a designer? *Not at all.* Why? He answers by using the illustration of a large off-the-rack clothing store.

"If there is a large stack of clothing, you're not surprised to find a suit that fits," he said. "If there are many universes, each governed by a different set of numbers, there will be one where there is a particular set of numbers suitable to life. We are in that one."[31]

The argument can be summarized this way: "There could have been millions and millions of different universes, each created with different dial settings of the fundamental ratios and constants, so many in fact that the right set was bound to turn up by sheer chance. We just happened to be the lucky ones."[32]

In other words, if ours is the only universe in existence, then the fine-tuning is powerful—many would say, conclusive—evidence that an intelligence had tinkered with the dials. There seems to be no other reasonable possibility. But that conclusion evaporates if there are many or an infinite number of universes. With enough random dial spinning, the odds are that at least one—our own—would win the cosmic lottery and be a livable habitat.

Rees is not the only skeptic to escape the theistic implications of the finely tuned universe by speculating about the existence of other worlds. In fact, that's exactly the approach Weinberg took after expressing amazement at the unexpected precariousness of the cosmological constant.[33]

Many physicists subscribe to some sort of multiple universe, or "multiverse," theory, although others scoff at the idea, charging that it's little more than a metaphysical escape hatch to avoid the fine-tuning evidence for a designer. Said one writer:

> Originally the many-worlds hypothesis was proposed for strictly scientific reasons as a solution to the so-called quantum-measurement problem in physics. Though its efficacy as an explanation within quantum physics remains controversial among physicists, its use there does have an empirical basis. More recently, however, it has been employed to serve as an alternate non-theistic explanation for the fine-tuning of the

physical constants. This use of the [hypothesis] does seem to betray a metaphysical desperation.[34]

"It's purely a concept, an idea, without scientific proof," William Lane Craig, coauthor of *Theism, Atheism and Big Bang Cosmology*, told me in an interview. "Look—this is pure metaphysics.[35] There's no real reason to believe such parallel worlds exist. The very fact that skeptics have to come up with such an outlandish theory is because the fine-tuning of the universe points powerfully toward an intelligent designer—and some people will hypothesize anything to avoid reaching that conclusion."[36]

Similarly, Cambridge's Polkinghorne, a former professor of mathematical physics, has called the hypothesis "pseudo-science" and "a metaphysical guess."[37] He put it this way in his book *Science and Theology*: "The many universes account is sometimes presented as if it were purely scientific, but in fact a sufficient portfolio of different universes could only be generated by speculative processes that go well beyond what sober science can honestly endorse."[38]

Davies has concluded that "the many-universes theory can at best explain only a limited range of features, and then only if one appends some metaphysical assumptions that seem no less extravagant than design."[39] Observed Clifford Longley: "The sight of scientific atheists clutching at such desperate straws has put new spring in the step of theists."[40]

Rees conceded the tenuous nature of the multiverse theory in a 2000 interview with a science journalist. Rees admitted the calculations are "highly arbitrary" (though he suggests someday they might not be), and that the theory itself "hangs on assumptions," remains speculative, and is not amenable to direct investigation. "The other universes are unavailable to us, just as the interior of a black hole is unavailable," he said. He added that we cannot even know if the universes are finite or infinite in number. Even so, he said the multiverse theory "genuinely lies within the province of science."[41]

All of this was swirling in my mind as I prepared to question Collins on the possibility that a multi-universe scenario could extinguish the evidence for a designer of our universe. I was genuinely curious: Can the hypothesis provide a reasonable refuge for skeptics who balk at the idea of God? Or would the anthropic argument withstand the challenge?

THE COSMIC HOCKEY PUCK

I have to admit that I was taken aback by Collins's initial response when I asked him about the viability of the many-universes hypothesis.

"Well," he said, taking a sip of tea and putting the mug on the table, "most of these hypotheses are entirely speculative and have little basis in physics. They're not worth considering. However, the most popular theory, inflationary cosmology, has more credibility. I have to say that I'm at least sympathetic to it. I'm trying to keep an open mind."

Collins was referring to the "self-reproducing inflationary universe" model proposed by André Linde of Stanford University, which is based on advanced principles of quantum physics. This was the theory that Weinberg cited when he tried to explain away the apparent fine-tuning of the cosmological constant. In a stunning example of understatement, one science writer said that Linde's concept "defies easy visualization."[42] However, at the risk of too much simplicity, a basic illustration can be used.

Linde postulates a preexisting superspace that is rapidly expanding. A small part of this superspace is blown up by a theoretical *inflaton* field, sort of like soap bubbles forming in an infinite ocean full of dish detergent. Each bubble becomes a new universe. In what's known as "chaotic inflation theory," a huge number of such universes are randomly birthed, thanks to quantum fluctuations, along various points of superspace. Thus, each universe has a beginning and is finite in size, while the much larger superspace is infinite in size and endures forever.

I mentioned to Collins that in an earlier interview on cosmology, William Lane Craig had little use for this kind of theory. "Granted, it's highly speculative," Collins said. "There are an awful lot of loose ends with it. But since it's by far the most popular theory today—and I believe it should be taken seriously—let's not critique it right now. Let's just make the assumption that it's true."

"All right," I said, nodding. "That's fine."

"Now, here's my overarching point: even if Linde's theory could account for the existence of many universes, this would not destroy the case for design. It would just kick the issue up another level. In fact, I believe it would point *toward* design."

That was an interesting twist! "Why do you believe that?" I asked.

"I'll use an everyday example," he said. "My wife and I have a bread-making machine. Actually, it's defunct now, but we used to use it. To make edible bread, we first needed this well-designed machine that had the right circuitry, the right heating element, the right timer, and so forth. Then we had to put in the right ingredients in the right proportions and in the right order—water, milk, flour, shortening, salt, sugar, yeast. The flour had to have the right amount of a protein substance called gluten, or else it would need to be added.[43] Everything has to be just right to produce a loaf of bread—otherwise, you get what looks like a burnt hockey puck.

"Now, let's face it: a universe is far more complex than a loaf of bread. My point is that if a bread machine requires certain specific parameters to be set in order to create bread, then there has to be a highly designed mechanism or process to produce functional universes. In other words, regardless of which multiple-universe theory you use, in every case you'd need a 'many-universes generator'—and it would require the right structure, the right mechanism, and the right ingredients to churn out new universes.

"Otherwise," he said, stifling a chuckle, "you'd end up with a cosmic hockey puck!"

THE MANY-UNIVERSE MACHINE

Collins pushed back his chair and walked over to a chalkboard on the wall. "My students get a kick out of it when I draw a 'many universes generator,'" he said, sketching a whimsical cartoon of a manufacturing machine, complete with a billowing smokestack and a conveyor belt that brought in raw materials and then carried freshly minted universes out the other side.

"This machine," he said, putting the finishing touches on his artwork, "can only produce life-sustaining universes if it has the right components and mechanisms."

I leaned back and scrutinized his drawing. "What would you need, say, under Linde's theory?" I asked.

"First," Collins said as he strolled back to his chair, "you'd need a mechanism to supply the energy needed for the bubble universes. That would be the inflaton field that he has hypothesized, which effectively acts like a reservoir of unlimited energy. Second, he would need a mechanism to form the bubbles. This would be Einstein's equation of general relativity. Because of its peculiar form, this would supposedly cause the bubble universes to form and the ocean to keep expanding.

"Third, he would need a mechanism to convert the energy of the inflaton field to the normal mass/energy that we find in our universe. Fourth, he would need a mechanism to allow enough variation in the constants of physics among the various universes. In other words, he would need a way to vary the constants of physics so that by random chance he would produce some universes, like ours, that have the right fine-tuning to sustain life."

"Is there a candidate for that mechanism?" I asked.

"Well, yes—superstring theory," he replied. "This might work, though it's far too early to tell."

When I asked why he brought up superstrings, he explained: "According to superstring theory, the ultimate constituents of matter are strings of energy that undergo quantum vibrations in ten or eleven dimensions of space-time. Six or seven of these dimensions are 'rolled up' to an extremely small size. In the jargon of string theory, they are said to be *compactified*. Their shape determines the modes of vibration of the strings. This, in turn, would determine the types and masses of fundamental particles and the characteristics of the forces between them. So they would have different constants of physics and laws governing the forces."

"That sounds pretty iffy," I said.

"Well, both inflationary cosmology and superstring theory are *highly* speculative. In fact, theoretical physicist Michio Kaku said recently that 'not a shred of experimental evidence' has been found to confirm superstrings.[44] Physicists are a long way from even working out the equations. Right now it's just a theory whose main merits are that it's mathematically elegant and that it holds the promise of unifying quantum mechanics and general relativity, two branches of physics that physicists have struggled to reconcile for over fifty years."

I summed up what Collins had said so far. "So the many-universes generator would need all these factors if it ever hoped to produce a functioning universe," I said.

"Right," he replied. "For example, without Einstein's equation and the inflaton field working together harmoniously, it wouldn't work. If the universe obeyed Newton's theory of gravity instead of Einstein's, it wouldn't work. But that's not all.

"You would also have to have the right background laws in place. For instance, without the so-called principle of quantization, all of the electrons in an atom would be sucked into the atomic nuclei. That would make atoms impossible. Further, as eminent Princeton physicist Freeman Dyson has noted, without the Pauli-exclusion principle, electrons would occupy the lowest orbit around the nucleus, and that would make complex atoms impossible.[45] Finally, without a universally attractive force between all masses—such as gravity—stars and planets couldn't form. If just one of these components was missing or different, it's highly improbable that any life-permitting universes could be produced.

"And keep in mind," he added, "you would need to make trillions upon trillions upon trillions upon trillions of universes in order to increase the odds that the cosmological constant would come out right at least once, since it's finely tuned to an incomprehensible degree. And that's just one parameter."

"What's your conclusion then?" I asked.

"It's highly unlikely that such a universe-generating system would have all the right components and ingredients in place by random chance, just like random chance can't account for how a bread-maker produces loaves of edible bread. So if a many-universe-generating system exists, it would be best explained by design."

"That means," I said, "that when scientists appeal to the theoretical existence of many universes to avoid the implications of the fine-tuning of our universe, they still can't escape design."

"Exactly," he declared. "Theists have nothing to fear from the idea that there may be multiple universes. There would still need to be an intelligent designer to make the finely tuned universe-generating process work. To modify a phrase from philosopher Fred Dretske: these are inflationary times, and the cost of atheism has just gone up."

THE SUPERMIND

I thought for a few moments about Collins's explanation. Certainly it made sense that generating universes would require the right mechanisms, the right ingredients, and the right precision—all earmarks of intelligent design. But I was still mentally wrestling with something else. To me—admittedly, not a physicist—the whole concept of multiple universes seemed absurd.

I found myself agreeing with the iconoclastic Gregg Easterbrook, a contributing editor for the *Atlantic Monthly*, who researched the discoveries and theories of modern science. He was characteristically blunt in his assessment. "The multiverse idea rests on assumptions that would be laughed out of town if they came from a religious text," he wrote. "[The theory] requires as much suspension of disbelief as any religion. *Join the church that believes in the existence of invisible objects fifty billion galaxies wide!*"[46]

When I mentioned my skepticism to Collins, he listened carefully. "There's a reason you feel that way," he said. "You see, everything else being equal, we tend to prefer hypotheses that are natural extrapolations of what we already know."

I wasn't sure what he was driving at. "Could you give me an illustration of that?" I asked.

"Sure," he said. "Let's say you found some dinosaur bones. You would naturally consider them to be very strong evidence that dinosaurs lived in the past. Why? Because even though nobody has ever seen dinosaurs, we do have the experience of other animals leaving behind fossilized remains. So the dinosaur explanation is a natural extrapolation from our common experience. It makes sense.

"Let's say there was a dinosaur skeptic, however. He was trying to rationalize away the bones you found. Let's suppose he claimed he could explain the bones by proposing that a 'dinosaur-bone-producing field' simply caused them to materialize out of thin air."

"That's ridiculous," I said.

"And that's exactly what you would tell the skeptic," Collins continued. "You'd say: 'Wait a second—there are no known laws of physics that would allow that field to conjure up bones out of nothing.' But the skeptic would be ready for you. He'd reply, 'Aha—we just haven't discovered these laws yet. We simply haven't detected these fields yet. Give us more time, Lee, and I'm sure we will.'

"My guess is that nothing could deter you from inferring that dinosaurs existed, because this would be a natural extrapolation from what you already know," Collins concluded. "On the other hand, the skeptic needs to invent a whole new set of physical laws and a whole new set of mechanisms that are *not* a natural extrapolation from anything we know or have experienced. You wouldn't buy his story. No way."

"You're saying, then, that an intelligent designer *is* a natural extrapolation of what we already know?"

"Yes, I am," he replied. "Think about it, Lee—we already know that intelligent minds produce finely tuned devices. Look at the space shuttle. Look at a television set. Look at an internal combustion engine. We see minds producing complex, precision machinery all the time.

"So postulating the existence of a supermind—or God—as the explanation for the fine-tuning of the universe makes all the sense in the world. It would simply be a natural extrapolation of what we already know that minds can do. And, what's more, unlike the hypothesis that there are many universes, we have independent evidence of God's existence, such as a personal experience of the Creator and the other sort of evidence you're talking about in your book."

THE BEAUTY OF PHYSICS

Collins took his last sip of tea at about the same time I finished my glass of water. "Let's go get some refills," he said, motioning for me to follow him down the hall.

Without students or faculty, the building was eerily quiet, our voices echoing slightly as we ambled down the empty corridor. "The day is too beautiful to be spending so much time indoors," I commented as we arrived at a self-serve kitchen area.

"Yeah, perfect for a run," Collins said.

I filled my glass with water while he blended his tea. Silence prevailed for a few moments, then Collins remarked: "Talking about beauty reminds me of another line of reasoning that points toward a designer," he said.

"Really?" I asked. "Tell me about it."

"Think about the extraordinary beauty, elegance, harmony, and ingenuity that we find in the laws of nature," he replied as we headed back to the conference room.

"Whole books have been written about it. Weinberg once spent an entire chapter explaining how the criteria of beauty and elegance have been used to guide physicists in formulating the right laws.[47] The theoretical physicist Alan Guth said that the original construction of the gauge theories of fundamental particle physics 'was motivated mainly by their mathematical elegance.'[48]

"One of the most influential scientists of the twentieth century, Paul Dirac, the Nobel Prize winner from Cambridge, even claimed that 'it is more important to have beauty in one's equations than to have them fit experiment.'[49] One historian said mathematical beauty was 'an integral part' of Dirac's strategy. He said Dirac believed physicists 'first had to select the most beautiful mathematics—not necessarily connected to the existing basis of theoretical physics—and then interpret them in physical terms.'[50]

"And you see beauty in the laws and principles of nature?" I asked.

"Oh, absolutely," he declared. "They're beautiful, and they're also elegant in their simplicity. Surprisingly so. When scientists are trying to construct a new law of nature, they routinely look for the simplest law that adequately accounts for the data."

I interrupted with an objection. "Isn't beauty in the eye of the beholder?" I asked. "What's beautiful seems so subjective."

"Subjectivity can't explain the success of the criterion of beauty in science," he replied. "We wouldn't expect purely subjective patterns to serve as the basis of theories that make highly accurate predictions, such as the success of quantum electrodynamics to predict the quantum correction to the g-factor of the electron.

"Besides, not all beauty is subjective; there are also objective aspects of it, at least in the classical sense. In his book *The Analysis of Beauty*, written in the mid-1700s, William Hogarth said the defining feature of beauty or elegance is 'simplicity with variety.' And that's what scientists have found—a world where fundamental simplicity gives rise to the enormous complexity needed for life."

I ventured another alternative. "Maybe the concept of beauty is merely the product of evolution," I said. "Perhaps it has survival value, and so our sense of what's beautiful has been shaped by natural selection."

"That would only apply to things we can see, touch, or hear— things in our everyday world that are necessary for survival. But evolution can't explain the beauty that exists in the underlying world of physical laws and mathematics," he said.

"In physics, we see an uncanny degree of harmony, symmetry, and proportionality. And we see something that I call 'discoverability.' By that, I mean that the laws of nature seem to have been carefully arranged so that they can be discovered by beings with our level of intelligence. That not only fits the idea of design, but it also suggests a providential purpose for humankind—that is, to learn about our habitat and to develop science and technology."

Collins mentioned that Davies had also commented about the beauty of nature in his book *Superforce*. Later I found the passage:

A common reaction among physicists to remarkable discoveries ... is a mixture of delight at the subtlety and elegance of nature, and of stupefaction: "I would never have thought of doing it that way." If nature is so "clever" it can exploit mechanisms that amaze us with their ingenuity, is that not persuasive evidence for the existence of intelligent design behind the physical universe? If the world's finest minds can unravel only with difficulty the deeper workings of nature, how could it be supposed that those workings are merely a mindless accident, a product of blind chance? . . . Uncovering the laws of physics resembles completing a crossword [puzzle] in a number of ways. . . . In the case of the crossword, it would never occur to us to suppose that the words just happened to fall into a consistent interlocking pattern by accident.[51]

"Under an atheistic viewpoint," Collins continued, "there's no reason to expect that the fundamental laws would be beautiful or elegant, because they easily could have been otherwise. Even Weinberg, who's an atheist, conceded that 'sometimes nature seems more beautiful than strictly necessary.'[52]

"However, the fine-tuning for simplicity, beauty, and elegance *does* make sense under the God hypothesis. Think of the classical conception of God—he is the greatest possible being, and therefore a being with perfect aesthetic sensibility. It wouldn't be surprising at all for God to want to create a world of great subtlety and beauty at its most fundamental level."

"ALL OTHER THEORIES FALL SHORT"

We walked back into the conference room, knowing that we were getting close to finishing. Collins leaned against the wall, a mug in one hand, the other arm casually folded across his chest, while I perched atop the back of a chair, my feet resting on its seat.

The intersection of faith and physics was a fascinating crossroads to me, and I was curious about the impact of Collins's research on his personal life.

"What has your study of the fine-tuning of the universe done for your faith?" I asked.

Collins put down his tea. "Oh, it has strengthened it, absolutely," he replied. "Like everybody, I've gone through some hard times in life, and all of the scientific evidence for God has been an important anchor for me."

That sounded like science displacing faith. "Isn't that what faith is supposed to do?" I asked.

"I *am* taking about faith," he insisted. "God doesn't usually appear supernaturally somewhere and say, 'Here I am.' He uses preachers to bring people his message of redemption through Christ. And sometimes he uses natural means. Romans 1:20 tells us that God's eternal power and divine nature can be seen and understood through things that are made, and that this is the reason humanity is without excuse. I see physics as uncovering the evidence of God's fingerprint at a deeper and more subtle level than the ancients could have dreamed of. He has used physics to enable me to see the evidence of his presence and creative ability. The heavens really do declare the glory of God, even more so for someone trained with physics and with eyes to see. That has been a tremendous encouragement to me.

"Of course," he continued, "the fine-tuning by itself can't tell us whether God is personal or not. We have to find out in other ways. But it does help us conclude that he exists, that he created the world, and that therefore the universe has a purpose. He made it very carefully and quite precisely as a habitat for intelligent life."

"How do you assess the persuasiveness of the anthropic evidence?" I asked.

"It's not conclusive in the sense that mathematics tells us two plus two equals four," he said. "Instead, it's a cumulative argument. The extraordinary fine-tuning of the laws and constants of nature, their beauty, their discoverability, their intelligibility—all of this combines to make the God hypothesis the most reasonable choice we have. All other theories fall short."

I picked up a newspaper clipping from the conference table, then said to Collins: "The *New York Times* recently published that famous quote by physicist Freeman Dyson, who looked at the evidence for fine-tuning and said: 'The universe in some sense must have known that we were coming.' But then the author added: 'This notion horrifies some physicists, who feel it is their mission to find a mathematical explanation of nature that leaves nothing to chance or the whim of the Creator.' Obviously, that's not how you see the mission of physics, is it?"[53]

"No, not at all," he said. "That attitude reflects an antitheistic bias. I don't mind scientists trying to find naturalistic explanations, but I wouldn't say it's the mission of physics to explain everything naturalistically. The mission of physics is to pursue a naturalistic explanation as far as we can; but since physics can only explain one set of laws by invoking a more fundamental set of laws, it can never itself explain the most fundamental laws. Explaining these laws is where one moves from physics to metaphysics. Though invoking God may not be strictly part of science, it is in the spirit of science to follow the evidence and its implications wherever they lead us. We shouldn't shrink back from the God hypothesis if that's what the facts fit."

He wasn't alone in that perspective. Said Harvard's Gingerich: "I believe that . . . the Book of Nature, with its astounding details—the blade of grass, the *Conus cedonulli,* or the resonance levels of the carbon atom—suggests a God of purpose and a God of design. And I think my belief makes me no less of a scientist."[54]

With that, one last question came to mind. "As you dig deeper and deeper into physics," I said to Collins, "do you have a sense of wonder and awe at what you find?"

"I really do," he said, a grin breaking on his face. "Not just with the fine-tuning but in lots of areas, like quantum mechanics and the ability of our minds to understand the world. The deeper we dig, we see that God is more subtle and more ingenious and more creative than we ever thought possible. And I think that's the way God created the universe for us—to be full of surprises."

HEADS OR TAILS

Whichever way I looked, the inference of design seemed inescapable. If ours is the only universe in existence, which is a logical conclusion based on the evidence, then its highly sophisticated fine-tuning cries out for a designer. On the other hand, if the esoteric theories of physicists turn out to be true and our universe is one of many others, then the need for a universe-generating mechanism also would demand a designer.

Heads or tails, the Creator wins.

As Vera Kistiakowski, professor of physics *emerita* at the Massachusetts Institute of Technology and former president of the Association of Women in Science, summarized the implications of the evidence: "The exquisite order displayed by our scientific understanding of the physical world calls for the divine."[55]

That was also the conclusion that dissolved Patrick Glynn's atheism. The anthropic evidence, he said . . .

... does offer as strong an indication as reason and science alone could be expected to provide that God exists.... Ironically, the picture of the universe bequeathed to us by the most advanced twentieth-century science is closer in spirit to the vision presented in the Book of Genesis than anything offered by science since Copernicus.[56]

So far, after the one-two punch of my interviews with Craig and Collins, the evidence was clearly pointing in that direction. In fact, my imagination was captivated by one particular implication.

In *The Case for Christ*, I described the historical evidence for the miracles of Jesus of Nazareth, especially his resurrection from the dead. The ability to supernaturally intervene in the normal affairs of the world, to momentarily suspend the natural functioning of the universe, is certainly powerful affirmation that he is the Son of God.

However, having heard about the meticulous fine-tuning of the laws of nature, I now realized that the everyday functioning of the universe is, *in itself*, a kind of ongoing miracle. The "coincidences" that allow the fundamental properties of matter to yield a habitable environment are so improbable, so far-fetched, so elegantly orchestrated, that they require a divine explanation.

In other words, the momentary abrogation of the laws of nature in a sudden, visible, and direct way—what we usually call a "miracle"—obviously points toward an all-powerful deity. Yet even if God *doesn't* supernaturally intervene, the otherwise inexplicable fine-tuning of physics, operating day in and day out ever since creation, also seems to warrant the term "miraculous."

And miracles are the province of God.

I was pondering this thought as Collins and I emerged from the building, taking deep breaths of the fragrant autumn air and basking in the sunshine. Looking up, I could see the blazing sun on one side of the blue sky and the faint moon on the other. My mind turned from the abstract world of physics to the planets and moons and stars and galaxies that populate the universe.

What other evidence of fine-tuning, I wondered, might be waiting in the cosmos? Could our very existence on a life-sustaining rock on the outskirts of the Milky Way tell us anything about the Creator who has thus far been so highly suggested by cosmology and physics?

I made my decision as I drove away from the campus: it was time to quiz an astronomer about what we can learn from the mystery and grandeur of the heavens.

FOR FURTHER EVIDENCE
More Resources on This Topic

Collins, Robin. "The Argument from Design and the Many-Worlds Hypothesis." In *Philosophy of Religion: A Reader and Guide*, ed. William Lane Craig. New Brunswick, N. J.: Rutgers University Press, 2002.

———. "The Evidence for Fine-Tuning." *In God and Design: The Teleological Argument and Modern Science*, ed. Neil Manson. New York: Routledge, 2003.

———. "A Scientific Argument for the Existence of God: The Fine-Tuning Design Argument." In *Reason for the Hope Within*, ed. Michael J. Murray. Grand Rapids, Mich.: Eerdmans, 1999.

———. "The Teleological Argument." In *The Rationality of Theism*, ed. Paul Copan and Paul Moser. New York: Routledge, 2003.

Dubay, Thomas. *The Evidential Power of Beauty*. San Francisco: Ignatius, 1999.

Leslie, John. *Universes*. New York: Routledge, 1989.

THE EVIDENCE OF ASTRONOMY: THE PRIVILEGED PLANET

As we survey all the evidence, the thought insistently arises that some supernatural agency—or, rather, Agency—must be involved. Is it possible that suddenly, without intending to, we have stumbled upon scientific proof of the existence of a Supreme Being? Was it God who stepped in and so providentially crafted the cosmos for our benefit?

Astronomer George Greenstein[1]

Astronomy leads us to a unique event, a universe which was created out of nothing, one with the very delicate balance needed to provide exactly the conditions required to permit life, and one which has an underlying (one might say "supernatural") plan.

Nobel laureate Arno Penzias[2]

There's nothing unusual about Earth. It's an average, unassuming rock that's spinning mindlessly around an unremarkable star in a run-of-the-mill galaxy—"a lonely speck in the great enveloping cosmic dark," as the late Carl Sagan put it.[3]

The fact that life flourishes on our planet isn't exceptional. Creatures of all kinds undoubtedly abound, we're told, in countless locations among the ten trillion billion stars in the universe. Some scientists have estimated there are up to ten trillion advanced civilizations.[4] Sagan put the number at one million for our Milky Way galaxy alone.[5]

After all, the forces of nature are so automatic that life is sure to have evolved wherever water exists. That's why whenever scientists raise new speculation about liquid water being present on another celestial body—the underground worlds of Jupiter's frozen moons

Europa and Ganymede are currently the most fashionable examples—then the automatic assumption is that living organisms must necessarily and inexorably follow.

If life can emerge from nonlife so quickly and efficiently on a planet as undistinguished as ours, they reason, then why not throughout the universe's hundreds of billions of galaxies? To them, life is like a soup mix: just add water!

The very title of astrobiologist David Darling's recent book nicely encapsulates this optimistic philosophy: *Life Everywhere*.[6] He's enthusiastic about claims that "life may arise inevitably whenever a suitable energy source, a concentrated supply of organic (carbon-based) material and water occur together." These ingredients, he said, "are starting to look ubiquitous in space."[7] Consequently, he believes microbial life, at least, "is widespread."[8]

In short, Earth has no privileged status. Polish scientist Nicholas Copernicus deflated our oversized ego by putting us in our place long ago—the universe doesn't revolve around us; instead, we're just living in a humdrum hamlet off the beaten path in a nondescript suburb of the vast Milky Way. We have no grand role, no meaning, no significance, no reason for being other than . . . well, just being.

"The universe that we observe," said Oxford's Richard Dawkins, "has precisely the properties we should expect if there is, at bottom, no design, no purpose, no evil and no good, nothing but blind, pitiless indifference."[9]

This is the essence of what I was taught as I studied science. Of course, these conclusions neatly bolstered my atheistic values. Somehow I managed to avoid getting too depressed by the personal implications of all of this, strangely finding hope and inspiration in the belief that we are not alone in the universe. Even if God didn't exist, at least there were millions of advanced civilizations out there.

BEAMING MESSAGES TO HERCULES

Ever since I first watched the classic movie *The Day the Earth Stood Still* as a child, I've been enthralled by the fanciful images of teeming inter-galactic life portrayed in science fiction. Sure, *Star Trek* and *Star Wars* were silly—but still, the idea of other exotic creatures living in the strange nooks and crannies of the universe was always intriguing and even comforting to me.

Later I became fascinated by the Drake Equation, an attempt by astronomer Frank Drake to quantify the number of civilizations that might exist in our galaxy. The equation factors in such variables as how many of the two hundred to three hundred billion stars in our Milky Way might resemble our own sun, the percentage of stars that may have planets in habitable zones, and so forth.

Though the specific numbers that scientists then plugged into Drake's equation mostly amounted to rank conjecture fueled by their own biases—one scientist admitted it was "a way of compressing a large amount of ignorance into a small space"[10]—this did lend an air of scientific certainty to a highly speculative issue.

Then I cheered from afar in the mid-1970s as Drake and Sagan beamed a message of greeting to the great globular cluster M13, which is a concentration of a quarter million stars in the constellation Hercules. While I knew there wasn't much practical science involved with this intragalactic phone call—it would take more than twenty-two thousand years for the message to reach its destination—nevertheless there was something romantic and adventurous about trying to communicate with the civilizations that most assuredly populated those distant stars.

All of this helped form my perspective as I would gaze over the years at the twinkling stars in the dark heavens. But now my attitude was changing. After studying the latest evidence from various scientific disciplines—from astronomy to cosmology to geology to oceanography to microbiology—my conclusions were being tugged in the opposite direction.

It's turning out that the Earth is anything but ordinary, that our sun is far from average, and that even the position of our planet in the galaxy is eerily fortuitous. The idea that the universe is a flourishing hothouse of advanced civilizations is now being undermined by surprising new scientific discoveries and fresh thinking.

In short, new findings are suggesting that we *are* special. More and more scientists are studying the mind-boggling convergence of scores of extraordinary "coincidences" that make intelligent life possible on Earth and concluding that this can't possibly be an accident. They're seeing signs of design, a kind of unlikely fine-tuning for life similar to the fine-tuning of physics that we explored in the previous chapter.

In fact, said one noted researcher, "new evidence which could potentially have refuted the [design] hypothesis has only ended up confirming it."[11] Once again, we find the evidence of science pointing in the direction of a Creator.

And rather than our lives being purposeless, scientists for the first time are uncovering concrete evidence that suggests at least one surprising purpose for which we were created—that is, to discover and learn about the surroundings in which we have been placed.

In other words, as we'll see in this chapter, one purpose for which we were designed is to do science itself.

RIGHT PLACE, RIGHT TIME

As the new millennium dawned, geologist Peter D. Ward and astronomer Donald Brownlee, both professors at the University of Washington in Seattle, published a provocative and highly successful book that raised this disquieting question about Earth: "What if it is utterly unique: the only planet with animals in this galaxy or even in the visible universe . . . ?"[12]

Their book, *Rare Earth*, marshals evidence from a wide range of scientific disciplines to build its case that "not only intelligent life, but even the simplest of animal life, is exceedingly rare in our galaxy and in the universe."[13] They called the conclusion "inescapable" that "Earth is a rare place indeed."[14]

Although Ward and Brownlee uncritically buy into the idea that microbial life may very well be more prevalent, a view they draw from the way life seemed to have effortlessly developed on Earth "about as soon as environmental conditions allowed its survival,"[15] their conviction that the existence of complex life is "extraordinarily rare" is bolstered by convincing data divorced from any theological framework.

Calling their book "carefully reasoned and scientifically astute," Don Johanson, director of the Institute of Human Origins at Arizona State University, remarked: "In spite of our wishful thinking, there just may not be other Mozarts or Monets."[16] David Levy, of comet Shoemaker-Levy fame, added, "As we know it on Earth, complex life might be very rare, and very precious."[17] Said the *Times of London*: "If they are right it could be time to reverse a process that has been going on since Copernicus."[18]

More and more scientists are observing the stunning ways in which our planet—against all odds—manages to fulfill a large number of finely balanced criteria that are absolutely crucial to supporting a habitat suitable for humankind.

"Rather than being one planet among billions, Earth now appears to be the uncommon Earth," said science educators Jimmy H. Davis and Harry L. Poe. "The data imply that Earth may be the only planet 'in the right place at the right time.'"[19]

A BOLD AND AUDACIOUS CLAIM

Earth's location, its size, its composition, its structure, its atmosphere, its temperature, its internal dynamics, and its many intricate cycles that are essential to life—the carbon cycle, the oxygen cycle, the nitrogen cycle, the phosphorous cycle, the sulfur cycle, the calcium cycle, the sodium cycle, and so on—testify to the degree to which our planet is exquisitely and precariously balanced.[20]

As they begin their influential textbook *Earth*, Frank Press of the National Academy of Sciences and Raymond Siever of Harvard University write about what they call "the uniqueness of planet Earth."[21]

They note how its atmosphere filters out harmful ultraviolet radiation while working with the oceans to moderate the climate through the storing and redistributing of solar energy, and how the Earth is just large enough so that its gravity retains the atmosphere and yet just small enough not to keep too many harmful gases. Then they describe the Earth's interior as . . .

> . . . a gigantic but delicately balanced heat engine fueled by radioactivity. . . . Were it running more slowly . . . the continents might not have evolved to their present form. . . . Iron may never have melted and sunk to the liquid core, and the magnetic field would never have developed. . . . If there had been more radioactive fuel, and therefore a faster running engine, volcanic dust would have blotted out the sun, the atmosphere would have been oppressively dense, and the surface would have been racked by daily earthquakes and volcanic explosions.[22]

These kind of highly choreographed geological processes—and there are lots of them—leave me shaking my head at the astounding ways in which our biosphere is precisely tuned for life. Even more interesting, though, is the "why" question behind them. What accounts for all of these astounding "coincidences?"

Press and Siever, while marveling that Earth "is a very special place," don't broach the possibility of design.[23] Ward and Brownlee skirt the issue in *Rare Earth*, preferring instead to occasionally pepper in words like "sheer luck" and "a rare chance happening."[24] At a conference, Ward remarked: "We are just incredibly lucky. Somebody had to win the big lottery, and we were it."

But does luck really explain why Earth enjoys this incredible convergence of extremely unlikely circumstances that have allowed human beings to flourish? Going far back into time, Christians have reached a far different conclusion: Earth was created by God as the stage upon which the human drama would be played out. What's amazing about modern science, including new discoveries just within the last few years, is that this view of the universe seems to be far better supported today than in ancient times.

Consider the conclusion of Michael J. Denton, a senior research fellow in human molecular genetics at the University of Otago in New Zealand, in his 1998 book *Nature's Destiny*:

> No other theory or concept ever imagined by man can equal in boldness and audacity this great claim . . . that all the starry heavens, that every species of life, that every characteristic of reality exists [to create a livable habitat] for mankind. . . . But most remarkably, given its audacity, it is a claim which is very far from a discredited prescientific myth. In fact, no observation has ever laid the presumption to rest. And today, four centuries after the scientific revolution, the doctrine is again reemerging. In these last decades of the twentieth century, its credibility is being enhanced by discoveries in several branches of fundamental science.[25]

How true are those words? Do the special conditions that allow for life on Earth demand a designer? To pursue reliable answers, I arranged a rendezvous at O'Hare International Airport in Chicago with two experts who had just collaborated on a ground-breaking book concerning this very topic. This would be a perfect opportunity to explore the stunning uniqueness of our planet.

INTERVIEW #5: GUILLERMO GONZALEZ, PHD, AND JAY WESLEY RICHARDS, PHD

Tall, blond Jay Wesley Richards, dressed in a navy blazer, is an Ivy League philosopher who speaks in rapid-fire bursts with unflagging enthusiasm. Guillermo Gonzalez, clad in a short-sleeve shirt, his thin-ning hair cropped short, is a nuts-and-bolts astronomer who talks in professorial tones on such topics as, "Chemical Abundance Trends among RV Tauri Stars."

Together, they authored *The Privileged Planet*, which documents astonishing evidence pointing toward a designer for Earth—and toward at least one apparent purpose for humankind.

Gonzalez is informally known as a "star guy." After graduating *summa cum laude* with degrees in astronomy and physics from the University of Arizona, he later earned his master's degree and doc-torate in astronomy from the University of Washington at Seattle. Now an assistant professor at Iowa State University, his research centers on low and intermediate mass stars and theories about stellar and planetary evolution.

He's a hands-on and yet conceptually sophisticated scientist, hav-ing logged countless hours doing research through telescopes at Cerro Tololo International Observatory, located at an altitude of 6,600 feet in Chile, and four other locations. He is adept at analyzing photo-metric and spectroscopic data. A member of the International Astro-nomical Union and the American Scientific Affiliation, the low-key but engaging Gonzalez has seen dozens of his articles published in technical journals and featured on the covers of such popular maga-zines as *Scientific American*.

An academic overachiever with a sincere, self-effacing personal-ity, Richards holds three advanced degrees in philosophy and theol-ogy, including a doctorate from Princeton Theological Seminary. He authored *The Untamed God* and has edited or contributed to such books as *Unapologetic Apologetics*, *Signs of Intelligence*, and *Are We Spiritual Machines?* His articles have appeared in publications rang-ing from *Perspectives on Science and Christian Faith* to the *Washing-ton Post* to the *Princeton Theological Review*. As vice president of the Discovery Institute, Richards is considered a bright star in the bur-geoning Intelligent Design movement.

Each of us clutching a soft drink, we met in an airlines hospital-ity suite, with Richards and Gonzalez sitting across from me at a gran-ite conference table under florescent lights in a simple room devoid of character. Anxious to proceed, I barely let them settle into their chairs before unleashing my first question.

THE COPERNICAN PRINCIPLE

I turned toward Richards. "I was taught in school that our planet is unexceptional, that we revolve around a typical star in an average, mundane part of the universe, and that there's nothing particularly unusual or special about Earth," I began. "Isn't that the view of most scientists today?"

"Yes, that's the so-called Principle of Mediocrity or the Copernican Principle," Richards replied. "Open any introductory astronomy textbook and you'll see it stated over and over that we should assume there's nothing special about our situation, our location in the universe, or the particular features of the Earth, the solar system, or humans themselves."

"But," I interjected, "isn't that appropriate in some sense?"

"Yes, of course," he said. "We shouldn't assume that the Earth, our solar system, or our sun is unique in every possible way. We wouldn't be able to do science if every place in the universe had a different law of gravity or atoms had a different mass. That's fine."

"Then where does the problem come in?" I asked.

"The problem is that the Copernican Principle has taken a metaphysically bloated form, which essentially says our metaphysical status is as insignificant as our astronomical location. In other words, we're not here for a purpose, we're not special in any way, and we don't occupy a privileged place in the cosmos."

I interrupted again. "Yet isn't it true that Copernicus's discovery—that the sun doesn't revolve around the Earth, but that the Earth revolves around the sun—quite naturally demoted humankind?"

Richards nodded wearily as if he had heard that comment a lot. "Let's go back to the beginning," he said. He stood, removed his jacket, and draped it over an unoccupied chair. Sitting back down, he continued.

"The story is that the ancients—Aristotle, Ptolemy, medieval Christians—all thought we were at the center of the universe, sort of the throne of the cosmos, the most important place that everything revolved around. Then Copernicus and Kepler came along and said they can explain the movement of the planets better by assuming that the sun is at the center and that the planets—including Earth—revolve around it. So we've been displaced from the center and removed from our position of privilege.

"This was the start of a long march of science that continued to demote us. Scientists later determined the sun isn't at the center of the universe; that we aren't at the center of the galaxy; and that the universe ultimately had no center, because scientists came to believe in the nineteenth century that it was infinite and eternal. You can see how this trend helped us to see ourselves as less and less significant, less and less at the center of things.

"So the Copernican Revolution came to represent the conflict between science and religion. Religious superstition maintained the Earth and humankind are the center of the universe, both physically and metaphysically, but modern science has disproved that.

"Humans have been stripped of their false sense of uniqueness and importance. While religious folk continued to insist there is something unique, special, intentional, and purposeful about our existence, scientists maintain that the material world is all there is, and that chance and impersonal natural law alone explain its existence."

I was following along in full agreement. Richards's assessment was entirely consistent with what I had been taught in school. But then he added the clincher.

"The problem," he said, a slight smile playing at the corner of his mouth, "is that this historical description is simply false."

SETTING THE RECORD STRAIGHT

Richards's claim startled me. "False?" I declared. "What do you mean? In what way?"

"Read Ptolemy, Galileo, Copernicus, Kepler. Read Dante," he said. "In Dante's *Divine Comedy*, the surface of the Earth is an intermediate place. This was true in Aristotelian cosmology, which was Christianized in the Middle Ages. For Aristotle, the world was made of air, earth, fire, and water. Earth is heaviest, so it naturally falls to the bottom.

"So the Earth was not so much at the *center* as it was at the *bottom* of the universe. It was sort of the cosmic sump. It was the place where things decay and die. Everything above the moon was made of a different type of matter—quintessence—and God dwelled in the heavenly sphere outside the celestial sphere of the stars. Man was in an intermediate place."

Gonzalez spoke up. "Dante then inverted these levels as you go the other way, down to hell," he said.

"Exactly," continued Richards. "You had nine levels going up toward God and getting closer to perfection, and then there were nine levels getting closer to absolute depravity, down to hell. Thus, in medieval cosmology, what we would call the center of the universe is Satan's throne. That's a very important point. If you imagine the center of the universe is Satan's throne and that the Earth itself is the cosmic sump, then clearly this is not the stereotype that we've been given that the center of the universe prior to Copernicus was the preeminent spot."

Gonzalez added: "The Enlightenment later retold the story by saying the church, because of its arrogance, put humans in the center."

Richards nodded. "That's the irony," he said. "It was the Enlightenment that made man the measure of all things. When you really think about it, Christian theology never actually put man literally in the center. We have a very important role to play in this cosmic drama, so much so that God even becomes incarnate. But it was never the case that everything was literally created solely for us.

"Many centuries ago, Augustine said God didn't create the world 'for man' or because of some sort of compulsion, but 'because he wanted to.'[26] In *The Divine Comedy*, the reader learns that the actual sense of us being in the center was merely a bias. We discover, in fact, that everything was arranged so that God is at the metaphysical center—that is, the place of supreme importance.

"Instead of denigrating Earth, actually Copernicus, Galileo, and Kepler saw their new scheme as exalting it. For instance, Galileo waxes poetic about how the Earth, like the other planets, reflects the glory of the sun and is no longer just a cosmic sump.[27] So in the transformation from medieval cosmology to the Renaissance view, this new perspective elevated man in some ways."

Other historical researchers have come to the same conclusion. Said one: "The Copernican system, far from demoting man, destroyed Aristotle's vision of the earth as a kind of cosmic sink, and if it did anything, it elevated humanity. In making the earth a planet, a heavenly body, Copernicus infinitely *ennobled* its status."[28]

But something didn't add up to me. "Didn't the church persecute Copernicus, Galileo, and Giordano Bruno for their view that the Earth revolved around the sun?" I asked.

"First of all," Richards said, "some claim Copernicus was persecuted, but history shows he wasn't; in fact, he died of natural causes the same year his ideas were published. As for Galileo, his case can't be reduced to a simple conflict between scientific truth and religious superstition. He insisted the church immediately endorse his views rather than allow them to gradually gain acceptance, he mocked the Pope, and so forth. Yes, he was censured, but the church kept giving him his pension for the rest of his life."

Indeed, historian William R. Shea said, "Galileo's condemnation was the result of the complex interplay of untoward political circumstances, political ambitions, and wounded prides."[29] Historical researcher Philip J. Sampson noted that Galileo himself was convinced that the "major cause" of his troubles was that he had made "fun of his Holiness"—that is, Pope Urban VIII—in a 1632 treatise.[30] As for his punishment, Alfred North Whitehead put it this way: "Galileo suffered an honorable detention and a mild reproof, before dying peacefully in his bed."[31]

"Bruno's case was very sad," Richards continued. "He was executed in Rome in 1600. Certainly this is a stain on church history. But again, this was a complicated case. His Copernican views were incidental. He defended pantheism and was actually executed for his heretical views on the Trinity, the Incarnation, and other doctrines that had nothing to do with Copernicanism.

"Now, here's the point I want to make: it's very important if you're going to advance the Copernican Principle that you make it look like it's grounded in the historical march of science. But when you actually look at the data, it's just not true. Writers of astronomy textbooks just keep recycling the myth, sort of like the flat-Earth myth, which was the idea that Columbus was told the Earth was flat and he thought it was round. That's just wrong too."

"Scholars at the time knew it was a sphere," added Gonzalez. "Even the ancient Greeks knew it was a sphere."

"They'd known it for a thousand years or more," said Richards.

I knew they were right about that. David Lindberg, former professor of the history of science and currently director of the Institute for Research in the Humanities at the University of Wisconsin, said in a recent interview:

One obvious [myth] is that before Columbus, Europeans believed nearly unanimously in a flat Earth—a belief allegedly drawn from certain biblical statements and enforced by the medieval church. This myth seems to have had an eighteenth century origin, elaborated and popularized by Washington Irving, who flagrantly fabricated evidence for it in his four-volume history of Columbus. . . . The truth is that it's almost impossible to find an educated person after Aristotle who doubts that the Earth is a sphere. In the Middle Ages, you couldn't emerge from any kind of education, cathedral school or university, without being perfectly clear about the Earth's sphericity and even its approximate circumference.[32]

Now in addition to the flat-Earth myth being exploded, here were Richards and Gonzalez asserting that the Copernican Principle was based on faulty history as well.

"So," continued Richards, "Guillermo and I embarked on a project to document whether there are important ways in which Earth is special or exceptional. To do this we had to show that there's not this long historical march of science showing how unimportant we are. We had to point out that the history is wrong and that what we're doing stands in the good tradition of science, which says, 'Let's find out what the world is like to the best of our ability.'"

"And," I said, "what did you find?"

Richards and Gonzalez exchanged glances. "Well, scientists have generally followed the Copernican Principle by saying that our planet is ordinary and that therefore life undoubtedly abounds in the universe," Richards began. "We believe, however, the evidence is quite to the contrary." He gestured toward his colleague to continue.

"We've found that our location in the universe, in our galaxy, in our solar system, as well as such things as the size and rotation of the Earth, the mass of the moon and sun and so forth—a whole range of factors—conspire together in an amazing way to make Earth a habitable planet," Gonzalez said. "And even beyond that, we've found that the very same conditions that allow for intelligent life on Earth also make it strangely well-suited for viewing and analyzing the universe."

"And we suspect this is not an accident," Richards added. "In fact, we raise the question of whether the universe has been literally designed for discovery."

THE INGREDIENTS FOR LIFE

With that framework set, I moved ahead to discuss one of the main attitudes of scientists who embrace the Copernican Principle. "They believe if you can just find a place anywhere in the universe where water stays liquid for a long enough period of time, then life will develop, just as it did on Earth," I said. "I assume you don't agree with that."

"No, I don't," Gonzalez said. "It's true that in order to have life you need water—which is the universal solvent—for reactions to take place, as well as carbon, which serves as the core atom of the information-carrying structural molecules of life. But you also need a lot more. Humans require twenty-six essential elements; a bacterium about sixteen. Intermediate life forms are between those two numbers. The problem is that not just any planetary body will be the source of all those chemical ingredients in the necessary forms and amounts."

I interrupted to point out that science fiction writers have managed to speculate about extra-terrestrial life that's built in a radically different form—for instance, creatures based on silicon instead of carbon.

Gonzalez was shaking his head before I had even finished my question. "That just won't work," he insisted. "Chemistry is one of the better understood areas of science. We know that you just can't get certain atoms to stick together in sufficient number and complexity to give you large molecules like carbon can. You can't get around it. And you just can't get other types of liquids to dissolve as many different kinds of chemicals as you can with water. There's something like half a dozen different properties of both water and carbon that are optimal for life. Nothing else comes close. Silicon falls far short of carbon.

"Unfortunately, people see life as being easy to create. They think it's enough merely to have liquid water, because they see life as an epiphenomenon—just a piece of slime mold growing on an inert piece of granite. Actually, the Earth's geology and biology interact very tightly with each other. You can't think of life as being independent of the geophysical and meteorological processes of the planet. They interact in a very intimate way. So you need not only the right chemicals for life but also a planetary environment that's tuned to life."

That sparked a related issue. Scientists have dreamed of terra-forming a planet like Mars, essentially making over its environment to create a planet that's more conducive to settlement by humans. "Would that be very difficult?" I asked.

"Absolutely. From the magnetic field to plate tectonics to the carbon dioxide cycle—ongoing life depends on a variety of very complicated interactions with the planet," he said.

Richards jumped in. "People generally think that because they plant a seed and it grows that it's easy to create the right environment for life, but that's misleading," he said. "A good example is the hermetically sealed biosphere that some people constructed in Arizona several years ago. They thought it would be relatively easy to create a self-contained environment conducive to life, but they had a devil of a time trying to make it work."

"But life can also exist in some terribly harsh conditions," I pointed out. "For instance, there are life forms that live off of deep-sea thermal vents. They don't seem to need oxygen or any particular support from the broader environment."

"On the contrary," Gonzalez said, "the only things down there that don't need oxygen are some microorganisms that breathe methane. But larger organisms, which need to regulate their metabolism, are invariably oxygen-breathers. The oxygen comes from surface life and marine algae. The oxygen gets mixed in with the ocean and transported into deep waters. So those organisms are very directly tied to the surface and the overall ecosystem of the planet."

Astounded by the Earth's fine-tuned physical, chemical, and biological interrelationships, some writers have gone so far as to liken our biosphere to a "superorganism" that is quite literally alive. In fact, James Lovelock's pantheistic Gaia Hypothesis even seeks to deify our planet. However, Gonzalez and Richards said it's unnecessary to go that far.

"Despite these admittedly incredible interrelationships, there's nothing that requires anyone to see the Earth itself as being an organism, especially a god or goddess," Richards said.

Then he turned to an image quite familiar to those who see the earmarks of design in Earth's complex and interconnected machinery. "That's sort of like deifying a watch because of its amazing properties," he said, "rather than looking beyond the watch to the one who made it."

THE HOSTILE WORLD OF M13

I granted the point that only certain kinds of planetary environments can play host to life. On the other hand, the universe is salted with trillions of stars, with countless terrestrial bodies undoubtedly revolving around them. Surely the mathematical odds favor many stars spawning Earth-like habitats—a point that argues against the idea that Earth is special and therefore designed.

But while my untrained eyes see each star as having equal potential to preside over a civilization-bearing solar system, I was soon to learn differently as I pursued questions concerning the conditions that are necessary for life to flourish.

I turned toward Gonzalez. "As we look out at the billions of stars that constitute our Milky Way galaxy," I said, "can't we logically assume that planets teeming with life are strewn all over the place?"

"No," he said unequivocally, "that's not a logical assumption based on the evidence. Along with Don Brownlee and Peter Ward of the University of Washington, I developed a concept called the Galactic Habitable Zone—that is, a zone in the galaxy where habitable planets might be possible. You see, you just can't form a habitable planet anywhere; there's a large number of threats to life as you go from place to place."

My mind flashed back to when Drake and Sagan beamed their message to the large concentration of stars called globular cluster M13. Their theory was that by transmitting their greeting toward a place packed with stars, there would be a higher chance of detection by an intelligent civilization. When I asked Gonzalez what he thought of that experiment, his reply was immediately dismissive.

"The problem is that if the probability of life at any one star is zero, then the probability for all the stars remains zero," he said.

"Zero?" I replied. "There are more than a quarter million stars in that globular cluster. Don't you think *any* of them harbor planets with life?"

Gonzalez stood his ground. "A globular cluster is one of the worst places in the entire galaxy to expect any life," he replied.

"Why?"

"Two reasons," he said. "First, globular clusters are among the most ancient things in our galaxy. Since they're extremely old, their stars have a very low abundance of heavy elements—carbon, nitrogen, oxygen, phosphorous, calcium, and so on. Instead, they're made up almost entirely of hydrogen and helium. In contrast, Earth is composed of iron, oxygen, magnesium, and silicone. Next comes sulfur.

"You see, the Big Bang produced basically hydrogen and helium. That's what the earliest stars were made of. The heavier elements were synthesized—cooked, if you will—in the interior of stars. Eventually, when these stars exploded as supernovae, these elements got expelled into the interstellar medium. They coalesced into other stars, where more heavy elements were cooked. Then they were expelled again and again, with stars subsequently containing ever-greater amounts of these 'metals,' or heavier elements.

"Now, you need these elements to eventually build terrestrial planets like Earth. Because the very old stars in globular clusters formed so early that they're composed virtually exclusively of hydrogen and helium, they're not going to have planets accompanying them. Maybe there will be dust, or grains, or boulders, but that's about it. You're not going to have Earth-size planets.

"The second problem is that globular clusters are so densely packed with stars that they wouldn't allow for stable, circular orbits to exist around them. The gravitational pull of the stars would create elliptical orbits that would take a hypothetical planet into extremes of cold and heat, which would create a life-prohibitive situation."

His assessment made sense, but it caused me to wonder why Sagan and Drake, both knowledgeable astronomers, would waste their time trying to communicate with the stars of M13. Gonzalez shook his head when I asked him about it.

"It's really surprising that they would think there would be any chance of a civilization receiving their message in a globular cluster," Gonzalez said. "They should have known better! Frankly, I think they were so deluded by their complete belief in the metaphysical Copernican Principle—that life was just going to be everywhere in the galaxy—that they overlooked the facts."

LIVING IN THE SAFE ZONE

Gonzalez's explanation made me wonder about the suitability of other places to harbor intelligent life. I knew that there are three basic types of galaxies in our universe. First, there are *spiral galaxies* like our own Milky Way. These are dominated by a central spherical bulge and a disk with "spiral arms" extending outward from the nucleus in a spiral pattern, resembling a celestial pinwheel. Second, there are *elliptical galaxies*, which are sort of egg-shaped. And, third, there are *irregular galaxies*, which appear disorganized and distorted. I asked Gonzalez to assess the life-bearing potential of each one.

"Certainly, our type of galaxy optimizes habitability, because it provides safe zones," he said, his tone professorial. "And Earth happens to be located in a safe area, which is why life has been able to flourish here.

"You see, galaxies have varying degrees of star formation, where interstellar gases coalesce to form stars, star clusters, and massive stars that blow up as supernovae. Places with active star formation are very dangerous, because that's where you have supernovae exploding at a fairly high rate. In our galaxy, those dangerous places are primarily in the spiral arms, where there are also hazardous giant molecular clouds. Fortunately, though, we happen to be situated safely between the Sagittarius and Perseus spiral arms.

"Also, we're very far from the nucleus of the galaxy, which is also a dangerous place. We now know that there's a massive black hole at the center of our galaxy. In fact, the Hubble space telescope has found that nearly every large nearby galaxy has a giant black hole at its nucleus. And believe me—these are dangerous things!

"Most black holes, at any given time, are inactive. But whenever anything gets near or falls into one, it gets torn up by the strong tidal forces. Lots of high energy is released—gamma rays, X-rays, particle radiation—and anything in the inner region of the galaxy would be subjected to high radiation levels. That's very dangerous for life forms. The center of the galaxy is also dangerous because there are more supernovae exploding in that region.

"One more thing: the composition of a spiral galaxy changes as you go out from the center. The abundance of heavy elements is greater towards the center, because that's where star formation has been more vigorous over the history of the galaxy. So it has been able to cook the hydrogen and helium into heavy elements more quickly, whereas in the outer disk of the galaxy, star formation has been going on more slowly over the years and so the abundance of heavy elements isn't quite as high. Consequently, the outer regions of the disk are less likely to have Earth-type planets.

"Now, put all of this together—the inner region of the galaxy is much more dangerous from radiation and other threats; the outer part of the galaxy isn't going to be able to form Earth-like planets because the heavy elements are not abundant enough; and I haven't even mentioned how the thin disk of our galaxy helps our sun stay in its desirable circular orbit. A very eccentric orbit could cause it to cross spiral arms and visit the dangerous inner regions of the galaxy, but being circular it remains in the safe zone.

"All of this," he said, his voice sounding a bit triumphant, "works together to create a narrow safe zone where life-sustaining planets are possible."

SCANNING THE STARS FOR LIFE

Suddenly, the Earth was sounding pretty special, nestled as it is in a sliver of space that gives it safe haven from the otherwise menacing conditions of the Milky Way. But what about other types of galaxies? Might they also provide threat-free neighborhoods for life-populated planets?

"What about elliptical galaxies?" I asked Gonzalez. "Do they have the potential to harbor life?"

"Elliptical galaxies look amorphous and are sort of egg-shaped, with stars having very random orbits, like bees swarming a beehive," he explained. "The problem for life in these galaxies is that the stars visit every region, which means they'll occasionally visit the dangerous, dense inner regions, where a black hole may be active. In any event, you're less likely to find Earth-like planets in elliptical galaxies because most of them lack the heavy elements needed to form them."

This was an important point, because I knew that most galaxies fall into the elliptical category.

"Most elliptical galaxies are less massive and luminous than our galaxy," Gonzalez continued. "Our galaxy is on the top one or two percent of the most massive and luminous. The bigger the galaxy, the more heavy elements it can have, because its stronger gravity can attract more hydrogen and helium and cycle them to build heavy elements. In the low-mass galaxies, which make up the vast majority, you can have whole galaxies without a single Earth-like planet. They just don't have enough of the heavy elements to construct Earths. Just like a globular cluster—you can have a whole globular cluster with hundreds of thousands of stars, and yet there won't be a single Earth.

"If you look at the deepest pictures ever taken by the Hubble Space Telescope, they show literally thousands of galaxies when the universe was really young. People have commented, 'Wow, look at all those galaxies! I wonder how many civilizations there are looking back at us?' In that picture, I'd say zero. Thousands and thousands and thousands of galaxies—but zero Earths, because the heavier elements haven't built up enough yet."

Richards interrupted to say, "Of course, we're not looking at these galaxies as they exist now; we're looking back in time, say, nine billion years ago. It's possible that some of those galaxies are now at the state where the Milky Way is. We don't know for sure."

"But," added Gonzalez, "this was back when it was much more dangerous, because it's the era of quasars, supernovae going off, and black holes. Even if you had a few regions in the galaxy where there were sufficient heavy elements to build Earths, they would have been so irradiated that life wouldn't be possible."

With elliptical galaxies being unlikely sites for budding civilizations, I turned to the last category of galaxy, called irregulars. "What's their potential for life?" I asked.

"Like the ellipticals, they also don't provide a safe harbor. In fact, they're worse. They're distorted and ripped apart, with supernovae going off throughout their volume. There are no safe places where there are fewer supernovae exploding, like we have between our spiral arms.

"In fact, astronomers keep finding new threats to life. For example, we're learning more about gamma ray bursts, which are more powerful than a supernova. If one of these goes off near you, the lights go out. So the probability for there being civilizations elsewhere actually keeps declining as we learn about the new threats that we didn't know about before."

"What's your opinion, then, about where Earth is located in the universe?" I asked.

"In terms of habitability, I think we are in the best possible place," Gonzalez said. "That's because our location provides enough building blocks to yield an Earth, while providing a low level of threats to life. I really can't come up with an example of another place in the galaxy that is as friendly to life as our location. Sometimes people claim you can be in any part of any galaxy. Well, I've studied other regions—spiral arms, galactic centers, globular clusters, edge of disks—and no matter where it is, it's worse for life. I can't think of any better place than where we are."

"That's ironic," I said. "It's the reverse of the Copernican Principle."

Richards agreed. "The propaganda of the Copernican Principle has been that the long march of science has shown how common and ordinary our situation is. But the trend is in the opposite direction. The more you pile on the threats we're discovering in most places in the universe, and you contrast that with the many ways we're in a cocoon of safety, the more our situation appears special."

"The most famous example is our own solar system," Gonzalez said. "At one time or another, scientists have speculated that there are civilizations on just about every body in our solar system—the moon, Mars, Jupiter.

"Percival Lowell built his own observatory in Arizona to find these civilizations on Mars. He actually quoted Copernicus to justify his belief that we can't be the only civilization. Now they've backtracked to the point of saying, well, maybe there's some very simple slime mold beneath the surface of Mars or Europa. And even that is extremely questionable. That's how far back they've had to retreat."

"Very often," observed Richards, "the Copernican Principle describes properties that don't matter. Who really cares whether we're in the physical center of the galaxy? It's irrelevant! What really matters is being in the place that's most conducive to life. And that's exactly where Earth finds itself."

PLANETS CIRCLING OTHER STARS

Within the last few years, astronomers finally have been able to discover planets orbiting other stars—a major confirmation of what was once merely widespread speculation. "Doesn't this confirm that there's nothing particularly out of the ordinary about our nine-planet system?" I asked.

"I'll concede," said Gonzalez, "that it demonstrates our solar system is not unique when it comes to having planets circling a star. But prior to the detection of the first planet orbiting another sun-like star in 1995, the expectation was that astronomers would find giant gas planets in large circular orbits, much like Jupiter. Jupiter orbits the sun in twelve years in a nearly circular orbit, far out from the terrestrial planets—Mercury, Venus, Earth, and Mars.

"However, we're finding that the planets circling other stars are quite different from Jupiter. They orbit over a full range of distances, from just a tiny fraction of an Astronomical Unit—which is the distance between the Earth and the sun—out to several Astronomical

Units. Most of their orbits are highly elliptical; very few are circular. These strongly non-circular orbits utterly surprised astronomers. Because they strongly subscribed to the Copernican Principle, they had expected that other planetary systems would be just like ours. And that expectation was basically dashed."

"What's wrong with an elliptical orbit for those kind of planets?" I asked.

"It poses a problem for the habitability of any terrestrial planets in their system, because it would make them less likely to have stable circular orbits," Gonzalez replied. "For example, Earth's orbit is almost a perfect circle. A planet with the mass of the Earth would be sensitive to any of the gas giant planets if they had more eccentric orbits. The Earthlike planet's own orbit would be affected, making it less circular and therefore subjecting the planet to dangerous surface temperature variations."

"So," I said, "if our own Jupiter had a more elliptical orbit, the Earth wouldn't be able to maintain as circular an orbit and have the steady temperature and predictable climate that come with that."

"That's right," he said. "In fact, even small variations in our nearly circular orbit can cause ice ages, because of temperature shifts on the surface of the planet. We have to maintain a circular orbit as much as possible to maintain a relatively steady temperature. That's only possible because Jupiter's orbit isn't very elliptical and therefore doesn't threaten to distort our round orbit."

TAKING HITS FOR EARTH

Now that we were discussing our solar system, I wanted to delve into other "local" factors that make our planet habitable. "What is it about our solar system that contributes to life on Earth?" I asked.

"A surprising amount," said Gonzalez. "More and more, astronomers are learning how the other planets tie into the habitability of Earth. For example, George Wetherill of the Carnegie Institution showed in 1994 that Jupiter—which is huge, more than three hundred times the mass of the Earth—acts as a shield to protect us from too many comet impacts. It actually deflects comets and keeps many of them from coming into the inner solar system, where they could collide with Earth with life-extinguishing consequences.

"This was illustrated very nicely by the impact of Comet Shoemaker-Levy 9 into Jupiter in July, 1994. This comet was attracted by Jupiter's tremendous gravitational pull and broke into fragments, with all of them hitting Jupiter. Even Saturn and Uranus participate in that kind of comet-catching.

"In addition, the other planets in our inner solar system protect us from getting bombarded by asteroids from the asteroid belt. The asteroids are mostly between the orbits of Mars and Jupiter. Our first line of defense is Mars, being at the edge of the asteroid belt. It takes a lot of hits for us. Venus does too. If you want to get an idea of the stuff that probably would have hit the Earth, look at the surface of the moon. The moon, unfortunately, has too little surface area to provide much protection, but it's a nice record."

"What about the Earth's position in the solar system?" I asked. "How much does that contribute to its habitability?"

"There's a concept invented by astrobiologists called the Circumstellar Habitable Zone. That's the region around a star where you can have liquid water on the surface of a terrestrial planet. This is determined by the amount of light you get from the host star.

"You can't be too close, otherwise too much water evaporates into the atmosphere and it causes a runaway greenhouse effect, and you boil off the oceans. We think that might be what happened to Venus. But if you get too far out, it gets too cold. Water and carbon dioxide freeze and you eventually develop runaway glaciation.

"The main point is that as you go further out from the sun, you have to increase the carbon dioxide content of the planet's atmosphere. This is necessary in order to trap the sun's radiation and keep water liquid. The problem is that there wouldn't be enough oxygen to have mammal-like organisms. It's only in the very inner edge of the Circumstellar Habitable Zone where you can have low enough carbon dioxide and high enough oxygen to sustain complex animal life. And that's where we are."

"So if the Earth's distance from the sun were moved by, say, five percent either way, what would happen?" I asked.

"Disaster," came his quick reply. "Animal life would be impossible. The zone for animal life in the solar system is much narrower than most people think."

"And that's why you need a circular orbit like the one Earth has," Richards added. "You don't just want to be in the Circumstellar Habitable Zone part of the time; you want to be in it continuously. It doesn't do you any good to have melted water for four months and then have the whole planet freeze up again."

OUR OVERACHIEVING SUN

Obviously, the key to continued life on Earth is the sun, whose nuclear fusion, taking place at twenty-seven million degrees Fahrenheit at its core, provides us with consistent warmth and energy ninety-three million miles away. Ever since witnessing a solar eclipse as a child, carefully protecting my eyes by observing the phenomenon through a projected image inside a cardboard box, I have been fascinated by this fiery behemoth, whose mass is an incomprehensible three hundred thousand times greater than the Earth's.

However, I had always been told that there was nothing out of the ordinary about the sun. As one text says flatly: "The sun is a common fixed star."[33] And if the sun is truly so average, so typical, so undistinguished, then the logical implication would be that lots of life-bearing Earths must be orbiting around lots of similar suns throughout the universe.

"Today, astronomers know a lot more about stars than they did when I was growing up," I said to Gonzalez. "Is the consensus still that the sun is just a common star?"

"No, not at all," Gonzalez replied. "It's just recently that some new astronomy textbooks are finally starting to say that, well, the sun really is unusual after all. For instance, it's among the ten percent most massive stars in the galaxy. In fact, if you pick a star at random, you're likely to pick one that's far less massive than the sun, usually red dwarfs, which make up about eighty percent of stars. Another eight or nine percent are called G dwarfs, most of which also are less massive than the sun. The sun is a yellow dwarf; technically, it has a G2 Spectral Type."

His comment about the ubiquity of red dwarfs piqued my curiosity. "Since red dwarfs dominate the universe, let's talk about them for a moment. Are they conducive to having life-bearing planets orbiting them?" I asked.

"I don't think they are," Gonzalez said.

"Why not?"

"Several reasons. First, red dwarfs emit most of their radiation in the red part of the spectrum, which makes photosynthesis less efficient. To work well, photosynthesis requires blue and red light. But a much greater problem is that as you decrease the mass of a star, you also decrease its luminosity. A planet would have to orbit this kind of star much closer in order to have sufficient heat to maintain liquid water on its surface.

"The problem is the tidal force between the star and the planet gets stronger as you move in, so the planet will spin down and eventually end up in what's called a tidally locked state. This means it always presents the same face towards the star. That's very bad, because it causes large temperature differences between the lit side and the unlit side. The lit side would be terribly dry and hot, while the unlit side would be prohibitively icy and cold. And there's another problem—red dwarfs have flares."

"But," I said, "the sun has flares too."

"That's right. And the intensity of flares on red dwarfs is about the same as on our sun. The difference is that red dwarfs as a whole emit much less total light, so they're much less luminous. That means in comparison to the luminosity of the star, the output of the flare is high."

"Whoa!" I said, putting up my hand in protest. "You've lost me."

Gonzalez regrouped. "Okay, let me get to the bottom line: for this kind of star, flares cause the star's total luminosity to vary. In fact, astronomers call them 'flare stars,' and they watch as they get much brighter for a while and then dimmer again. We don't pay too much attention to the solar flares of our sun, because the sun is so luminous that the flares are like a little blip. You barely notice them."

"And remember we're ninety-three million miles from the sun," Richards said. "With a red dwarf, your planet would have to be much closer to the star."

"Right," said Gonzalez. "The luminosity increase would cause temperature spikes on the surface of an orbiting planet. But just as bad would be the increased particle radiation that would result from the flares. On Earth, we get a very mild effect called the aurora borealis. This is where there's a flare on the sun, the particles eventually reach the Earth, they're funneled down the magnetic field to the north and south poles, and we see the aurora borealis as these beautiful lights in the northern hemisphere.

"However, particle radiation has the effect of quickly stripping away the atmosphere, increasing the surface radiation levels, but most importantly, destroying the ozone layer, which we need to protect from radiation. All of this would be deadly for any life on a planet near a red dwarf.

"And then red dwarfs have one more problem: they don't produce much ultraviolet light, which you need early on to build up oxygen in the atmosphere. Scientists believe that the oxygen in the Earth's atmosphere was built up at first by the ultraviolet radiation that broke up water into oxygen and hydrogen. The oxygen was allowed to build up in the atmosphere, while the hydrogen escaped into space, because it's lighter. But you get very little blue light from a red dwarf, so this phenomenon wouldn't occur as rapidly and you wouldn't get the build up of the oxygen you need to sustain life.

"Fortunately, our sun is not only the right mass, but it also emits the right colors—a balance of red and blue. As a matter of fact, if we were orbiting a more massive star, called an F dwarf, there would be much more blue radiation that would build up the oxygen and ozone layer even faster. But any momentary interruption of the ozone layer would subject the planet to an immediate flood of highly intense ultraviolet radiation, which would be disastrous to life.

"Also, the more massive stars don't live as long—that's the major problem. Stars that are even just a little more massive than the sun live only a few billion years. Our sun is expected to last a total of about ten billion years on its main sequence, burning hydrogen steadily, whereas stars just a few tens of percent more massive have considerably less lifetime on the main sequence. And while on the main sequence, they change luminosity much faster. Everything on their lifecycle happens faster."

"Anything else that makes our sun unusual?" I asked.

"Yes, the sun is metal-rich; in other words, it has a higher abundance of heavy elements compared to other stars of its age in this region of the galaxy. As it turns out, the sun's metallicity may be near the golden mean for building Earth-size habitable terrestrial planets.

"And the sun is highly stable, more so than most comparable stars. Its light output only varies by one-tenth of one percent over a full sunspot cycle, which is about eleven years. This prevents wild climate swings on Earth.

"Another way it's anomalous is that the sun's orbit is more nearly circular in the galaxy than most other stars of its age. That helps by keeping us away from the galaxy's dangerous spiral arms. If the sun's orbit were more eccentric, we could be exposed to the kind of galactic dangers I mentioned earlier, such as explosions of supernovae."

I realized after Gonzalez's comments that I would never look at the bejeweled night sky as I had in the past. I used to see stars as being fungible, which is a legal term meaning one is just as good as the other. But now I understood why the vast majority of stars would be automatically ruled out as being capable of supporting life-bearing planets.

It would take a star with the highly unusual properties of our sun—the right mass, the right light, the right composition, the right distance, the right orbit, the right galaxy, the right location—to nurture living organisms on a circling planet. That makes our sun, and our planet, rare indeed.

As much as I have been fascinated by the sun, I've also frequently stared in wonder at the other dominant celestial body in our sky—the moon. Curious to find out whether this barren, rocky satellite contributes anything to its host planet—other than inspiration for poets and other romantics—I proceeded to turn our discussion toward lunar issues.

OUR LIFE-SUPPORTING MOON

Centuries ago, the dark patches on the moon—low-lying areas that had been flooded with basaltic lava—were thought to be oceans that provided life-giving water to its unseen population. They were called *maria*, Latin for "seas."[34] The name has stuck; to this day, for example, we still refer to *Mare Tranquilitatis*, or the Sea of Tranquility.

Johannes Kepler, the seventeenth-century astronomer who fanned the flames of the Copernican Revolution, gazed at the moon and believed he discerned caves that were populated by moon people. He even wrote a book in which he fantasized about what their lives might be like.[35] A century later, William Herschel, who gained fame by discovering Uranus, thought he made out cities, highways, and pyramids on the lunar landscape."[36]

As scientific knowledge grew, dreams of finding lunar civilizations dissipated. Everyone came to agree that the moon cannot support life. Yet surprising discoveries in recent years have shown the opposite to be true: the moon really *does* support life—ours! Scientific evidence confirms how this parched, airless satellite actually contributes in unexpected ways to creating a lush and stable environment a quarter of a million miles away on Earth.

When I asked Gonzalez about how the moon helps support life on our planet, the first thing he brought up was a discovery that only dates back to 1993.

"There was a remarkable finding that the moon actually stabilizes the tilt of the Earth's axis," he said. "The tilt is responsible for our seasons. During the summer, in the northern hemisphere the north pole axis is pointed more toward the sun. Six months later, when the Earth is on the other side of the sun, then the south pole is more pointed toward the sun. With the Earth's tilt at 23.5 degrees, this gives us very mild seasons. So in a very real way, the stability of our climate is attributable to the moon."

"What would happen," I asked, "if the moon were not there?"

"Then our tilt could swing wildly over a large range, resulting in major temperature swings. If our tilt were more like ninety degrees, the north pole would be exposed to the sun for six months while the south pole would be in darkness, then vice-versa. Instead, it varies by only about one and a half degrees—just a tiny variation, because the gravity from the moon's orbit keeps it stabilized.

"The moon's large size compared to its host planet is unique in the inner solar system," he continued. "Mercury and Venus have no moons. Mars has two tiny moons—probably captured asteroids—and they don't do anything to stabilize the axis of Mars. Its axis is pretty close to Earth's right now, but that's only by coincidence. It actually varies over a huge range. In fact, all three of these planets have chaotic variations in their tilt.

"The moon also helps in another crucial way, which is to increase our tides. The moon contributes sixty percent to the tides; the sun accounts for the other forty percent. Tides serve an important role by flushing out nutrients from the continents to the oceans, which keeps them more nutrient-rich than they otherwise would be. Scientists discovered just a few years ago that the lunar tides also help to keep large-scale ocean circulation going. That's important because the oceans carry a lot of heat, which is necessary to keep the temperature of the higher latitudes relatively mild."

I asked, "What if the moon were larger than it is?"

"If it were more massive and in the same place, the tides would be much too strong, which would create serious difficulties. You see, the moon is slowing down the Earth's rotation. The tides pull on the Earth and slow it down a little bit, while at the same time the moon moves out in its orbit. We can actually measure this. Astronauts left mirrors on the moon and astronomers have been bouncing lasers off them since the early 1970s. They've documented that the moon is moving out in its orbit at 3.82 centimeters a year.

"If the moon were more massive, it would slow down the Earth much more. That would be a problem because if the days became too long, then you could have large temperature differences between day and night."

James Kasting, a professor of geosciences and meteorology at Pennsylvania State University, has confirmed that "Earth's climatic stability is dependent to a large extent on the existence of the moon." Without the moon, he said, the Earth's tilt could "vary chaotically from zero to eighty-five degrees on a time scale of tens of millions of years," with devastating results.

To me, it was amazing enough that the moon "just happens" to be the right size and in the right place to help create a habitable environment for Earth. Again, it was piling on more and more "coincidences" that were making it harder to believe mere chance could be responsible for our life-sustaining biosphere.

But then Kasting made one more intriguing observation that adds yet another mind-blowing improbability to already extraordinary circumstances. "The moon is now generally believed to have formed as a consequence of a glancing collision with a Mars-sized body during the later stages of the Earth's formation," he said. "If such moon-forming collisions are rare . . . habitable planets might be equally rare."[37]

THE DANGERS OF A WATER WORLD

Having explored the moon's contribution to the Earth's life-support system, I decided it was time to focus on our planet itself. I had studied enough geology to know that the Earth is more than just an undifferentiated spinning rock, but that its interior is a dynamic and complex system eight thousand miles in diameter, with a solid iron core surrounded by iron that has been rendered liquid by the heat. At its center, where the pressure is more than three million times greater than at the planet's surface, temperatures soar to nine thousand degrees Fahrenheit.

"What," I said to Gonzalez, "are some of the phenomena on Earth that contribute to its ability to sustain life?"

"First let's talk about the Earth's mass," Gonzalez said. "A terrestrial planet must have a minimum mass to retain an atmosphere. You need an atmosphere for the free exchange of the chemicals of life and to protect inhabitants from cosmic radiation. And you need an oxygen-rich atmosphere to support big-brained creatures like humans. Earth's atmosphere is twenty percent oxygen—just right, it turns out.

"And the planet has to be a minimum size to keep the heat from its interior from being lost too quickly. It's the heat from its radioactive decaying interior that drives the critically important mantle convection inside the Earth. If Earth were smaller, like Mars, it would cool down too quickly; in fact, Mars cooled down and basically is dead."

"What if the Earth were a little more massive than it is?" I asked.

"The bigger the planet, the higher the surface gravity, and the less surface relief between the ocean basins and the mountains," he said. "The rocks at the bases of mountains can only withstand so much weight before they fracture. The higher the surface gravity of a planet, the greater the pull of the gravity on the mountains, and the tendency would be toward creating a smooth sphere.

"Think what would happen if our planet were a smooth sphere. The Earth has a lot of water in its crust. The only reason we're not a water world right now is because we have continents and mountains to rise above it. If you were to smooth out all the land, water would be at a depth of two kilometers. You would have a water world—and a water world is a dead world."

That perplexed me. "If you need water for life," I said, "why doesn't more water mean more life?"

Gonzalez replied, "We have life on Earth because we have the energy-rich sunlit surface of the oceans, which is teeming with mineral nutrients. Tides and weathering wash the nutrients from the continents into the oceans, where they feed organisms. In a water world, many of the life-essential minerals would sink to the bottom. That's the basic problem. Besides, the salt concentration in a water world would be prohibitively high. Life can only tolerate a certain level of saltiness."

"Our oceans and seas are salty," I said. "How does Earth manage to regulate this?"

"We have large, marshy areas along some coasts. Because these are shallow, water comes in from the ocean and evaporates quickly, leaving salt behind. So you get huge salt deposits accumulating on the continents, and the salt content of the ocean doesn't get out of control. But in a water world, eventually the excess salt would saturate the water and settle to the bottom. This would create a super-saturated salt solution that would be inhospitable to life."

Even so, I said, some scientists have theorized that life might exist inside Jupiter's frozen moon Europa, where a theoretical ocean might be located. "It doesn't sound like you think life would be possible in an environment like that," I said.

"No, I don't think so," he replied. "I don't believe it would be habitable. There would be no way to regulate the salt, so I certainly don't imagine there are any dolphins swimming around in there."

Mountains and continents, then, are crucial for a life-flourishing planet. But where did they come from? I soon learned that they are partly the product of elaborate choreography involving radioactive elements and plate tectonics—absolutely essential ingredients for any planet to sustain a thriving biosphere.

THE ENGINE OF THE EARTH

Scientists over the last several decades have established the surprising centrality of plate tectonics, and the related continental drift, to the sustaining of life on Earth. Continental drift refers to the movement of a dozen or more massive plates in the Earth's lithosphere, which is the outer, rigid shell of the planet. One crucial byproduct of plate tectonics is the development of mountain ranges, which are generally created over long periods of time as the plates collide and buckle.

Scientists are finding that the importance of plate tectonics is difficult to overstate. "It may be," said Ward and Brownlee in *Rare Earth*, "that plate tectonics is the central requirement for life on a planet."[38] Interestingly, they added that "of all the planets and moons in our solar system, plate tectonics is found only on Earth."[39] In fact, any heavenly body would need oceans of water as a prerequisite to having plate tectonics, in order to lubricate and facilitate the movement of the plates.

When I asked Gonzalez why plate tectonics is so crucial, he launched into describing an improbable series of highly coordinated natural processes that left me amazed once more at how finely tuned our planet really is.

"Not only does plate tectonics help with the development of continents and mountains, which prevent a water world, but it also drives the Earth's carbon dioxide–rock cycle," he said. "This is critical in regulating the environment through the balancing of greenhouse gases and keeping the temperature of the planet at a livable level.

"You see, greenhouse gases, like carbon dioxide, absorb infrared energy and help warm the planet. So they're absolutely crucial. The problem is that their concentration in the atmosphere needs to be regulated as the sun slowly brightens. Otherwise, the Earth would not be able to stabilize its surface temperature, which would be disastrous.

"Plate tectonics cycles fragments of the Earth's crust—including limestone, which is made up of calcium, carbon dioxide, and oxygen atoms—down into the mantle. There, the planet's internal heat releases the carbon dioxide, which is then continually vented to the atmosphere through volcanoes. It's quite an elaborate process, but the end result is a kind of thermostat that keeps the greenhouse gases in balance and our surface temperature under control.

"What's driving plate tectonics is the internal heat generated by radioactive isotopes—Potassium-40, Uranium-235, Uranium-238, Thorium-232. These elements deep inside the Earth were originally produced in supernovae, and their production in the galaxy is declining with time because the supernova rate is declining with time. That will limit the production of Earth-like planets in the future, because they won't generate as much internal heat as the Earth does.

"This radioactive decay also helps drive the convection of the liquid iron surrounding the Earth's core, which results in an amazing phenomenon: the creation of a dynamo that actually generates the planet's magnetic field. The magnetic field is crucial to life on Earth, because it shields us from low-energy cosmic rays. If we didn't have a magnetic shield, there would be more dangerous radiation reaching the atmosphere. Also, solar wind particles would directly interact with the upper atmosphere, stripping it away, especially the molecules of hydrogen and oxygen from water. That would be bad news because water would be lost more quickly.

"Now, remember how I said that plate tectonics helps regulate global temperatures by balancing greenhouse gases? Well, there's also another natural thermostat, called the Earth's *albedo*. *Albedo* refers to the proportion of sunlight a planet reflects. The Earth has an especially rich variety of albedo sources—oceans, polar ice caps, continental interiors, including deserts—which is good for regulating the climate. Whatever light isn't reflected by Earth is absorbed, which means the surface gets heated.

"This is self-regulated through one of the Earth's natural feedback mechanisms. To give you an example, some marine algae produce dimethyl sulfide. This helps to build cloud condensation nuclei, or CCN, which are small particles in the atmosphere around which water can condense to form cloud droplets.

"If the ocean gets too warm, then this algae reproduce more quickly and release more dimethyl sulfide, which leads to a greater concentration of CCN and a higher albedo for the marine stratus clouds. Higher cloud albedo, in turn, cools the ocean below, which then reduces the rate at which the algae reproduce. So this provides a natural thermostat.[40]

"On the other hand, Mars lacks oceans, so it doesn't have this albedo component. It only has deserts, small polar caps, and very thin, occasional clouds. So Mars is far less capable of adjusting its albedo as its more eccentric orbit takes it closer and then further from the sun. That's one of the reasons why it experiences larger temperature swings than Earth."

Giant plates of shifting rock that precariously balance greenhouse gases; decaying radioactive isotopes acting as a life-sustaining underground furnace; an internal dynamo that generates a magnetic field which deflects cosmic dangers; precision feedback loops that unite biology and meteorology—I had to pause and marvel at the complex and interconnected processes that orchestrate our planet's environment.

And that was just the beginning. I knew Gonzalez could go on and on about scores of other fine-tuned phenomena. Among them are the elaborate physical processes that resulted in valuable ores being deposited near the planet's surface, enabling them to be efficiently mined for our technological development. Geologist George Brimhall of the University of California at Berkeley has observed:

> The creation of ores and their placement close to the Earth's surface are the result of much more than simple geologic chance. Only an exact series of physical and chemical events, occurring in the right environment and sequence and followed by certain climatic conditions, can give rise to a high concentration of these compounds so crucial to the development of civilization and technology.[41]

When I took this together with all of the various "serendipitous" circumstances involving our privileged location in the universe, I was left without a vocabulary to describe my sense of wonder. The suggestion that all of this was based on fortuitous chance had become absurd to me. The tell-tale signs of design are evident from the far reaches of the Milky Way down to the inner core of our planet.

And yet there was more—a whole new dimension of evidence that suggests this astounding world was created, in part, so we could have the adventure of exploring it.

THE POWER OF AN ECLIPSE

The story begins with an unabashed love for solar and lunar eclipses that helped drive a young Guillermo Gonzalez into a life-long study of stellar mysteries.

Mesmerized by the partial eclipses he had witnessed as an amateur astronomer, Gonzalez longed to see the zenith of them all: a total eclipse of the sun, where the moon just barely covers the sun's photosphere. He finally got his chance in 1995. Aware that an eclipse was going to occur on October 24 of that year, he scheduled his research so he could witness the event in northern India, one of the few places where it was going to be fully visible.

"One thing about eclipses," he told me, "is that a seasoned astronomer could be standing next to someone from a remote village, and they would both have tears in their eyes. They're both in awe. At my eclipse camp, as soon as the total phase of the eclipse ended, when you could see the sun's beautiful corona and it was relatively dark, people spontaneously applauded as if rewarding a show. It was just so beautiful!"

Gonzalez photographed the eclipse and made scientific measurements. But he wasn't done. His mind wouldn't let go of an insight: *eclipses are better viewed on Earth than they would be from any other planet in our solar system.*

"There's a striking convergence of rare properties that allow people on Earth to witness perfect solar eclipses," he said. "There's no law of physics that would necessitate this. In fact, of the nine planets with their more than sixty-three moons in our solar system, the Earth's surface is the best place where observers can witness a total solar eclipse, and that's only possible for the 'near-term' future.[42]

"What's really amazing is that total eclipses are possible because the sun is four hundred times larger than the moon, but it's also four hundred times further away. It's that incredible coincidence that creates a perfect match. Because of this configuration, and because the Earth is the innermost planet with a moon, observers on Earth can discern finer details in the sun's chromosphere and corona than from any other planet, which makes these eclipses scientifically rich.

"What intrigued me," he said, "was that the very time and place where perfect solar eclipses appear in our universe also corresponds to the one time and place where there are observers to see them."

That "coincidence" was so fascinating to me that I asked him to repeat his last statement before we continued. After he did, he added: "What's more, perfect solar eclipses have resulted in important scientific discoveries that would have been difficult if not impossible elsewhere, where eclipses don't happen."

"What discoveries?" I asked.

"I'll give you just three examples," he said. "First, perfect solar eclipses helped us learn about the nature of stars. Using spectroscopes, astronomers learned how the sun's color spectrum is produced, and that data helped them later interpret the spectra of distant stars.

"Second, a perfect solar eclipse in 1919 helped two teams of astronomers confirm the fact that gravity bends light, which was a prediction of Einstein's general theory of relativity. That test was only possible during a total solar eclipse, and it led to general acceptance of Einstein's theory.

"Third, perfect eclipses provided a historical record that has enabled astronomers to calculate the change in the Earth's rotation over the past several thousand years. This enabled us to put ancient calendars on our modern calendar system, which was very significant."

Richards, who had been listening intently, spoke up. "What's mysterious," he said, "is that the same conditions that give us a habitable planet also make our location so wonderful for scientific measurement and discovery. So we say there's a correlation between *habitability* and *measurability*.

"Not only does the specific configuration of the Earth, sun, and moon allow for perfect eclipses, but that same configuration is also vital to sustaining life on Earth. We've already discussed how the size and location of the moon stabilizes our tilt and increases our tides, and how the size of the sun and our distance from it also make life possible here.

"Our main point," he concluded, "is that there's no obvious reason to assume that the very same rare properties that allow for our existence would also provide the best overall setting to make discoveries about the world around us. In fact, we believe that the conditions for making scientific discoveries on Earth are so fine-tuned that you would need a great amount of faith to attribute them to mere chance."

HABITABILITY AND MEASURABILITY

Prompted by the study of perfect solar eclipses, Gonzalez and Richards began to investigate the incredible convergence of habitability and measurability in scores of other settings. They came up with a wide range of examples that merely served to amplify their amazement.

"For example," said Gonzalez, "not only do we inhabit a location in the Milky Way that's fortuitously optimal for life, but our location also happens to provide us with the best overall platform for making a diverse range of discoveries for astronomers and cosmologists. Our location away from the galaxy's center and in the flat plane of the disk provides us with a particularly privileged vantage point for observing both nearby and distant stars.

"We're also in an excellent position to detect the cosmic background radiation, which is critically important because it helped us realize our universe had a beginning in the Big Bang. The background radiation contains invaluable information about the properties of the universe when it was only about three hundred thousand years old. There's no other way of getting that data. And if we were elsewhere in the galaxy, our ability to detect it would have been greatly hindered."

Richards offered a few other illustrations. "The moon stabilizes the Earth's tilt, which gives us a livable climate—and it also consistently preserves the deep snow deposits in the polar regions. These deposits are a tremendously valuable data recorder for scientists," he said.

"By taking core samples from the ice, researchers can gather data going back hundreds of thousands of years. Ice cores can tell us about the history of snowfall, temperatures, winds near the polar regions, and the amount of volcanic dust, methane, and carbon dioxide in the atmosphere. They record the sunspot cycle through variations in the concentration of beryllium-10. They even record the temporary weakening of the Earth's magnetic field forty thousand years ago. In 1979, scientists identified a tentative link between nitrate spikes in an Antarctic ice core with nearby supernovae. By taking deeper cores, it might be possible to catalog all nearby supernovae of the last few hundred thousand years—something that would be otherwise impossible."

Another example of the strange correlation between habitability and measurability, Richards said, is the clarity of our atmosphere. "The metabolisms of higher organisms require from ten to twenty percent oxygen in the atmosphere—which is also the amount needed to facilitate fire, allowing for the development of technology," Richards said.[43] "But it just so happens that the very composition of our atmosphere also gives it transparency, which it wouldn't have if it were rich in carbon-containing atoms, like methane. And a transparent atmosphere allows the science of astronomy and cosmology to flourish."

"Wait a second," I said. "Doesn't the water vapor in our atmosphere cause cloudiness that can hinder astronomy? That's why putting a telescope in space has been such a breakthrough."

"Actually, astronomers prefer a partly cloudy atmosphere to one that's completely cloudy or always windy and dusty," Gonzalez said. "Besides, we're not saying that every condition of measurability is uniquely and individually optimized on Earth. Our argument depends on what's called an optimal negotiation of competing conditions.

"As Henry Petroski said in his book *Invention by Design*, 'All design involves conflicting objectives and hence compromise, and the best designs will always be those that come up with the best compromise.'[44] To come up with discoveries in a wide range of scientific disciplines, our environment must be a good compromise of competing factors—and we find that it is."

Another interesting connection between habitability and measurability involves plate tectonics. As Gonzalez and Richards explained earlier, plate tectonics is essential to having a livable planet. One byproduct of the movement of these crustal plates is earthquakes, which, in turn, have provided scientists with research data that would otherwise be difficult to obtain.

"Thousands of seismographs all over the planet have measured earthquakes through the years," Richards said. "In the past few decades, scientists have been able to use that data to produce a three-dimensional map of the structure of the Earth's interior."

Over and over again, he said, the extraordinary conditions that create a hospitable environment on Earth also happen to make our planet strangely well-suited for viewing, analyzing, and understanding the universe.

"Is that merely some sort of cosmic quirk?" Richards asked. "Are we just lucky? I think wisdom entails the ability to discern the difference between mere coincidence and a meaningful pattern. We have more than a coincidence here. Much more."

THE TRILEMMA OF LIFE

When trying to explain the existence of life, said Gonzalez and Richards, we face a trilemma. One possibility is that some natural necessity, like the laws of physics, inexorably leads to life. Advocates of SETI—the Search for Extra-Terrestrial Intelligence—like that possibility. However, more and more scientific discoveries are showing how incredibly improbable it is to marshal the right conditions for life. Many scientists are concluding that intelligent life is, at minimum, far rarer than was once thought. In fact, it may very well be unique to Earth.

The second possible explanation is chance: life is a fluke. Create enough planets circling enough stars and the odds say at least one of them will have life. Brownlee and Ward, who wrote *Rare Earth*, seem to gravitate toward this explanation.

But there's also a third possibility: life was created. After studying all of the extraordinarily rare circumstances that have contributed to life on Earth, and then overlaying the amazing way in which these conditions also open the door to scientific discoveries, Gonzalez and Richards have landed in this camp.

"To find that we have a universe where the very places where we find observers are also the very best overall places for observing—*that's* surprising," Richards said. "I see design not just in the rarity of life in the universe, but also in this very pattern of habitability and measurability."

I turned toward Gonzalez. "What's your conclusion?" I asked.

"My conclusion, frankly, is that the universe was designed for observers living in places where they can make scientific discoveries," he replied. "There may be other purposes to the universe, but at least we know that scientific discovery was one of them."

Ever the theologian, Richards jumped back in. "In the Christian tradition, this is quite at home," he said. "Christians have always believed that God testifies to his existence through the book of nature and the book of Scripture. In the nineteenth century, science effectively closed the book of nature. But now, new scientific discoveries are reopening it."

"But if the universe was designed with us in mind, why is it so incredibly vast?" I asked. "There's a lot of empty space out there. Isn't that wasteful and unnecessary?"

"Because the universe was designed for discovery, we need something to discover," Richards replied. "The universe is vast and we're small, but we have access to it. That's what is amazing. We can see background radiation that has come from more than ten billion light years away."

"Plus," added Gonzalez, "we needed supernovae to build up the heavy elements so life-bearing planets could develop. And one particular type of supernovae is incredibly useful as a 'standard candle.' Type 1a supernovae have 'calibratable liminosities' so we can use them to determine distances and to probe the expansion history of the universe. So, again, we see the connection between habitability and measurability."

Richards made one other interesting observation. "Darwin once complained that pollen couldn't have been designed. After all, he said, look at the waste! Millions upon millions of particles are produced, but very, very few are used in the development of flowers.

"However, what he didn't realize was that pollen is one of the most useful tools we have in the scientific exploration of the past, in part, because it can be dated through Carbon 14. When we find pollen in lake sediments and ice cores, we can use it to gauge how old the layered deposits are and what the ancient climate was like.

"Darwin only looked at pollen from a biological standpoint; when we look at the big picture, we see it has another use he never anticipated. Perhaps the same is true in many other instances throughout the universe."

A CHERISHED GROUP OF CREATURES

I pushed my chair back from the table as if I had just consumed a hearty meal. In a sense, I had. Gonzalez and Richards had served me a remarkable feast—fact upon fact, evidence upon evidence, discovery upon discovery that compelled an incredible conclusion. As I sat there and digested the data, my mind turned to the book *God and the Astronomers*, which I had been reading on the airplane just prior to our interview.

In one chapter, John A. O'Keefe describes how he went away to school at the age of fourteen and began to get into arguments with his roommate about God. These encounters turned him toward astronomy, a field where scientists were beginning to find new and exciting evidence about the possibility of a Creator.

After earning degrees from Harvard and the University of Chicago, O'Keefe went on to become a renowned astronomer and pioneer in space research. The late Eugene Shoemaker called him "the godfather of astrogeology." He was awarded many honors, including the Goddard Space Flight Center's highest award, and is credited with numerous breakthrough discoveries in his scientific research at NASA.[45]

It was the discoveries of astronomy that bolstered O'Keefe's faith in God. He once ran calculations estimating the likelihood of the right conditions for life existing elsewhere. He concluded that if his assumptions were correct, then based on the mathematical probabilities "only one planet in the universe is likely to bear intelligent life. We know of one—the Earth—but it is not certain that there are many others, and perhaps there are no others."[46]

O'Keefe said he would have no theological problem if, indeed, other civilizations existed. That's the position of many Christians.[47] God certainly could have created other life-populated planets that the Bible doesn't reveal. But it was the sheer improbability of the coincidences that conspired to create life on Earth that led O'Keefe to this conclusion:

> We are, by astronomical standards, a pampered, cossetted, cherished group of creatures; our Darwinian claim to have done it all ourselves is as ridiculous and as charming as a baby's brave efforts to stand on its own feet and refuse his mother's hand. If the universe had not been made with the most exacting precision we could never have come into existence. *It is my view that these circumstances indicate the universe was created for man to live in.*[48]

And for humankind to explore. The findings of Gonzalez and Richards that the cosmos was designed for discovery have added a compelling new dimension to the evidence for a Creator. And frankly, their analysis makes sense.

If God so precisely and carefully and lovingly and amazingly constructed a mind-boggling habitat for his creatures, then it would be natural for him to want them to explore it, to measure it, to investigate it, to appreciate it, to be inspired by it—and ultimately, and most importantly, to find him through it.

FOR FURTHER EVIDENCE
More Resources on This Topic

Denton, Michael. *Nature's Destiny*. New York: The Free Press, 1998.

Gonzalez, Guillermo and Jay Wesley Richards. *The Privileged Planet*. Washington, D.C.: Regnery, 2004.

Jastrow, Robert. *God and the Astronomers*. New York: W. W. Norton, second edition, 1992.

Sampson, Philip. *Six Modern Myths*. Downer's Grove, Ill.: InterVarsity, 2000.

Ward, Peter and Donald Brownlee. *Rare Earth*. New York: Copernicus, 2000.

THE EVIDENCE OF BIOCHEMISTRY: THE COMPLEXITY OF MOLECULAR MACHINES

We have always underestimated the cell.... The entire cell can be viewed as a factory that contains an elaborate network of interlocking assembly lines, each of which is composed of a set of large protein machines.... Why do we call [them] machines? Precisely because, like machines invented by humans to deal efficiently with the macroscopic world, these protein assemblies contain highly coordinated moving parts.

Bruce Alberts, President, National Academy of Sciences[1]

We should reject, as a matter of principle, the substitution of intelligent design for the dialogue of chance and necessity; but we must concede that there are presently no detailed Darwinian accounts of the evolution of any biochemical system, only a variety of wishful speculations.

Biochemist Franklin M. Harold[2]

Michael Behe was taught in parochial school that God had set up the universe, knew what was going to happen, and intended for life to come into existence, but from our perspective the entire process unfolded through Darwinian evolution. And that pretty much satisfied the young Behe.

Later as a student in biochemistry, when Behe would encounter enormously complicated biological systems, his response was to scratch his head and say, "Gee, I wonder how evolution created that? Well, *somebody* must know!" He always moved on, assuming someone did.

Then one day, while doing post-doctorate research on DNA at the National Institutes of Health, he and a colleague were pondering what it would take for life to begin by naturalistic processes. As they enumerated the components that would be needed—proteins, a genetic code, a membrane, and so on—they looked at each other and said, "Naaaaahhhhhh!" They knew there was no way life could have sprung into existence unaided. Seeds of skepticism were planted.

Subsequently, he read geneticist Michael Denton's groundbreaking book *Evolution: A Theory in Crisis*. For the first time, Behe was exposed to a well-reasoned scientific critique of Darwinism—and he was astounded. Until then, he only knew of "religious nuts" who doubted Darwin. Now, here was a thoughtful, agnostic scientist who was powerfully challenging whether Darwin's mechanism of natural selection could really explain how life started and developed through the ages.

Spurred on by Denton's book, Behe began scouring the scientific literature in search of the detailed Darwinian explanations he had always assumed were there. Time after time, he found scientists describing complex, interlocking biological systems and basically saying, "Isn't it wonderful how natural selection put this together?" The *how* was always missing.

That's when Behe realized that as a biochemist, he was perfectly situated to investigate whether the evidence points toward Darwinism or God as the source for living organisms. After all, life is essentially a molecular phenomenon. If Darwinian evolution is going to work, it has to succeed at the microscopic level of amino acids, proteins, and DNA. On the other hand, if there really was a designer of the world, then his fingerprints were going to be all over the cell.

And the cell is Behe's world—an incredible, intricate, Lilliputian world where a typical cell takes ten million million atoms to build. One scientist described a single-cell organism as a high-tech factory, complete with

> artificial languages and their decoding systems, memory banks for information storage and retrieval, elegant control systems regulating the automated assembly of parts and components, error fail-safe and proof-reading devices utilized for quality control, assembly processes involving the principle of prefabrication and modular construction . . . [and] a capacity not equaled in any of our own most advanced machines, for it would be capable of replicating its entire structure within a matter of a few hours.[3]

Shaking off his preconceptions as best he could, Behe began to scrutinize the molecular evidence with new eyes. Ultimately, he would summarize his stunning conclusions in what the *National Review* would call one of the most important non-fiction books of the twentieth century.

INTERVIEW #6: MICHAEL J. BEHE, PHD

Lehigh University's "Mountaintop Campus," a seventy-two-acre, eight-building research complex overlooking the hardscrabble city of Bethlehem, Pennsylvania, was littered with brown, brittle leaves when I arrived one autumn afternoon in my search for Michael Behe.

After parking in front of Iacocca Hall, a modern, tan-and-green glass building, I walked up to the second floor. I strolled down a long hallway with laboratories on both sides—the Complex Carbohydrate Research Lab, the Core Chromatography/Electrophoresis Lab, the Molecular Microbiology Research Lab, the Neuroendocrinology Lab, the Core DNA Lab, and the ominous-sounding Virology Lab, with an orange biohazard sign plastered on its door.

The hallway's wall featured scintillating reading—an oversized reproduction of a technical article by two Lehigh scientists, asking the provocative question: "How Does Testosterone Affect Hippocampal Plasticity in Black-Capped Chickadees?"

I knocked on the door of a nondescript office and was greeted cheerfully by Behe, dressed in blue jeans and a lumberjack shirt. He's enthusiastic, energetic, and engaging, with a quick smile and a crackling sense of humor. He always seems to be moving; even when perched on his swivel chair, he would roll back and forth ever so slightly. Wiry and balding, with wispy gray hair, a beard, and round glasses, he has a gentle and self-effacing manner that tends to put visitors at ease.

Behe credits his casual manner to being the father of eight (at the time, going on nine) children, who keep him from taking himself too seriously. He laughed when I asked if he had any hobbies. "Mostly, I drive kids places," he said.

Behe grew up on the other side of Pennsylvania. He received a degree in chemistry with honors from Drexel University and a doctorate in biochemistry at the University of Pennsylvania. After post-doctorate research at the University of Pennsylvania and the National Institutes of Health, he joined Lehigh's faculty in 1985. He also has served on the

Molecular Biochemistry Review Panel of the Division of Molecular and Cellular Biosciences at the National Science Foundation.

He has authored forty articles for such scientific journals as *DNA Sequence*, *The Journal of Molecular Biology*, *Nucleic Acids Research*, *Biopolymers*, *Proceedings of the National Academy of Sciences USA*, *Biophysics*, and *Biochemistry*. He has lectured at the Mayo Clinic and dozens of schools, including Yale, Carnegie-Mellon, the University of Aberdeen, Temple, Colgate, Notre Dame, and Princeton. He is a member of the American Society for Biochemistry and Molecular Biology, the Society for Molecular Biology and Evolution, and other professional organizations.

Behe has contributed to several books, including *Mere Creation*, *Signs of Intelligence*, and *Creation and Evolution*. He was catapulted into the national spotlight, however, by his enigmatically titled and award-winning best-seller, *Darwin's Black Box*. According to David Berlinski, author of *A Tour of the Calculus*, Behe's book "makes an overwhelming case against Darwin on the biochemical level" through an argument "of great originality, elegance, and intellectual power." Added Berlinski: "No one has done this before."[4]

In fact, it was this book that lured me to Lehigh. I knew that Behe's theories could provide strong support for the idea that a designer created the tiny but complex molecular machines that drive the cellular world—that is, *if* his arguments could withstand the objections of skeptical Darwinists.

PEERING INSIDE THE BLACK BOX

The "black box" in the title of Behe's book is a term scientists use when describing a system or machine that they find interesting but they don't know how it works. As an example, Behe gestured toward the Dell computer on his desk. "A computer is a black box for most people," he explained. "You type on the keyboard and you can do word processing or play electronic games, but most of us don't have the foggiest idea of how the computer actually works."

"And to Darwin, the cell was a black box," I commented.

"That's right," he replied. "In Darwin's day, scientists could see the cell under a microscope, but it looked like a little glob of Jello, with a dark spot as the nucleus. The cell could do interesting things— it could divide, it could move around—but they didn't know *how* it did anything."

"There must have been speculation," I said.

"Of course," Behe said. "Electricity was a big deal back then, and some believed that all you had to do was to zap some gelatinous material and it would come alive. Most scientists speculated that the deeper they delved into the cell, the more simplicity they would find. But the opposite happened.

"Now we've probed to the bottom of life, so to speak—we're at the level of molecules—and there's complexity all the way down. We've learned the cell is horrendously complicated, and that it's actually run by micromachines of the right shape, the right strength, and the right interactions. The existence of these machines challenges a test that Darwin himself provided."

"A test?" I asked.

"Darwin said in his *Origin of Species*, 'If it could be demonstrated that any complex organ existed which could not possibly have been formed by numerous, successive, slight modifications, my theory would absolutely break down.'[5] And that was the basis for my concept of irreducible complexity.

"You see, a system or device is irreducibly complex if it has a number of different components that all work together to accomplish the task of the system, and if you were to remove one of the components, the system would no longer function. An irreducibly complex system is highly unlikely to be built piece-by-piece through Darwinian processes, because the system has to be fully present in order for it to function. The illustration I like to use is a mousetrap."

I chuckled. "Do you have problems with mice at your house?"

"Actually, yes, we do," he said with a laugh. "But a mousetrap has turned out to be a great example."

He stood and walked over to a filing cabinet, removing a run-of-the-mill mousetrap and putting it down on the desk next to me. "You can see the interdependence of the parts for yourself," he said, pointing to each component as he described them.

"First, there's a flat wooden platform to which the other parts are attached. Second, there's a metal hammer, which does the job of crushing the mouse. Third, there's a spring with extended ends to press against the platform and the hammer when the trap is charged. Fourth, there's a catch that releases when a mouse applies a slight bit of pressure. And, fifth, there's a metal bar that connects to the catch and holds the hammer back when the trap is charged.

"Now, if you take away any of these parts—the spring or the holding bar or whatever—then it's not like the mousetrap becomes half as efficient as it used to be or it only catches half as many mice. Instead, it doesn't catch *any* mice. It's broken. It doesn't work at all."

He pointed down at the trap again. "And notice that you don't just need to have these five parts, but they also have to be matched to each other and have the right spatial relationship to each other. See—the parts are stapled in the right place. An intelligent agent does that for a mousetrap. But in the cell, who tells the parts where they should go? Who staples them together? Nobody—they have to do it on their own. You have to have the information resident in the system to tell the components to get together in the right orientation, otherwise it's useless."

Behe sat back down. "So the mousetrap does a good job of illustrating how irreducibly complex biological systems defy a Darwinian explanation," he continued. "Evolution can't produce an irreducibly complex biological machine suddenly, all at once, because it's much too complicated. The odds against that would be prohibitive. And you can't produce it directly by numerous, successive, slight modifications of a precursor system, because any precursor system would be missing a part and consequently couldn't function. There would be no reason for it to exist. And natural selection chooses systems that are already working."

I studied the mousetrap. "You said an irreducibly complex system can't be produced *directly* by numerous, successive, slight modifications," I said. "Does that mean there couldn't be an indirect route?"

Behe shook his head. "You can't absolutely rule out all theoretical possibilities of a gradual, circuitous route," he said. "But the more complex the interacting system, the far less likely an indirect route can account for it. And as we discover more and more of these irreducibly complex biological systems, we can be more and more confident that we've met Darwin's criterion of failure."

I asked, "Are there a lot of different kinds of biological machines at the cellular level?"

"Life is actually based on molecular machines," he replied. "They haul cargo from one place in the cell to another; they turn cellular switches on and off; they act as pulleys and cables; electrical machines let current flow through nerves; manufacturing machines build other machines; solar-powered machines capture the energy from light and store it in chemicals. Molecular machinery lets cells move, reproduce, and process food. In fact, every part of the cell's function is controlled by complex, highly calibrated machines."

Behe motioned toward the mousetrap. "And if the creation of a simple device like this requires intelligent design," he said, "then we have to ask, 'What about the finely tuned machines of the cellular world?' If evolution can't adequately explain them, then scientists should be free to consider other alternatives."

Before I began investigating that issue any further, though, I wanted to stay focused a while longer on Behe's whimsical use of the mousetrap to illustrate irreducible complexity. Ever since *Darwin's Black Box* was published, the lowly rodent-catcher has become something of a new icon in the debate over evolution versus design. As such, it has been pelted by opposition from Darwinists—and I needed to know if Behe could fend off the best challenges.

MESSING WITH THE MOUSETRAP

"Your mousetrap has generated quite a bit of controversy," I began. "For instance, John McDonald of the University of Delaware said mousetraps can work well with fewer parts than yours—and he even drew a picture of a trap that's simpler than the one you drew. Doesn't this undermine your point that your mousetrap is irreducibly complex?"

"No, not a bit," he said with a good-natured smile. "I *agree* there are mousetraps with fewer parts than mine. As a matter of fact, I said so in my book! I said you can just prop open a box with a stick, or you can use a glue trap, or you can dig a hole for the mouse to fall into, or you can do any number of things.

"The point of irreducible complexity is not that one can't make some other system that could work in a different way with fewer parts. The point is that the trap we're considering right now needs all of its parts to function. The challenge to Darwinian gradualism is to get to my trap by means of numerous, successive, slight modifications. You can't do it. Besides, you're using your intelligence as you try. Remember, the audacious claim of Darwinian evolution is that it can put together complex systems with no intelligence at all."

Behe's simple explanation seemed sufficient to defeat McDonald's critique.[6] But there was a stronger challenge to consider. I reached down into my briefcase and removed a copy of *Natural History* magazine.

"Kenneth Miller of Brown University has another objection to your trap," I said. Then I read him Miller's comments:

> Take away two parts (the catch and the metal bar), and you may not have a mousetrap but you do have a three-part machine that makes a fully functional tie clip or paper clip. Take away the spring, and you have a two-part key chain. The catch of some mousetraps could be used as a fishhook, and the wooden base as a paperweight; useful applications of other parts include everything from toothpicks to nutcrackers and clipboard holders. The point, which science has long understood, is that bits and pieces of supposedly irreducibly complex machines may have different—but still useful—functions.[7]

"That's a strong point," I said. "Maybe an irreducibly complex system could develop gradually over time, because each of its components could have another function that natural selection would preserve on the way toward developing a more complex machine."

"That's an interesting argument," he said.

I leaned forward. "Doesn't this dismantle your case?" I asked.

Behe didn't flinch. "The problem," he replied, "is that it's not an argument against anything I've ever said. In my book, I explicitly point out that some of the components of biochemical machines can have other functions. But the issue remains—can you use numerous, slight, successive modifications to get from those other functions to where we are?

"Some of this objection seems a bit silly. Could a component of a mousetrap function as a paperweight? Well, what do you need to be a paperweight? You need mass. You need to exist. An elephant, or my computer, or a stick can be a paperweight. But suppose you go buy a paperweight. What would it look like? Most of them are nondescript, roundish things. None of them look anything like a precursor to a mousetrap. Besides, look at what he's doing: he's starting from the finished product—the mousetrap—and disassembling it and moving a few things around to use them for other purposes. Again, that's intelligent design!

"The question for evolution is not whether you can take a mousetrap and use its parts for something else; it's whether you can start with something else and make it into a mousetrap. The problem for evolutionists is to start with a less complex system and build a more complex system. Even if every component could theoretically have a useful function prior to its assembly into the mousetrap, you'd still have the problem of how the mousetrap becomes assembled."

"Explain further," I said.

"When people put together a mousetrap, they have the disassembled components in different drawers or something, and they grab one from each drawer and put it together. But in the cell, there's nobody there to do that.

"In molecular machines, components have portions of their shape that are complementary to each other, so they connect with each other in the right way. A positive charge can attract a negative charge, and an oily region can attract another oily region. So if we use the mousetrap as an analogy, one end of the spring would have to have a certain shape or magnetism that just happened to attract and fit with another component of the trap. They'd all have to fit together that way until you had the whole trap assembled by itself.

"In other words, if you just had the components themselves without the ability to bring the other pieces into position, you'd be far from having a functioning mousetrap. Nobody ever addresses this problem in the evolutionary literature. If you do any calculations about how likely this could occur by itself, you find it's very improbable. Even with small machines, you wouldn't expect them to self-assemble during the entire lifetime of the earth. That's a severe problem that evolutionists don't like to address."

THE AMAZING, MOVING CILIUM

The mousetrap emerged unscathed. But of course, it was only intended to be an illustration to help people understand irreducibly complex cellular systems. I decided to press forward by asking about some specific examples of molecular machines to see whether they could have developed by the step-by-step evolutionary process envisioned by Darwin. When I asked Behe for a specimen of irreducible complexity, he quickly cited the cilium.

"Cilia are whiplike hairs on the surface of cells. If the cell is stationary, the cilia move fluid across the cell's surface. For instance," he said, pointing toward my throat, "you've got cilia lining your respiratory tract. Every cell has about two hundred of them, and they beat in synchrony in order to sweep mucus toward your throat for elimination. That's how your body expels little foreign particles that you accidentally inhale.

But cilia also have another function: if the cell is mobile, the cilia can row it through a fluid. Sperm cells would be an example; they're propelled forward by the rowing action of cilia."

"That sounds fairly simple," I remarked.

"That's what scientists used to think when they examined cilia under a light microscope. They just looked like little hairs. But now that we have electron microscopes, we've found that cilia are, in fact, quite complicated molecular machines. Think about it: most hairs don't beat back and forth. What enables cilia to do this? Well, it turns out a cilium is made up of about two hundred protein parts."

"How does it function?"

He smiled. "I'll try to keep this basic," he said. "There are nine pairs of microtubules, which are long, thin, flexible rods, which encircle two single microtubules. The outer microtubules are connected to each other by what are called nexin linkers. And each microtubule has a motor protein called *dynein*. The motor protein attaches to one microtubule and has an arm that reaches over, grabs the other one, and pushes it down. So the two rods start to slide lengthwise with respect to each other. As they start to slide, the nexin linkers, which were originally like loose rope, get stretched and become taut. As the dynein pushes farther and farther, it starts to bend the apparatus; then it pushes the other way and bends it back. That's how you get the rowing motion of the cilium.

"That doesn't begin to do justice to the complexity of the cilium. But my point is that these three parts—the rods, linkers, and motors—are necessary to convert a sliding motion into a bending motion so the cilium can move. If it weren't for the linkers, everything would fall apart when the sliding motion began. If it weren't for the motor protein, it wouldn't move at all. If it weren't for the rods, there would be nothing to move. So like the mousetrap, the cilium is irreducibly complex."

"Why can't Darwinian evolution account for that?"

"You only get the motion of the cilium when you've got everything together. None of the individual parts can do the trick by themselves. You need them all in place. For evolution to account for that, you would have to imagine how this could develop gradually—but nobody has been able to do that."

I ventured a possibility. "Maybe these three components were being used for other purposes in the cell and eventually came together for this new function," I said. "For instance, microtubules look a bit like girders. Maybe they were used in the structure of primitive cells. Or maybe they formed the cellular highways along which the motor proteins moved material within the cell."

Behe didn't look impressed. "A motor protein that has been transporting cargo along a cellular highway might not have the strength necessary to push two microtubules relative to each other," he replied. "A nexin linker would have to be exactly the right size before it was useful at all. Creating the cilium inside the cell would be counterproductive; it would need to extend from the cell. The necessary components would have to come together at the right place at the right time, even assuming they were all pre-existing in the cell."

"Isn't it possible that they might all come together by chance?" I asked.

"It's extraordinarily improbable," he replied. "Let me illustrate it for you. Say there are ten thousand proteins in a cell. Now, imagine you live in a town of ten thousand people, and everyone goes to the county fair at the same time. Just for fun, everyone is wearing blindfolds and is not allowed to speak. There are two other people named Lee, and your job is to link hands with them. What are the odds that you could go grab two people at random and create a link of Lees? Pretty slim. In fact, it gets worse. In the cell, the mutation rate is extremely low. In our analogy, that would mean you could only change partners at the county fair one time a year.

"So you link with two other people—sorry, they're not the other Lees. Next year, you link with two other people. Sorry, no Lees again. How long would it take you to link with the other Lees? A very, very long time—and the same is true in the cell. It would take an enormous amount of time—a *prohibitive* amount of time—even to get three proteins together.

"To make it even more difficult, a recent study in *Science* magazine found that half the proteins in a simple yeast cell don't function alone, but they function as complexes of half a dozen proteins or more. Up to fifty proteins are stuck together like cogs in a machine. Of the other fifty percent, most are in complexes of three or four. Very few work as single, Lone Ranger proteins. So this is a huge problem not only in cilia but in other cells too."

"Some scientists have pointed out that there are examples of other cilia that don't have some of the parts that you contend are essential,"

I said. "One said, 'In nature, we can find scores of cilia lacking one or more of the components supposedly essential to the function of the apparatus.' Doesn't the existence of simpler cilia refute your contention that they are irreducibly complex?"

"If you could point to a series of less complex structures that progress from one to the other in order to create the cilia I've described, then, yes, that would refute me. But that isn't the case," he said. "What the critics say is that you can take away one of the several microtubules and the cilium would still function. That's fine. You still need all the basic components—microtubules, nexin, and dynein.

"Let me give you an analogy. Some big mousetraps—actually, they're rat traps—have double springs to make them stronger. You can take one spring away and it would still work to a degree. In a sense, the second spring is a redundant component. The cilium is the same way; it's got some redundant components. You can take one of the microtubules away and it will still function, though maybe not as well.

"But evolution does not start with the completed trap or completed cilium and take parts away; it has to build things up from the bottom. And all cilia have the three critical components that I've mentioned. There have been experiments where scientists have removed one of the three and the cilium doesn't work. It's broken—just like you'd expect it to be, since it's an irreducibly complex machine."

THE WORLD'S MOST EFFICIENT MOTOR

As amazing as the cilium is, I was even more fascinated by another biological machine for propelling cells—the bacterial flagellum. "While cilia act like oars to move cells, it was discovered in 1973 that the flagellum performs like a rotary propeller," Behe explained. "Only bacteria have them."

"How does it work?" I asked.

"Extremely efficiently," he said. "Just picture an outboard motor on a boat and you get a pretty good idea of how the flagellum functions, only the flagellum is far more incredible. The flagellum's propeller is long and whiplike, made out of a protein called *flagellin*. This is attached to a drive shaft by hook protein, which acts as a universal joint, allowing the propeller and drive shaft to rotate freely. Several types of proteins act as bushing material to allow the drive shaft to penetrate the bacterial wall and attach to the rotary motor."[8]

"Where does it get its energy?" I asked.

"That's an interesting phenomenon," he replied. "Some other biological systems that generate movement, like muscles, use energy that has been stored in what's called a 'carrier molecule.' But the flagellum uses another system—energy generated by a flow of acid through the bacterial membrane. This is a complex process that scientists are still studying and trying to understand. The whole system works really well—the flagellum's propeller can spin at ten thousand revolutions per minute."

As a car aficionado, I was staggered by that statistic! A friend had recently given me a ride in his exotic high-performance sports car, and I knew it wasn't capable of generating that many rpms. Even the notoriously high-revving Honda S2000, with a state-of-the-art, four-cylinder, two-liter, dual-overhead-cam aluminum block engine, featuring four valves per cylinder and variable intake and exhaust valve timing, has a redline of only nine thousand rpms.[9]

"Not only that," Behe continued, "but the propeller can stop spinning within a quarter turn and instantly start spinning the other way at ten thousand rpms. Howard Berg of Harvard University called it the most efficient motor in the universe. It's way beyond anything we can make, especially when you consider its size."

"How small is it?"

"A flagellum is on the order of a couple of microns. A micron is about 1/20,000 of an inch. Most of its length is the propeller. The motor itself would be maybe 1/100,000ths of an inch. Even with all of our technology, we can't even begin to create something like this. Sometimes in my lectures I show a drawing of the flagellum from a biochemistry textbook, and people say it looks like something from NASA. If you think about it, we've discovered machines inside ourselves. On *Star Trek* they had a creature called the Borg, which has tiny machines inside. Well, it turns out everybody does!"

Drawings of the flagellum are, indeed, very impressive, since they look uncannily like a machine that human beings would construct. I remember a scientist telling me about his father, an accomplished engineer who was highly skeptical about claims of intelligent design. The dad could never understand why his son was so convinced that the world had been designed by an intelligent agent. One day the scientist put a drawing of the bacterial flagellum in front of him. Fascinated, the engineer studied it silently for a while, then looked up and said to his son with a sense of wonder: "Oh, now I get what you've been saying."

"Think of this too," Behe continued. "Imagine a boat with its motor running. Uh-oh! Nobody's steering it. It goes out and crashes—*boom!* Well, who's steering the bacterial cell? It turns out it has sensory systems that feed into the bacteria flagellum and tell it when to turn on and when to turn off, so that it guides it to food, light, or whatever it's seeking. In a sense, it's like those smart missiles that have guidance systems to help them find their target, except there's no explosion at the end!"

"And the flagellum is irreducibly complex?"

"That's right," he said. "Genetic studies have shown that between thirty and thirty-five proteins are needed to create a functional flagellum. I haven't even begun to describe all of its complexities; we don't even know the roles of all its proteins. But at a minimum you need at least three parts—a paddle, a rotor, and a motor—that are made up of various proteins. Eliminate one of those parts and you don't get a flagellum that only spins at five thousand rpms; you get a flagellum that simply doesn't work at all. So it's irreducibly complex— and a huge stumbling block to Darwinian theory."

I asked, "Has anyone been able to propose a step-by-step evolutionary explanation of how a gradual process could have yielded a flagellum?"

"In a word—no," he said with a chuckle. "For most irreducibly complex systems, the best you get is a sort of hand-waving, cartoonish explanation, but certainly nothing that approaches being realistic. Even evolutionary biologist Andrew Pomiankowski admitted: 'Pick up any biochemistry textbook, and you will find perhaps two or three references to evolution. Turn to one of these and you will be lucky to find anything better than 'evolution selects the fittest molecules for their biological function.'[10]

"But for the flagellum, there aren't even any cartoon explanations. The best the Darwinists have been able to muster is to say that the flagellum has components that look like the components of other systems that don't have as many parts, so maybe somehow this other system had something to do with the flagellum. Nobody knows where this subsystem came from in the first place, or how or why the subsystem may have turned into a flagellum. So, no, there's no reasoned explanation anyone has been able to offer."

I tried another approach. "What about Darwinists who say, 'Maybe it's merely too early for us to come up with a road map of how these gradual changes developed. Someday we'll better understand the flagellum, so have patience—in the end, science is going to figure it out.'"

Behe leaned back in his chair. "You know, Darwinists always accuse folks in the Intelligent Design movement of making an argument from ignorance. Well, that's a pure argument from ignorance! They're saying, 'We have no idea how this could have happened, but let's assume evolution somehow did it.' You've heard of 'God-of-the-gaps'—inserting God when you don't have another explanation? Well, this is 'evolution-of-the-gaps.' Some scientists merely insert evolution when they don't understand something.

"Look—we may not understand everything about these biological systems, but we do know some things. We do know that these systems have a number of very specifically matched components that do not lend themselves to a gradualistic explanation. We know that intelligence can assemble complex systems, like computers and mousetraps and things like that. The complexity we see is not going to be alleviated by the more we learn; it can only get more complicated. We will only discover more details about the systems.

"Here's an illustration. Let's say you have a car in a dark garage. You shine a flashlight on one part of the engine and you see all of its components and its obvious complexity. Shining the flashlight on another part of the motor isn't going to make the first part go away. It isn't going to make the problem any simpler; it's going to make it more complicated. And as we discover more about the flagellum, it won't negate the complexity we've already found. All we'll have is an even more complicated, more impressive, more interdependent machine— and an even greater challenge to Darwinian theory."

MOLECULAR TRUCKS AND HIGHWAYS

According to Behe, the cilium and bacterial flagellum are just the beginning of the Darwin-defying complexity in the microscopic world of the cell. One of his other favorites is the "intra-cellular transport system."

"The cell is not a simple bag of soup, with everything sloshing around," he said. "Instead, eukaryotic cells—cells of all organisms except bacteria—have a number of compartments, sort of like rooms in a house.

"There's the nucleus, where the DNA resides; the mitochondria, which produce energy; the endoplasmic reticulum, which processes proteins; the Golgi apparatus, which is a way station for proteins that are being transported elsewhere; the lysosome, which is a garbage disposal unit; secretory vesicles, which store cargo before it's sent out of the cell; and the peroxisome, which helps metabolize fats. Each compartment is sealed off by a membrane, just like a room has walls and a door. In fact, the mitochondrion has four separate sections. Counting everything, there are more than twenty different sections in each cell.

"Cells are constantly getting rid of old stuff and manufacturing new components, and these components are designed to work in one room but not others. Most new components are made at a central location in the cell on things called *ribosomes*."

Denton has described the ribosome, a collection of some fifty large molecules containing more than one million atoms, as an automated factory that can synthesize any protein that it is instructed to make by DNA. Given the correct genetic information, in fact, it can construct any protein-based biological machine, including another ribosome, regardless of the complexity. Denton marveled:

> It is astonishing to think that this remarkable piece of machinery, which possesses the ultimate capacity to construct every living thing that has ever existed on Earth, from a giant redwood to the human brain, can construct all its own components in a matter of minutes and ... is of the order of several thousand million million times smaller than the smallest piece of functional machinery ever constructed by man.[11]

"Not only is the ribosome amazing," Behe said, "but now you're faced with the challenge of getting these new components into the right rooms where they can operate. In order to do that, you need to have another complicated system, just like you need a lot of things in place for a Greyhound bus to take someone from Philadelphia to Pittsburgh.

"First of all, you've got to have molecular trucks, which are enclosed and have motors attached to them. You've got to have little highways for them to travel along. You've got to be able to identify which components are supposed to go into which truck—after all, it doesn't do any good if you just grab any protein that comes along, because each one needs to go to a specific room. So there has to be a signal attached to the protein—sort of a ticket—to let the protein onto the right molecular truck. The truck has to know where it's going, which means having a signal on the truck itself and a complementary signal on the compartment where the truck is supposed to unload its cargo.

"When the truck arrives where it's supposed to go, it's kind of like a big ocean liner that has crossed from London to New York. It pulls up at the dock and everyone's waving—but, oops, they forgot the gang plank. Now what are you going to do? You see, you've got to have a way for the cargo to get out of the truck and into the compartment, and it turns out this is an active process that involves other components recognizing each other, physically opening things up, and allowing the material to go inside.

"So you've got numerous components, all of which have to be in place or nothing works. If you don't have the signal, if you don't have the truck, you're pretty much out of luck. Now, does this microscopic transportation system sound like something that self-assembled by gradual modifications over the years? I don't see how it could have been. To me, it has all the earmarks of being designed."

THE BLOOD-CLOTTING CASCADE

There was a pause in our conversation as my mind processed the stupefying complexity of the cilium, flagellum, and intracellular transport system. As I began to formulate my next line of questioning, Behe noticed a Band-Aid on one of my fingers, covering a cut I had received while picking up pieces of broken glass the previous day.

"Irreducible complexity is a very relevant topic," he commented as he gestured toward the bandage. "An irreducibly complex system just saved your life."

"What do you mean?" I asked.

"Blood clotting," he said. "If your blood hadn't clotted in the right place and in the right amount and at the right time, you would have bled to death. As it turns out, the system of blood clotting involves a highly choreographed cascade of ten steps that use about twenty different molecular components. Without the whole system in place, it doesn't work."

Suddenly, I felt a personal stake in the topic. "Tell me more," I said.

"The real trick with blood clotting isn't so much the clot itself— it's just a blob that blocks the flow of blood—but it's the regulation of the system," he continued.

"If you make a clot in the wrong place—say, the brain or lung—you'll die. If you make a clot twenty minutes after all the blood has drained from your body, you'll die. If the blood clot isn't confined to the cut, your entire blood system might solidify, and you'll die. If you make a clot that doesn't cover the entire length of the cut, you'll die. To create a perfectly balanced blood-clotting system, clusters of protein components have to be inserted all at once. That rules out a gradualistic Darwinian approach and fits the hypothesis of an intelligent designer."

Surely, I thought to myself, there must be another way. "Some scientists have proposed that a process called 'gene duplication' can account for the creation of new components for complex biological systems," I said. "Why wouldn't that work with blood clotting?"

Gene duplication can happen during the process of cell division when DNA is being copied from the original cell for use in the new cell. Occasionally, the process goes awry and a piece of DNA, perhaps a gene, is copied twice. This creates an extra gene. While the original gene can go about its pre-assigned role, the extra gene can drift and perhaps create a new function. Some scientists have theorized that this is how new components might be created for irreducible systems.

"Sure, gene duplication happens," Behe replied. "But what the fans of gene duplication rarely recognize is that when you get a duplicated gene, you don't get a new protein with new properties. You've got the same protein as before. And that's a problem."

I was having difficulty seeing why. "Could you explain that?" I asked.

He glanced down at the mousetrap, which was still sitting on his desk. "Let's go back to the mousetrap analogy," he said. "Suppose you have a one-component mousetrap, with two ends of a metal spring being bent and pressing against each other under tension so that if a mouse disturbs them, they'll slip and spring and hopefully catch a paw or tail. And say you wanted to develop a more efficient two-component trap that has a wooden base as well as the spring.

"According to the concept of gene duplication, you would make a copy of the first spring. Now you've got two springs—except the second spring somehow becomes a wooden base. Do you see the conceptual disconnect? You can't just say the spring somehow morphs into a wooden base without doing more than just saying, 'gene duplication did it.' The problem is, Darwinists don't provide the details of how this can actually happen in the real world.

"When one scientist tried to come up with a step-by-step scenario of how blood-clotting could have developed, he couldn't avoid generalizing by saying a component suddenly 'appears,' or 'is born,' or, 'arises,' or, 'springs forth,' or 'is unleashed.'[12] What's causing all of this springing forth and unleashing? There's no meaningful explanation of what could have caused these steps to take place. These are details that doom these scenarios.

"And there are a lot more problems than that. How can blood clotting develop over time, step by step, when in the meantime the animal has no effective way to stop from bleeding to death whenever it's cut? And when you've only got part of a system in place, the system doesn't work, so you've got the components sitting around doing nothing—and natural selection only works if there is something useful right now, not in the future.

"Besides, at best the explanations that some people attempt are mere word pictures. In science we're supposed to do experiments to show something is true. Nobody has ever done experiments to show how blood-clotting could have developed. Nobody has been able to show how a duplicated gene can develop some new function where it starts to make a new and irreducibly complex pathway."

SURVIVING THE ACID TEST

There *is* a scientific way, however, to establish through experimental data whether Behe's concept of irreducible complexity is really an insuperable barrier for Darwinism. I was anxious to see whether Behe's ideas could survive this formidable challenge from Miller, a biology professor who's an ardent and outspoken evolutionist.

The "true acid test," explained Miller, would be to use "the tools of molecular genetics to wipe out an existing multi-part system and then see if evolution can come to the rescue with a system to replace it."[13] If the system can be replaced purely by naturalistic evolutionary processes, then Behe's theory has been disproved.

After describing Miller's challenge, I asked Behe: "Do you agree this would be a fair test?"

Without hesitation, he said: "Yes, I agree. That's a terrific test."

Then I said: "Miller went on to describe an experiment by scientist Barry Hall of the University of Rochester to show how this apparently was done in the laboratory. Miller concluded: 'No doubt about it—the evolution of biochemical systems, even complex multi-part ones, is explicable in terms of evolution. Behe is wrong.'"[14]

I faced Behe squarely. "Tell me, has Hall proved through his experiment that your theory is incorrect?"

Unflustered, Behe replied: "No, not really. Actually, Hall is very modest about what his experiment shows. He didn't knock out a complex system and then show how evolution can replace it. Instead, he knocked out one component of a system that has five or six components. And replacing one component in a complex system is a lot easier than building one from scratch.

"For instance, suppose someone told you that natural processes could produce a working television set. You'd say, 'That's interesting. Why don't you show me?' He would then unplug a thousand television sets. Eventually, a strong wind would come along and blow one plug back into the outlet, and the TV would come on. He would say, 'See? I told you that natural processes could produce a working TV.' But that's not exactly what happened. He wasn't producing a new complex system; there was a glitch introduced and he showed that on occasion this can be fixed by random processes.

"That's a little like what went on with Hall's experiment with the bacterium *E. coli*. There was a complex system with a number of different parts, he knocked out one of them, and after a while he showed that random processes came up with a fix for that one part. That's a far cry from producing a brand new system from scratch.

"But there's something equally important: Hall made it clear that he had intervened to keep the system going while evolution was trying to come up with a replacement for the missing part. In other words, he added a chemical to the mixture that gave it the time to come up with the mutation that fixed the glitch. The result never would have actually happened in nature without his intelligent intervention in the experiment.

"Here's another analogy. Suppose you say you can make a three-legged stool by random processes. You take a three-legged stool and break off one leg. Then you hold up the stool so it won't fall over. Finally, a wind comes along, knocks down a tree branch, and it accidentally falls right where the missing leg had been. You're intervening to help the stool through the stage where it would otherwise have fallen over and you've made it possible for the branch to fit in the right place.

"Back to Hall's experiment. Without going into the technical details, which I've done in more formal responses,[15] in nature you couldn't have gotten just the mutation that he got in the laboratory. You would have had to have simultaneously gotten a *second* mutation—and the odds of that would have been prohibitive. Hall made it clear that he intervened so that he would get results that would never have actually happened in the natural world. And that is injecting intelligence into the system.

"When you analyze the entire experiment, the result is exactly what you would expect of irreducible complexity requiring intelligent intervention. Unintentionally, he has shown the limits of Darwinism and the need for design."

WHIRLPOOLS AND TORNADOES

"What about other alternatives to Darwinian gradualism?" I asked. "How about self-organization? Maybe there's some sort of self-organizational property in biochemistry that encourages the parts of molecular machines to self-assemble."

"Just like natural selection explains some things, self organization explains some things too. The controversy arises when they're used to explain big things or everything," Behe said.

"It's true that if you pull out the plug in your bathtub, the water forms a little whirlpool. That's self-organization: the water is moving in an organized fashion whereas it wasn't before. Tornadoes organize themselves. If you mix chemicals together in a certain way, you get a system that acts like a clock. It will turn blue, five seconds later it will turn colorless, and it will oscillate back and forth. So it's clear that there is such a thing as self-organization.

"The question is, can it explain more complicated phenomena? Can it explain the genetic code? Scientists trying to solve the riddle of the origin of life have been exploring self-organizational properties for decades. Yet today they're more confused about the origin of life than fifty years ago. They haven't come up with any explanation for how self-organization could account for something as complex as even the first primitive living organism.

"Right now, there's only one principle that we know can come up with complex interactive systems, and that's intelligence. Natural selection has been proposed, but there's little or no evidence backing that claim. Some people had high hopes for self-organizational properties or complexity theory, but there's no evidence that these can explain something as complicated as the cell. The only force known to be able to make irreducibly complex machines is intelligent design.

"So scientists are in the curious position of ignoring something they know to be capable of explaining what they see in biology, in favor of phantom or totally unproven explanations. Why ignore intelligent design when it's a good match to the data? Yes, we have to keep an open mind in science, but we shouldn't be ignoring the most obvious explanation for all the evidence we have today."

"One reason some scientists are reluctant," I said, "is because they claim intelligent design is not falsifiable." I was referring to the belief among many philosophers and scientists that a theory cannot truly be scientific unless there are potential ways to prove it false through experiments or other means.[16]

"That's silly," Behe replied.

"But I hear it over and over," I insisted. "The National Academy of Sciences said: 'Intelligent design . . . [is] not science because [it's] not testable by the methods of science.'"[17]

"Yes, I know," he said, "but what's really ironic is that intelligent design is routinely called unfalsifiable by the very people who are busy trying to falsify it! As you just pointed out, Miller proposed a test that would falsify the claim that intelligence is needed to produce an irreducibly complex system. So I don't see the problem. Intelligent design's strong point is that it's falsifiable, just like a good scientific theory should be. Frankly, I'd say it's more falsifiable than Darwinism is."

"Come on," I said. "Do you really believe that?"

"Yes, I do, and I'll give you an example," he replied. "My claim is that there is no unintelligent process that could produce the bacterial flagellum. To falsify that claim, all you would have to do would be to find one unintelligent process that could produce that system. On the other hand, Darwinists claim that *some* unintelligent process could produce the flagellum. To falsify that, you'd have to show that the system could not possibly have been created by any of a potentially infinite number of possible unintelligent processes. That's impossible to do. So which claim is falsifiable? I'd say the claim for intelligent design."

That isn't the only objection that Behe has turned on its head. While Darwinists often accuse intelligent design proponents of letting their religious beliefs color their science, Behe once told a newspaper reporter: "It has been my experience ... that the ones who oppose the theory of design most vociferously do so for religious reasons."[18]

"What did you mean by that?" I asked.

"It seems that the folks who get the most animated when talking about Darwinian evolution are the ones most concerned with the philosophical and theological ramifications of the theory, not the science itself," he explained.

"Scientists propose hypotheses all the time. No big deal. But if I say, 'I don't think natural selection is the driving force for the development of life; I think it was intelligent design,' people don't just disagree; many of them jump up and down and get red in the face. When you talk to them about it, invariably they're not excited because they disagree with the science; it's because they see the extra-scientific implications of intelligent design and they don't like where it's leading."

Behe shrugged. "I guess that's okay," he added. "These are important issues and people can get emotional about them. But we should not use what we want to be true to dismiss arguments or try to avoid them."

THE ARROW OF PROGRESS

Behe's concept of irreducible complexity is at once a negative and a positive argument. First, he has taken Darwin at his own word and demonstrated how these interconnected biological systems could not have been created through the numerous, successive, slight modifications that his theory demands. The result has been a staggering— some say lethal—blow to Darwinism.

Second, Behe has pointed out that there is an alternative that does sufficiently explain how complex biological machines could have been created. Once again, as with the previous experts I had interviewed on cosmology, physics, and astronomy, the evidence conspires to point toward a transcendent Creator.

"My conclusion can be summed up in a single word: *design*," Behe said as we came to the end of our interview. "I say that based on science. I believe that irreducibly complex systems are strong evidence of a purposeful, intentional design by an intelligent agent. No other theory succeeds; certainly not Darwinism.

"Based on the empirical evidence—which is continuing to mount—I'd agree with Joseph Cardinal Ratzinger that 'the great projects of the living creation are not the products of chance and error. . . . [They] point to a creating Reason and show us a creating Intelligence, and they do so more luminously and radiantly today than ever before.'"[19]

"Your book has been out for several years now," I said. "How well do you think it has endured so far?"

"I'm very pleased with how things stand," he said, leaning back in his chair and casually folding his arms over his chest. "It has attracted a lot of attention from people who have tried to knock it down, but they haven't been able to do it. Complex biological systems have yet to be explained by naturalistic means. That's a fact. Even Darwinists admit that in their candid moments. And as science advances, we're continuing to find more and more complexity in the cellular world. This, Lee, is the arrow of progress.

"I do hear occasional complaints that science needs to pretend that everything works by natural law and that intelligent design is 'giving up.' I've never seen the logic of that. The purpose of science, it seems to me, is to find out how things got here and how they work. Science should be the search for truth, not merely the search for materialistic explanations. The great scientists of history—Newton and Einstein, for instance—never thought science's job was to come up with some sort of self-sufficient explanation for nature. This is a recent innovation, and not a good one—especially in light of discoveries during the last fifty years that have pointed in the exact opposite direction."

Behe and I continued to talk for a while, then we shook hands and parted ways. As I lingered in the hallway, peering through the glass into various laboratories where scientists were hard at work, I thought of the concession by microbiologist James Shapiro of the University of Chicago in his review of Behe's book: "There are no detailed Darwinian accounts for the evolution of any fundamental biochemical or cellular system, only a variety of wishful speculations."[20]

Shapiro might not be amenable to Behe's ultimate conclusions, but personally I wasn't ready to bank on wishful speculations. Connecting the dots from my interviews with William Lane Craig, Robin Collins, Guillermo Gonzalez, Jay Richards, and now Michael Behe, I was coming up with a picture that was squarely at odds with the icons that had once led me into atheism. In the words of Allan Sandage, one of the most highly respected scientists of our age:

The world is too complicated in all its parts and interconnections to be due to chance alone. I am convinced that the existence of life with all its order in each of its organisms is simply too well put together. Each part of a living thing depends on all its other parts to function. How does each part know? How is each part specified at conception? The more one learns of biochemistry the more unbelievable it becomes unless there is some type of organizing principle—an architect for believers, a mystery to be solved by science (even as to *why*) sometime in the indefinite future for materialist reductionalists.[21]

That mystery was going to take me even deeper inside the awe-inspiring, microscopic realm of the cell. As I started my rental car and began to drive down the asphalt road from Lehigh's Mountaintop Campus, I remembered that Stephen Meyer, the philosopher of science I had already interviewed about the relationship between science and faith, has written extensively on DNA. This seemed like a good time for a new chat about where the arrow of genetics might be pointing.

FOR FURTHER EVIDENCE
More Resources on This Topic

Behe, Michael J. *Darwin's Black Box: The Biochemical Challenge to Evolution*. New York: Touchstone, 1996.
——. "Darwin's Breakdown: Irreducible Complexity and Design at the Foundation of Life." In *Signs of Intelligence*, eds. William A. Dembski and James M. Kushiner. Grand Rapids, Mich: Brazos, 2001.
——. "Evidence for Design at the Foundation of Life" and "Answering Scientific Criticisms of Intelligent Design." In *Science and Evidence for Design in the Universe*, eds. Michael J. Behe, William A. Dembski, and Stephen C. Meyer. San Francisco: Ignatius, 2000.
——. "Intelligent Design Theory as a Tool for Analyzing Biochemical Systems." In *Mere Creation*, ed. William A. Dembski. Downer's Grove, Ill.: InterVarsity Press, 1998.

THE EVIDENCE OF BIOLOGICAL INFORMATION: THE CHALLENGE OF DNA AND THE ORIGIN OF LIFE

Human DNA contains more organized information than the Encyclopedia Britannica. If the full text of the encyclopedia were to arrive in computer code from outer space, most people would regard this as proof of the existence of extraterrestrial intelligence. But when seen in nature, it is explained as the workings of random forces.

George Sim Johnson[1]

Einstein said, "God does not play dice." He was right. God plays Scrabble.

Philip Gold[2]

In 1953, when Francis Crick told his wife Odile that he and a colleague had discovered the secret of life—the chemical structure of DNA, where the instructions for building proteins were encoded—she didn't believe him. Years later, she confessed to her husband: "You were always coming home and saying things like that, so naturally I thought nothing of it."[3]

This time, he wasn't exaggerating. He and James D. Watson would win the Nobel Prize for discovering the now-famous double helix of deoxyribonucleic acid, where the "language of life" is stored.

For more than fifty years, as scientists have studied the six feet of DNA that's tightly coiled inside every one of our body's one hundred trillion cells, they have marveled at how it provides the genetic information necessary to create all of the proteins out of which our bodies are built. In fact, each one of the thirty thousand genes that are embedded in our twenty-three pairs of chromosomes can yield as many as 20,500 different kinds of proteins.[4]

The astounding capacity of microscopic DNA to harbor this mountain of information, carefully spelled out in a four-letter chemical alphabet, "vastly exceeds that of any other known system," said geneticist Michael Denton.

In fact, he said the information needed to build the proteins for all the species of organisms that have ever lived—a number estimated to be approximately one thousand million—"could be held in a teaspoon and there would still be room left for all the information in every book ever written."[5]

DNA serves as the information storehouse for a finely choreographed manufacturing process in which the right amino acids are linked together with the right bonds in the right sequence to produce the right kind of proteins that fold in the right way to build biological systems. The documentary *Unlocking the Mystery of Life*, which has aired on numerous PBS television stations, describes the elaborate operation this way:

> In a process known as transcription, a molecular machine first unwinds a section of the DNA helix to expose the genetic instructions needed to assemble a specific protein molecule. Another machine then copies these instructions to form a molecule known as messenger RNA. When transcription is complete, the slender RNA strand carries the genetic information . . . out of the cell nucleus. The messenger RNA strand is directed to a two-part molecular factory called a ribosome. . . . Inside the ribosome, a molecular assembly line builds a specifically sequenced chain of amino acids. These amino acids are transported from other parts of the cell and then linked into chains often hundreds of units long. Their sequential arrangement determines the type of protein manufactured. When the chain is finished, it is moved from the ribosome to a barrel-shaped machine that helps fold it into the precise shape critical to its function. After the chain is folded into a protein, it is then released and shepherded by another molecular machine to the exact location where it is needed.[6]

It was this "absolutely mind-boggling" procedure that helped lead biology professor Dean Kenyon to repudiate the conclusions of his own book on the chemical origin of life and conclude instead that nothing short of an intelligence could have created this intricate cellular apparatus. "This new realm of molecular genetics [is] where we see the most compelling evidence of design on the Earth," he said.[7]

It seemed fitting that when scientists announced that they had finally mapped the three billion codes of the human genome—a project that filled the equivalent of 75,490 pages of *The New York Times*—divine references abounded. President Clinton said scientists were "learning the language in which God created life," while geneticist Francis S. Collins, head of the Human Genome Project, said DNA was "our own instruction book, previously known only to God."[8]

Are such public bows to a Creator merely a polite social custom, meant only as a nodding courtesy to a predominantly theistic country? Or does the bounty of information in DNA really warrant the conclusion that an intelligent designer must have infused genetic material with its protein-building instructions? Are there any naturalistic processes that can account for the appearance of biological data in the earliest cells?

I knew where to go to get answers. One of the country's leading experts on origin-of-life issues, who has written extensively on the implications of the information in DNA, resides in Washington state. He and I had already discussed the intersection of faith and science for Chapter Four of this book; now it was time to sit down with him again, this time in his new quarters at the Discovery Institute in downtown Seattle.

INTERVIEW #7: STEPHEN C. MEYER, PHD

Since our last discussion, philosopher and scientist Stephen Meyer had moved with his wife and three children to the outskirts of Seattle so he could focus on his role as Director and Senior Fellow at the Discovery Institute's Center for Science and Culture.[9] He continues to keep one foot in academia, however, as professor of the Conceptual Foundations of Science at Palm Beach Atlantic University.

Meyer earned his doctorate at Cambridge University, where he analyzed scientific and methodological issues in origin-of-life biology. For his master's degree, also from Cambridge, he studied the history of molecular biology and evolutionary theory.

He has written about DNA and the problem of the origin of biological information for the books *Debating Design*, published by Cambridge University Press; *Darwinism, Design, and Public Education*, published by Michigan State University Press; *Science and Evidence for Design in the Universe*; *Signs of Intelligence*; and *Mere Creation*. Lately he has been finishing a book called *DNA by Design: The Signature in the Cell*, which further expands on his analysis of biological information.

We got together on an unusually sultry summer day, had a pleasant lunch in an avant-garde Asian restaurant, and then settled into an office at the Discovery Institute. Meyer lowered his lanky frame into a plain wooden chair, his back to a half-opened window through which random traffic noises could be heard. It was nearly midafternoon before we got started with our discussion.

It was clear that Meyer likes the give-and-take of interviews. Although Meyer is typically more professorial than pugnacious, I've never heard of him shying away from tough questions or even rhetorically bloody debates with fervent Darwinists.

In fact, I once hosted the videotaping of an intellectual shoot-out between Meyer and an atheistic anthropologist on the legitimacy of intelligent-design theories, and I remember walking away amazed at Meyer's finesse in deftly dismantling the professor's case while at the same time forcefully presenting his own. Maybe that's a throwback to Meyer's earlier years when he trained as a boxer, learning to overcome fears of taking a punch and how to jab away at an opponent's weaknesses.

As for me, I wasn't after blood in this interview; I was merely seeking straightforward answers to an issue that has befuddled origin-of-life scientists for the last five decades. Even though most Darwinists concede they are stumped on the question of how DNA and life itself came into existence,[10] they don't like Meyer's conclusions on the matter. I didn't care much about that; my criterion was simple: what makes the most sense from a purely scientific perspective?

THE DNA-TO-DESIGN ARGUMENT

I began our discussion by reading Meyer a quote that I had encountered in my research and scribbled in my notes. "According to Bernd-Olaf Küppers, the author of *Information and the Origin of Life*, 'The problem of the origin of life is clearly basically equivalent to the problem of the origin of biological information,'"[11] I said. "Do you agree with him?"

"Oh, absolutely, yes," Meyer replied. "When I ask students what they would need to get their computer to perform a new function, they reply, 'You have to give it new lines of code.' The same principle is true in living organisms.

"If you want an organism to acquire a new function or structure, you have to provide information somewhere in the cell. You need instructions for how to build the cell's important components, which are mostly proteins. And we know that DNA is the repository for a digital code containing the instructions for telling the cell's machinery how to build proteins. Küppers recognized that this was a critical hurdle in explaining how life began: where did this genetic information come from?

"Think of making soup from a recipe. You can have all the ingredients on hand, but if you don't know the proper proportions, or which items to add in what order, or how long to cook the concoction, you won't get a soup that tastes very good.

"Well, a lot of people talk about the 'prebiotic soup'—the chemicals that supposedly existed on the primitive Earth prior to life. Even if you had the right chemicals to create a living cell, you would also need information for how to arrange them in very specific configurations in order to perform biological functions. Ever since the 1950s and 1960s, biologists have recognized that the cell's critical functions are usually performed by proteins, and proteins are the product of assembly instructions stored in DNA."

"Let's talk about DNA, then," I said. "You've written that there's a 'DNA-to-design argument.' What do you mean by that?"

Meyer removed a pair of gold-rimmed glasses from his shirt pocket and put them on as he began to give his answer. "Very simply," he said, "I mean that the origin of information in DNA—which is necessary for life to begin—is best explained by an intelligent cause rather than any of the types of naturalistic causes that scientists typically use to explain biological phenomena."

"When you talk about 'information' in DNA, what exactly do you mean?" I asked.

"We know from our experience that we can convey information with a twenty-six-letter alphabet, or twenty-two, or thirty—or even just two characters, like the zeros and ones used in the binary code in

computers. One of the most extraordinary discoveries of the twentieth century was that DNA actually stores information—the detailed
instructions for assembling proteins—in the form of a four-character
digital code.

"The characters happen to be chemicals called *adenine, guanine,
cytosine,* and *thymine*. Scientists represent them with the letters A, G,
C, and T, and that's appropriate because they function as alphabetic
characters in the genetic text. Properly arranging those four 'bases,' as
they're called, will instruct the cell to build different sequences of
amino acids, which are the building blocks of proteins. Different
arrangements of characters yields different sequences of amino acids."

With that, Meyer decided to show me an illustration he often uses
with college students. Reaching over to a desk drawer, he took out
several oversized plastic snap-lock beads of the sort that young children play with. "It says on the box that these are for kids ages two to
four, so this is advanced chemistry," he joked.

He held up orange, green, blue, red, and purple beads of different shapes. "These represent the structure of a protein. Essentially, a
protein is a long linear array of amino acids," he said, snapping the
beads together in a line. "Because of the forces between the amino
acids, the proteins fold into very particular three-dimensional
shapes," he added as he bent and twisted the line of beads.

"These three-dimensional shapes are highly irregular, sort of like
the teeth in a key, and they have a lock-key fit with other molecules
in the cell. Often, the proteins will catalyze reactions, or they'll form
structural molecules, or linkers, or parts of the molecular machines
that Michael Behe writes about. This specific three-dimensional
shape, which allows proteins to perform a function, derives directly
from the one-dimensional sequencing of amino acids."

Then he pulled some of the beads apart and began rearranging
their order. "If I were to switch a red one and a blue one, I'd be setting up a different combination of force interactions and the protein
would fold completely differently. So the sequence of the amino acids
is critical to getting the long chain to fold properly to form an actual
functional protein. Wrong sequence, no folding—and the sequence
of amino acids is unable to serve its function.

"Proteins, of course, are the key functional molecule in the cell; you
can't have life without them. Where do they come from? Well, that question forces a deeper issue—what's the source of the assembly instructions

in DNA that are responsible for the one-dimensional sequential arrangements of amino acids that create the three-dimensional shapes of proteins? Ultimately," he emphasized, "the functional attributes of proteins derive from information stored in the DNA molecule."

THE LIBRARY OF LIFE

I was fascinated by the process that Meyer had described. "What you're saying is that DNA would be like a blueprint for how to build proteins," I said, using an analogy I had heard many times before.

Meyer hesitated. "Actually, I don't like the blueprint metaphor," he said. "You see, there are probably other sources of information in the cell and in organisms. As important as DNA is, it doesn't build everything. All it builds are the protein molecules, but they are only sub-units of larger structures that themselves are informatively arranged."

"Then what's a better analogy?" I asked.

"DNA is more like a library," he said. "The organism accesses the information that it needs from DNA so it can build some of its critical components. And the library analogy is better because of its alphabetic nature. In DNA, there are long lines of A, C, G, and T's that are precisely arranged in order to create protein structure and folding. To build one protein, you typically need 1,200 to 2,000 letters or bases—which is a lot of information."

"And this raises the question again of the origin of that information," I said.

"It's not just that a question has been raised," he insisted. "This issue has caused all naturalistic accounts of the origin of life to break down, because it's *the* critical and foundational question. If you can't explain where the information comes from, you haven't explained life, because it's the information that makes the molecules into something that actually functions."

I asked, "What does the presence of information tell you?"

"I believe the presence of information in the cell is best explained by the activity of an intelligent agent," he replied. "Bill Gates said, 'DNA is like a software program, only much more complex than anything we've ever devised.' That's highly suggestive, because we know that at Microsoft, Gates uses intelligent programmers to produce software. Information theorist Henry Quastler said as far back as the 1960s that the 'creation of new information is habitually associated with conscious activity.'"[12]

"But we're talking about something—the origin of information and life—that happened a long time ago," I said. "How can scientists reconstruct what happened in the distant past?"

"By using a scientific principle of reasoning that's called *uniformitarianism*," Meyer replied. "This is the idea that our present knowledge of cause-and-effect relationships should guide our reconstruction of what caused something to arise in the past."

"For example . . . ," I said and paused, hoping to prompt an illustration that would help me follow him.

"For instance, let's say you find a certain kind of ripple marks preserved from the ancient past in sedimentary strata. And let's say that in the present day you see the same sort of ripple marks being formed in lake beds as the water evaporates. You can reasonably infer, then, using uniformitarian logic, that the ripple marks in the sedimentary strata were produced by a similar process.

"So let's go back to DNA. Even the very simplest cell we study today, or find evidence of in the fossil record, requires information that is stored in DNA or some other information-carrier. And we know from our experience that information is habitually associated with conscious activity. Using uniformitarian logic, we can reconstruct the cause of that ancient information in the first cell as being the product of intelligence."

As my mind tracked his line of reasoning, everything seemed to click into place—except one thing. "However," I said, "there's a caveat."

Meyer cocked an eyebrow. "Like what?" he asked.

"All of that is true—unless you can find some better explanation."

"Yes, of course," he said. "You have to rule out other causes of the same effect. Origin-of-life scientists have looked at other possibilities for decades and, frankly, they've come up dry."

Before we went any further, though, I needed to satisfy myself that the other major possible scenarios fall short of the intelligent design theory.

THE MISSING SOUP

In 1871, Charles Darwin wrote a letter in which he speculated that life might have originated when "a protein compound was chemically formed . . . in some warm little pond, with all sorts of ammonia and phosphoric salts, light, heat, electricity, etc. present."[13] A few years ago a scientist summarized the basic theory this way:

> The first stage on the road to life is presumed to have been the build-up, by pure chemical synthetic processes occurring on the surface of the early Earth, of all the basic organic compounds necessary for the formation of a living cell. These are supposed to have accumulated in the primeval oceans, creating a nutrient broth, the so-called "prebiotic soup." In certain specialized environments these organic compounds were assembled into large macromolecules, proteins and nucleic acids. Eventually, over millions of years, combinations of these macromolecules occurred which were then endowed with the property of self-reproduction. Then driven by natural selection ever more efficient and complex self-reproducing molecular systems evolved until finally the first simple cell system emerged.[14]

"I hear scientists talk a lot about this prebiotic soup," I said. "How much evidence is there that it actually existed?"

"That's a very interesting issue," he replied. "The answer is there isn't any evidence."

That's highly significant, because most origin-of-life theories presuppose the existence of this ancient chemical ocean. "What do you mean, 'there isn't any'?"

"If this prebiotic soup had really existed," Meyer explained, "it would have been rich in amino acids. Therefore, there would have been a lot of nitrogen, because amino acids are nitrogenous. So when we examine the earliest sediments of the Earth, we should find large deposits of nitrogen-rich minerals."

That seemed logical to me. "What have scientists found?"

"Those deposits have never been located. In fact, Jim Brooks wrote in 1985 that 'the nitrogen content of early organic matter is relatively low—just .015 percent.' He said in *Origins of Life*: 'From this we can be reasonably certain that there never was any substantial amount of 'primitive soup' on Earth when pre-Cambrian sediments were formed; if such a soup ever existed it was only for a brief period of time.'"[15]

This was an astounding conclusion! "Don't you find that surprising, since scientists routinely talk about the prebiotic soup as if it were a given?" I asked.

"Yes, certainly it's surprising," he replied. "Denton commented on this in *Evolution: A Theory in Crisis*, when he said: 'Considering the way the prebiotic soup is referred to in so many discussions of the origin of life as an already established reality, it comes as something of a shock to realize that there is absolutely no positive evidence for its existence.'[16] And even if we were to assume that the prebiotic soup did exist, there would have been significant problems with cross-reactions."

"What do you mean?"

"Take Stanley Miller's origin-of-life experiment fifty years ago, when he tried to recreate the early Earth's atmosphere and spark it with electricity. He managed to create two or three of the protein-forming amino acids out of the twenty-two that exist."

I interrupted to let Meyer know that biologist Jonathan Wells had already told me how Miller's experiment used an atmosphere that scientists now recognize was unrealistic, and that using the correct environment doesn't yield any biologically relevant amino acids.

"That's right," Meyer continued. "What's also interesting, however, is that Miller's amino acids reacted very quickly with the other chemicals in the chamber, resulting in a brown sludge that's not life-friendly at all. That's what I mean by cross-reactions—even if amino acids existed in the theoretical prebiotic soup, they would have readily reacted with other chemicals. This would have been another tremendous barrier to the formation of life. The way that origin-of-life scientists have dealt with this in their experiments has been to remove these other chemicals in the hope that further reactions could take the experiment in a life-friendly direction.

"So instead of simulating a natural process, they interfered in order to get the outcome they wanted. And *that*," Meyer concluded, "is intelligent design."

Undoubtedly, obstacles to the formation of life on the primitive Earth would have been extremely formidable, even if the world were awash with an ocean of biological precursors. Still, is there *any* reasonable naturalistic route to life? Like a homicide detective rounding up the usual suspects, I decided to run down the three possible scenarios to see if any of them made sense.

SCENARIO #1: RANDOM CHANCE

I began with an observation. "I know that the idea of life forming by random chance is out of vogue right now among scientists," I said.

Meyer agreed. "Virtually all origin-of-life experts have utterly rejected that approach," he said with a wave of his hand.

"Even so, the idea is still very much alive at the popular level," I pointed out. "For many college students who speculate about these things, chance is still the hero. They think if you let amino acids randomly interact over millions of years, life is somehow going to emerge."

"Well, yes, it's true that this scenario is still alive among people who don't know all the facts, but there's no merit to it," Meyer replied.

"Imagine trying to generate even a simple book by throwing Scrabble letters onto the floor. Or imagine closing your eyes and picking Scrabble letters out of a bag. Are you going to produce *Hamlet* in anything like the time of the known universe? Even a simple protein molecule, or the gene to build that molecule, is so rich in information that the entire time since the Big Bang would not give you, as my colleague Bill Dembski likes to say, the 'probabilistic resources' you would need to generate that molecule by chance."

"Even," I asked, "if the first molecule had been much simpler than those today?"

"There's a minimal complexity threshold," he replied. "There's a certain level of folding that a protein has to have, called tertiary structure, that is necessary for it to perform a function. You don't get tertiary structure in a protein unless you have at least seventy-five amino acids or so. That may be conservative. Now consider what you'd need for a protein molecule to form by chance.

"First, you need the right bonds between the amino acids. Second, amino acids come in right-handed and left-handed versions, and you've got to get only left-handed ones. Third, the amino acids must link up in a specified sequence, like letters in a sentence.

"Run the odds of these things falling into place on their own and you find that the probabilities of forming a rather short functional protein at random would be one chance in a hundred thousand trillion trillion trillion trillion trillion trillion trillion trillion trillion trillion. That's a ten with 125 zeroes after it!

"And that would only be one protein molecule—a minimally complex cell would need between three hundred and five hundred protein molecules. Plus, all of this would have to be accomplished in a mere 100 million years, which is the approximate window of time between the Earth cooling and the first microfossils we've found.

"To suggest chance against those odds is really to invoke a naturalistic miracle. It's a confession of ignorance. It's another way of saying,

'We don't know.' And since the 1960s, scientists, to their credit, have been very reluctant to say that chance played any significant role in the origin of DNA or proteins—even though, as you say, it's still unfortunately a live option in popular thinking."

SCENARIO #2: NATURAL SELECTION

Random chance might not account for the origin of life, but zoologist Richard Dawkins says that when natural selection acts on chance variations, then evolution is capable of scaling otherwise impossibly high peaks. In fact, that was the premise of his 1996 book *Climbing Mount Improbable*.

He suggested that a complex biological structure is like a sheer cliff that cannot be scaled in one big bound without intermediate stepping stones, as chance must do. People look at this towering peak and think evolutionary processes could never get them to the top.

The backside of that same mountain, however, has a gradual slope that makes for much easier climbing. This represents the Darwinian idea that nature provides small chance variations and then natural selection chooses the ones that are most advantageous. Over long periods of time, little changes accumulate into major differences. So while the mountain looks impossible to climb from the cliff side, it's quite easy to scale via the smaller Darwinian steps of natural selection on the backside.[17]

In light of that insight, I asked Meyer: "Can natural selection explain how evolution managed to scale the mountain of building the first living cell?"

"Whether natural selection really works at the level of biological evolution is open to debate, but it most certainly does not work at the level of *chemical* evolution, which tries to explain the origin of the first life from simpler chemicals," Meyer replied. "As Theodosius Dobzhansky said, 'Prebiological natural selection is a contradiction in terms.'"[18]

"How so?" I asked.

"Darwinists admit that natural selection requires a self-replicating organism to work," he explained. "Organisms reproduce, their offspring have variations, the ones that are better adapted to their environment survive better, and so those adaptations are preserved and passed on to the next generation.

"However, to have reproduction, there has to be cell division. And that presupposes the existence of information-rich DNA and proteins. But that's the problem—those are the very things they're trying to explain!

"In other words, you've got to have a self-replicating organism for Darwinian evolution to take place, but you can't have a self-replicating organism until you have the information necessary in DNA, which is what you're trying to explain in the first place. It's like the guy who falls into a deep hole and realizes he needs a ladder to get out. So climbs out, goes home, gets a ladder, jumps back into the hole, and climbs out. It begs the question."

I raised another possibility. "Maybe replication first began in a much simpler way and then natural selection was able to take over," I said. "For example, some small viruses use RNA as their genetic material. RNA molecules are simpler than DNA, and they can also store information and even replicate. What about the so-called 'RNA first hypothesis' that says reproductive life originated in a realm that's much less complex than DNA?"

"There's a mountain of problems with that," he said. "Just to cite a couple of them, the RNA molecule would need information to function, just as DNA would, and so we're right back to the same problem of where the information came from. Also, for a single strand of RNA to replicate, there must be an identical RNA molecule close by. To have a reasonable chance of having two identical RNA molecules of the right length would require a library of ten billion billion billion billion billion billion RNA molecules—and that effectively rules out any chance origin of a primitive replicating system."[19]

Although popular for a while, the RNA theory has generated its share of skeptics. Evolutionist Robert Shapiro, a chemistry professor at New York University, said the idea at this point "must be considered either a speculation or a matter of faith."[20] Origin-of-life researcher Graham Cairns-Smith said the "many interesting and detailed experiments in this area" have only served to show that the theory is "highly implausible."[21] As Jonathan Wells noted in my earlier interview with him, biochemist Gerald Joyce of the Scripps Research Center was even more blunt: "You have to build straw man upon straw man to get to the point where RNA is a viable first biomolecule."[22]

Jay Roth, former professor of cell and molecular biology at the University of Connecticut and an expert in nucleic acids, said whether the original template for the first living system was RNA or DNA, the same problem exists. "Even reduced to the barest essentials," he said, "this template must have been very complex indeed. For this template and this template alone, it appears it is reasonable at present to suggest the possibility of a creator."[23]

SCENARIO #3: CHEMICAL AFFINITIES AND SELF-ORDERING

Meyer pointed out that by the early 1970s, most origin-of-life scientists had become disenchanted with the options of random chance and natural selection. As a result, some explored a third possibility: various self-organizational theories for the origin of information-bearing macromolecules.

For example, scientists theorized that chemical attractions may have caused DNA's four-letter alphabet to self-assemble or that the natural affinities between amino acids prompted them to link together by themselves to create protein. When I broached these possibilities, Meyer's response was to bring up a name I had already encountered during my investigation.

"One of the first advocates of this approach was Dean Kenyon, who coauthored the textbook *Biochemical Predestination*," Meyer said. "The title tells it all. The idea was that the development of life was inevitable because the amino acids in proteins and the bases, or letters, in the DNA alphabet had self-ordering capacities that accounted for the origin of the information in these molecules."

I already knew that Kenyon had repudiated the conclusions of his own book, declaring that "we have not the slightest chance of a chemical evolutionary origin for even the simplest of cells" and that intelligent design "made a great deal of sense, as it very closely matched the multiple discoveries in molecular biology."[24] Still, I wanted to consider the evidence for myself.

"How did this chemical attraction supposedly work?" I asked.

"We'll use proteins as an example," he said. "Remember, proteins are composed of a long line of amino acids. The hope was that there would be some forces of attraction between the amino acids that would cause them to line up the way they do and then fold so that the protein can perform the functions that keep a cell alive."

I interrupted. "You have to admit that there are examples in nature where chemical attractions do result in a kind of self-ordering."

"That's right," Meyer said. "Salt crystals are a good illustration. Chemical forces of attraction cause sodium ions, Na+, to bond with chloride ions, Cl−, in order to form highly ordered patterns within a crystal of salt. You get a nice sequence of Na and Cl repeating over and over again. So, yes, there are lots of cases in chemistry where bonding affinities of different elements will explain the origin of their molecular structure. Kenyon and others hoped this would be the case for proteins and DNA."

"What turned out to be the problem?" I asked.

"As scientists did experiments, they found that amino acids didn't demonstrate these bonding affinities," Meyer replied.

"None at all?"

"There were some very, very slight affinities, but they don't correlate to any of the known patterns of sequencing that we find in functional proteins. Obviously, that's a major problem—but there was an even bigger theoretical difficulty. Information theorist Hubert Yockey and chemist Michael Polanyi raised a deeper issue: 'What would happen if we *could* explain the sequencing in DNA and proteins as a result of self-organization properties? Wouldn't we end up with something like a crystal of salt, where there's merely a repetitive sequence?'"[25]

When I asked Meyer to elaborate, he said: "Consider the genetic information in DNA, which is spelled out by the chemical letters A, C, G, and T. Imagine every time you had an A, it would automatically attract a G. You'd just have a repetitive sequence: A-G-A-G-A-G-A-G. Would that give you a gene that could produce a protein? Absolutely not. Self-organization wouldn't yield a genetic message, only a repetitive mantra.

"To convey information, you need irregularity in sequencing. Open any book; you won't see the word 'the' repeating over and over and over. Instead, you have an irregular sequencing of letters. They convey information because they conform to a certain known independent pattern—that is, the rules of vocabulary and grammar. That's what enables us to communicate—and that's what needs to be explained in DNA. The four letters of its alphabet are also highly irregular while at the same time conforming to a functional requirement—that is, the correct arrangement of amino acids to create a working protein.

"Here's an example. If you go north of here into Victoria Harbor in British Columbia, you'll see a pattern on a hillside. As the ferry approaches, you'll realize it's a message: red and yellow flowers spell out WELCOME TO VICTORIA. That's an example of an informational sequence.

"Notice you don't have mere repetition—a W followed by an E, followed by another W and another E, and so on. Instead, there's an irregular combination of letters that conform to an independent pattern or specific set of functional requirements—English vocabulary and grammar. So we immediately recognize this as informational. Whenever we encounter these two elements—irregularity that's specified by a set of functional requirements, which is what we call 'specified complexity'—we recognize this as information. And this kind of information is invariably the result of mind—not chance, not natural selection, and not self-organizational processes."

"And this is the kind of information we find in DNA?" I asked.

"That's correct. If all you had were repeating characters in DNA, the assembly instructions would merely tell amino acids to assemble in the same way over and over again. You wouldn't be able to build all the many different kinds of protein molecules you need for a living cell to function. It would be like handing a person an instruction book for how to build an automobile, but all the book said was 'the-the-the-the-the-the.' You couldn't hope to convey all the necessary information with that one-word vocabulary.

"Whereas information requires variability, irregularity, and unpredictability—which is what information theorists call complexity—self-organization gives you repetitive, redundant structure, which is known as simple order. And complexity and order are categorical opposites.

"Chemical evolutionary theorists are not going to escape this. The laws of nature, by definition, describe regular, repetitive patterns. For that reason one cannot invoke self-organizing processes to explain the origin of information, because informational sequences are irregular and complex. They exhibit the 'specified complexity' I talked about. Future discoveries aren't going to change this principle."

To me, this absolutely doomed the idea of chemical affinities accounting for the information in DNA. But Meyer wasn't through. There was yet another devastating problem with this theory.

"If you study DNA," he continued, "you will find that its structure depends on certain bonds that are caused by chemical attractions. For instance, there are hydrogen bonds and bonds between the sugar and phosphate molecules that form the two twisting backbones of the DNA molecule.

"However," he stressed, "there's one place where there are *no* chemical bonds, and that's between the nucleotide bases, which are the chemical letters in the DNA's assembly instructions. In other words, the letters that spell out the text in the DNA message do not interact chemically with each other in any significant way. Also, they're totally interchangeable. Each base can attach with equal facility at any site along the DNA backbone."

Sensing the need for an illustration, Meyer stood and reached over to the desk to grab another child's toy—a metal chalkboard with several magnetic letters sticking to it. Sitting back down, he put the chalkboard on his lap and maneuvered the letters until they spelled the word *INFORMATION*.

"My kids were young when I was first studying this, so I came up with this example," he said. "We know that there are magnetic affinities here; that's why the magnetic letters stick to the metal chalkboard." To demonstrate, he picked up the letter R and let the magnetism pull it back to the board.

"Notice, however, that the magnetic force is the same for each one of the letters, and so they're effectively interchangeable. You can use the letters to spell whatever you want. Now, in DNA, each individual base, or letter, is chemically bonded to the sugar-phosphate backbone of the molecule. That's how they're attached to the DNA's structure. But—and here's the key point—*there is no attraction or bonding between the individual letters themselves.* So there's nothing chemically that forces them into any particular sequence. The sequencing has to come from somewhere else.

"When I show students the magnetic letters sticking to the metal chalkboard, I ask, 'How did this word *INFORMATION* arise?' The answer, of course, is intelligence that comes from outside the system. Neither chemistry nor physics arranged the letters this way. It was my choice. And in DNA, neither chemistry nor physics arranges the letters into the assembly instructions for proteins. Clearly, the cause comes from outside the system."

He paused while the implications sunk in. "And that cause," he stressed, "is *intelligence*."

"ALMOST A MIRACLE"

Like a skillful boxer picking apart the defenses of his opponent, Meyer had adroitly dismantled the three categories of naturalistic explanations for the origin of life and information in DNA. We even discussed another option—the possibility that some external force might be responsible for creating organization, much in the same way gravity creates a vortex as water drains from a bathtub. Meyer quickly dismissed that notion, pointing out that such forces may produce order but they can't manufacture information.[26]

These dead-ends for naturalistic origin-of-life theories would not be a surprise to scientists in the field. When prominent origin-of-life researcher Leslie Orgel ran into another evolutionist at a Detroit conference several years ago, Orgel admitted the overwhelming difficulties he had encountered in trying to figure out how nucleic acids might have been naturally synthesized on the primitive Earth. Then Orgel candidly conceded, "There are equally overwhelming difficulties in the way of all theories."[27]

In short, no hypothesis has come close to explaining how information necessary to life's origin arose by naturalistic means. As Crick, a philosophical materialist, has conceded: "An honest man, armed with all the knowledge available to us now, could only state that in some sense, the origin of life appears at the moment to be almost a miracle, so many are the conditions which would have had to have been satisfied to get it going."[28]

For many researchers, the only recourse has been to continue to have faith that, as one scientist put it, some previously unknown "magic mineral" will be discovered to have had "exactly the right properties to cause the necessary reactions to occur to create a nucleic acid."[29]

"Maybe," I said to Meyer, "someday scientists will come up with another hypothesis."

"Maybe they will," he replied. "You can't prove something like this with one-hundred-percent certainty, because you don't know what new evidence will show. That's why all scientists reason in a way that's provisional. Having said that, though, we do know that some possibilities can be excluded categorically. They're dead ends. For example, I think you can categorically exclude the idea that self-organizational processes can provide new information. More evidence will simply not change that."

"Some skeptics would claim you're arguing from ignorance," I pointed out. "Scientists admit they don't know how life started, so you conclude there must have been an intelligent designer."

"No, not at all. I'm not saying intelligent design makes sense simply because other theories fail," he insisted. "Instead, I'm making an inference to the best explanation, which is how scientists reason in historical matters. Based on the evidence, the scientist assesses each hypothesis on the basis of its ability to explain the evidence at hand. Typically, the key criterion is whether the explanation has 'causal power,' which is the ability to produce the effect in question.

"In this case, the effect in question is information. We've seen that neither chance, nor chance combined with natural selection, nor self-organizational processes have the causal power to produce information. But we do know of one entity that does have the required causal powers to produce information, and that's intelligence. We're not inferring to that entity on the basis of what we *don't* know, but on the basis of what we *do* know. That's not an argument from ignorance."

"Isn't there a fundamental weakness to your argument, though?" I asked. "You're arguing by analogy, comparing the information in DNA to information we find in language. Arguments based on analogies are notoriously weak. Advocates might emphasize the similarities between two things, but opponents will stress the differences."

"I'll admit that there is a way of speaking about the information in DNA that goes too far and then becomes metaphorical," he began. "When people talk about DNA as being a message, that could imply there was a receiver who could 'understand' the message. I'm not saying that DNA is this sort of semantic information.

"However, I'm not arguing by analogy. The coding regions of DNA have *exactly* the same relevant properties as a computer code or language. As I said earlier, whenever you find a sequential arrangement that's complex and corresponds to an independent pattern or functional requirement, this kind of information is *always* the product of intelligence. Books, computer codes, and DNA all have these two properties. We know books and computer codes are designed by intelligence, and the presence of this type of information in DNA also implies an intelligent source.

"Scientists in many fields recognize this connection between information and intelligence. When archaeologists discovered the Rosetta stone, they didn't think its inscriptions were the product of random chance or self-organizational processes. Obviously, the sequential arrangements of symbols was conveying information, and it was a reasonable assumption that intelligence created it. The same principle is true for DNA."

THE BIOLOGICAL BIG BANG

Meyer had made a convincing case that intelligence—and intelligence alone—can explain the presence of precise information within genetic material. By itself, this was impressive evidence for the existence of a designer of life.

As I looked down at my hand and tried to comprehend the vast quantities of complex and specific information inscribed in each cell, a slight smile formed at the corners of my mouth. The answer to the monumental question of whether there's a Creator, I mused, might very well be as close as my own fingertips.

Meyer wasn't finished, however. As he mentioned in our previous interview, he is convinced that the so-called "Cambrian explosion"—in which a dazzling array of new life forms suddenly appears fully formed in the fossil record, without any of the ancestors required by Darwinism—also is powerful evidence of a designer. The reason: this phenomenon would have required the sudden infusion of massive amounts of new genetic and other biological information that only could have come from an intelligent source.

Among other places, Meyer makes that case in "The Cambrian Information Explosion: Evidence for Intelligent Design" in *Debating Design*, recently published by Cambridge University Press. Another extensive piece, "The Cambrian Explosion: Biology's Big Bang," appears in *Darwinism, Design, and Public Education*. Meyer coauthored this analysis with Paul Chien, chairman and professor in the biology department at the University of San Francisco, who worked with leading Chinese scientists on interpreting Cambrian fossils unique to China's Chengjiang region; Paul A. Nelson, a philosopher of biology who earned his doctorate at the University of Chicago; and paleontologist Marcus Ross.

"The fossils of the Cambrian Explosion absolutely cannot be explained by Darwinian theory or even by the concept called 'punctuated equilibrium,' which was specifically formulated in an effort to explain away the embarrassing fossil record," Meyer said. "When you look at the issue from the perspective of biological information, the best explanation is that an intelligence was responsible for this otherwise inexplicable phenomenon."

I leaned back in my chair and crossed my legs to get comfortable. "This sounds fascinating," I said. "Explain what you mean."

Meyer clearly relished the opportunity to elaborate. "New developments in embryology and developmental biology are telling us that DNA, as important as it is, is not the whole show," Meyer began.

"DNA provides some but not all of the information that's needed to build a new organism with a novel form and function. You see, DNA builds proteins, but proteins have to be assembled into larger structures. There are different kinds of cells, and those cells have to be arranged into tissues, and tissues have to be arranged into organs, and organs have to be arranged into overall body plans.

"According to neo-Darwinism, new biological forms are created from mutations in DNA, with natural selection preserving and building on the favorable ones. But if DNA is only part of the story, then you can mutate it indefinitely and you'll never build a fundamentally new body architecture.

"So when you encounter the Cambrian explosion, with its huge and sudden appearance of radically new body plans, you realize you need lots of new biological information. Some of it would be encoded for in DNA—although how that occurs is still an insurmountable problem for Darwinists. But on top of that, where does the new information come from that's not attributable to DNA? How does the hierarchical arrangement of cells, tissues, organs, and body plans develop? Darwinists don't have an answer. It's not even on their radar."

IN THE BLINK OF AN EYE

Using radiometric techniques to date zircon crystals in Siberia, scientists have recently been able to increase their accuracy in pinpointing the time frame of the Cambrian explosion, whose beginning they have determined to be some 530 million years ago.

Paleontologists now think that during a five-million-year (or even shorter) window of time, at least twenty and as many as thirty-five of the world's forty phyla, the highest category in the animal kingdom, sprang forth with unique body plans. In fact, some experts believe that "*all* living phyla may have originated by the end of the explosion."[30]

To put this incredible speed into perspective, if you were to compress all of the Earth's history into twenty-four hours, the Cambrian explosion would consume only about one minute.[31]

"The Cambrian explosion represents an incredible quantum leap in biological complexity," Meyer said. "Before then, life on Earth was pretty simple—one-celled bacteria, blue-green algae, and later some sponges and primitive worms or mollusks. Then without any ancestors in the fossil record, we have a stunning variety of complex creatures appear in the blink of an eye, geologically speaking.

"For example the trilobite—with an articulated body, complicated nervous system, and compound eyes—suddenly shows up fully formed at the beginning of the explosion. It's amazing! And this is followed by stasis, which means the basic body plans remained distinct over the eons.

"All of this totally contradicts Darwinism, which predicted the slow, gradual development in organisms over time. Darwin admitted the Cambrian explosion was 'inexplicable' and 'a valid argument' against his theory. He insisted *natura non facit saltum*—nature takes no leaps.' He thought he would be vindicated, however, as more fossils were discovered, but the picture has only gotten worse.

"The big issue is where did the information come from to build all these new proteins, cells, and body plans? For instance, Cambrian animals would have needed complex proteins, such as *lysyl oxidase*. In animals today, lysyl oxidase molecules require four hundred amino acids. Where did the genetic information come from to build those complicated molecules? This would require highly complex, specified genetic information of the sort that neither random chance, nor natural selection, nor self-organization can produce."

In my interview for Chapter Three, biologist Jonathan Wells had satisfactorily answered my objections to the Cambrian explosion, one of which was that transitional organisms may have been too small or soft to have left a legacy of fossils. Still, another possibility came to mind.

"Maybe," I suggested, "some unexplained environmental phenomenon caused a sudden spate of mutations that accelerated the creation of new organisms."

"That doesn't solve the problem," Meyer replied. "First, even assuming a generous mutation rate, the Cambrian explosion was far too short to have allowed for the kind of large-scale changes that the fossils reflect.

"Second, only mutations in the earliest development of organisms have a realistic chance of producing large-scale macroevolutionary change. And scientists have found that mutations at this stage typically have disastrous effects. The embryo usually dies or is crippled."

Geneticist John F. McDonald has called this "a great Darwinian paradox."[32] The kind of mutations that macroevolution needs—namely, large-scale, beneficial ones—*don't* occur, while the kind it doesn't need—large-scale mutations with harmful effects or small-scale mutations with limited impact—*do* occur, though infrequently.

I brought up another idea that has been offered by some evolutionists. "Why couldn't mutations have occurred in an inactive part of the DNA, sort of a neutral area that wouldn't have had any immediate impact on the organism?" I asked. "Then, after a long period of time during which these mutations could accumulate, a new gene sequence could have suddenly kicked in and created an entirely new protein. Natural selection would then preserve any beneficial effects this would have on the organism."

This theory wasn't new to Meyer. He responded by saying, "Keep in mind that these mutations would have had to occur by random chance, since natural selection can't preserve anything until it confers a positive benefit on the organism. The problem is that the odds of creating a novel functional protein without the help of natural selection would be vanishingly small. There are now a number of studies in molecular biology that establish this. So this so-called 'neutral theory' of evolution is another dead end.

"There's really only one explanation that accounts for all the evidence. In any other field of endeavor, it would be obvious, but many scientists shy away from it in biology. The answer," he said, "is an intelligent designer."

FITTING THE "TOP DOWN" PATTERN

The puzzle of the Cambrian Explosion quickly falls into place once the possibility of a purposeful Creator is allowed as one of the explanatory options. Even one of the explosion's most vexing features—its so-called "top down" pattern of appearance—is efficiently explained by intelligent design.

Said Meyer: "Neo-Darwinism predicts a 'bottom up' pattern in which small differences in form between evolving organisms appear prior to large differences in form and body plan organization. For instance, you might imagine that pre-Cambrian sponges would have given rise to several different varieties. These varieties would have evolved over time to produce different species. As this process continued, wholly different creatures with completely new body plans would have emerged in the Cambrian era.

"Instead, however, fossils from the Cambrian explosion show a radically different 'top down' pattern. Major differences in form and body plans appear first, with no simpler transitions before them. Later, some minor variations arise within the framework of these separate and disparate body plans.

"This has completely stumped neo-Darwinists. Others have tried to explain it away by proposing big leaps of evolutionary change—the so-called punctuated equilibrium idea—but even this can't account for the 'top down' phenomenon. In fact, punctuated equilibrium predicts a 'bottom up' pattern; it just asserts that the increments of evolutionary change would be larger. Yet if you postulate intelligent design, the 'top down' pattern makes sense, because it's the same pattern we see in the history of human technological design."

"Can you give me an example?" I asked.

"Sure—think about cars or airplanes," Meyer replied. "They also manifest a 'top down' pattern of appearance. In both cases, the major blueprint or plan appears fairly suddenly and remains essentially constant over history.

"For instance, all cars have a basic organizational plan that includes a motor, a drive shaft, two axles, four wheels, and so forth. After the basic invention came about, then variations have occurred on the theme over time. That's an example of 'top down' change. The original blueprint was the product of intelligence, and the continuity through the years is explained by an idea being passed from generation to generation of automotive engineers.

"In a similar way, why couldn't the body plans of the Cambrian animals have originated as an idea in the mind of a designer? This would explain why the major differences in form appear first and then subsequent small-scale variations only come later. In fact, intelligence is the only cause we know that produces the kind of 'top down' pattern we see in both the fossil record and in human technology, as illustrated by everything from cars and airplanes to guns and bicycles.[33]

"Intelligence also explains the origin of the layers of information necessary to create the new body plans in the Cambrian animals. As I mentioned earlier, to build a new animal you need DNA to create the proteins and additional information to arrange the proteins into higher level structures. We find the same layering or hierarchical form of organization in human technologies, like a computer's circuit board. Humans use intelligence to produce complex components, such as transistors and capacitors, as well as their specific arrangement and connection within an integrated circuit.

"Once you allow intelligent design as an option, you can quickly see how it accounts for the key features of the Cambrian phenomenon. No other entity explains the sudden appearance of such complex new creatures. No other entity produces 'top down' patterns. No other entity can create the complex and functionally specific information needed for new living forms. No other explanation suffices."

"But intelligent design sounds like such an outmoded concept," I said. "William Paley famously compared biological systems to the workings of a watch more than two hundred years ago. That's old news."

I had struck a nerve. Meyer uncrossed his legs, planted both feet on the floor, and spoke with conviction. "I think the opposite is true," he insisted. "We've learned a lot about biology since the Civil War. Evolutionists are still trying to apply Darwin's nineteenth-century thinking to a twenty-first century reality, and it's not working. Explanations from the era of the steamboat are no longer adequate to explain the biological world of the information age.

"Darwinists say they're under some sort of epistemological obligation to continue trying, because to invoke design would be to give up on science. Well, I say it's time to redefine science. We should not be looking for only the best naturalistic explanation, but the best explanation, period. And intelligent design is the explanation that's most in conformity with how the world works."

A HALLMARK OF MIND

As our interview was drawing to a close, Meyer's reference to the twenty-first century prompted one last line of inquiry. "Fast forward ten or twenty years," I said. "What do you see?"

"I think the information revolution taking place in biology is sounding the death knell for Darwinism and chemical evolutionary theories," he said as he removed his glasses and slipped them into his pocket.

"The attempt to explain the origin of life solely from chemical constituents is effectively dead now. Naturalism cannot answer the fundamental problem of how to get from matter and energy to biological function without the infusion of information from an intelligence.

"Information is not something derived from material properties; in a sense, it transcends matter and energy. Naturalistic theories that rely solely on matter and energy are not going to be able to account for information. Only intelligence can. I think that realization is going to progressively dawn on more and more people, especially younger scientists who have grown up in the age of information technology.

"Today we buy information, we sell it, we regard it as a commodity, we value it, we send it down wires and bounce it off satellites— and we know it invariably comes from intelligent agents. So what do we make of the fact that there's information in life? What do we make of the fact that DNA stores far more information in a smaller space than the most advanced supercomputer on the planet?

"Information is the hallmark of mind. And purely from the evidence of genetics and biology, we can infer the existence of a mind that's far greater than our own—a conscious, purposeful, rational, intelligent designer who's amazingly creative. There's no getting around it."

The cacophony of street noise coming through the half-opened window was getting louder now that rush hour was approaching. Meyer's wife was graciously cooking a salmon dinner for us at their house, and it was time to get on the highway before it got clogged with traffic. As we ended our discussion, Meyer excused himself for a quick meeting in another office, giving me some time to reflect.

Meyer's two rhetorical questions near the conclusion of our discussion effectively summed up the issue. The data at the core of life is not disorganized, it's not simply orderly like salt crystals, but it's complex and specific information that can accomplish a bewildering task—the building of biological machines that far outstrip human technological capabilities.

What else can generate information but intelligence? What else can account for the rapid appearance of a staggering variety of fully formed, complex creatures that have absolutely no transitional intermediates in the fossil record? The conclusion was compelling: an intelligent entity has quite literally spelled out evidence of his existence through the four chemical letters in the genetic code. It's almost as if the Creator autographed every cell.

I sighed and slumped back in my chair, a bit exhausted from my whirlwind of travel and interviews. The case for a Creator was accumulating at a remarkable pace, and I could sense I was approaching the conclusion of my quest. But I also knew there was at least one more expert I needed to consult.

In the closing minutes of our conversation, Meyer had mentioned the word "mind" and referred to conscious activity. As beguiled as I was by DNA, I was equally intrigued by the human brain. Weighing just three pounds, it has ten thousand million nerve cells, each sending out enough fibers to create a thousand million million connections. That's equal to the number of leaves in a dense forest covering a million square miles.[34]

Yet how does all of that circuitry create the unique phenomenon of human consciousness? How does raw biological processing power enable me to reflect, or form beliefs, or make free choices? Is my consciousness only attributable to the physics and chemistry of my brain, or have I also been endowed with an immaterial mind and soul? And if there is persuasive evidence of a soul, what could this tell me about the existence of a Creator—and an afterlife?

I pulled out a small notebook and scribbled myself a note to contact an expert on consciousness as soon as I returned to Los Angeles. I started to slip the pad into my shirt pocket, but instead I stopped and looked at the reminder I had just written.

It was also a reminder of something else. Those few words—a fragment of a sentence—represented information that has its source in my intelligence. How intuitively obvious that a dense array of far more complicated biological assembly instructions must, too, have their origin in a mind.

FOR FURTHER EVIDENCE
More Resources on This Topic

Meyer, Stephen C. "The Cambrian Information Explosion: Evidence for Intelligent Design." In *Debating Design*, eds. Michael Ruse and William Dembski. Cambridge, England: Cambridge University Press, 2004.

———. "DNA and the origin of Life: Information, Specification, and Explanation" and "The Cambrian Explosion:

Biology's Big Bang." In *Darwinism, Design, and Public Education*, eds. John Angus Campbell and Stephen C. Meyer. Lansing, Mich.: Michigan State University Press, 2003.

———. "Evidence for Design in Physics and Biology." In *Science and Evidence for Design in the Universe*, eds. Michael J. Behe, William A. Dembski, and Stephen C. Meyer. San Francisco: Ignatius Press, 1999.

———. "The Explanatory Power of Design: DNA and the Origin of Information." In *Mere Creation*, ed. William A. Dembski. Downer's Grove, Ill.: InterVarsity, 1998, 113–47.

10

THE EVIDENCE OF CONSCIOUSNESS: THE ENIGMA OF THE MIND

Cogito ergo sum—"I think, therefore I am."

René Descartes

Why should a bunch of atoms have thinking ability? Why should I, even as I write now, be able to reflect on what I am doing and why should you, even as you read now, be able to ponder my points, agreeing or disagreeing, with pleasure or pain, deciding to refute me or deciding that I am just not worth the effort? No one, certainly not the Darwinian as such, seems to have any answer to this. . . . The point is that there is no scientific answer.

Darwinist philosopher Michael Ruse[1]

The intelligence of machines will exceed human intelligence early in this century," predicted techno-prophet Ray Kurzweil, recipient of the prestigious National Medal of Technology and called "the ultimate thinking machine" by *Forbes*. "By intelligence, I include all of the diverse and subtle ways in which humans are intelligent—including musical and artistic aptitude, creativity, physically moving, and even responding to emotion.

"By 2019, a thousand-dollar computer will match the processing power of the human brain. . . . By 2050, a thousand dollars of computing will equal the processing power of all human brains on Earth. . . . Will these future machines be capable of having spiritual experiences? They certainly will claim to. *They will claim to be people, and to have the full range of emotional and spiritual experiences that people claim to have.*"[2]

In envisioning the future, Kurzweil's book *The Age of Spiritual Machines* raises the controversial question of whether computers will not only become smarter than people but might also achieve consciousness—and thus become virtually indistinguishable from their biologically based counterparts.

In a sense, Kurzweil's theories are a logical extension of Darwinian evolution. According to Darwinists, the physical world is all that there is. At some point, the human brain evolved, with its raw processing power increasing over the eons. When the brain reached a certain level of structure and complexity, people became "conscious"—that is, they suddenly developed subjectivity, feelings, hopes, a point of view, self-awareness, introspection, that "hidden voice of our private selves."

As far back as 1871, Darwin advocate Thomas Huxley said: "Mind [or consciousness] is a function of matter, when that matter has attained a certain degree of organization."[3] Darwinists today agree that "conscious experience is a physical and not a supernatural phenomenon," as sociobiologist Edward O. Wilson said.[4]

If consciousness really is the automatic byproduct of increasingly sophisticated brain power, then why couldn't super-smart robots become conscious when they achieve a bigger brain capacity than people? Once the basic Darwinian premise is accepted, then Kurzweil's futuristic scenario suddenly seems possible.

"If you can get a computer to take on any structure you like, and if consciousness is generated by structure, then by definition that kind of structure is going to eventually give you consciousness," said David Chalmers, codirector of the Center for Consciousness Studies at the University of Arizona.[5]

Kurzweil's predictions, however, have been assailed by critics who say computer consciousness is absurd. "I cannot recall reading a book in which there is such a huge gulf between the spectacular claims advanced and the weakness of the arguments given in their support," scoffed John Searle, a professor of mind at the University of California at Berkeley.[6] "You can expand the power all you want, hooking up as many computers as you think you need, and they still won't be conscious, because all they'll ever do is shuffle symbols."[7]

Said William Dembski of the Conceptual Foundations of Science at Baylor University: "Kurzweil is peddling science fiction and bad philosophy."[8]

As fascinating as this debate over futuristic computers has been, there still remains a much more important controversy over *human* consciousness. Amazingly, many scientists and philosophers are now concluding that the laws of physics and chemistry cannot explain the experience of consciousness in human beings. They are convinced that there is more than just the physical brain at work, but there also is a nonmaterial reality called the "soul," "mind," or "self" that accounts for our sentience.

In fact, they cite its very existence as strong evidence against the purely naturalistic theory of Darwinian evolution and in favor of a Creator who imbued humankind with his image.

THE CONTROVERSY OVER CONSCIOUSNESS

One scientist whose opinions were reversed on the issue is Wilder Penfield, the renowned father of modern neurosurgery. He started out suspecting that consciousness somehow emanated from the neural activities in the brain, where synapses can fire an astounding ten million billion times a second. "Through my own scientific career, I, like other scientists, have struggled to prove that the brain accounts for the mind," he said.[9]

But through performing surgery on more than a thousand epileptic patients, he encountered concrete evidence that the brain and mind are actually distinct from each other, although they clearly interact. Explained one expert in the field:

> Penfield would stimulate electrically the proper motor cortex of conscious patients and challenge them to keep one hand from moving when the current was applied. The patient would seize this hand with the other hand and struggle to hold it still. Thus one hand under the control of the electrical current and the other hand under the control of the patient's mind fought against each other. Penfield risked the explanation that the patient had not only a physical brain that was stimulated to action but also a nonphysical reality that interacted with the brain.[10]

In other words, Penfield ended up agreeing with the Bible's assertion that human beings are both body and spirit. "To expect the highest brain mechanism or any set of reflexes, however complicated, to carry out what the mind does, and thus perform all the functions of the mind, is quite absurd,"[11] he said. "What a thrill it is, then, to discover that the scientist, too, can legitimately believe in the existence of the spirit."[12]

Similarly, Oxford University professor of physiology Sir Charles Sherrington, a Nobel Prize winner described as "a genius who laid the foundations of our knowledge of the functioning of the brain and spinal cord,"[13] declared five days before his death: "For me now, the only reality is the human soul."[14]

As for his one-time student John C. Eccles, himself an eminent neurophysiologist and Nobel laureate, his ultimate conclusion is the same. "I am constrained," he said, "to believe that there is what we might call a supernatural origin of my unique self-conscious mind or my unique selfhood or soul."[15]

But is it really rational in the twenty-first century to believe in John Calvin's sixteenth-century claim that "the endowments we possess cannot possibly be from ourselves," but that they must have a divine source?[16] Is the Bible's insistence that people consist of both body and spirit—a belief called "dualism"—a defensible assertion?[17] Or is the human brain simply, in the famous words of MIT's Marvin Minsky, "a computer made of meat," with conscious thought as its wholly mechanical output?

Consciousness, declared Searle, is "the single most important fact about our existence, except for life itself."[18] It was clear to me that the answer to the mystery of our mind would either be a powerful confirmation of Darwinian naturalism or a persuasive affirmation of a far greater mind in whose likeness we were created.

SURPASSING THE BRAIN'S BOUNDARIES

It was a news dispatch from the front lines of the scientific investigation of human consciousness. Published by the journal *Resuscitation* and presented to scientists at the California Institute of Technology in 2001, the year-long British study provided evidence that consciousness continues after a person's brain has stopped functioning and he or she has been declared clinically dead.[19] It was dramatic new evidence that the brain and mind are not the same, but they're distinct entities.

"The research," said Reuters journalist Sarah Tippit, "resurrects the debate over whether there is life after death and whether there is such a thing as the human soul."[20]

In their journal article, physician Sam Parnia and Peter Fenwick, a neuropsychiatrist at the Institute of Psychiatry in London, describe their study of sixty-three heart attack victims who were declared clinically dead but were later revived and interviewed. About ten percent reported having well-structured, lucid thought processes, with memory formation and reasoning, during the time that their brains were not functioning. The effects of oxygen starvation or drugs—objections commonly offered by skeptics—were ruled out as factors. Later, the researchers found numerous cases that were similar.[21]

While large-scale studies are still needed, the once-skeptical Parnia said the scientific findings so far "would support the view that mind, 'consciousness,' or the 'soul' is a separate entity from the brain."[22]

He speculated that the brain might serve as a mechanism to manifest the mind, much in the same way a television set manifests pictures and sounds from waves in the air. If an injury to the brain causes a person to lose some aspects of his mind or personality, this doesn't necessarily prove that the brain was the source of the mind. "All it shows is that the apparatus is damaged," he said.[23]

Active research is continuing in this area and into other aspects of human consciousness.[24] Meanwhile, the scientists who are committed to finding a purely physical answer—appropriately called "physicalists"—are candid in admitting that they currently have no explanation for how the brain might spawn consciousness.

Conceded Searle: "We don't have an adequate theory of how the brain causes conscious states, and we don't have an adequate theory of how consciousness fits into the universe."[25]

Still, Searle and many others find refuge in their unshakable faith that science will eventually discover a completely naturalistic explanation. Given Darwinism as a non-negotiable starting point, there's really no other choice.

"I am firmly in the confident camp—a substantial explanation for the mind's emergence from the brain will be produced and perhaps soon," predicted professor of neurology Antonio R. Damasio. "The giddy feeling, however, is tempered by the acknowledgment of some sobering difficulties."[26]

Eccles calls this kind of attitude "promissory materialism . . . extravagant and unfulfillable."[27] Instead, many researchers are following Eccles's example by pursuing the evidence of science and the logic of philosophy wherever they lead, even if they point toward dualism. Said anthropologist Marilyn Schlitz:

I would take the position of a radical empiricist, in that I am driven by data, not theory. And the data I see tell me that there are ways in which people's experience refutes the physicalist position that the mind is the brain and nothing more. There are solid, concrete data that suggest that our consciousness, our mind, may surpass the boundaries of the brain.[28]

As for the Bible, both the Old and New Testaments consistently teach that humans are "a hyphenate creature, a spirit/body dichotomy," said anthropologist Arthur C. Custance. Then, quite significantly, he added: "To this extent there is no quarrel between theology and the findings of recent research."[29] Custance continued:

[The Bible] makes it very clear that when the soul or spirit leaves the body, the body is dead and that if the spirit is somehow returned to the body, the whole person comes back to life.[30] This duality is repeated in hundreds of places in the Bible[31]. . . . Indeed the formation of Adam as the first human being is expressly stated as the result of the animation of a body by a spirit, constituting it as a living soul.[32]

Do Christianity and contemporary research really support each other, while at the same time contradicting the Darwinian claim that the brain is solely responsible for consciousness? As I went looking for answers, I didn't have to travel far from my home in Southern California. It was just a short drive to the house of a prominent professor trained in science, philosophy, and theology, who has pondered and written about these topics for years.

INTERVIEW #8: J. P. MORELAND, PHD

When I pulled up to J. P. Moreland's house on a cool and foggy morning, he was outside with a cup of coffee in his hand, having just walked home from a chat with some neighbors. His graying hair was close-cropped, his mustache neatly trimmed, and he was looking natty in a red tie, blue shirt, and dark slacks.

"Good to see you again," he said as we shook hands. "Come on in."

We walked into his living room, where he settled into a floral-patterned chair and I eased into an adjacent couch. The setting was familiar to me, since I had previously interviewed him on other challenging topics for *The Case for Christ* and *The Case for Faith*.[33] Both times I found him to have an uncanny ability to discuss abstract issues and technical matters in understandable but accurate language. That's unusual for a scientist, uncommon for a theologian, and downright rare for a philosopher!

Moreland's science training came at the University of Missouri, where he received a degree in chemistry. He was subsequently awarded the top fellowship for a doctorate in nuclear chemistry at the University of Colorado but declined the honor to pursue a different career path. He then earned a master's degree in theology at Dallas Theological Seminary and a doctorate in philosophy at the University of Southern California.

Moreland developed an early interest in issues relating to human consciousness, returning to that theme time after time in his various books. He has written, edited, or coauthored *Christianity and the Nature of Science, Body and Soul, The Life and Death Debate, Beyond Death, Does God Exist? Christian Perspectives on Being Human, The Creation Hypothesis, Scaling the Secular City, Love Your God with All Your Mind, Naturalism: A Critical Analysis,* and other books.

Also, he has authored more than fifty technical articles for *Perspectives on Science and Christian Faith, Philosophy and Phenomenological Research, American Philosophical Quarterly, Journal of Psychology and Theology, Metaphilosophy,* and a host of other journals. Moreland's memberships include national scientific, philosophical, and theological societies. Currently, he's a professor in the highly respected philosophy program at the Talbot School of Theology, where he teaches on numerous topics, including philosophy of mind.

As we began our interview, I thought it would be a good idea to get straight on some key definitions—something that's not always easy when discussing consciousness.

REGAINING CONSCIOUSNESS

U.S. Supreme Court Justice Potter Stewart once said it may be difficult to define pornography, "but I know it when I see it."[34] Similarly, consciousness can be a challenging concept to describe, even though our own conscious thoughts are quite tangible to ourselves. As J. R. Smythies of the University of Edinburgh put it: "The consciousness of other people may be for me an abstraction, but my own consciousness is for me a reality."[35]

"What is consciousness?" Moreland said, echoing the opening question that I had just posed to him. "Well, a simple definition is that consciousness is what you're aware of when you introspect. When you pay attention to what's going on inside of you, that's consciousness."

He looked at me and apparently could see from my expression that I needed a fuller description. "Think of it like this," he continued. "Suppose you were having an operation on your leg, and suddenly you begin to be aware of people talking about you. Someone says, 'I think he's recovering.' You start to feel an ache in your knee. You say to yourself, 'Where am I? What's going on?' And you start to remember you were operated on. What you're doing is regaining consciousness. In short, consciousness consists of sensations, thoughts, emotions, desires, beliefs, and free choices that make us alive and aware."

"What if consciousness didn't exist in the world?" I asked.

"I'll give you an example," Moreland replied. "Apples would still be red, but there would be no awareness of red or any sensations of red."

"What about the soul?" I asked. "How would you define that?"

"The soul is the ego, the 'I,' or the self, and it contains our consciousness. It also animates our body. That's why when the soul leaves the body, the body becomes a corpse. The soul is immaterial and distinct from the body."

"At least," I observed, "that's what the Bible teaches."

"Yes, Christians have understood this for twenty centuries," he said. "For example, when Jesus was on the cross, he told the thief being crucified next to him that he would be with Jesus immediately after his death and before the final resurrection of his body.[36] Jesus described the body and soul as being separate entities when he said, 'Do not be afraid of those who kill the body but cannot kill the soul.'[37] The apostle Paul says that to be absent from the body is to be present with the Lord."[38]

I was curious about whether belief in the soul is a universal phenomenon. "What about beyond Christianity?" I asked. "Is this concept present in other cultures as well?"

"We know that dualism was taught by the ancient Greeks, although, unlike Christians, they believed the body and soul were alien toward each other," he explained. "In contemporary terms, I'd agree with physicalist Jaegwon Kim, who acknowledged that 'something like this dualism of personhood, I believe, is common lore shared across most cultures and religious traditions.'"[39]

Still, there are those who deny dualism and instead believe we are solely physical beings who are, as geneticist Francis Crick said, "no more than the behavior of a vast assembly of nerve cells and their associated molecules."[40] To explore this issue, I decided to take an unusual approach in my interview with Moreland by asking him to imagine—for just a few minutes—that these physicalists are right.

WHAT IF PHYSICALISM IS TRUE?

"Let's face it," I said, "some people flatly deny that we have an immaterial soul. John Searle said, 'In my worldview, consciousness is caused by brain processes.'[41] In other words, they believe consciousness is purely a product of biology. As brain scientist Barry Beyerstein said, just as the kidneys produce urine, the brain produces consciousness."[42]

Moreland was listening carefully as I spoke, his head slightly cocked. I continued by saying, "Do me a favor, J. P.—assume for a moment that the physicalists are right. What are the logical implications if physicalism is true?"

His eyes widened. "Oh, there would be several key ones," he replied.

"Give me three," I said.

Moreland was more than willing. "First, if physicalism is true, then consciousness doesn't really exist, because there would be no such thing as conscious states that must be described from a first-person point of view," he said.

"You see, if everything were matter, then you could capture the entire universe on a graph—you could locate each star, the moon, every mountain, Lee Strobel's brain, Lee Strobel's kidneys, and so forth. That's because if everything is physical, it could be described entirely from a third-person point of view. And yet we know that we have first-person, subjective points of view—so physicalism can't be true."

Clearly, Moreland was warming up to this exercise. "The second implication," he continued, "is that there would be no free will. That's because matter is completely governed by the laws of nature. Take any physical object," he said as he glanced out the window, where the fog was breaking up. "For instance, a cloud," he said. "It's just a material object, and its movement is completely governed by the laws of air pressure, wind movement, and the like. So if I'm a material object, all of the things I do are fixed by my environment, my genetics, and so forth.

"That would mean I'm not really free to make choices. Whatever's going to happen is already rigged by my makeup and environment. So how could you hold me responsible for my behavior if I wasn't free to choose how I would act? This is one of the reasons we lost the Vietnam War."

I was following him until that last statement, which seemed oddly incongruous to me. "What has this got to do with Vietnam?" I asked.

Moreland explained: "I heard a former advisor to the president say that B. F. Skinner's behaviorism influenced the Pentagon's strategy. Skinner believed that we're just physical objects, so you can condition people, just like you can condition a laboratory animal by applying electric shocks. Keep doing certain things over and over, and you can change behavior. So in Vietnam, we bombed, we came back, we bombed, we came back, we bombed, and so forth. We assumed that after we gave the North Vietnamese shock after shock, pretty soon we could manipulate their behavior. After all, they're just physical objects responding to stimuli. Eventually they *had* to give in."

"But they didn't," I said.

"That's right. It didn't work."

"Why?"

"Because there was more to the Vietnamese than their physical brains responding to stimuli. They have souls, desires, feelings, and beliefs, and they could make free choices to suffer and to stand firm for their convictions despite our attempt to condition them by our bombing.

"So if the materialists are right, kiss free will good-bye. In their view, we're just very complicated computers that behave according to the laws of nature and the programming we receive. But, Lee, obviously they're wrong—we *do* have free will. We all know that deep down inside. We're more than just a physical brain.

"Third, if physicalism were true, there would be no disembodied intermediate state. According to Christianity, when we die, our souls leave our bodies and await the later resurrection of our bodies from the dead. We don't cease to exist when we die. Our souls are living on.

"This happens in near-death experiences. People are clinically dead, but sometimes they have a vantage point from above, where they look down at the operating table that their body is on. Sometimes they gain information they couldn't have known if this were just an illusion happening in their brain. One woman died and she saw a tennis shoe that was on the roof of the hospital. How could she have known this?

"If I am just my brain, then existing outside the body is utterly impossible. When people hear of near-death experiences, they don't think that if they looked up at the hospital ceiling, they'd see a pulsating brain with a couple of eyeballs dangling down, right? When people hear near-death stories, Lee, they are intuitively attributing to that person a soul that could leave the body. And clearly these stories make sense, even if we're not sure they're true. We've got to be more than our bodies or else these stories would be ludicrous to us."

Moreland seemed to be sidestepping this issue a bit. "How about you personally?" I asked. "Do you think near-death experiences are true?"

"We have to be careful with the data and not overstate things, but I do think they provide at least a minimalist case for consciousness surviving death," he said. "In fact, as far back as 1965, psychologist John Beloff wrote in *The Humanist* that the evidence of near-death experiences already indicates 'a dualistic world where mind or spirit has an existence separate from the world of material things.' He conceded that this could 'present a challenge to humanism as profound in its own way as that which Darwinian evolution did to Christianity a century ago.'"[43]

Moreland paused before adding one other comment. "Regardless of what anyone thinks about near-death experiences, we do have confirmation that Jesus was put to death and was later seen alive by credible eyewitnesses," he said.[44] "Not only does this provide powerful historical corroboration that it's possible to survive after the death of our physical body, but it also gives Jesus great credibility when he teaches that we have both a body and an immaterial spirit."

THE INNER AND PRIVATE MIND

At this point, having considered Moreland's critique of physicalism, I wanted to hear his affirmative case that consciousness and the soul are immaterial entities. "What positive evidence is there that consciousness and the self are not merely a physical process of the brain?" I asked.

"We have experimental data, for one thing," he replied. "For example, neurosurgeon Wilder Penfield electrically stimulated the brains of epilepsy patients and found he could cause them to move their arms or legs, turn their heads or eyes, talk, or swallow. Invariably the patient would respond by saying, 'I didn't do that. You did.'[45] According to Penfield, 'the patient thinks of himself as having an existence separate from his body.'[46]

"No matter how much Penfield probed the cerebral cortex, he said, 'There is no place . . . where electrical stimulation will cause a patient to believe or to decide.'[47] That's because those functions originate in the conscious self, not the brain.

"A lot of subsequent research has validated this. When Roger Sperry and his team studied the differences between the brain's right and left hemispheres, they discovered the mind has a causal power independent of the brain's activities. This led Sperry to conclude materialism was false.[48]

"Another study showed a delay between the time an electric shock was applied to the skin, its reaching the cerebral cortex, and the self-conscious perception of it by the person.[49] This suggests the self is more than just a machine that reacts to stimuli as it receives them. In fact, the data from various research projects are so remarkable that Laurence C. Wood said, 'many brain scientists have been compelled to postulate the existence of an immaterial mind, even though they may not embrace a belief in an after-life.'"[50]

"What about beyond the laboratory?" I asked.

"There are valid philosophical arguments as well," he said. "For instance, I know that consciousness isn't a physical phenomenon because there are things that are true of my consciousness that aren't true of anything physical."

"For instance . . . ," I said, prompting him further.

"For example, some of my thoughts have the attribute of being true. Tragically, some of my thoughts have the attribute of being false—like the Chicago Bears are going to go to the Super Bowl," he said with a chuckle. "However, none of my brain states are true or false. No scientist can look at the state of my brain and say, 'Oh, that particular brain state is true and that one's false.' So there's something true of my conscious states that are not true of any of my brain states, and consequently they can't be the same thing.

"Nothing in my brain is *about* anything. You can't open up my head and say, 'You see this electrical pattern in the left hemisphere of

J. P. Moreland's brain? That's about the Bears.' Your brain states aren't *about* anything, but some of my mental states are. So they're different.

"Furthermore, my consciousness is inner and private to me. By simply introspecting, I have a way of knowing about what's happening in my mind that is not available to you, my doctor, or a neuroscientist. A scientist could know more about what's happening in my brain than I do, but he couldn't know more about what's happening in my mind than I do. He has to ask me."

When I asked Moreland for an illustration of this, he said, "Have you heard of Rapid Eye Movement?"

"Sure," I replied.

"What does it indicate?"

"Dreaming."

"Exactly. How do scientists know that when there is a certain eye movement that people are dreaming? They've had to wake people and ask them. Scientists could watch the eyes move and read a printout of what was physically happening in the brain, so they could correlate brain states with eye movements. But they didn't know what was happening in the mind. Why? Because that's inner and private.

"So the scientist can know about the brain by studying it, but he can't know about the mind without asking the person to reveal it, because conscious states have the feature of being inner and private, but the brain's states don't."

THE REALITY OF THE SOUL

For centuries, the human soul has enchanted poets, intrigued theologians, challenged philosophers, and dumbfounded scientists. Mystics, like Teresa of Àvila in the sixteenth century, have described it eloquently: "I began to think of the soul as if it were a castle made of a single diamond or of very clear crystal, in which there are many rooms, just as in heaven there are many mansions."[51]

Moreland was understandably more precise in analyzing the soul, though unfortunately less poetic. He had already clarified that the soul contains our consciousness. Still, he hadn't offered any reason to believe that the soul is an actual entity. It was time, I felt, to press him on this issue. "What makes you think that the soul is real?" I asked.

Moreland replied by saying, "First, we're aware that we're different from our consciousness and our body. We know that we're beings who have consciousness and a body, but we're not merely the same thing as our conscious life or our physical life.

"Let me give you an illustration of how we're not the same thing as our personality traits, our memories, and our consciousness. I had a student a few years ago whose sister had a terrible accident on her honeymoon. She was knocked unconscious and lost all of her memories and a good bit of her personality. She did not believe she had been married. As she began to recover, they showed her videos of the wedding to convince her that she had actually married her husband. She eventually got to the point where she believed it, and she got remarried to him.

"Now, we all knew this was the same person all along. This was Jamie's sister. She was not a different person, though she was behaving differently. But she had totally different memories. She had lost her old memories and she didn't even have the same personality. What that proves is you can be the same person even if you lose old memories and gain new memories, or you lose some of your old personality traits and gain new personality traits.

"Now, if I were just my consciousness, when my consciousness was different, I'd be a different person. But we know that I can be the same person even though my consciousness changes, so I can't be the same thing as my consciousness. I've got to be the 'self,' or soul, that contains my consciousness.

"Same with my body. I can't be the same thing as my body or brain. There was a story on television about an epileptic who underwent an operation in which surgeons removed fifty-three percent of her brain. When she woke up, nobody said, 'We have forty-seven percent of a person here.' A person can't be divided into pieces. You are either a person or you're not. But your brain and your body can be divided. So that means I can't be the same thing as my body."

Those illustrations helped, though I said, "The fact that the soul and consciousness are invisible makes it difficult to conceptualize them."

"Sure, that's true," he replied. "My soul and my consciousness are invisible, though my body is visible. That's another distinction. In fact, I remember the time when my daughter was in the fifth grade and we were having family prayers. She said, 'Dad, if I could see God, it would help me believe in him.' I said, 'Well, honey, the problem isn't that you've never seen God. The problem is that you've never seen your mother.' And her mother was sitting right next to her!

"My daughter said, 'What do you mean, Dad?' I said, 'Suppose without hurting your mom, we were able to take her apart cell by cell and peek inside each one of them. We would never come to a moment where we would say, 'Look—here's what Mommy's thinking about doing the rest of the day.' Or 'Hey, this cell contains Mommy's feelings.' Or 'So this is what Mom believes about pro football.' We couldn't find Mommy's thoughts, beliefs, desires, or her feelings.

"'Guess what else we would never find? We'd never find Mommy's ego or her self. We would never say, 'Finally, in this particular brain cell, *there's* Mommy. There's her ego, or self.' That's because Mommy is a person, and persons are invisible. Mommy's ego and her conscious life are invisible. Now, she's small enough to have a body, while God is too big to have a body—so let's pray!'

"The point is this, Lee: I *am* a soul, and I *have* a body. We don't learn about people by studying their bodies. We learn about people by finding out how they feel, what they think, what they're passionate about, what their worldview is, and so forth. Staring at their body might tell us whether they like exercise, but that's not very helpful. That's why we want to get 'inside' people to learn about them.

"So my conclusion is that there's more to me than my conscious life and my body. In fact, I am a 'self,' or an 'I,' that cannot be seen or touched unless I manifest myself through my behavior or my talk. I have free will because I'm a 'self,' or a soul, and I'm not just a brain."

OF COMPUTERS AND BATS

Moreland's denial that the brain produces consciousness made me think of the debate over whether future computers can become sentient. I decided to ask him to weigh in on the issue—although his ultimate conclusion was never in doubt.

"If a machine can achieve equal or greater brain power as human beings, then some physicalists say the computer would become conscious," I said. "I assume you would disagree with that."

Moreland chuckled. "One atheist said that when computers reach the point of imitating human behavior, only a racist would deny them full human rights. But of course that's absurd. Nobel-winner John Eccles said he's 'appalled by the naiveté' of those who foresee computer sentience. He said there's 'no evidence whatsoever for the statement made that, at an adequate level of complexity, computers also would achieve self-consciousness.'[52]

"Look, we have to remember that computers have artificial intelligence, not intelligence. And there's a huge difference. There's no 'what it's like to be a computer.' A computer has no 'insides,' no awareness, no first-person point of view, no insights into problems. A computer doesn't think, 'You know what? I now see what this multiplication problem is really like.' A computer can engage in behavior if it's wired properly, but you've got to remember that consciousness is *not* the same as behavior. Consciousness is being alive; it's what *causes* behavior in really conscious beings. But what causes behavior in a computer is electric circuitry.

"Let me illustrate my point. Suppose we had a computerized bat that we knew absolutely everything about from a physical point of view. We would have exhaustive knowledge of all its circuitry so that we could predict everything this bat would do when it was released into the environment.

"Contrast that with a real bat. Suppose we knew everything about the organs inside the bat—its blood system, nervous system, brain, heart, lungs. And suppose that we could predict everything this bat would do when released into the environment. There would still be one thing that we would have no idea about: *what it's like to be a bat.* What it's like to hear, to feel, to experience sound and color. That stuff involves the 'insides' of the bat, its point of view. That's the difference between a conscious, sentient bat and a computerized bat.

"So in general, computers might be able to imitate intelligence, but they won't ever have consciousness. We can't confuse behavior with what it's like to be alive, awake, and sentient. A future superintelligent computer might be programmed to say it's conscious or even behave as if it were conscious, but it can never truly become conscious, because consciousness is an immaterial entity apart from the brain."

Moreland's choice of a bat for his illustration was an oblique reference to New York University philosopher Thomas Nagel's famous 1974 essay "What Is it Like to Be a Bat?"[53] Thinking about life from a bat's perspective prompted me to briefly pursue another line of inquiry on a tangential topic. "What about animals—do they have souls or consciousness?" I asked.

"Absolutely," came his quick answer. "In several places the Bible uses the word 'soul' or 'spirit' when discussing animals.[54] Animals are not simply machines. They have consciousness and points of view.

But the animal soul is much simpler than the human soul. For example, the human soul is capable of free moral action, but I think the animal soul is determined. Also, Augustine said animals have thoughts, but they don't think about their thinking. And while we have beliefs about our beliefs, animals don't.

"You see, the human soul is vastly more complicated because it's made in the image of God. So we have *self*-reflection and *self*-thinking. And while the human soul survives the death of its body, I don't think the animal soul outlives its body. I could be wrong, but I think the animal soul ceases to exist at death."

Bad news, it seems, for the bat.

CONSCIOUSNESS AND EVOLUTION

Moreland had made a cogent case for consciousness and the soul being independent of our brain and body. "How does this present a problem for Darwinists?" I asked.

Moreland glanced down at some notes he had brought along. "As philosopher Geoffrey Medell said, 'The emergence of consciousness, then, is a mystery, and one to which materialism fails to provide an answer.' Atheist Colin McGinn agrees. He asks, 'How can mere matter originate consciousness? How did evolution convert the water of biological tissue into the wine of consciousness? Consciousness seems like a radical novelty in the universe, not prefigured by the aftereffects of the Big Bang. So how did it contrive to spring into being from what preceded it?'"

Moreland looked squarely at me. "Here's the point: *you can't get something from nothing*," he declared. "It's as simple as that. If there were no God, then the history of the entire universe, up until the appearance of living creatures, would be a history of dead matter with no consciousness. You would not have any thoughts, beliefs, feelings, sensations, free actions, choices, or purposes. There would be simply one physical event after another physical event, behaving according to the laws of physics and chemistry."

Moreland stopped for a moment to make sure this picture was vivid in my mind. Then he leaned forward and asked pointedly: "How, then, do you get something totally different—conscious, living, thinking, feeling, believing creatures—from materials that don't have that? That's getting something from nothing! And that's the main problem.

"If you apply a physical process to physical matter, you're going to get a different arrangement of physical materials. For example, if you apply the physical process of heating to a bowl of water, you're going to get a new product—steam—which is just a more complicated form of water, but it's still physical. And if the history of the universe is just a story of physical processes being applied to physical materials, you'd end up with increasingly complicated arrangements of physical materials, but you're not going to get something that's completely nonphysical. That is a jump of a totally different kind.

"At the end of the day, as Phillip Johnson put it, you either have 'In the beginning were the particles,' or 'In the beginning was the Logos,' which means 'divine mind.' If you start with particles, and the history of the universe is just a story about the rearrangement of particles, you may end up with a more complicated arrangement of particles, but you're still going to have particles. You're not going to have minds or consciousness.

"However—and this is really important—if you begin with an *infinite* mind, then you can explain how finite minds could come into existence. That makes sense. What doesn't make sense—and which many atheistic evolutionists are conceding—is the idea of getting a mind to squirt into existence by starting with brute, dead, mindless matter. That's why some of them are trying to get rid of consciousness by saying it's not real and that we're just computers."

He smiled after that last statement, then added: "However, that's a pretty difficult position to maintain while you're conscious!"

THE EMERGENCE OF THE MIND

"Still," I protested, "some scientists maintain that consciousness is just something that happens as a natural byproduct of our brain's complexity. They believe that once evolution gave us sufficient brain capacity, consciousness inexorably emerges as a biological process."

"Let me mention four problems with that," Moreland insisted. "First, they are no longer treating matter as atheists and naturalists treat matter—namely, as brute stuff that can be completely described by the laws of chemistry and physics. Now they're attributing spooky, soulish, or mental potentials to matter."

"What do you mean by 'potentials'?"

"They're saying that prior to this level of complexity, matter contained the potential for mind to emerge—and at the right moment, guess what happened? These potentials were activated and consciousness was sparked into existence."

"What's wrong with that theory?"

"That is no longer naturalism," he said. "That's panpsychism."

That was a new term to me. "Pan *what*?"

"*Panpsychism*," he repeated. "It's the view that matter is not just inert physical stuff, but that it also contains proto-mental states in it. Suddenly, they've abandoned a strict scientific view of matter and adopted a view that's closer to theism than to atheism. Now they're saying that the world began not just with matter, but with stuff that's mental *and* physical at the same time. Yet they can't explain where these pre-emergent mental properties came from in the first place. And this also makes it hard for them to argue against the emergence of God."

"The *emergence* of God?" I asked. "What do you mean by that?"

"If a finite mind can emerge when matter reaches a certain level of complexity, why couldn't a far greater mind—God—emerge when millions of brain states reach a greater level of consciousness? You see, they want to stop the process where they want it to stop—at themselves—but you can't logically draw that line. How can they know that a very large God hasn't emerged from matter, because, after all, haven't a lot of people had religious experiences with God?"

"That wouldn't be the God of Christianity," I pointed out.

"Granted," he replied. "But this is still a problem for atheists. And there's a second problem: they would still be stuck with determinism, because if consciousness is just a function of the brain, then I'm my brain, and my brain functions according to the laws of chemistry and physics. To them, the mind is to the brain as smoke is to fire. Fire causes smoke, but smoke doesn't cause anything. It's just a byproduct. Thus, they're locked into determinism.

"Third, if mind emerged from matter without the direction of a superior Intelligence, why should we trust anything from the mind as being rational or true, especially in the area of theoretical thinking?

"Let me give you an analogy. Let's say you had a computer that was programmed by random forces or by nonrational laws without a mind being behind it. Would you trust a printout from that machine? Of course not. Well, same with the mind—and that's a problem for Darwinists. And by the way, you can't use evolution as an explanation for why the mind should be considered trustworthy, because theoretical thinking does not contribute to survival value."

Moreland's comments reminded me of the famous quote from British evolutionist J. B. S. Haldane: "If my mental processes are determined wholly by the motions of the atoms in my brain, I have no reason to suppose that my beliefs are true . . . and hence I have no reason for supposing my brain to be composed of atoms."[55]

"Here's the fourth problem," Moreland went on, "If my mind were just a function of the brain, there would be no unified self. Remember, brain function is spread throughout the brain, so if you cut the brain in half, like the girl who lost fifty-three percent of her brain, then some of that function is lost. Now you've got forty-seven percent of a person. Well, nobody believes that. We all know she's a unified self, because we all know her consciousness and soul are separate entities from her brain.

"There's one other aspect of this, called the 'binding problem.' When you look around the room, you see many things at the same time," he said, gesturing around at various objects in our field of vision. "You see a table, a couch, a wall, a painting in a frame. Every individual thing has light waves bouncing off of it and they're striking a different location in your eyeball and sparking electrical activity in a different region of the brain. That means there is no single part of the brain that is activated by all of these experiences. Consequently, if I were simply my physical brain, I would be a crowd of different parts, each having its own awareness of a different piece of my visual field.

"But that's not what happens. I'm a unified 'I' that has all of these experiences at the same time. There is something that binds all of these experiences and unifies them into the experience of oneself—me—even though there is no region of the brain that has all these activation sites. That's because my consciousness and my 'self' are separate entities from the brain."

Moreland was on a roll, but I jumped in anyway. "What about recent brain studies that have shown activity in certain areas of the brain during meditation and prayer?" I asked. "Don't those demonstrate that there's a physical basis for these religious experiences, as opposed to an immaterial basis through the soul?"

"No, it doesn't. All it shows is a physical *correlation* with religious experiences," he replied.

"You'll have to explain that," I said.

"Well, there's no question that when I'm praying, smelling a rose, or thinking about something, my brain still exists. It doesn't pop out of existence when I'm having a conscious life, including prayer. And I would be perfectly happy if scientists were to measure what was going on in my brain while I'm praying, feeling forgiveness, or even thinking about lunch. But remember: just because there is a correlation between two things, that doesn't mean they're the same thing. Just because there's a correlation between fire and smoke, this doesn't mean smoke is the same as fire.

"Now, sometimes your brain states can cause your conscious states. For example, if you lose brain functioning due to Alzheimer's disease, or you get hit over the head, you lose some of your mental conscious life. But there's also evidence that this goes the other way as well. There are data showing that your conscious life can actually reconfigure your brain.

"For example, scientists have done studies of the brains of people who worried a lot, and they found that this mental state of worry changed their brain chemistry. They've done studies of the brain patterns of little children who were not nurtured and loved, and their patterns are different than children who have warm experiences of love and nurture. So it's not just the brain that causes things to happen in our conscious life; conscious states can also cause things to happen to the brain.

"Consequently, I wouldn't want to say there's a physical basis for religious experiences, even though they might be correlated. Sometimes it could be cause-and-effect from brain to mind, but it could also be cause-and-effect from mind to brain. How do the scientists know it isn't actually my prayer life that's causing something to happen in my brain, rather than the other way around?"[56]

THE RETURN OF OCKHAM'S RAZOR

As we talked about the human mind, mine was drifting back to my first interview with William Lane Craig, during which he brought up a scientific principle called Ockham's razor. As I listened to Moreland defend the concept of dualism, it dawned on me that Ockham's razor would argue in the opposite direction—toward the view that only the brain exists—because it says science prefers simpler explanations where possible. It was a challenge I decided to pose to Moreland.

"You're familiar with the scientific principle called Ockham's razor," I said to him.

As soon as the question left my mouth, Moreland knew where I was headed. "Yes, it says that we shouldn't multiply entities beyond what's needed to explain something. And I assume your objection is that Ockham's razor would favor a simple alternative, such as the brain accounting for everything, rather than more complicated explanation like the two entities of dualism."

"That's right," I said. "Surely this undercuts the case for dualism."

He was ready with an answer. "No, it really doesn't. Actually, Ockham's razor favors dualism, and here's why," he said. "What's the intent of Ockham's razor? The thrust of this principle is that when you're trying to explain a phenomenon, you should only include the elements that are necessary to explain the phenomenon. And as I've demonstrated through scientific evidence and philosophical reasoning, dualism is necessary to explain the phenomenon of consciousness. Only dualism can account for all of the evidence—and, hence, it does not violate Ockham's razor."

I wasn't ready to give up. "But maybe we just don't have all the evidence yet," I said. "Maybe your conclusions are premature. Physicalists are confident that the day will come when they'll be able to explain consciousness solely in physical terms."

Moreland's reply was adamant: "There will never, ever be a scientific explanation for mind and consciousness."

His forceful and unequivocal statement startled me. "Why not?" I asked.

"Think about how scientists go about explaining things: they show that something had to happen due to antecedent conditions. For example, when scientists explain why gases behave the way they do, they show that if you hold the volume constant and increase the temperature, the pressure has to increase. That is, when we heat a pressure cooker, the pressure goes up.

"When scientists explain that, they don't just correlate temperature and pressure. They don't just say that temperature and pressure tend to go together. They try to show why the pressure has *got* to increase, why it couldn't have done anything other than that, given the temperature increase. Scientists want to show why something *has* to happen given the cause; they're not content simply to correlate things and leave it at that.

"And this will never work with consciousness, because the relationship between the mind and the brain is contingent, or dependent.

In other words, the mind is not something that *had* to happen. One atheist asked, 'How could a series of physical events, little particles jostling against one another, electric currents rushing to and fro, blossom into conscious experience? Why shouldn't pain and itches be switched around? Why should any experience emerge when these neurons fire in the brain?' He's pointing out that there's no necessary connection between conscious states and the brain.

"So in the future scientists will be able to develop more correlations between conscious states and states of the brain, and that's wonderful. But my point is this: *correlation is not explanation.* To explain something scientifically, you've got to show *why* the phenomenon *had* to happen given the causes. And scientists cannot explain the 'why' behind consciousness, because there's no necessary connection between the brain and consciousness. It didn't have to happen this way."

DEDUCTIONS ABOUT GOD

It's no wonder that Alvin Plantinga of Notre Dame University, a dualist who is frequently called the greatest living American philosopher, surveyed the current body/mind debate and concluded: "Things don't look hopeful for Darwinian naturalists."[57]

Faced with data and logic that support dualism, and unable to offer a plausible theory for how consciousness could have erupted from mindless matter, atheists are pinning their hopes on some as-yet-undetermined scientific discovery to justify their faith in physicalism. And some aren't even so sure about that—physicist and atheist Steven Weinberg said scientists may have to "bypass the problem of human consciousness" altogether, because "it may just be too hard for us."[58] In other words, it's failing to give them the answers they want.

As for Moreland, he agrees with Plantinga's bleak assessment for atheists. "Darwinian evolution will never be able to explain the origin of consciousness," he told me. "Perhaps Darwinists can explain how consciousness was shaped in a certain way over time, because the behavior that consciousness caused had survival value. But it can't explain the *origin* of consciousness, because it can't explain how you can get something from nothing.

"In Darwin's notebooks, he said if there was anything his theory can't explain, then there would have to be another explanation—a creationist explanation. Well, he can't explain the origin of mind. He tried to reduce consciousness down to the brain, because he could tell a story about how the brain evolved. But as we've discussed, Lee, consciousness cannot be reduced merely to the physical brain. This means the atheist creation story is inadequate and false. And yet there is an alternative explanation that makes sense of all the evidence: our consciousness came from a greater Consciousness.

"You see, the Christian worldview begins with thought and feeling and belief and desire and choice. That is, God is conscious. God has thoughts. He has beliefs, he has desires, he has awareness, he's alive, he acts with purpose. We start there. And because we start with the mind of God, we don't have a problem with explaining the origin of our mind."

I asked, "What, then, can we deduce about God from this?"

"That he's rational, that he's intelligent, that he's creative, that he's sentient. And that he's invisible, because that's the way conscious beings are. I have no inclination to doubt that this very room is teeming with the presence of God, just because I can't see or touch or smell or hear him. As I explained earlier, I can't even see my own wife! I can't touch, see, smell, or hear the *real* her.

"One more thing. The existence of my soul gives me a new way to understand how God can be everywhere. That's because my soul occupies my body without being located in any one part of it. There's no place in my body where you can say, 'Here I am.' My soul is not in the left part of my brain, it's not in my nose, it's not in my lungs. My soul is fully present everywhere throughout my body. That's why if I lose part of my body, I don't lose part of my soul.

"In a similar way, God is fully present everywhere. He isn't located, say, right outside the planet Mars. God occupies space in the same way the soul occupies the body. If space were somehow cut in half, God wouldn't lose half his being. So now I have a new model, based on my own self, for God's omnipresence. And shouldn't we expect this? If we were made in the image of God, wouldn't we expect there to be some parallels between us and God?"

I asked, "Do you foresee more scientists coming to the conclusion that the soul, though immaterial, is very real?"

"The answer is yes—if they are willing to open themselves up to nonscientific knowledge," he replied. "I believe in science; it's wonderful and gives us some very important information. But there are other ways of knowing things as well. Because, remember, most of the evidence for the reality of consciousness and the soul is from our own first-person awareness of ourselves and has nothing to do with the study of the brain. The study of the brain allows us to correlate the brain with conscious states, but it tells us nothing about what consciousness itself is."

"But, J. P., aren't you asking scientists to do the unthinkable—to ignore scientific knowledge?"

"No, not at all," he insisted. "I'm only asking that they become willing to listen to *all* the evidence and see where it leads—which is what the quest for truth should be about."

"And if they do that?"

"They will come to believe in the reality of the soul and the immaterial nature of consciousness. And this could open them up personally to something even more important—to a much larger Mind and a much bigger Consciousness, who in the beginning was the Logos, and who made us in his image."

COGITO ERGO SUM

A ringing telephone ended our conversation, although I was wrapping up the interview anyway. A colleague was calling to remind Moreland of a faculty meeting. I thanked Moreland for his time and insights, gathered my things, and strolled out to my car. I was just about to start the engine, but instead I let go of the key, leaned back in my seat, and took a few moments (as Moreland would say) to introspect.

Interestingly, this very act of introspection intuitively affirmed to me what Moreland's facts and logic had already established—my ability to ponder, to reason, to speculate, to imagine, and to feel the emotional brunt of the interview showed that my mind surely could not have been the evolutionary byproduct of brute, mindless matter.

"Selfhood . . . is not explicable in material or physical terms," said philosopher Stuart C. Hackett. "The essential spiritual selfhood of man has its only adequate ground in the transcendent spiritual Selfhood of God as Absolute Mind."[59]

In other words, I am more than just the sum total of a physical brain and body parts. Rather, I *am* a soul, and I *have* a body. I think—therefore, I am. Or as Hackett said: "With modest apology to Descartes: *Cogito, ergo Deus est!* I think, therefore God is."[60]

I found myself wholeheartedly agreeing with philosopher Robert Augros and physicist George Stanciu, who explored the depths of the mind/body controversy and concluded that "physics, neuroscience, and humanistic psychology all converge on the same principle: mind is not reducible to matter." They added: "The vain expectation that matter might someday account for mind . . . is like the alchemist's dream of producing gold from lead.[61]

I leaned forward and started the car. After months of investigating scientific evidence for God—traveling a total of 26,884 miles, which is the equivalent of making one lap around the Earth at the equator— I had finally reached a critical mass of information. It was time to synthesize and digest what I had learned—and ultimately to come to a conclusion that would have vast and life-changing implications.

FOR FURTHER EVIDENCE
More Resources on This Topic

Cooper, John W. *Body, Soul, and Life Everlasting*. Grand Rapids, Mich.: Eerdmans, 1989.

Habermas, Gary and J. P. Moreland. *Beyond Death*. Wheaton, Ill.: Crossway, 1998.

Moreland, J. P. "God and the Argument from Mind." In *Scaling the Secular City*. Grand Rapids, Mich.: Baker, 1987.

———. *What Is the Soul?* Norcross, Ga.: Ravi Zacharias International Ministries, 2002.

———. and Scott B. Rae. *Body and Soul*. Downer's Grove, Ill.: InterVarsity, 2000.

Taliaferro, Charles. *Consciousness and the Mind of God*. Cambridge, England: Cambridge University Press, 1994.

Witham, Larry. "Mind and Brain." In *By Design: Science and the Search for God*. San Francisco: Encounter Books, 2003.

11

THE CUMULATIVE
CASE FOR A CREATOR

The vast mysteries of the universe should only confirm our belief in the certainty of its Creator. I find it as difficult to understand a scientist who does not acknowledge the presence of a superior rationality behind the existence of the universe as it is to comprehend a theologian who would deny the advances of science.

Werner von Braun, the father of space science[1]

Faith does not imply a closed, but an open mind. Quite the opposite of blindness, faith appreciates the vast spiritual realities that materialists overlook by getting trapped in the purely physical.

Sir John Templeton [2]

Standing boldly in front of the national media, his posture like a boxer ready to pounce, the cocky prosecutor shook his finger at five television cameras and taunted renowned defense attorney William F. Neal.

"I defy Mr. Neal," he declared, *"to stop that Pinto!"* His words became a rally cry, challenging Neal to establish that a Ford Pinto containing three teenage girls had come to a halt on an Indiana highway before being struck from behind by a Chevy van.

It was yet another moment of high drama in a ground-breaking criminal trial that had captivated the nation. In the first case of its kind in U.S. history, prosecutors blamed the girls' deaths on the car's manufacturer, charging Ford Motor Company with reckless homicide for allegedly designing a vehicle that was prone to explode in low- to moderate-speed rear crashes.

If the Pinto had been safe, the prosecutors contended, the three teenagers would have walked away virtually unscathed from the relatively minor collision. But, they said, because the car's gas tank had been located in a vulnerable position, the car erupted in a fireball that consumed them all.

A pivotal issue was the severity of the crash. Neal maintained that the Pinto had been stopped on the highway and the van was traveling at fifty miles an hour. "No subcompact could have withstood the assault of the van in this case," Neal told the jurors.

The prosecutor, however, countered that the Pinto had been moving in the same direction as the van, which meant the force of the impact would have been much less. Indeed, a few eyewitnesses testified the car had been in motion, though their accounts varied and during cross-examination Neal sought to raise doubts about the vantage points from which they saw the Pinto.

Then the prosecutor presented his star witness: the shaggy-haired, twenty-one-year-old driver of the van, who had not been criminally charged for the crash and was cooperating with the prosecution. He testified that the Pinto had been moving at fifteen to twenty miles an hour when they collided. Neal scoffed, pointing out that the distracted driver had only seen the Pinto for one-sixth of a second before hitting it. But the driver, who had five previous traffic convictions in three years, stuck to his story.

In the glare of the television cameras, the prosecutor was ebullient. Feeling confident in the thoroughness of his investigation and believing Neal could offer no contradictory testimony, he defiantly challenged Neal to make good on his promise that he would stop the Pinto.

Surprisingly, however, the prosecutor's bravado was short-lived. A few days later, to the astonishment of the prosecution, Neal used both negative and positive evidence to accomplish what the prosecutor was convinced he could never do.

First, Neal undermined the testimony of the van's driver. The physician who had treated him for minor injuries said the driver had admitted to him that the Pinto had been stopped. That was damaging enough for the prosecution.

Even more devastating, Neal then presented two surprise witnesses that police had somehow overlooked during their supposedly exhaustive investigation. Both were hospital workers who testified that the driver of the Pinto told them independently before her death that she had been stopped on U.S. Highway 133 when the van struck her car.

The prosecutor was stunned. In a flash, these two unforeseen witnesses changed the entire momentum of the trial. "Nobody knew anything about them," the prosecutor sputtered. "They came out of the blue."

Outside the courtroom, Neal was ecstatic. "The prosecutor challenged us to stop that Pinto," he said, stifling a chuckle. "Well, now we've stopped it *twice*."

The once-confident prosecutor, now publicly embarrassed, found himself on the defensive as reporters pelted him with questions about why his investigation had failed to unearth these witnesses. Ultimately, after several judicial rulings further eroded the prosecutor's case, jurors voted to acquit the automaker.

Neal's performance, which I documented in my book *Reckless Homicide*, was among the most masterful I had ever seen in my years as a legal affairs journalist.[3] His success was not the product of adroit legal maneuvering, clever arguments, or courtroom slight-of-hand. Plain and simple, it was old-fashioned, dogged detective work that uncovered the surprise witnesses. Defense investigators went beyond the obvious, posed questions that others weren't asking, out-hustled police investigators, and followed the clues wherever they led.

Years later, I would understand exactly how the prosecutor felt that day. I was once full of confidence that Darwinism justified my atheism. I felt I had investigated the issue sufficiently, having studied biology, chemistry, geology, anthropology, and other sciences in school and having read books that reenforced my beliefs. No doubt about it—natural selection acting on random variation had put God out of a job.

When Christians approached me about the evidence for their faith, I was as defiant as the combative prosecutor on the courthouse steps. *The Origin of Species* trumped the Bible. The critical thinking of scientists overpowered the wishful thinking of theists. To me, the case was closed.

But then, prompted by the positive changes in my wife after she became a follower of Jesus, I began to go beyond the obvious, to set aside my prejudices, to ask questions I had never posed before, and to pursue the clues of science and history wherever they led. Instead of letting naturalism limit my search, I opened myself to the full range of possibilities. And, frankly, I wasn't prepared for what would happen.

Like the negative evidence that undermined the van's driver in the Pinto case, the facts of science systematically eroded the foundation of Darwinism until it could no longer support the weight of my atheistic conclusions. Suddenly, the intellectual basis for my skepticism was collapsing.

That was disconcerting enough. But then—like the surprise witnesses who suddenly shifted the momentum at the Indiana trial—my wide-ranging research was building an unexpected affirmative case for the existence of a Creator.

Yes, I was stunned; yes, I felt like the wind was being knocked out of me; yes, it was unnerving to wrestle with the implications. But I had vowed to follow the facts regardless of the cost—even at the cost of my own smug self-sufficiency.

A FRESH EXAMINATION OF THE EVIDENCE

I was reminded of the Pinto trial as I sat in my home office and glanced over at a shelf where my eye caught the book I had written on the case. As I started reminiscing about the unanticipated turnaround in that courtroom drama, my thoughts drifted to the emotions I felt on November 8, 1981.

It was on that day, after nearly two years of intensive research, that I sat alone in my room and wrote down the key evidence I had discovered during my original investigation into the credibility of Christianity. Much of it concerned the facts regarding the life, teachings, miracles, death, and resurrection of Jesus of Nazareth, as I described in my book *The Case for Christ*, and the answers to the "Big Eight" objections to Christianity, as I recounted in *The Case for Faith*.

But also very important at the time were the corroborating scientific facts. Even though there was less evidence than is readily available today, there was still plenty upon which to reach a verdict. I can remember analyzing the scientific research and coming to the startling conclusion that the data of the physical world point powerfully toward the existence of a Creator.

What seemed impossible two years earlier now seemed not just possible, not just likely—but obvious. Like the Pinto prosecutor, I was dismayed and disoriented—and yet at the same time I felt confident and even strangely comforted by the conclusion.

Now, more than two decades later, having spent over a year reevaluating and updating the case for a Creator by interviewing experts on the latest scientific discoveries, I sat at my desk once more and mentally reviewed the most current evidence I had encountered.

I was amazed at how new findings in physics, astronomy, bio-chemistry, and other disciplines have added so much to the pool of scientific knowledge. As I considered the evidence afresh, I tried to honestly weigh which hypothesis—Darwinism or Design—best accounted for the most current data of science.

POSSIBILITY #1: THE DARWINISM HYPOTHESIS

To start with, I considered how the facts fit the hypothesis that all of life can be explained by the undirected, purely naturalistic processes of evolution. "Like all other scientific theories, Darwinian evolution must be continually compared with the evidence," said biol-ogist Jonathan Wells. "If it does not fit the evidence, it must be reeval-uated or abandoned—otherwise it is not science, but myth."[4]

Looking at the doctrine of Darwinism, which undergirded my atheism for so many years, it didn't take me long to conclude that it was simply too far-fetched to be credible. I realized that if I were to embrace Darwinism and its underlying premise of naturalism, I would have to believe that:

- Nothing produces everything
- Non-life produces life
- Randomness produces fine-tuning
- Chaos produces information
- Unconsciousness produces consciousness
- Non-reason produces reason

Based on this, I was forced to conclude that Darwinism would require a blind leap of faith that I was not willing to make. Simply put, the central pillars of evolutionary theory quickly rotted away when exposed to scrutiny.

For example, naturalistic processes have utterly failed to explain how non-living chemicals could somehow self-assemble into the first living cell. Not only are there no viable theories, but none are on the horizon. Biochemist Klaus Dose, one of the leading origin-of-life experts, conceded: "At present all discussions on principle theories and experiments in the field either end in stalemate or in a confes-sion of ignorance."[5]

Science writer Robert Roy Britt cast the problem more colorfully: "Have you ever had one of those dreams where you try to run from a monster and your legs go round and round but you don't get anywhere? The quest to understand the origin of life isn't much different."[6]

Stephen C. Meyer pointed out in my interview that there are insurmountable hurdles involving the origin of biological information that simply cannot be resolved by more research and effort. In other words, origin-of-life scientists are not going to wake up from their nightmare. To me, this constitutes the Achilles' heel of evolutionary theory. As biochemist Michael Denton observed, the idea that undirected processes could somehow turn dead chemicals into all the extraordinary complexity of living things is surely "no more nor less than the great cosmogenic myth" of our times.[7]

In addition, the overall fossil record has stubbornly refused to confirm the grand claims of Darwinian transitions. Despite innumerable discoveries since Darwin's day, "the intermediates have remained as elusive as ever," said Denton.[8] Rather than harmonize into a consistent case for Darwin's theory, the fossils are a discordant cacophony that cannot reasonably account for the monumental leaps Darwinism must make, for example, between fish and amphibians or amphibians and reptiles.

The most glaring deficiency of the fossil record is biology's Big Bang, the Cambrian explosion. The majority—or, according to some experts, all—of the world's forty phyla, the highest category in the animal kingdom, virtually sprang forth with unique body plans more than five hundred million years ago. The sudden appearance of these radically new life forms, devoid of prior transitions, has turned Darwin's Tree of Life on its head.

Like the overconfident prosecutor in the Pinto case, Darwin predicted that new discoveries would explain away this quantum leap in biological complexity. In reality, they have only made matters worse. The excuse that the transitionary creatures were too soft or small to be fossilized withers under examination. Alternate theories, like Stephen Jay Gould's "punctuated equilibrium," dash themselves on the rocks of reason. Darwin's assessment is still accurate more than a century and a half later: the Cambrian explosion is "inexplicable" under his hypothesis. This remains, in my opinion, a fatal shortcoming.

When I examined these and other deficiencies of Darwinism as objectively as I could, I became firmly convinced that evolution *is* a confirmed fact—as long as it's defined as the micro-evolutionary variations we see in the animal and plant world. Undeniably, a considerable amount of change and diversification has taken place over time. However, there is simply insufficient evidence from which to draw the radical conclusion that large-scale, macro-evolutionary transitions have occurred.

As award-winning author Roger Lewin, a former editor with *Science* and *New Scientist* magazines, summarized a historic scientific conference on macroevolution: "The central question . . . was whether the mechanisms underlying microevolution can be extrapolated to explain the phenomenon of macroevolution. At the risk of doing violence to the position of some people at the meeting, the answer can be given as a clear, No."[9]

In short, the amount of faith needed to maintain belief in the most sweeping and controversial claims of Darwinism far exceeded what I believed was reasonably warranted by the hard evidence of science. On top of that, naturalism has absolutely no credible explanation for how the universe came into being in the first place. This failure of the naturalistic and Darwinist ideas opened the door to considering the other hypothesis—that both the universe and the life it contains are the product of an intelligent designer.

POSSIBILITY #2: THE DESIGN HYPOTHESIS

"A big, fundamental question, like belief in God (or disbelief), is not settled by a single argument," said physicist-turned-theologian John Polkinghorne. "It's too complicated for that. What one has to do is to consider lots of different issues and see whether or not the answers one gets add up to a total picture that makes sense."[10]

That's the approach I took in my investigation. I probed six different scientific disciplines to see whether they point toward or away from the existence of an intelligent designer.

When I opened my mind to the possibility of an explanation beyond naturalism, I found that the design hypothesis most clearly accounted for the evidence of science. The "explanatory power" of the design hypothesis outstripped every other theory. Consider some of the facts that were adduced in my investigation:

• *The Evidence of Cosmology*

Thanks to scientific discoveries of the last fifty years, the ancient *kalam* cosmological argument has taken on a powerful and persuasive new force. As described by William Lane Craig, the argument is simple yet elegant: *first, whatever begins to exist has a cause*. Even renowned skeptic David Hume didn't deny this first premise. In fact, atheist Quentin Smith's contention that "we came from nothing, by nothing, and for nothing" seems intuitively absurd.

Second, the universe had a beginning. Based on the data, virtually all cosmologists now agree the universe began in the Big Bang at some specific point in the past. Craig stressed that even alternate theories for the origin of the universe require a beginning. For instance, Stephen Hawking's use of "imaginary numbers" merely conceals the beginning point in his own model, which Hawking admits is not really a description of reality.

The conclusion then follows inexorably from the two premises: *therefore, the universe has a cause.* Even once-agnostic astronomer Robert Jastrow conceded the essential elements of Christianity and modern cosmology are the same: "The chain of events leading to man commenced suddenly and sharply, at a definite moment in time, in a flash of light and energy."

• *The Evidence of Physics*

One of the most striking discoveries of modern science has been that the laws and constants of physics unexpectedly conspire in an extraordinary way to make the universe habitable for life. For instance, said physicist-philosopher Robin Collins, gravity is fine-tuned to one part in a hundred million billion billion billion billion billion.

The cosmological constant, which represents the energy density of space, is as precise as throwing a dart from space and hitting a bulls-eye just a trillionth of a trillionth of an inch in diameter on Earth. One expert said there are more than thirty physical or cosmological parameters that require precise calibration in order to produce a universe that can sustain life.

Collins demonstrated that chance cannot reasonably account for this "anthropic principle" and that the most-discussed alternative— that there are multiple universes—lacks any evidential support and ultimately collapses upon the realization that these other worlds would owe their existence to a highly designed process.

This evidence was so powerful that it was instrumental in Patrick Glynn abandoning his atheism. "Today the concrete data point strongly in the direction of the God hypothesis," he said. "It is the simplest and most obvious solution to the anthropic puzzle."

• *The Evidence of Astronomy*

Similar to the fine-tuning of physics, Earth's position in the universe and its intricately choreographed geological and chemical processes work together with exquisite efficiency to create a safe place for humans to live.

For example, astronomer Guillermo Gonzalez and science philosopher Jay Wesley Richards said it would take a star with the highly unusual properties of our sun—the right mass, the right light, the right age, the right distance, the right orbit, the right galaxy, the right location—to nurture living organisms on a circling planet. Numerous factors make our solar system and our location in the universe just right for a habitable environment.

What's more, the exceptional conditions that make life possible also happen to make our planet strangely well-suited for viewing and analyzing the universe and our environment. All of this suggests our planet may be rare, if not unique, and that the Creator wanted us to be able to explore the cosmos.

"If the universe had not been made with the most exacting precision we could never have come into existence," said Harvard-educated astrophysicist John A. O'Keefe of NASA. "It is my view that these circumstances indicate the universe was created for man to live in."

• *The Evidence of Biochemistry*

Darwin said, "If it could be demonstrated that any complex organ existed which could not possibly have been formed by numerous, successive, slight modifications, my theory would absolutely break down." Biochemist Michael Behe has demonstrated exactly that through his description of "irreducibly complex" molecular machines.

These complicated, microscopic contraptions, such as cilia and bacterial flagella, are extremely unlikely to have been built piece-by-piece through Darwinian processes, because they had to be fully present in order to function. Other examples include the incredible system of transporting proteins within cells and the intricate process of blood-clotting.

More than just a devastating challenge to Darwinism, these amazing biological systems—which far exceed the capacity of human technology—point toward a transcendent Creator. "My conclusion," said Behe, "can be summed up in a single word: design. I say that based on science. I believe that irreducibly complex systems are strong evidence of a purposeful, intentional design by an intelligent agent."

Behe's argument has proven impervious to challenges by skeptics. While obviously there will be future discoveries in biochemistry, Behe pointed out that they will not be able to negate the complexity that has already been discovered—and which is best explained by a Creator.

• *The Evidence of Biological Information*

The six-feet of DNA coiled inside every one of our body's one hundred trillion cells contains a four-letter chemical alphabet that spells out precise assembly instructions for all the proteins from which our bodies are made. Cambridge-educated Stephen Meyer demonstrated that no hypothesis has come close to explaining how information got into biological matter by naturalistic means.

On the contrary, he said that whenever we find a sequential arrangement that's complex and corresponds to an independent pattern or function, this kind of information is *always* the product of intelligence. "Books, computer codes, and DNA all have these two properties," he said. "We know books and computer codes are designed by intelligence, and the presence of this type of information in DNA also implies an intelligent source."

In addition, Meyer said the Cambrian explosion's dazzling array of new life forms, which suddenly appeared fully formed in the fossil record, with no prior transitions, would have required the infusion of massive amounts of new biological information. "Information is the hallmark of mind," said Meyer. "And purely from the evidence of genetics and biology, we can infer the existence of a mind that's far greater than our own—a conscious, purposeful, rational, intelligent designer who's amazingly creative."

• *The Evidence of Consciousness*

Many scientists are concluding that the laws of chemistry and physics cannot explain our experience of consciousness. Professor J. P. Moreland defined consciousness as our introspection, sensations, thoughts, emotions, desires, beliefs, and free choices that make us alive and aware. The "soul" contains our consciousness and animates our body.

According to a researcher who showed that consciousness can continue after a person's brain has stopped functioning, current scientific findings "would support the view that 'mind,' 'consciousness,' or the 'soul' is a separate entity from the brain."

As Moreland said, "You can't get something from nothing." If the universe began with dead matter having no conscious, "how, then, do you get something totally different—consciousness, living, thinking, feeling, believing creatures—from materials that don't have that?" But if everything started with the mind of God, he said, "we don't have a problem with explaining the origin of our mind."

Darwinist philosopher Michael Ruse candidly conceded that "no one, certainly not the Darwinian as such, seems to have any answer" to the consciousness issue. Nobel Prize–winning neurophysiologist John C. Eccles concluded from the evidence "that there is what we might call a supernatural origin of my unique self-conscious mind or my unique selfhood or soul."

THE IDENTITY OF THE DESIGNER

As I reviewed the avalanche of information from my investigation, I found the evidence for an intelligent designer to be credible, cogent, and compelling. Actually, in my opinion the combination of the findings from cosmology and physics by themselves were sufficient to support the design hypothesis. All of the other data simply built an even more powerful cumulative case that ended up overwhelming my objections.

But who or what is this master Designer? Like playing a game of connect-the-dots, each one of the six scientific disciplines I investigated contributed clues to unmasking the identity of the Creator.

As Craig explained during our interview, the evidence of cosmology demonstrates that the cause of the universe must be an uncaused, beginningless, timeless, immaterial, personal being endowed with freedom of will and enormous power. In the area of physics, Collins established that the Creator is intelligent and has continued to be involved with his creation after the Big Bang.

The evidence of astronomy, showing that the Creator was incredibly precise in creating a livable habitat for the creatures he designed, logically implies that he has care and concern for them. Also, Gonzalez and Richards presented evidence that the Creator has built at least one purpose into his creatures—to explore the world he has designed, and therefore to perhaps discover him through it.

Not only do biochemistry and the existence of biological information affirm the Creator's activity after the Big Bang, but they also show he's incredibly creative. Evidence for consciousness, as Moreland said, helps establish that the Creator is rational, gives us a basis for understanding his omnipresence, and even suggests that life after death is credible.

This is not a picture of the god of deism, who supposedly formed the universe but then abandoned it. As Meyer explained in my first interview with him, the abundant evidence for the Creator's continued activity in the universe after the initial creation event discredits deism as a credible possibility.

Pantheism, the idea that the Creator and universe are co-existent, also falls short of accounting for the evidence, because it cannot explain how the universe came into existence. After all, if the pantheistic god didn't exist prior to the physical universe, then it would not be capable of bringing the universe into being.

Also, Craig explained how the scientific principle of Ockham's razor shaves away the multiple gods of polytheism, leaving us with a single Creator. In addition, the personal nature of the Creator argues against the impersonal divine force that's at the center of some New Age religions.

In contrast, however, the portrait of the Creator that emerges from the scientific data is uncannily consistent with the description of the God whose identity is spelled out in the pages of the Bible.

- *Creator?* "In the beginning you laid the foundations of the earth, and the heavens are the work of your hands."[11]
- *Unique?* "You were shown these things so that you might know that the Lord is God; besides him there is no other."[12]
- *Uncaused and timeless?* "Before the mountains were born or you brought forth the earth and the world, from everlasting to everlasting you are God."[13]
- *Immaterial?* "God is spirit."[14]
- *Personal?* "I am God Almighty."[15]
- *Freedom of will?* "And God said, 'Let there be light,' and there was light."[16]
- *Intelligent and rational?* "How many are your works, O Lord! In wisdom you made them all; the earth is full of your creatures."[17]
- *Enormously powerful?* "The Lord is . . . great in power."[18]
- *Creative?* "For you created my inmost being; you knit me together in my mother's womb. I praise you because I am fearfully and

wonderfully made; your works are wonderful, I know that full well."[19]

- *Caring?* "The earth is full of his unfailing love."[20]
- *Omnipresent?* "The heavens, even the highest heaven, cannot contain you."[21]
- *Has given humankind purpose?* "For everything, absolutely everything, above and below, visible and invisible, . . . everything got started in him and finds its purpose in him."[22]
- *Provides for life after death?* "He will swallow up death forever."[23]

As the apostle Paul wrote two millennia ago: "For since the creation of the world God's invisible qualities—his eternal power and divine nature—have been clearly seen, being understood from what has been made [that is, his creation], so that men are without excuse."[24]

The question of whether these qualities might also describe the deities of any other world religions became moot once I added the evidence that I discovered through the study of ancient history and archaeology.

As I described in my book *The Case for Christ*—a summary of which is included as an appendix to this book—the convincing evidence establishes the essential reliability of the New Testament, demonstrates the fulfillment of ancient prophecies in the life of Jesus of Nazareth against all odds, and supports Jesus' resurrection as being an actual event that occurred in time and space. Indeed, his return from the dead is an unprecedented and supernatural feat that authenticated his claim to being the one-and-only Son of God.

To me, the range, the variety, the depth, and the breathtaking persuasive power of the evidence from both science and history affirmed the credibility of Christianity to the degree that my doubts were simply washed away.

Unlike Darwinism, where my faith would have to swim upstream against the strong current of evidence flowing the other way, putting my trust in the God of the Bible was nothing less than the most rational and natural decision I could make. I was merely permitting the torrent of facts to carry me along to their most logical conclusion.

THE FUSION OF SCIENCE AND FAITH

Unfortunately, there's a lot of misunderstanding about faith. Some believe faith actually contradicts facts. "The whole point of faith," scoffed Michael Shermer, editor of *The Skeptical Inquirer*, "is to believe regardless of the evidence, which is the very antithesis of science."[25]

However, that's certainly not my understanding. I see faith as being a reasonable step in the same direction that the evidence is pointing. In other words, faith goes beyond merely acknowledging that the facts of science and history point toward God. It's responding to those facts by investing trust in God—a step that's fully warranted due to the supporting evidence.

Oxford's Alister McGrath pointed out that all worldviews require faith. "The truth claims of atheism simply cannot be proved," he said. "How do we know that there is no God? The simple fact of the matter is that atheism is a faith, which draws conclusions that go beyond the available evidence."[26]

On the other hand, the available evidence from the latest scientific research is convincing more and more scientists that facts support faith as never before. "The age-old notion that there is more to existence than meets the eye suddenly looks like fresh thinking again," said journalist Gregg Easterbrook. "We are entering the greatest era of science-religion fusion since the Enlightenment last attempted to reconcile the two."[27]

To many people, including physicist Paul Davies, this is a shocking and unexpected development. "It may seem bizarre," he said, "but in my opinion science offers a surer path to God than religion."[28]

Added nanoscientist James Tour of Rice University: "Only a rookie who knows nothing about science would say science takes away from faith. If you really study science, it will bring you closer to God."[29] Astrophysicist and priest George Coyne put it this way: "Nothing we learn about the universe threatens our faith. It only enriches it."[30]

For Polkinghorne, who achieved acclaim as a mathematical physicist at Cambridge before becoming a full-time minister, the same kind of thinking he uses in science has helped him draw life-changing conclusions about God:

> No one has ever seen a quark, and we believe that no one ever will. They are so tightly bound to each other inside the protons and neutrons that nothing can make them break out on their own. Why, then, do I believe in these invisible quarks? ... In summary, it's because quarks make sense of a lot of direct physical evidence. ... I wish to engage in a similar strategy

with regard to the unseen reality of God. His existence makes sense of many aspects of our knowledge and experience: the order and fruitfulness of the physical world; the multilayered character of reality; the almost universal human experiences of worship and hope; the phenomenon of Jesus Christ (including his resurrection). I think that very similar thought processes are involved in both cases. I do not believe that I shift in some strange intellectual way when I move from science to religion.... In their search for truth, science and faith are intellectual cousins under the skin."[31]

He added, however, an important distinction. "Religious knowledge is more demanding than scientific knowledge," he said. "While it requires scrupulous attention to matters of truth, it also calls for the response of commitment to the truth discovered."[32]

According to McGrath, the Hebrew word for "truth" suggests "something which can be relied upon." Thus, he said, truth is more than about simply being right. "It is about trustworthiness," he explained. "It is a relational concept, pointing us to someone who is totally worthy of our trust. We are not being asked to know yet another fact but to enter into a relationship with the one who is able to sustain and comfort us."[33]

The facts of science and history, then, can only take us so far. At some point, the truth demands a response. When we decide not merely to ponder the abstract concept of a designer but to embrace him as our own—to make him our "true God"—then we can meet him personally, relate to him daily, and spend eternity with him as he promises.

And that, as a young medical doctor and his wife learned, changes everything.

FROM SCIENCE TO GOD

No one was more surprised by the scientific evidence for God than the soft-spoken, silver-haired, seventy-seven-year-old physician who was sitting across from me in a booth at a Southern California restaurant.

His story, like the one Craig told me earlier about the Eastern European physicist who found God through cosmology, is yet another testimony to the power of science to point seekers toward God. However, it's something else too—a road map for how you might want to proceed if you're personally interested in seeing whether faith in God is warranted by the facts.

Viggo Olsen is a brilliant surgeon whose life was steeped in science. Graduating *cum laude* from medical school, he later became a diplomate of the American Board of Surgery and a fellow of the American College of Surgeons. In fact, his name has a whole raft of letters after it—M.S., M.D., Litt.D., D.H., F.A.C.S., F.I.C.S., and D.T.M.&H. He attributes his former spiritual skepticism to his knowledge of the scientific world.

"I viewed Christianity and the Bible through agnostic eyes," he said. "My wife Joan was a skeptic too. We believed there was no independent proof that any Creator exists. Rather, we believed life came into being through evolutionary processes."

The problem was Joan's parents, both devout Christians. When Viggo and Joan visited them in 1951 on their way to starting his first internship at a New York City hospital, they got an earful of religious propaganda. In late-night discussions, Viggo and Joan would patiently explain why Christianity was inconsistent with contemporary science. Finally, in frustration at two o'clock one morning around the kitchen table, they agreed to examine the Christian faith for themselves.

Olsen implied his search would be sincere and honest, but inwardly he had already hatched a plan. "My intent was not to do an objective study at all," he recalled. "Just like a surgeon incises a chest, we were going to slash into the Bible and dissect out all its embarrassing scientific mistakes."

At their new home, Viggo and Joan labeled a piece of paper: "Scientific Mistakes in the Bible," figuring they could easily fill it. They worked out a system under which they would discuss with each other what they were learning in their investigation. At the end, there would always be more unanswered questions. While Viggo was working at the hospital, Joan would research the issues left hanging. Then, on alternate nights and weekends, when Viggo was off duty, they studied together, analyzed, discussed, and argued.

Problems quickly emerged—but not the kind they were anticipating. "We were having trouble finding those scientific mistakes," he said. "We'd find something that seemed to be an error, but on further reflection and study, we saw that our understanding had been shallow. That made us sit up and take notice."

Then a student passed along a 1948 book called *Modern Science and Christian Faith*.[34] Each of its thirteen chapters was written by a different scientist about the evidence in his field that pointed toward

God. Even though it was published before many of the eye-popping scientific discoveries that I've described in this book, the evidence was nevertheless sufficient to stun Viggo and Joan.

"It blew our minds!" Olsen said. "For the first time we began to see there were reasons behind Christianity. Deciding to believe would definitely not be committing intellectual suicide."

THE ADVENTURE OF A LIFETIME

They devoured that book, plus many others that were cited in its bibliography. As they analyzed the evidence, they came to several conclusions.

First, they knew on scientific grounds that the universe was not eternal. Rather, it came into being at a certain point. Since the universe is packed with power—heat energy, atomic energy, and so forth—they reasoned that it must have been brought into being by some mighty force.

Second, they looked at the obvious design of the universe and the human body, all the way down to organs and cells, concluding that the power that brought the universe into existence must also be intelligent.

Third, they decided that as great as the human intellect is, there is something even higher—the ability of people to empathize, to love, and to have compassion. Since the Creator must be greater than his creatures, he must also be imbued with those same qualities.

Based on evidence and reasoning independent of the Bible, they were able to answer the first of the three questions that formed the basis of their investigation: "Is there a God who created the universe?" They surprised themselves with their verdict: yes, a personal Creator-God does exist.

With this established, they began exploring their next two broad questions: "Did God reveal himself to humankind through the Bible or other sacred scriptures? And is Jesus the Son of God—deity united with humanity—and can he help us as he claimed?"

The investigation continued into those topics. One day, while Viggo was working at the hospital, he formulated what he thought was a powerful argument against Christianity. "I was really proud of it," he told me, reliving the scene as if it were last month. "I spent all day mentally honing it. I couldn't wait to tell Joan!"

At the end of his shift, he walked the three blocks to their small apartment. "To this day I remember the thought that struck me as Joan opened the door and gave me a kiss—*what a neat little pregnant wife I've got.*"

He walked in and closed the door. Standing in the entryway, he explained his new objection to Christianity. Finally, he asked, "What do you think?"

"There was silence for a moment," he recalled. "Then Joan looked up at me with her beautiful blue eyes and said, 'But, Vic, haven't you, after all our studies, really come to believe Christ is the Son of God?'

"There was something about the way she said it and the way she looked at me that almost instantaneously knocked down all the barriers remaining in my mind," he said. "The evidence was no longer obstructed. All we had learned came together into a wonderful, magnificent, glowing, fabulous picture of Jesus.

"I hesitated, and then I said, 'Yes, I really do. I know it's true. I do believe!' I hadn't believed up until that point—but with the barriers torn down, I knew she was right. We moved into the living room and sat down on the couch. I said, 'So what about you?'

"She said, "I settled the matter several days ago, but I was afraid to tell you. All the things we studied and learned finally convinced me about the Bible, about Christ, and about my need—*our* need—for him. A few days ago, I knew I was completely convinced.' She had already prayed to receive God's gift of forgiveness and eternal life. And that started the biggest adventure of our lives!"

Wanting to maximize the impact they would have, Viggo and Joan prayed a bold prayer in which they asked God to send them to a place devoid of both Christians and medical care. He obliged—and they ended up spending thirty-three years in the poverty-wracked nation of Bangladesh.

There, they founded Memorial Christian Hospital as a center of medical care and spiritual light, where countless people have found healing and hope. They and their colleagues helped establish 120 churches. They were warmly embraced by the people and the government of Bangladesh—in fact, Viggo was honored with Visa #001 in gratitude for his contributions to the country.

"It must have been difficult to live in an underdeveloped nation like that," I said.

"Actually," he told me with a smile, "it was the greatest adventure we could ever have. When you're in a hard place, when you're over your head again and again, when you're sinking and beyond yourself and praying your heart out—then you see God reach out, and touch your life, and resolve the situation beyond anything you could have ever hoped."

His eyes sparkled. "That's living it up!" he declared. "There's nothing that can match that. We got to experience that again and again and again. We wouldn't have missed it for the world. In my opinion, finding the purpose for which God made you—whatever it may be— and then fully pursuing it is simply the very best way to live."

Viggo eventually wrote three books about his experiences. I especially like the title of one of them—*The Agnostic Who Dared to Search*[35]—because it suggests there is a risk involved with investigating the evidence for God. At some point, the truth you uncover is going to demand a response.

And that could change everything.

YOU WERE DESIGNED FOR DISCOVERY

Though Viggo Olsen has a stronger science background than I do, there were definite similarities in the way we both approached the issue of faith and science. We read books, we asked questions, we tracked down leads, and we pursued the evidence regardless of where it was taking us. We investigated systematically and enthusiastically, as if our lives depended on it.

And in the end, our lives, our attitudes, our philosophies, our worldviews, our priorities, and our relationships were revolutionized— for the better.

If you're a spiritual skeptic or seeker, I hope you'll resolve to investigate the evidence for yourself. Actually, Olsen's three-pronged approach would provide a good outline to follow:

- First, is there a God who created the universe?
- Second, did God reveal himself to humankind through the Bible or other sacred scriptures?
- Third, is Jesus the Son of God—deity united with humanity— and can he help us as he claimed?

You'll soon find that the universe is governed by both physical laws and spiritual laws. The physical laws point us toward the Creator; the spiritual laws tell us how we can know him personally, both today and forever.

After all, he's not just the Creator in a broad sense; he's *your* creator. You were made to relate to him in a vibrant, dynamic, and intimate way. And if you seek him wholeheartedly, he promises to provide all the clues you need to find him.[36] In fact, you may even have sensed as you've been reading this book that he's already pursuing you in a subtle but very real way.

You were, as the research by Gonzalez and Richards suggests, designed for discovery—and the greatest discovery of your life awaits you. So I hope you'll pursue scientific knowledge, but that you won't stop there. Don't let its allure become a destination; instead, allow it to guide you beyond itself to the incredible implications it offers for your life and eternity.

My suggestion is this: take a few quiet moments to soak in these closing words, so eloquently expressed by Alister McGrath, and let them become an impetus toward your adventure of a lifetime:

> Many have found that the awesome sight of the star-studded heavens evoke a sense of wonder, an awareness of transcendence, that is charged with spiritual significance. Yet the distant shimmering of stars does not itself create this sense of longing; it merely exposes what is already there. They are catalysts for our spiritual insights, revealing our emptiness and compelling us to ask whether and how this void might be filled.
>
> Might our true origins and destiny somehow lie beyond those stars? Might there not be a homeland, from which we are presently exiled and to which we secretly long to return? Might not our accumulation of discontentment and disillusionment with our present existence be a pointer to another land where our true destiny lies and which is able to make its presence felt now in this haunting way?
>
> Suppose that this is not where we are meant to be but that a better land is at hand? We don't belong here. We have somehow lost our way. Would not this make our present existence both strange and splendid? Strange, because it is not where our true destiny lies; splendid, because it points ahead to where that real hope might be found. The beauty of the night skies or a glorious sunset are important pointers to the origins and the ultimate fulfillment of our heart's deepest desires. But if we mistake the signpost for what is signposted, we will attach our hopes and longings to lesser goals, which cannot finally quench our thirst for meaning.[37]

APPENDIX:
A SUMMARY OF
THE CASE FOR CHRIST

Here is a summary of the historical evidence for Jesus Christ from thirteen leading experts who were interviewed for my book *The Case for Christ:*

CAN THE BIOGRAPHIES OF JESUS BE TRUSTED?

I once thought that the gospels were merely religious propaganda, hopelessly tainted by overactive imaginations and evangelistic zeal. But Craig Blomberg of Denver Seminary, one of the country's foremost authorities on the biographies of Jesus, built a convincing case that they reflect eyewitness testimony and bear the unmistakable earmarks of accuracy. So early are these accounts of Jesus' life that they cannot be explained away as legendary inventions. "Within the first two years after his death," Blomberg said, "significant numbers of Jesus' followers seem to have formulated a doctrine of the atonement, were convinced that he had been raised from the dead in bodily form, associated Jesus with God, and believed they found support for all these convictions in the Old Testament." A study indicates that there was nowhere enough time for legend to have developed and wiped out a solid core of historical truth.

DO JESUS' BIOGRAPHIES STAND UP TO SCRUTINY?

Blomberg argued persuasively that the gospel writers intended to preserve reliable history, were able to do so, were honest and willing to include difficult-to-explain material, and didn't allow bias to unduly color their reporting. The harmony among the gospels on essential facts, coupled with divergence on some incidental details, lends historical credibility to the accounts. What's more, the early church could not have taken root and flourished right there in Jerusalem if it had been teaching facts about Jesus that his own contemporaries could have exposed as exaggerated or false. In short, the gospels were able to pass all eight evidential tests, demonstrating their basic trustworthiness as historical records.

WERE JESUS' BIOGRAPHIES
RELIABLY PRESERVED FOR US?

World-class scholar Bruce Metzger, professor emeritus at Princeton Theological Seminary, said that compared to other ancient documents, there is an unprecedented number of New Testament manuscripts and that they can be dated extremely close to the original writings. The modern New Testament is 99.5 percent free of textual discrepancies, with no major Christian doctrine in doubt. The criteria used by the early church to determine which books should be considered authoritative have ensured that we possess the best records about Jesus.

IS THERE CREDIBLE EVIDENCE
FOR JESUS OUTSIDE HIS BIOGRAPHIES?

"We have better historical documentation for Jesus than for the founder of any other ancient religion," said Edwin Yamauchi of Miami University, a leading expert on ancient history. Sources from outside the Bible corroborate that many people believed Jesus performed healings and was the Messiah, that he was crucified, and that despite this shameful death, his followers, who believed he was still alive, worshiped him as God. One expert documented thirty-nine ancient sources that corroborate more than one hundred facts concerning Jesus' life, teachings, crucifixion, and resurrection. Seven secular sources and several early Christian creeds concern the deity of Jesus, a doctrine "definitely present in the earliest church," according to Gary Habermas, the scholar who wrote *The Historical Jesus*.

DOES ARCHAEOLOGY CONFIRM
OR CONTRADICT JESUS' BIOGRAPHIES?

John McRay, a professor of archaeology for more than fifteen years and author of *Archaeology and the New Testament*, said there's no question that archaeological findings have enhanced the New Testament's credibility. No discovery has ever disproved a biblical reference. Further, archaeology has established that Luke, who wrote about one-quarter of the New Testament, was an especially careful historian. Concluded one expert: "If Luke was so painstakingly accurate in his historical reporting [of minor details], on what logical basis may we assume he was credulous or inaccurate in his reporting of matters that were far more important, not only to him but to others as well?" Like, for instance, the resurrection of Jesus—the event that authenticated his claim to being the unique Son of God.

IS THE JESUS OF HISTORY THE SAME AS THE JESUS OF FAITH?

Gregory Boyd, a Yale- and Princeton-educated scholar who wrote the award-winning *Cynic Sage or Son of God*, offered a devastating critique of the Jesus Seminar, a group that questions whether Jesus said or did most of what's attributed to him. He identified the Seminar as "an extremely small number of radical-fringe scholars who are on the far, far left wing of New Testament thinking." The Seminar ruled out the possibility of miracles at the outset, employed questionable criteria, and some participants have touted myth-riddled documents of extremely dubious quality. Further, the idea that stories about Jesus emerged from mythology fails to withstand scrutiny. Said Boyd: "The evidence for Jesus being who the disciples said he was . . . is just light years beyond my reasons for thinking that the left-wing scholarship of the Jesus Seminar is correct." In sum, the Jesus of faith is the same as the Jesus of history.

WAS JESUS REALLY CONVINCED HE WAS THE SON OF GOD?

By going back to the very earliest traditions, which were safe from legendary development, Ben Witherington III, author of *The Christology of Jesus*, was able to show that Jesus had a supreme and transcendent self-understanding. Based on the evidence, Witherington said: "Did Jesus believe he was the Son of God, the anointed one of God? The answer is yes. Did he see himself as the Son of Man? The answer is yes. Did he see himself as the final Messiah? Yes, that's the way he viewed himself. Did he believe that anybody less than God could save the world? No, I don't believe he did." Scholars said that Jesus' repeated reference to himself as the Son of Man was not a claim of humanity, but a reference to Daniel 7:13–14, in which the Son of Man is seen as having universal authority and everlasting dominion and who receives the worship of all nations. Said one scholar: "Thus, the claim to be the Son of Man would be in effect a claim to divinity."

WAS JESUS CRAZY WHEN HE CLAIMED TO BE THE SON OF GOD?

Gary Collins, a professor of psychology for twenty years and author of forty-five books on psychology-related topics, said Jesus exhibited no inappropriate emotions, was in contact with reality, was brilliant and had amazing insights into human nature, and enjoyed deep and abiding relationships. "I just don't see signs that Jesus was suffering from any known mental illness," he concluded. In addition, Jesus backed up his claim to being God through miraculous feats of healing, astounding demonstrations of power over nature, unrivaled teaching, divine understanding of people, and with his own resurrection, which was the ultimate evidence of his deity.

DID JESUS FULFILL THE ATTRIBUTES OF GOD?

While the incarnation—God becoming man, the infinite becoming finite—stretches our imaginations, prominent theologian D. A. Carson pointed out that there's lots of evidence that Jesus exhibited the characteristics of deity. Based on Philippians 2, many theologians believe Jesus voluntarily emptied himself of the independent use of his divine attributes as he pursued his mission of human redemption. Even so, the New Testament specifically confirms that Jesus ultimately possessed every qualification of deity, including omniscience, omnipresence, omnipotence, eternality, and immutability.

DID JESUS—AND JESUS ALONE— MATCH THE IDENTITY OF THE MESSIAH?

Hundreds of years before Jesus was born, prophets foretold the coming of the Messiah, or the Anointed One, who would redeem God's people. In effect, dozens of these Old Testament prophecies created a fingerprint that only the true Messiah could fit. This gave Israel a way to rule out imposters and validate the credentials of the authentic Messiah. Against astronomical odds—by one estimate, one chance in a trillion, trillion, trillion, trillion, trillion, trillion, trillion, trillion, trillion, trillion, trillion, trillion, trillion—Jesus, and only Jesus throughout history, matched this prophetic fingerprint. This confirms Jesus' identity to an incredible degree of certainty. The expert I interviewed on this topic, Louis Lapides, is an example of someone raised in a conservative Jewish home and who came to believe Jesus is the

Messiah after a systematic study of the prophecies. Today, he's a pastor of a church in California and former president of a national network of fifteen messianic congregations.

WAS JESUS' DEATH A SHAM, AND HIS RESURRECTION A HOAX?

By analyzing the medical and historical data, Dr. Alexander Metherell, a physician who also holds a doctorate in engineering, concluded Jesus could not have survived the gruesome rigors of crucifixion, much less the gaping wound that pierced his lung and heart. In fact, even before the crucifixion he was in serious to critical condition and suffering from hypovolemic shock as the result of a horrific flogging. The idea that he swooned on the cross and pretended to be dead lacks any evidential basis. Roman executioners were grimly efficient, knowing that they themselves would face death if any of their victims were to come down from the cross alive. Even if Jesus had somehow lived through the torture, his ghastly condition could never have inspired a worldwide movement based on the premise that he had gloriously triumphed over the grave.

WAS JESUS' BODY REALLY ABSENT FROM HIS TOMB?

William Lane Craig, who has earned two doctorates and written several books on the Resurrection, presented striking evidence that the enduring symbol of Easter—the vacant tomb of Jesus—was a historical reality. The empty grave is reported or implied in extremely early sources—Mark's Gospel and a creed in 1 Corinthians 15—which date so closely to the event that they could not possibly have been products of legend. The fact that the Gospels report that women discovered the empty tomb bolsters the story's authenticity, because women's testimony lacked credibility in the first century and thus there would have been no motive to report they found the empty tomb if it weren't true. The site of Jesus' tomb was known to Christians, Jews, and Romans, so it could have been checked by skeptics. In fact, nobody—not even the Roman authorities or Jewish leaders—ever claimed that the tomb still contained Jesus' body. Instead, they were forced to invent the absurd story that the disciples, despite having no motive or opportunity, had stolen the body—a theory that not even the most skeptical critic believes today.

WAS JESUS SEEN ALIVE AFTER
HIS DEATH ON THE CROSS?

The evidence for the post-Resurrection appearances of Jesus didn't develop gradually over the years as mythology distorted memories of his life. Rather, said renowned Resurrection expert Gary Habermas, his resurrection was "the central proclamation of the early church from the very beginning." The ancient creed from 1 Corinthians 15 mentions specific individuals who encountered the risen Christ, and Paul, in effect, challenged first-century doubters to talk with these individuals personally to determine the truth of the matter for themselves. The Book of Acts is littered with extremely early affirmations of Jesus' resurrection, while the Gospels describe numerous encounters in detail. Concluded British theologian Michael Green: "The appearances of Jesus are as well authenticated as anything in antiquity. . . . There can be no rational doubt that they occurred."

ARE THERE ANY SUPPORTING FACTS THAT
POINT TOWARD THE RESURRECTION?

Professor J. P. Moreland presented circumstantial evidence that provided strong documentation for the Resurrection. First, the disciples were in a unique position to know whether the Resurrection happened, and they went to their deaths proclaiming it was true. Nobody knowingly and willingly dies for a lie. Second, apart from the Resurrection, there's no good reason why such skeptics as Paul and James would have been converted and would have died for their faith. Third, within weeks of the Crucifixion, thousands of Jews became convinced Jesus was the Son of God and began following him, abandoning key social practices that had critical sociological and religious importance for centuries. They believed they risked damnation if they were wrong. Fourth, the early sacraments of Communion and Baptism affirmed Jesus' resurrection and deity. And fifth, the miraculous emergence of the church in the face of brutal Roman persecution "rips a great hole in history, a hole the size and shape of Resurrection," as C. F. D. Moule put it.

Taken together, I concluded that this expert testimony constitutes compelling evidence that Jesus Christ was who he claimed to be— the one and only Son of God. For details that support this summary, as well as other evidence, please refer to *The Case for Christ*.

DELIBERATIONS: QUESTIONS FOR REFLECTION OR GROUP STUDY

CHAPTER ONE: WHITE-COATED SCIENTISTS VERSUS BLACK-ROBED PREACHERS

1. Have you ever met someone who was as hostile toward Christianity as the author was? What are the various factors that might have been driving that person's skepticism? Is there any part of the author's attitude that you can personally relate to? How so?

2. What's your current viewpoint concerning Christianity? How would you rank its credibility on a scale of one to ten, with one being "none" and ten being "absolute"? Specifically, what are your opinions based on? Have your attitudes changed over the years? If so, how? What prompted those changes?

3. Do you believe that Christianity is being eclipsed or enhanced by modern science? Why? On what do you base your assessment?

4. William Provine, professor of history and biological sciences at Cornell University, listed five implications if Darwinism is true: there's no evidence for God; there's no life after death; there's no absolute foundation for right and wrong; there's no ultimate meaning for life; and people don't really have free will. Why do you think he's right or wrong? Which one of these implications concerns you the most and why?

CHAPTER TWO: THE IMAGES OF EVOLUTION

1. Can you recall when you first were exposed to Darwin's theory of evolution? What was the setting? What was your reaction at the time? Have your attitudes toward Darwinism changed since then? Why or why not? To what degree do you consider yourself to be open-minded on the issue?

2. Were any of the "images of evolution" described in the chapter instrumental in shaping your opinions? How so?

3. The author said that his belief in Darwinism was pivotal in his decision to become an atheist. In what way has your opinion about evolution affected your spiritual outlook?

4. How do you respond to Harvard geneticist Richard Lewontin's opinion that science should be seen as "the only begetter of truth"? Is that a scientific or a philosophical statement? How much confidence do you put in science? What do you believe are the limits of science? What ways are there to know about something apart from the scientific method?

5. What preconceptions or prejudices might inhibit your investigation of the scientific evidence for a Creator? What can you do to set them aside and keep an open mind? What do you hope this investigation of the case for a Creator will personally accomplish for you?

CHAPTER THREE: DOUBTS ABOUT DARWINISM

1. On a scale of one to ten, with one representing "total disbelief" and ten representing "complete agreement," what was your personal opinion about Darwinism before you read the interview with Jonathan Wells? Why did you choose that number? Did the number change after reading Wells's critique of evolutionary theory? How so?

2. Which one of biologist Jonathan Wells's disclosures was the most surprising to you? Why?

3. Consider each of the various icons of evolution that Wells discussed. As you evaluate each one, discuss whether you now think it provides viable support for Darwinism. What makes you reach that conclusion? If you were a juror and the icons were presented to you as evidence for the truth of Darwinism, would you say you have a reasonable doubt? Why or why not?

4. In Wells's opinion, the evidence for Darwinism "is not only grossly inadequate, it's systematically distorted," and that in twenty or thirty years "people will look back in amazement and say, 'How could anyone have believed this?'" In your opinion, what would need to happen before most people would reach that conclusion? How likely do you believe it is that this will occur?

CHAPTER FOUR: WHERE SCIENCE MEETS FAITH

1. Re-read the quotations that begin this chapter. They represent radically different viewpoints. Which position more accurately reflects

your current position? What influences or factors prompted you to arrive at this perspective?

2. What was your first reaction to Stephen Jay Gould's so-called NOMA principle, which says science and faith occupy distinct realms that shouldn't overlap? Was your opinion buttressed or changed by Stephen Meyer's analysis?

3. Meyer lists six ways in which modern science supports belief in God. Which one of these areas is most intriguing to you? Which, if any, engendered the most skepticism? If Meyer is correct concerning these six categories of evidence, how strong is the case for a Creator? How well do you believe Meyer responded to the objections to intelligent design theory? Which of his answers were the most convincing and why?

4. Every scientist has a motive, Meyer said, "but motives are irrelevant to assessing the validity of scientific theories." Why do you agree or disagree with him?

5. Meyer said that he once resonated with Nietzsche's question: *Why should God rule and I serve?* "Why should a condition of my happiness be submission to the will of God?" Meyer asked. "I sensed I couldn't be happy without him; I knew my bad lifestyle only brought misery. So I ended up literally shaking my fist at God in a wheat field in Washington State." Have you ever figuratively shaken your fist at God? What circumstances prompted that reaction? What has happened since then to resolved this issue? How might your current view of God—positive or negative—affect the way you assess the scientific evidence for his existence?

CHAPTER FIVE: THE EVIDENCE OF COSMOLOGY

1. How convincing is the first premise of the *kalam* cosmological argument—that whatever begins to exist has a cause? Can you think of any exceptions to that rule? How well do you believe William Lane Craig responded to the possibility that the universe might have emerged, uncaused, from a sea of quantum energy?

2. The second premise of the *kalam* argument says that the universe began to exist. Do you think the evidence from mathematics and cosmology sufficiently supports the claim that the universe had a beginning at some point in the past? Why or why not? How do you assess the strength of the arguments that seek to avoid the beginning of the universe?

3. The *kalam* argument says that if its two premises are true, then it's logical to conclude that the universe has a cause. Can you think of any alternate theory that would support another conclusion?

4. Craig explains several characteristics of the cause of the universe that can be deduced from the evidence: "A cause of space and time must be an uncaused, beginningless, timeless, spaceless, immaterial, personal being endowed with freedom of will and enormous power." How well do you believe Craig has argued for this list of qualities?

CHAPTER SIX: THE EVIDENCE OF PHYSICS

1. Robin Collins said the evidence for the fine-tuning of the universe is widely regarded as "by far the most persuasive current argument for the existence of God." How do you personally assess the evidence? What facts were the most important in reaching your conclusion?

2. Do you think that the finely balanced parameters of physics could be the result of random happenstance? Why or why not?

3. Do you believe that ours is the only universe in existence, or that other universes also exist? What specific evidence prompts your belief? How do you assess Collins's position that even if multiple universes exist, there must be an intelligently designed mechanism for creating them?

4. According to an article in the *New York Times*, some physicists "feel it is their mission to find a mathematical explanation of nature that leaves nothing to chance or the whim of the Creator." Collins disagreed, saying, "We shouldn't shrink back from the God hypothesis if that's what the facts fit." Which position best reflects your attitude? What prompts you to hold the opinion that you do?

5. Atheist Patrick Glynn cites the evidence from physics as being one of the reasons why he came to believe in God. How persuasive must the evidence be in order for you to come to the conclusion that a Creator exists? How close does the evidence presented in the first two chapters—cosmology and physics—come to meeting that test?

CHAPTER SEVEN: THE EVIDENCE OF ASTRONOMY

1. What were you taught in school concerning the Earth—that it's most likely unique or that it's only one of countless other inhabited planets? Did the interview with Guillermo Gonzalez and Jay Wesley Richards change your perspective? How so?

2. What fact about the universe, our galaxy, the solar system, the sun, or the Earth intrigued you the most? Why?

3. Gonzalez and Richards said there are essentially three options concerning the existence of life. One is that some natural necessity, like the laws of physics, inexorably leads to life. A second is pure chance: life is a fluke. The third is that life was intentionally created. When you compile all of the evidence presented by Gonzalez and Richards, where does the preponderance of the evidence point? What facts back up your conclusion?

4. The late John A. O'Keefe, a prominent pioneer in space research, said the evidence of astronomy led him to conclude that "the universe was created for man to live in." Assume for a moment that he's right. What are three or four reasons why God might have been motivated to create the Earth and then populate it with creatures of his design, including humankind? What relevance do those reasons have for you personally?

CHAPTER EIGHT: THE EVIDENCE OF BIOCHEMISTRY

1. Early in this chapter, a scientist is quoted as describing a single-cell organism as a high-tech factory. After reading how organisms operate on a microscopic level, do you believe that "design" or some other explanation is most appropriate? What factors helped you reach your conclusion?

2. If someone asked you to summarize Michael Behe's argument in your own words, using a mousetrap as an illustration, how would you do it?

3. Charles Darwin conceded that his theory would "absolutely break down" if it could be shown that any complex organ "could not possibly have been formed by numerous, slight modifications." Behe claims he has passed this test. Why do you agree or disagree? If you believe Behe has failed, what else would he need to do in order to meet Darwin's challenge?

4. Which of the biological systems described by Behe—cilia, bacterial flagella, the cellular transport system, or blood-clotting— was the most impressive to you? How well do you believe Behe responded to objections?

5. Behe said that when he concludes life was intelligently designed, some people "don't just disagree; many of them jump up

and down and get red in the face." Why do you believe this issue generates so much controversy? Do you feel an emotional investment in the matter? How so?

CHAPTER NINE: THE EVIDENCE OF BIOLOGICAL INFORMATION

1. If you were a teacher evaluating Stephen Meyer on how well he defended his thesis that DNA is best explained by an intelligent cause, what grade would you give him? What two or three reasons would you give in defending that grade?

2. While scientists are virtually unanimous in ruling out random chance for the origin of life, this theory is still prevalent in popular opinion. What's your assessment of the odds that life could have assembled by chance? Do you agree or disagree with Meyer's conclusion that believing in chance is like invoking a "naturalistic miracle"?

3. Meyer also critiqued two other scenarios—that natural selection or self-ordering tendencies could have been responsible for the origin of life. In light of his analysis, do you believe either of those possibilities has merit? Why or why not? What's your response to Meyer's assertion that only intelligent entities produce information—including the information that's spelled out in DNA's four-letter chemical alphabet?

4. Darwin admitted that the Cambrian explosion was "inexplicable" and a "valid argument" against his theory, but he predicted future fossil discoveries would vindicate macroevolution. Today, do you believe that the direction of the fossil evidence is pointing toward or away from Darwinism? In what ways does Darwinism successfully account for the Cambrian phenomenon? In what ways is the phenomenon consistent with intelligent design?

CHAPTER TEN: THE EVIDENCE OF CONSCIOUSNESS

1. Imagine you were asked to debate the question of whether people consist of both body and spirit or, conversely, that we are essentially "a computer made of meat." Which proposition, in your view, carries the most weight? What evidence would you present for your side?

2. One expert said that although there's no adequate theory of how the brain causes consciousness, he has faith that science will eventually discover a completely naturalistic explanation. Nobel-winner John Eccles calls this hope "extravagant and unfulfillable." In light of the

interview with J. P. Moreland, who do you think is most likely correct and why?

3. Moreland said, "You can't get something from nothing," and therefore human consciousness is inexplicable if the universe only consists of physical matter. However, he said that if everything were brought into being by a divine mind, then the existence of finite minds makes sense. Do you find this argument compelling? Why or why not?

4. Techno-prophet Ray Kurzweil raised the question of whether computers might someday develop consciousness. Based on the evidence and arguments by Moreland, what's your opinion on this issue and why?

CHAPTER ELEVEN: THE CUMULATIVE CASE FOR A CREATOR

1. After recapping the evidence, the author concludes that Darwinism "was simply too far-fetched to be credible." After reading through his summary of the scientific data, do you agree or disagree? What evidence prompts you to come to your conclusion?

2. The author reiterates discoveries from six scientific disciplines and says, in his opinion, the positive evidence for an intelligent designer is "credible, cogent, and compelling." As you consider the testimony by experts presented in this book, do you believe a sufficient case has been made for a Creator? Why? What facts tipped the scale for you in one direction or the other?

3. The portrait of the Creator that emerges from the scientific data, says the author, is "uncannily consistent" with the description of God in the Bible. Do you believe his analysis is reasonable? Why or why not? When you add the historical information about Jesus contained in the appendix, what's your assessment of the credibility of Christianity?

4. Physicist and theologian John Polkinghorne says "religious knowledge is more demanding than scientific knowledge" because it calls for "the response of commitment to the truth discovered." How do you believe you should personally respond to the evidence you've encountered in this book? If you decide to pursue the three-pronged approach that Viggo Olsen discussed, what specific steps do you plan to take? What do you think your biggest obstacle will be and how will you overcome it? Or are you at a point where you feel you should respond to the evidence like Olsen and the author did—by praying to receive Jesus as your forgiver and leader? What implications would such a decision hold for you personally?

NOTES

Chapter 1: White-Coated Scientists Versus Black-Robed Preachers

1. Quote of German atheistic philosopher Ludwig Feuerbach in: Hans Küng, *Freud and the Problem of God*, enlarged edition, translated by Edward Quinn (New Haven: Yale University Press, 1990), 3.
2. Lee Strobel, "Textbook Battle Rages in Bible Belt County," *Chicago Tribune* (October 20, 1974) and "Hidden Issues Seen Behind Textbook Split," *Chicago Tribune* (October 21, 1974).
3. Phillip E. Johnson, *Darwin on Trial* (Downers Grove, Ill.: InterVarsity Press, second edition, 1993), 126–27.

Chapter 2: The Images of Evolution

1. Review of: Carl Sagan, *The Demon-Haunted World: Science as a Candle in the Dark* (New York: Ballantine, 1997) in the *New York Review of Books* (January 9, 1997). Emphasis in original.
2. Phillip E. Johnson, "The Church of Darwin," *Wall Street Journal* (August 16, 1999).
3. J. P. Moreland, *Christianity and the Nature of Science* (Grand Rapids, Mich.: Baker, 1989), 19.
4. Eugenie Scott, "Keep Science Free from Creationism," *Insight* (February 21, 1994).
5. Richard Dawkins, *The Blind Watchmaker* (New York: Norton, 1986), 6.
6. Neil Campbell, Jane Reece, and Lawrence Mitchell, *Biology* (Menlo Park, Calif.: Benjamin/Cummings, 1999), 419.
7. Alan Feduccia, *The Origin and Evolution of Birds* (New Haven: Yale University Press, 1996), 38.
8. Phillip E. Johnson, *Darwin on Trial*, 80.
9. Dean E. Murphy of the *New York Times*, "Eagle Scout Faces Ultimatum over Atheism," *Orange County Register* (November 3, 2002).
10. Richard Dawkins, "On Debating Religion," *The Nullifidian* (December 1994).
11. Quoted in Gregg Easterbrook, "The New Convergence," *Wired* (December 2002).
12. Quoted in Holly J. Morris, "Life's Grand Design," *U.S. News and World Report* (July 29, 2002).
13. Michael Ruse, *Can a Darwinian Be a Christian?* (Cambridge, England: Cambridge University Press, 2001), 217, 128.
14. Richard F. Carlson, editor, *Science and Christianity: Four Views* (Downers Grove, Ill.: InterVarsity Press, 2000), 81.
15. Ibid., 187.

16. Douglas Futuyma, *Evolutionary Biology* (Sunderland, Mass.: Sinauer, 1986), 3.
17. William A. Dembski and James M. Kushiner, editors, *Signs of Intelligence* (Grand Rapids, Mich.: Brazos, 2001), 44.
18. Quoted in Michael Ruse, *Can a Darwinian Be a Christian?* 98.
19. Romans 1:20.
20. Richard F. Carlson, editor, *Science and Christianity: Four Views*, 139.
21. Ibid., 118.
22. George Gaylord Simpson, *The Meaning of Evolution* (Cambridge, Mass.: Harvard University Press, 1967), 345.
23. Richard F. Carlson, editor, *Science and Christianity: Four Views*, 118.
24. Nancy Pearcey, "Design and the Discriminating Public: Gaining a Hearing from Ordinary People," in William A. Dembski and James M. Kushiner, editors, *Signs of Intelligence*, 44. Emphasis in original.
25. Ibid., quoting: Gertrude Himmelfarb, *Darwin and the Darwinian Revolution* (Garden City, N.Y.: Doubleday Anchor, 1959), 329–30.
26. Phillip E. Johnson, quoted in *World* (July/August 2002).
27. Ernst Mayr, foreword to *Darwinism Defended*, by Michael Ruse (New York: Addison-Wesley, 1982), xi-xii.
28. See: Gordy Slack, "A Good Life," *UCI Journal* (Spring 1999), available at: *www.today.uci.edu/journal/99spring/f2.html* (January 2, 2002).
29. John H. Campbell and J. William Schopf, editors, *Creative Evolution?!* (Boston: Jones and Bartlett, 1994), 4–5.
30. William Provine, "Scientists Face It! Science and Religion Are Incompatible," *The Scientist* 2 (1988).
31. Edward O. Wilson, *On Human Nature* (Cambridge, Mass.: Harvard University Press, 1978), 1. Emphasis added.
32. "Iconoclast of the Century: Charles Darwin (1809–1882)," *Time* (December 31, 1999).
33. *World Book Encyclopedia*, Volume 5 (Chicago: Field Enterprises Educational Corp., 1962 edition), 334.
34. Quoted in: Phillip E. Johnson, "The Intelligent Design Movement: Challenging the Modernist Monopoly on Science," in: William A. Dembski and James M. Kushiner, editors, *Signs of Intelligence*, 34.
35. Bertrand Russell, *Why I Am Not a Christian* (New York: Simon & Schuster, 1957), 106.
36. Ibid., 107.
37. Robert W. Funk, Roy W. Hoover, and The Jesus Seminar, *The Five Gospels* (San Francisco: HarperSanFrancisco, 1993), 2.
38. See: Lee Strobel, *The Case for Christ* (Grand Rapids, Mich.: Zondervan. 1998).
39. See: Lee Strobel, *The Case for Faith* (Grand Rapids, Mich.: Zondervan, 2000).

40. Linus Pauling, *No More War!* (New York: Dodd, Mead & Co., 1958), 209.

41. Available at *search.nap.edu/readingroom/books/evolution98/ evol4.html* (January 5, 2003).

42. Robert M. Augros and George N. Stanciu, *The New Story of Science* (New York: Bantam, 1986), xiv.

43. Ibid., xv.

Chapter 3: Doubts about Darwinism

1. Quoted in *Scientific American* (July 2000).

2. Larry Hatfield, "Educators Against Darwin," *Science Digest* (Winter 1979).

3. "A Scientific Dissent From Darwinism," two-page advertisement, *The Weekly Standard* (October 1, 2001).

4. See: *Getting the Facts Straight* (Seattle: Discovery Institute Press, 2001), 11.

5. Ibid., 9.

6. Jonathan Wells, *Charles Hodge's Critique of Darwinism: An Historical-Critical Analysis of Concepts Basic to the 19th Century Debate* (Lewiston, N.Y.: Edwin Mellen, 1988).

7. What Wells called his "faith journey" even brought him to the Unification Church, partly because he shared its strong anticommunist stance. For critiques of this group, whose theology I thoroughly disagree with, see: Ruth A. Tucker, *Another Gospel* (Grand Rapids, Mich.: Zondervan 1989), 245–66.

8. See: Jonathan Wells, *Icons of Evolution* (Washington, D.C.: Regnery, 2000).

9. Note that all interviews have been edited for conciseness, clarity, and content.

10. While Wells's definition of neo-Darwinism is valid, I generally have used the term "Darwinism" in this book to encompass the concept of neo-Darwinism.

11. See: Philip H. Abelson, "Chemical Events on the Primitive Earth," *Proceedings of the National Academy of Sciences USA* 55 (1966), 1365–72.

12. See: Michael Florkin, "Ideas and Experiments in the Field of Prebiological Chemical Evolution," *Comprehensive Biochemistry* 29B (1975), 231–60.

13. See: Sidney W. Fox and Klaus Dose, *Molecular Evolution and the Origin of Life* (New York: Marcel Dekker, revised edition 1977), 43, 74–76.

14. John Cohen, "Novel Center Seeks to Add Spark to Origins of Life," *Science* 270 (1995), 1925–26.

15. See: Gerald F. Joyce, "RNA Evolution and the Origins of Life," *Nature* 338 (1989), 217–24; and Robert Irion, "RNA Can't Take the Heat," *Science* 279 (1998), 1303.

16. Charles B. Thaxton, Walter L. Bradley, and Roger L. Olsen, *The Mystery of Life's Origin* (Dallas: Lewis and Stanley, 1984).

17. See: Lee Strobel, *The Case for Faith*, 87–112.

18. Gregg Easterbrook, "The New Convergence."

19. Lee Strobel, *The Case for Faith*, 108.

20. John Horgan, "A Holiday Made for Believing," *New York Times* (December 25, 2002).

21. Francis Crick, *Life Itself* (New York: Simon and Schuster, 1981), 88.

22. Lee Strobel, *The Case for Faith*, 108.

23. The biological classifications in ascending order are: species, genus, family, order, class, phylum, and kingdom. For example, for human beings, the classifications would be: species (sapiens); genus (homo); family (hominids); order (primates); class (mammals); phylum (chordates); and kingdom (animals).

24. The big bright spot, of course, was the Bears' 46–10 victory over New England in Super Bowl XX, which was played on January 26, 1986, at the Louisiana Superdome.

25. See: Jeffrey H. Schwartz, "Homeobox Genes, Fossils, and the Origin of Species," *Anatomical Record (New Anatomist)* 257 (1999), 15–31.

26. See: James W. Valentine and Douglas H. Erwin, "Interpreting Great Developmental Experiments: The Fossil Record," in: Rudolf A. Raff and Elizabeth C. Raff, editors, *Development as an Evolutionary Process* (New York: Alan R. Liss, 1987), 84–85.

27. See: Stephen Jay Gould, "Abscheulich! Atrocious!" *Natural History* (March, 2002).

28. For a description of how various textbooks use embryo drawings, see: Jonathan Wells, *Icons of Evolution*, 101–104.

29. *The World Book Encyclopedia*, Volume 2, 242.

30. See: Kenneth Miller, "What Does It Mean To Be One Of Us?" *Life* (November 1996).

31. See: Jonathan Wells, *Icons of Evolution*, 105.

32. Lewis Wolpert, *The Triumph of the Embryo* (Oxford: Oxford University Press, 1991), 185.

33. See: Tim Berra, *Evolution and the Myth of Creationism* (Stanford: Stanford University Press, 1990), 117–19.

34. R. Gore, "Dinosaurs," *National Geographic* (January 1993).

35. Michael Denton, *Evolution: A Theory in Crisis* (Chevy Chase, Md.: Adler and Adler, 1986), 162.

36. Ibid., 172.

37. Larry D. Martin, "The Relationship of *Archaeopteryx* to other Birds," in: M. K. Hecht, J. H. Ostrom, G. Viohl, and P. Wellnhofer, editors, *The Beginnings of Birds* (Eichstätt: Freunde des Jura-Museums, 1985), 182, quoted in: Jonathan Wells, *Icons of Evolution*, 116.

38. Pierre Lecomte du Nouy, *Human Destiny* (New York: Longmaus, Green and Co., 1947), quoted in: Hank Hanegraaff, *The Face That Demonstrates the Farce of Evolution* (Nashville: Word, 1998), 37.

39. Phillip E. Johnson, *Darwin on Trial*, 81.

40. Kathy A. Svitil, "Plucking Apart the Dino-Birds," *Discover* (February 2003).

41. Ibid.

42. Discovery of what news articles described as a "four-winged dinosaur" caused a stir in early 2003. In a letter to the *New York Times*, however, Howard Zimmerman, co-editor of *The Scientific American Book of Dinosaurs*, said he doubted whether this finding "will cast new light on the evolution of birds." He said that "since the geographic strata in which the fossils were found are about 125 million years old, this animal could not have been the progenitor of the avian line." In other words, Zimmerman indicated it was not "the missing evolutionary link." See: "Do Birds and Dinosaurs Flock Together?" *New York Times* (January 26, 2003).

43. See: Charles Darwin, *The Origin of Species* (New York: Grammercy, 1998).

44. "Ape Man: The Story of Human Evolution," hosted by Walter Cronkite, Arts and Entertainment network, September 4, 1994, quoted in: Hank Hanegraaff, *The Face That Demonstrates the Farce of Evolution*, 57.

45. Marvin L. Lubenow, *Bones of Contention* (Grand Rapids, Mich.: Baker, 1992), 86.

46. *World Book Encyclopedia*, Volume 10, 50.

47. Martin L. Lubenow, *Bones of Contention*, 87.

48. Hank Hanegraaff, *The Face That Demonstrates the Farce of Evolution*, 50.

49. See: Martin L. Lubenow, *Bones of Contention*, 86–99.

50. Hank Hanegraaff, *The Face That Demonstrates the Farce of Evolution*, 52.

51. Martin L. Lubenow, *Bones of Contention*, 87.

52. Michael D. Lemonick, "How Man Began," *Time* (March 14, 1994), quoted in: Hank Hanegraaff, *The Face That Demonstrates the Farce of Evolution*, 52.

53. See: Constance Holden, "The Politics of Paleoanthropology," *Science* 213 (1981).

54. See: Henry Gee, *In Search of Deep Time: Beyond the Fossil Record to a New History of Life* (New York: The Free Press, 1999).

55. See: Ian Tattersall, "Paleoanthropology and Preconception," in: W. Eric Meikle, F. Clark Howell, and Nina G. Jablonski, editors, *Contemporary Issues in Human Evolution*, Memoir 21 (San Francisco: California Academy of Sciences, 1996); Geoffrey A. Clark, "Through a Glass Darkly: Conceptual Issues in Modern Human Origins Research," in G. A. Clark and C. M. Willermet, editors, *Conceptual Issues in Modern Human Origins Research* (New York: Aldine de Gruyter, 1997), quoted in: Jonathan Wells, *Icons of Evolution*, 223.

56. See: Misia Landau, *Narratives of Human Evolution* (New Haven: Yale University Press, 1991).

57. F. Clark Howell, "Thoughts on the Study and Interpretation of the Human Fossil Record," in W. Eric Meikle, F. Clark Howell, and Nina G. Jablonski, editors, *Contemporary Issues in Human Evolution*, Memoir 21.

58. For a critique of "punctuated equilibrium," see: Phillip E. Johnson, *Darwin on Trial*, 50, 52, 58, 60–61, 120, 141, 153, 184–185, 187.

59. Jonathan Wells, *Icons of Evolution*, 188.

Chapter 4: Where Science Meets Faith

1. Steven Weinberg, "A Designer Universe?" *The New York Review of Books* (October 21, 1999), adapted from a talk given at the Conference on Cosmic Design of the American Association for the Advancement of Science, Washington, D.C., April 1999 (emphasis added).

2. John Polkinghorne, *Quarks, Chaos, and Christianity* (New York: Crossroad, 1994), xii.

3. Sharon Begley, "Science Finds God," *Newsweek* (July 20, 1998).

4. Ibid.

5. See: Dean H. Kenyon and Gary Steinman, *Biochemical Predestination* (New York: McGraw-Hill, 1969).

6. Allan Sandage, "A Scientist Reflects on Religious Belief," available at: *www.leaderu.com/truth/1truth15.html* (January 7, 2003).

7. J. P. Moreland, *Christianity and the Nature of Science*, 103.

8. Review of Carl Sagan, *The Demon-Haunted World: Science as a Candle in the Dark* (New York: Ballantine, 1997) in the *New York Review of Books* (January 9, 1997).

9. Stephen Jay Gould, "Nonoverlapping Magisteria," *Natural History* 106 (March 1997). See also: Stephen Jay Gould, *Rocks of Ages* (New York: Ballantine, 1999).

10. Stephen Jay Gould, *Rocks of Ages*, 14.

11. Phillip E. Johnson, "The Church of Darwin," *Wall Street Journal* (August 16, 1999).

12. See: Malcolm W. Browne, "Clues to Universe Origin Expected," *New York Times* (March 12, 1978).

13. Fred Hoyle, "The Universe: Past and Present Reflections," *Annual Review of Astronomy and Astrophyics* 20 (1982).

14. Paul Davies, *The Cosmic Blueprint* (New York: Simon & Schuster, 1988), 203.

15. Richard Dawkins, *River Out of Eden* (New York: Basic Books, 1995), 10.

16. Steven H. Gifis, *Law Dictionary* (Woodbury, N.Y.: Barron's Educational Series, 1975), 33–34.

17. David Briggs, "Science, Religion Are Discovering Commonality in Big Bang Theory," *Los Angeles Times* (May 2, 1992).

18. See: Michael Shermer, *How We Believe* (New York: W. H. Freeman, 2000), 72–73, 251.

19. Sharon Begley, "Science Finds God," *Newsweek* (July 20, 1998).

20. Michael Shermer, *How We Believe*, xxix.

21. Kenneth R. Miller, *Finding Darwin's God* (New York: Cliff Street Books, paperback edition, 2000), 28.

22. Ibid., 101.

23. Ibid.

24. G. C. Williams, *Natural Selection: Domains, Levels and Challenges* (Oxford: Oxford University Press, 1992), 73, 72.

25. George Ayoub, "On the Design of the Vertebrate Retina," *Origins & Design* 17:1, Winter, 1996.

26. Romans 8:22: "We know that the whole creation has been groaning as in the pains of childbirth right up to the present time."

Chapter 5: The Evidence of Cosmology: Beginning with a Bang

1. Gregg Easterbrook, "The New Convergence," *Wired* (December 2002).

2. C. J. Isham, "Creation of the Universe as a Quantum Process," in: R. J. Russell, W. R. Stoeger, and G. V. Coyne, editors, *Physics, Philosophy, and Theology* (Vatican City State: Vatican Observatory, 1988), 378, quoted in William Lane Craig, *Reasonable Faith* (Wheaton, Ill.: Crossway, revised edition, 1994), 328.

3. *Discover* (April 2002).

4. Genesis 1:1.

5. "And God said, 'Let there be light,' and there was light"—Genesis 1:3.

6. This is not to suggest that questions concerning the age of the universe aren't important. My goal at this point, however, was to sidestep biblical debates over this issue and instead see whether the evidence most widely conceded by non-Christian scientists pointed toward or away from God.

7. Steven Weinberg, *The First Three Minutes* (New York: Basic Books, updated edition, 1988), 5.

8. Ibid.

9. Ibid., 6.

10. Bill Bryson, *A Short History of Nearly Everything* (New York: Broadway, 2003), 10.

11. Ibid., 13.

12. Quoted in Robert Jastrow, *God and the Astronomers* (New York: W. W. Norton, second edition, 1992), 104.

13. Dennis Overbye, "Are They *a)* Geniuses or *b)* Jokers?" *New York Times* (November 9, 2002).

14. Bill Bryson, *A Short History of Nearly Everything*, 13.

15. See: Stuart C. Hackett, *The Resurrection of Theism* (Grand Rapids, Mich.: Baker, second edition, 1982).

16. William Lane Craig and Mark S. McLeod, editors, *The Logic of Rational Theism: Exploratory Essays* (Lewiston, N.Y.: Edwin Mellen, 1990), 11.

17. William Lane Craig, *Reasonable Faith*, 92.

18. William Lane Craig and Quentin Smith, *Theism, Atheism and Big Bang Cosmology* (Oxford: Clarendon Press, 1993), 135.

19. Timothy Ferris, *The Whole Shebang* (New York: Touchstone, 1998), 265.

20. Brad Lemley, "Guth's Grand Guess," *Discover* (April 2002).

21. Ibid., 35.

22. David Hume, *The Letters of David Hume*, Two Volumes, J.Y.T. Greig, editor (Oxford: Clarendon Press, 1932), 1:187, quoted in: William Lane Craig, *Reasonable Faith*, 93.

23. Stephen W. Hawking and Roger Penrose, *The Nature of Space and Time* (Princeton, N.J.: Princeton University Press, 1996), 20.

24. Kai Nielsen, *Reason and Practice* (New York: Harper & Row, 1971), 48.

25. Robert Jastrow, *God and the Astronomers* (New York: W.W. Norton, revised edition, 1992), 14.

26. George H. Smith, *Atheism* (Amherst, N.Y.: Prometheus, 1989), 239 (emphasis in original).

27. David M. Brooks, *The Necessity of Atheism* (New York: Freethought Press Association, 1933), 102–103, quoted in: Ibid.

28. For a summary of evidence for the Resurrection see: Lee Strobel, *The Case for Easter* (Grand Rapids, Mich.: Zondervan, 2004).

29. George H. Smith, *Atheism*, 237.

30. Edmund Whittaker, *The Beginning and End of the World* (Oxford: Oxford University Press, 1942), quoted in: Robert Jastrow, *God and the Astronomers*, 103, (emphasis added).

31. George H. Smith, *Atheism*, 237.

32. Einstein made this comment in a letter to Willem DeSitter. See: Robert Jastrow, *God and the Astronomers*, 21.

33. Robert Jastrow, *God and the Astronomers*, 21. Said Jastow of Einstein: "We know he had well-defined feelings about God, but not as the Creator or the Prime Mover. For Einstein, the existence of God was proven by the laws of nature; that is, the fact that there was order in the Universe and man could discover it."

34. Ibid., 104.

35. Ibid., 105.

36. Bill Bryson, *A Short History of Nearly Everything*, 13.

37. See: Joseph Silk, *The Big Bang* (San Francisco: W. H. Freeman, 1989), 311–12.

38. Carl Sagan, *Cosmos* (New York: Ballantine, 1993), 4.

39. See: Deborah Zabarenko, Reuters News Agency, "Princeton Physicist Offers Theory of Cyclic Universe," *Orange County (Calif.) Register* (April 26, 2002).

40. The Business Week Best-Seller List, *Business Week* (December 31, 2001).

41. See: Michael Shermer, *How We Believe*, 102.

42. Ibid.

43. Stephen Hawking, *A Brief History of Time* (New York: Bantam, 1988), 141.

44. As a side note, Craig said singularities do not have to be a mathematical point in time, but could theoretically have different geometries.

45. See: Michael White and John Gribbin, *Stephen Hawking: A Life in Science* (New York: Plume/Penguin, 1992).

46. Michael Shermer, *How We Believe*, 103.

47. See: Stephen W. Hawking and Roger Penrose, *The Nature of Space and Time* (Princeton, N.J.: Princeton University Press, 1996).

48. See: *www.hawking.org.uk/about/aindex.html* (accessed June 7, 2003).

49. The Four Spiritual Laws were written by the late Bill Bright, founder of Campus Crusade for Christ, as a summary of the gospel. Law No. 1: God loves you and created you to know him personally. He has a wonderful plan for your life (John 3:16; John 17:3). Law No. 2: People are sinful and separated from God, so we cannot know him personally or experience his life and plan (Romans 3:23; Romans 6:23). Law No. 3: Jesus Christ is God's only provision for our sin. Through him alone we can know God personally and experience God's love and plan (Romans 5:8; 1 Corinthians 15:3–6; John 14:6). Law No. 4: We must individually receive Jesus Christ as Savior and Lord; then we can know God personally and experience his love (John 1:12; Ephesians 2:8, 9; John 3:1–8, Revelation 3:20). See: *www.campuscrusadeforChrist.org* (accessed June 9, 2003).

Chapter 6: The Evidence of Physics: The Cosmos on a Razor's Edge

1. Paul Davies, *God and the New Physics* (New York: Simon and Schuster, 1983), 189.
2. John Templeton, *The Humble Approach: Scientists Discover God* (Philadelphia: Templeton Foundation, 1998), 19.
3. For a description of the dynamics between Christian and non-Christian spouses, based on the experiences that Leslie and I had during the era when she was a Christian and I was an atheist, see Lee and Leslie Strobel, *Surviving a Spiritual Mismatch in Marriage* (Grand Rapids, Mich.: Zondervan, 2002).
4. See: Patrick Glynn, "The Making and Unmaking of an Atheist," in: *God: The Evidence* (Rocklin, Calif.: Forum, 1997), 1–20.
5. Ibid., 22.
6. Ibid., 55, 53.
7. Alister McGrath, *Glimpsing the Face of God* (Grand Rapids, Mich.: Eerdmans, 2002), 19.
8. John Polkinghorne, *Belief in God in an Age of Science* (New Haven: Yale University Press, 1998), 10.
9. Walter L. Bradley, "The 'Just So' Universe," in William A. Dembski and James M. Kushiner, *Signs of Intelligence*, 170.
10. Paul Davies, *The Mind of God* (New York: Touchstone, 1992), 16, 232.
11. Edward Harrison, *Masks of the Universe* (New York: Collier, 1985), 263, 252.
12. Quoted in John Barrow and Frank Tipler, *The Anthropic Cosmological Principle* (Oxford: Oxford University Press, 1986), 22.
13. Owen Gingerich, "Dare a Scientist Believe in Design?" in John M. Templeton, editor, *Evidence of Purpose* (New York: Continuum, 1994), 25.
14. John Leslie, *Universes* (New York: Routledge, 1989), 198.
15. Robert M. Augros and George N. Stanciu, *The New Story of Science*, 70.
16. Robin Collins, "A Scientific Argument for the Existence of God: The Fine-Tuning Design Argument," in Michael J. Murray, editor, *Reason for the Hope Within* (Grand Rapids, Mich.: Eerdmans, 1999), 48.
17. Paul Davies, *The Cosmic Blueprint: New Discoveries in Nature's Creative Ability to Order the Universe* (New York: Simon and Schuster, 1988), 203.
18. Collins (and Gingerich in his earlier quote) was referring to a well-known comment by Sir Fred Hoyle: "A common sense interpretation of the facts suggests that a superintellect has monkeyed with the physics, as well as with chemistry and biology, and that there are no blind forces worth speaking about in nature. The numbers one calculates from the facts seem to me so overwhelming as to put this conclusion almost beyond question." Fred Hoyle, "The Universe: Past and Present Reflections," *Engineering & Science* (November 1981).

19.   The relative strength of the four forces in nature—gravity, electromagnetism, the weak force, and the strong nuclear force—is typically specified by a widely used dimensionless measure, which can roughly be thought of as the relative strengths of the respective forces between two protons in a nucleus. See: John Barrow and Frank Tipler, *The Anthropic Cosmological Principle* (Oxford: Oxford University Press, 1986), 293–95.

20.   Martin Rees, *Just Six Numbers: The Deep Forces That Shape the Universe* (New York: Basic, 2000), 30.

21.   Stephen C. Meyer, "Evidence for Design in Physics and Biology" in Michael J. Behe, William A. Dembski, and Stephen C. Meyer, editors, *Science and Evidence for Design in the Universe* (San Francisco: Ignatius, 2000), 60.

22.   Steven Weinberg, "A Designer Universe?" *New York Review of Books* (October 21, 1999).

23.   Ibid.

24.   Ibid.

25.   Roger Penrose, *The Emperor's New Mind* (New York: Oxford, 1989), 344, quoted in Stephen C. Meyer, "Evidence for Design in Physics and Biology" in Michael J. Behe, William A. Dembski, and Stephen C. Meyer, editors, *Science and Evidence for Design in the Universe*, 61.

26.   Brad Lemley, "Why Is There Life?" *Discover* (November 2002) emphasis added.

27.   Ibid. Also see Martin Rees, *Just Six Numbers: The Deep Forces That Shape the Universe*.

28.   Quoted in Larry Witham, *By Design* (San Francisco: Encounter, 2003), 55.

29.   Bill Bryson, *A Short History of Nearly Everything*, 16.

30.   Brad Lemley, "Why Is There Life?"

31.   Ibid.

32.   Clifford Longley, "Focusing on Theism," *London Times* (January 21, 1989).

33.   Steven Weinberg, "A Designer Universe?"

34.   Michael J. Behe, William A. Dembski, and Stephen C. Meyer, *Science and Evidence for Design in the Universe*, 104, referencing Clifford Longley, "Focusing on Theism."

35.   Paul Davies offers this definition of metaphysics: "In Greek philosophy, the term 'metaphysics' originally meant 'that which comes after physics.' It refers to the fact that Aristotle's metaphysics was found, untitled, placed after his treatise on physics. But metaphysics soon came to mean those topics that lie beyond physics (we would today say beyond science) and yet may have a bearing on the nature of scientific inquiry. So metaphysics means the study of topics about physics (or science generally), as opposed

to the scientific subject itself. Traditional metaphysical problems have included the origin, nature, and purpose of the universe, how the world of appearances presented to our senses relates to its underlying 'reality' and order, the relationship between mind and matter, and the existence of free will. Clearly science is deeply involved in such issues, but empirical science alone may not be able to answer them, or any 'meaning-of-life' questions." (Paul Davies, *The Mind of God*, 31.)

36. Lee Strobel, *The Case for Faith*, 78, 79.

37. John Polkinghorne, *Serious Talk: Science and Religion in Dialogue* (London: Trinity Press International, 1995), 6.

38. John Polkinghorne, *Science and Theology* (Minneapolis: Fortress Press, 1998), 38.

39. Paul Davies, *The Mind of God*, 220.

40. Clifford Longley, "Focusing on Theism."

41. Brad Lemley, "Why Is There Life?" In a subsequent interview, Rees said it's helpful for physicists to contemplate the possibility of other universes. He added: "I don't believe, but I think it's part of science to find out." See Dennis Overbye, "A New View of Our Universe: Only One of Many," *New York Times* (October 29, 2002).

42. Ibid.

43. According to *The Bread Factory Book*, produced by Sanyo: "Bread flour made from hard wheat is high in the protein substance called gluten. When mixed and kneaded, the gluten stretches and incorporates air bubbles to produce a light, fine textured loaf." In making whole-wheat bread, up to four tablespoons of gluten needs to be added to increase the height of the loaves.

44. Michio Kaku, *Introduction to Superstrings and M-Theory* (New York: Springer-Verlag, second edition, 1999), 17.

45. Freeman Dyson, *Disturbing the Universe* (New York: Harper and Row, 1979), 251.

46. Gregg Easterbrook, "The New Convergence," *Wired* (December 2002) emphasis added.

47. See: "Chapter Six: Beautiful Theories," in Steven Weinberg, *Dreams of a Final Theory* (New York, Vintage Books, 1992).

48. Alan Guth, *The Inflationary Universe* (New York: Helix, 1997), 124.

49. Paul Dirac, "The Evolution of the Physicist's Picture of Nature," *Scientific American* (May 1963).

50. Oliver Darrigol, *From c-Numbers to q-Numbers: The Classical Analogy in the History of Quantum Theory* (Los Angeles: University of California Press, 1992), 304.

51. Paul Davies, *Superforce: The Search for a Grand Unified Theory of Nature* (New York: Simon and Schuster, 1984), 235–36.

52. Steven Weinberg, *Dreams of a Final Theory*, 250.
53. Dennis Overbye, "A New View of Our Universe: Only One of Many."
54. Owen Gingerich, "Dare a Scientist Believe in Design?" in John M. Templeton, editor, *Evidence of Purpose* (New York: Continuum, 1994), 32.
55. Vera Kistiakowsky, "The Exquisite Order of the Physical World Calls for the Divine," in Henry Margenau and Roy Abraham Varghese, *Cosmos, Bios, Theos* (Chicago: Open Court, 1992), 52.
56. Patrick Glynn, *God: The Evidence*, 55, 26.

Chapter 7: The Evidence of Astronomy: The Privileged Planet
1. George Greenstein, *The Symbiotic Universe* (New York: William Morrow, 1988), 27.
2. Henry Margenau and Roy Abraham Varghese, editors, *Cosmos, Bios, and Theos* (LaSalle, Ill.: Open Court, 1992), 83.
3. Carl Sagan, *Pale Blue Dot* (New York: Ballantine, 1994), 7.
4. See: Peter D. Ward and Donald Brownlee, *Rare Earth* (New York: Copernicus, 2000), xxiv.
5. Ibid., xiv.
6. David Darling, *Life Everywhere* (New York: Basic Books, 2002).
7. Ibid., xii.
8. Ibid., xi.
9. *Science* 277 (1997), 892.
10. Bernard Oliver quoted in Steven J. Dick, *Life on Other Worlds* (Cambridge: Cambridge University Press, 1998), 217.
11. Michael J. Denton, *Nature's Destiny* (New York: The Free Press, 1998), 387.
12. Peter D. Ward and Donald Brownlee, *Rare Earth*, xxiv.
13. Ibid., xiv.
14. Ibid., 33.
15. Ibid., xix.
16. Ibid., back cover.
17. Ibid.
18. The *Times of London* (January 26, 2002), quoted in: David Darling, *Life Everywhere*, 91.
19. Jimmy H. Davis and Harry L. Poe, *Designer Universe* (Nashville: Broadman & Holman, 2002), 107.
20. See: Michael Denton, *Nature's Destiny* (New York: The Free Press, 1998), 88–89.
21. Frank Press and Raymond Siever, *Earth* (New York: W. H. Freeman, 1986), 3.
22. Ibid., 4.
23. Ibid., 3.
24. Peter D. Ward and Donald Brownlee, *Rare Earth*, 37, 229.

25. Michael J. Denton, *Nature's Destiny*, 3–4.

26. Quoted in Hans Blumenberg, *The Genesis of the Copernican Revolution*, translated by Robert M. Wallace (Cambridge, Mass.: MIT Press, 1987), xv.

27. Galileo Galilei, *Sidereus Nuncius*, quoted in Dennis Danielson, *The Book of the Cosmos* (Cambridge: Perseus, Helix, 2000), 150.

28. Philip J. Sampson, *Six Modern Myths* (Downers Grove, Ill.: InterVarsity, 2000), 33 (emphasis added).

29. William R. Shea, "Galileo and the Church" in: David C. Lindberg and Ronald L. Numbers, editors, *God and Nature* (Berkeley: University of California Press, 1986), 132.

30. Philip J. Sampson, *Six Modern Myths*, 38, citing Jerome J. Langford, *Galileo, Science and the Church* (Ann Arbor: University of Michigan Press, 1971), 134.

31. A. N. Whitehead, *Science and the Modern World* (Cambridge: Cambridge University Press, 1946), 2, quoted in Philip J. Sampson, *Six Modern Myths*, 38.

32. "Natural Adversaries?" *Christian History*, 76 (Volume XXI, No. 4), 44.

33. Gunter D. Roth, *Stars and Planets* (New York: Sterling, 1998), 89.

34. Pam Spence, general editor, *The Universe Revealed* (Cambridge: Cambridge University Press, 1999), 40.

35. David Koerner and Simon LeVay, *Here Be Dragons* (Oxford: Oxford University Press, 2000), 5.

36. Ibid., 5–6.

37. Quoted in Peter D. Ward and Donald Brownlee, *Rare Earth*, 266.

38. Ibid., 220. For an excellent discussion of the importance of plate tectonics, 191–220.

39. Ibid.

40. See: R. J. Charlson, J. E. Lovelock, M. O. Andrea, and S. G. Warren, "Oceanic phytoplankton, atmospheric sulfur, cloud albedo and climate," *Nature* 326 (1987); and R. J. Charlson et al., "Reshaping the theory of cloud formation," *Science* 293 (2001).

41. "The Genesis of Ores," *Scientific American*, May, 1991.

42. Gonzalez noted that one of Saturn's moons, Prometheus, comes close, but it's shaped like a potato and results in eclipses that last less than a second.

43. See Michael J. Denton, *Nature's Destiny*, 117.

44. Henry Petroski, *Invention by Design* (Cambridge, Mass.: Harvard University Press, 1996), 30.

45. See: *www.geocities.com/CapeCanaveral/Campus/4764/OKeefeObitEOS.pdf* (accessed June 1, 2003).

46. John A. O'Keefe, "The Theological Impact of the New Cosmology" in: Robert Jastrow, *God and the Astronomers* (New York: W. W. Norton, 1992), 122.

47. Astronomer Hugh Ross makes an interesting related observation. He cites seven reasons to believe why it's likely that micro-organisms from Earth have ended up on Mars. Based on "the transportability and survivability of Earth's life forms," he said that "there are many reasons to believe that millions of Earth's minute creatures have been deposited on the surface of Mars and other solar system planets." He said Mars's inhospitable environment would make germination of such life unlikely, and "thus 'adult' organisms should be quite rare on Mars." He added: "The discovery of microbial life and creatures perhaps as large as nematodes on Mars—a discovery we can expect as technology continues to advance—will probably be touted as proof of naturalistic evolution, when in truth it proves nothing of the kind. It will prove something, however, about the amazing vitality of what God created." See Hugh Ross, *The Creator and the Cosmos* (Colorado Springs: Navpress, 1993), 144–46.

48. John A. O'Keefe, "The Theological Impact of the New Cosmology," in Robert Jastrow, *God and the Astronomers*, 118 (emphasis added).

Chapter 8: The Evidence of Biochemisty: The Complexity of Molecular Machines

1. Bruce Alberts, "The Cell as a Collection of Protein Machines," *Cell* 92 (February 8, 1998).

2. Franklin M. Harold, *The Way of the Cell* (Oxford: Oxford University Press, 2001), 205.

3. Ibid., 329.

4. Michael Behe, *Darwin's Black Box* (New York: Touchstone, 1996), back cover.

5. Charles Darwin, *The Origin of Species* (New York: New York University Press, sixth edition, 1998), 154.

6. For a more in-depth response to McDonald, see Michael J. Behe, "A Mousetrap Defended," available at *www.arn.org/docs/behe/mb_mousetrapdefended.htm* (accessed November 2, 2002).

7. Kenneth R. Miller, "The Flaw in the Mousetrap," *Natural History* (April 2002).

8. See: Edward M. Purcell, "The Efficiency of Propulsion by a Rotating Flagellum," *Proceedings of the National Academy of Sciences USA* 94 (October 1997), available at *www.impa.br/~jair/pnas.pdf* (accessed July 1, 2003).

9. See: Joe Lorio, "Four of a Kind," *Automobile* (August, 2003).

10. Andrew Pomiankowski, "The God of the Tiny Gaps," *New Scientist* (September 14, 1996).

11. Michael Denton, *Evolution: A Theory in Crisis*, 338.

12. See: Michael J. Behe, *Darwin's Black Box*, 90–97.

13. Kenneth R. Miller, *Finding Darwin's God* (New York: Cliff Street, 1999), 145.

14. Ibid., 147.

15. See: Michael J. Behe, "A True Acid Test: Response to Ken Miller," available at: *www.arn.org/docs/behe/mb_trueacidtest.htm* (accessed July 3, 2003).

16. Not all philosophers and scientists agree with the falsification test. "The role of falsification in science is not clear," said philosopher J. P. Moreland. "Nevertheless, falsification is certainly relevant to science. Whether it constitutes a necessary or sufficient condition for science, however, is quite another matter." See: J. P. Moreland, *Christianity and the Nature of Science*, 32–35.

17. National Academy of Sciences, *Science and Creationism: A View from the National Academy of Sciences* (Washington, D.C.: National Academy Press, 1999), 25.

18. Pamela R. Winnick, interview with Michael Behe, *The Pittsburgh Post-Gazette* (February 8, 2001).

19. J. Ratzinger, *In the Beginning: A Catholic Understanding of the Story of Creation and the Fall* (Grand Rapids, Mich.: Eerdmans, 1986), 56.

20. J. A. Shapiro, "In the Details . . . What?" *National Review* (September 16, 1996).

21. Allan Sandage, "A Scientist Reflects on Religious Belief," Truth: An Interdisciplinary Journal of Christian Thought, Volume 1 (1985). Available at *www.clm.org/truth/1truth15.html* (accessed July 31, 2000).

Chapter 9: The Evidence of Biological Information: The Challenge of DNA and the Origin of Life

1. George Sim Johnson, "Did Darwin Get It Right?" *The Wall Street Journal* (October 15, 1999).

2. Quoted in Stephen C. Meyer, "Word Games: DNA, Design, and Intelligence," in William A. Dembski and James M. Kushiner, *Signs of Intelligence*, 102.

3. Nicholas Wade, "A Revolution at 50; DNA Changed the World. Now What?" *New York Times* (February 25, 2003).

4. See: Nancy Gibbs, "The Secret of Life," *Time* (February 17, 2003).

5. Michael Denton, *Evolution: A Theory in Crisis*, 334.

6. *Unlocking the Mystery of Life*, produced by Illustra Media, available at: *www.illustramedia.com*.

7. Ibid.

8. Quoted in Larry Witham, *By Design*, 172.

9. The Discovery Institute is a think tank that deals with a wide variety of projects in the fields of technology, science and culture, legal reform, national defense, the environment and the economy, the future of democratic institutions, transportation, religion and public life, foreign affairs, and other areas. See: *www.discovery.org*.

10. See: Fazale R. Rana and Hugh Ross, "Life from the Heavens? Not This Way," *Facts for Faith*, Quarter 1, 2002, an account of a 1999 international conference on the origin of life, where the mood among Darwinists was described as full of frustration, pessimism, and desperation.

11. See: Bernd-Olaf Küppers, *Information and the Origin of Life* (Cambridge, Mass.: MIT Press, 1990), 170–72.

12. Henry Quastler, *The Emergence of Biological Organization* (New Haven: Yale University Press, 1964), 16.

13. Francis Darwin, *The Life and Letters of Charles Darwin* (New York: D. Appleton, 1887), 202.

14. Michael Denton, *Evolution: A Theory in Crisis*, 260.

15. See: J. Brooks, *Origins of Life* (Sydney: Lion, 1985).

16. Michael Denton, *Evolution: A Theory in Crisis*, 261.

17. See: Richard Dawkins, *Climbing Mount Improbable* (New York: W. W. Norton, 1996).

18. See: S. W. Fox, editor, *The Origins of Prebiological Systems and of their Molecular Matrices* (New York: Academic Press, 1965), 309–15.

19. For a summary of other arguments against the "RNA first" hypothesis, see: "Stephen C. Meyer Replies," *First Things* (October 2000).

20. Robert Shapiro, *Origins: A Skeptic's Guide to the Creation of Life on Earth* (New York: Summit, 1986), 189.

21. Ibid.

22. See: Gerald F. Joyce, "RNA Evolution and the Origins of Life," *Nature* 338 (1989), 217–24, and Robert Irion, "RNA Can't Take the Heat," *Science* 279 (1998), 1303.

23. Jay Roth, "The Piling of Coincidence on Coincidence," in: Henry Margenau and Roy Abraham Varghese, editors, *Cosmos, Bios, Theos* (Chicago: Open Court, 1992), 199.

24. Interview in *Unlocking the Mystery of Life*.

25. See: Michael Polanyi, "Life's Irreducible Structure," *Science* 160 (1968), 1308–12.

26. For a more detailed critique of this theory, see Hubert P. Yockey, "Self-Organization, Origin of Life Scenarios, and Information Theory, *Journal of Theoretical Biology* 91 (1981), 13–31, and Stephen C. Meyer, "DNA and the Origin of Life: Information, Specification, and Explanation," in John Angus Campbell and Stephen C. Meyer, editors, *Darwinism, Design, and Public Education* (Lansing, Mich.: Michigan State Univ. Press, 2003), 252–55.

27. Robert Shapiro, *Origins: A Skeptic's Guide to the Creation of Life on Earth*, 188.
28. Francis Crick, *Life Itself*, 88.
29. Robert Shapiro, *Origins: A Skeptic's Guide to the Creation of Life on Earth*, 189.
30. See: J. W. Valentine et al., "Fossils, Molecules, and Embryos: New Perspectives on the Cambrian Explosion," *Development* 126 (1999).
31. See: Chi Lili, "Traditional Theory of Evolution Challenged," *Beijing Review* (March 31–April 6, 1997).
32. John F. McDonald, "The Molecular Basis of Adaptation: A Critical Review of Relevant Ideas and Observations," *Annual Review of Ecology and Systematics* 14 (1983).
33. See: Stuart Kauffman, *At Home in the Universe* (Oxford: Oxford University Press, 1995).
34. Michael Denton, *Evolution: A Theory in Crisis*, 330.

Chapter 10: The Evidence of Consciousness: The Enigma of the Mind
1. Michael Ruse, *Can a Darwinian Be a Christian?* (Cambridge: Oxford University Press, 2001), 73.
2. Ray Kurzweil, "The Evolution of Mind in the Twenty-First Century," in Jay W. Richards, editor, *Are We Spiritual Machines?* (Seattle: Discovery Institute, 2002), 12, 29, 44–45, (emphasis added).
3. Thomas Huxley, "Mr. Darwin's Critics," *Contemporary Review* (November 1871).
4. Edward O. Wilson, *Consilience* (New York: Vintage, 1998), 132.
5. "Do Brains Make Minds?" on the television program *Closer to Truth*, first aired October 2000.
6. John Searle, "I Married a Computer," in Jay W. Richards, editor, *Are We Spiritual Machines?* 76.
7. "Do Brains Make Minds?" on *Closer to Truth*.
8. Quoted in *World* magazine (July/August 2002).
9. Wilder Penfield, *The Mystery of the Mind* (Princeton: Princeton Univ. Press, 1975), xiii.
10. Lee Edward Travis, "Response," in Arthur C. Custance, *The Mysterious Matter of Mind* (Grand Rapids, Mich.: Zondervan; and Richardson, Texas: Probe Ministries, 1980), 95–96.
11. Wilder Penfield, *The Mystery of the Mind*, 79.
12. Ibid., 85.
13. *The British Medical Journal* (March 15, 1952), quoted in Arthur C. Custance, *The Mysterious Matter of Mind*, 51.
14. Karl R. Popper and John C. Eccles, *The Self and Its Brain* (New York: Springer-Verlag, 1977), 558.
15. Ibid., 559–60.

16. John Calvin, *Institutes of the Christian Religion*, 1536, quoted in J. P. Moreland, *Scaling the Secular City* (Grand Rapids, Mich.: Baker, 1987), 77.

17. There are two major species of dualism: substance dualism and property/event dualism. For a brief description of the distinctions between the two, see Gary R. Habermas and J. P. Moreland, *Beyond Death* (Wheaton: Crossway, 1998), 37–66. For purposes of this chapter, the term "dualism" refers to substance dualism.

18. "What Is Consciousness?" on the television program *Closer to Truth*, first aired June 2000.

19. See: S. Parnia, D.G. Waller, R. Yeates, and P. Fenwick, "A Qualitative and Quantitative Study of the Incidence, Features and Aetiology of Near-Death Experience in Cardiac Arrest Survivors," *Resuscitation* (February 2001).

20. Sarah Tippit, "Scientist Says Mind Continues After Brain Dies," *Reuters* (June 29, 2001).

21. Sam Parnia, "Near Death Experiences in Cardiac Arrest and the Mystery of Consciousness," available at *www.datadiwan.de/SciMedNet/library/articlesN75+/N76Parnia_nde.htm* (accessed June 13, 2003).

22. Ibid.

23. Sarah Tippit, "Scientist Says Mind Continues After Brain Dies."

24. For a discussion, see Gary R. Habermas and J. P. Moreland, *Beyond Death*, 155–218, and Patrick Glynn, *God: The Evidence* (Rocklin, Calif.: Forum, 1997), 99–137.

25. "What Is Consciousness?" on *Closer to Truth*.

26. Antonio R. Damasio, "How the Brain Creates the Mind," *Scientific American* (December 1999).

27. John C. Eccles, *The Human Mystery* (New York: Springer-Verlag, 1979), vii, quoted in: Robert M. Augros and George N. Stanciu, *The New Story of Science*, 171.

28. "Do Brains Make Minds?" on *Closer to Truth*.

29. Arthur C. Custance, *The Mysterious Matter of Mind*, 90.

30. See: James 2:26 and Luke 8:55.

31. For example see: Matthew 26:41; Romans 8:10; 1 Corinthians 5:5, 6:20, 7:34; 2 Corinthians 7:1; and Galatians 5:17.

32. See: Genesis 2:27. Quotation from: Arthur C. Custance, *The Mysterious Matter of Mind*, 93 (italics removed).

33. See: "The Circumstantial Evidence" in: Lee Strobel, *The Case for Christ*, 244–57, and "Objection #6: A Loving God Would Never Torture People in Hell," in: Lee Strobel, *The Case for Faith*, 169–94.

34. Justice Potter Stewart (concurring), Jacobellis v. Ohio, 378 U.S. 198 (1964).

35. J. R. Smythies, "Some Aspects of Consciousness," in Arthur Koestler and J. R. Smythies, editors, *Beyond Reductionism* (London: Hutchinson, 1969), 235, quoted in Arthur C. Custance, *The Mysterious Matter of Mind*, 35.

36. Luke 23:43: "Today you will be with me in paradise."

37. Matthew 10:28.

38. 2 Corinthians 5:8.

39. Jaegwon Kim, "Lonely Souls: Causality and Substance Dualism," in Kevin Corcoran, editor, *Soul, Body, and Survival* (Ithica, NY: Cornell Univ. Press, 2001), 30.

40. Francis Crick, *The Astonishing Hypothesis* (New York: Scribner's, 1994), 3.

41. "What Is Consciousness?" on *Closer to Truth*.

42. "Do Brains Make Minds?" on *Closer to Truth*.

43. Cited in David Winter, *Hereafter: What Happens after Death?* (Wheaton, Ill.: Harold Shaw, 1972), 33–34.

44. For a short description of the evidence for the Resurrection, see Gary R. Habermas and J. P. Moreland, *Beyond Death*, 111–54.

45. See: Wilder Penfield, *The Mystery of the Mind*, 76–77.

46. Wilder Penfield, "Control of the Mind" Symposium at the University of California Medical Center, San Francisco, 1961, quoted in Arthur Koestler, *Ghost in the Machine* (London: Hutchinson, 1967), 203.

47. Wilder Penfield, *The Mystery of the Mind*, 77–78.

48. See: Roger W. Sperry, "Changed Concepts of Brain and Consciousness: Some Value Implications," *Zygon* (March 1985).

49. Laurence W. Wood, "Recent Brain Research and the Mind-Body Dilemma," *The Asbury Theological Journal*, vol. 41, no. 1 (1986).

50. Ibid.

51. Mark Water, compiler, *The New Encyclopedia of Christian Quotations* (Grand Rapids, Mich.: Baker, 2000), 972. Teresa's reference to mansions is an allusion to John 14:2.

52. Quoted in Robert W. Augros and George N. Stanciu, *The New Story of Science*, 170.

53. See: Thomas Nagel, "What Is It Like to Be a Bat?" *Philosophical Review* 83 (October, 1974).

54. For example, see Genesis 1:30; Leviticus 24:18; Ecclesiastes 3:19; and Revelation 8:9.

55. J. B. S. Haldane, "When I am Dead," in *Possible Worlds and Other Essays* (London: Chatto and Winduw, 1927), 209, quoted in C. S. Lewis, *Miracles* (London: Fontana, 1947), 19.

56. For a further critique of "neurotheology," the idea that the brain is wired for religious experiences, see: Kenneth L. Woodward, "Faith Is More Than a Feeling," *Newsweek* (May 7, 2001).

57. Quoted in Larry Witham, *By Design*, 211.
58. Ibid., 192.
59. Stuart C. Hackett, *The Reconstruction of the Christian Revelation Claim* (Grand Rapids, Mich.: Baker, 1984), 111.
60. Ibid.
61. Robert W. Augros and George N. Stanciu, *The New Story of Science*, 168, 171.

Chapter 11: The Cumulative Case for a Creator

1. Quoted in Cal Thomas, "Gone Bananas," *World* (September 7, 2002).
2. John M. Templeton, *The Humble Approach*, 115.
3. See: Lee Strobel, *Reckless Homicide: Ford's Pinto Trial* (Sound Bend, Ind.: And Books, 1980).
4. Jonathan Wells, *Icons of Evolution*, 5.
5. Klaus Dose, "The Origin of Life: More Questions than Answers," *Interdisciplinary Science Review* 13 (1998).
6. Robert Roy Britt, "The Year's Top Ten Space Mysteries," available at *www.msnbc.com/news/851919.asp?vts=122820022235* (accessed December 28, 2002).
7. Michael Denton, *Evolution: A Theory in Crisis*, 358.
8. Ibid., 162.
9. Roger Lewin, "Evolutionary Theory Under Fire," *Science* 210 (November 1980).
10. John Polkinghorne, *Quarks, Chaos, and Christianity* (New York: Crossroad, 1994), 25.
11. Psalm 102:25
12. Deuteronomy 4:35
13. Psalm 90:2
14. John 4:24
15. Genesis 17:1. According to theologian Millard J. Erickson, "God is personal. He is an individual being, with self-consciousness and will, capable of feeling, choosing, and having a reciprocal relationship with other personal and social beings." Millard J. Erickson, *Christian Theology* (Grand Rapids, Mich.: Baker, 1985), 269.
16. Genesis 1:3
17. Psalm 104:24
18. Nahum 1:3
19. Psalm 139:13–14
20. Psalm 33:5
21. 1 Kings 8:27
22. Colossians 1:16 (*The Message*)
23. Isaiah 25:8
24. Romans 1:20

25. Michael Shermer, *How We Believe*, 123.
26. Alister McGrath, *Glimpsing the Face of God*, 22.
27. Gregg Easterbrook, "The New Convergence," *Wired* (December 2002).
28. Quoted in John Polkinghorne, *Quarks, Chaos and Christianity*, 35.
29. See: Candace Adams, "Leading Nanoscientist Builds Big Faith," *Baptist Standard* (March 15, 2002).
30. Quoted in Margaret Wertheim, "The Pope's Astrophysicist," *Wired* (December 2002).
31. John Polkinghorne, *Quarks, Chaos, and Christianity*, 98–100.
32. Ibid., 13.
33. Alister McGrath, *Glimpsing the Face of God*, 44.
34. See: American Scientific Affiliation, *Modern Science and Christian Faith* (Wheaton, Ill.: Van Kampen, 1948).
35. Viggo Olsen, *The Agnostic Who Dared to Search* (Chicago: Moody, 1974). His other books are *Daktar* and *Daktar II*, both published by Moody.
36. God said in Jeremiah 29:13: "You will seek me and find me when you seek me with all your heart."
37. Alister McGrath, *Glimpsing the Face of God*, 51, 53.

ACKNOWLEDGMENTS

I'm glad you paused to read this page, because I want to tell you about my deep appreciation for several people whose assistance was invaluable in producing this book.

Special gratitude goes to Mark Mittelberg, my ministry partner for more than fifteen years, whose guidance and friendship mean the world to me. My thanks also go to his wife, Heidi, and their children, Matthew and Emma Jean, for their faithful support and prayers.

The team at Zondervan has been terrific. My editor, John Sloan, is the one whose insights originally put me on the right track in writing my *Case* books. Bruce Ryskamp, Scott Bolinder, Stan Gundry, Lyn Cryderman, John Topliff, Greg Stielstra, John Raymond, Dave Lambert, Bob Hudson, and the rest of the Zondervan team are simply the best partners I could ever imagine.

Thanks also to Jane Vogel for co-laboring on the student edition; Marion Stilley for her excellent work as my assistant; Bob and Gretchen Passantino for their suggestions; Bill Hybels, Jim Mellado, and the Willow Creek Association for their partnership; Bill Dallas, Jay Mitchell, and the team at Church Communication Network for their support; Scott and Susan Evans, Doug Martinez, and the staff at Outreach, Inc., for their friendship; Brad Dennison for first exposing me to helpful resources on science issues; and Bill and Kathy Butterworth, Karl and Barbara Singer, Doug and Fay Slaybaugh, Rick and Kay Warren, Paul Braoudakis, Bob Gordon, Beverly Nelson, Brad Mitchell, Brad Johnson, Hank Hanegraaff, and Paul Young for their kindness and encouragement.

And this book would never have become a reality without the prayers and support of my wife, Leslie, my son, Kyle, and my daughter and her husband, Alison and Daniel Morrow, all of whom I love and cherish.

INDEX

ABOUT THE AUTHOR

Lee Strobel, who holds a Master of Studies in Law degree from Yale Law School, as well as a journalism degree from the University of Missouri, is the former legal affairs editor of the *Chicago Tribune*. His awards include Illinois's highest honors for both investigative reporting and public service journalism from United Press International.

His journey from atheism to faith has been documented in the Gold Medallion–winning books *The Case for Christ* and *The Case for Faith*. His other best-sellers include *Inside the Mind of Unchurched Harry and Mary*, which also won a Gold Medallion; *Surviving a Spiritual Mismatch in Marriage*, which he coauthored with his wife, Leslie; *God's Outrageous Claims*; and *What Jesus Would Say*, all published by Zondervan. His book *Reckless Homicide* has been used as a supplementary text at several law schools.

Lee has been a teaching pastor at two of America's largest churches: Willow Creek Community Church in suburban Chicago and Saddleback Valley Community Church in Orange County, California. He is a contributing editor and columnist for *Outreach* magazine and formerly taught First Amendment Law at Roosevelt University.

Lee and Leslie, who have been married for more than thirty years, reside in Southern California. Their daughter, Alison, is a teacher and novelist; their son, Kyle, received his master's degree in philosophy of religion and is pursuing a second master's degree in New Testament studies.

The Case for Christ

*A Journalist's Personal
Investigation of the
Evidence for Jesus*

Is Jesus really the divine Son of God? What reason is there to believe that he is?

In his bestseller *The Case for Christ*, the legally trained investigative reporter Lee Strobel examined the claims of Christ by retracing his own spiritual journey, reaching the hard-won yet satisfying verdict that Jesus is God's unique son.

Written in the style of a blockbuster investigative report, *The Case for Christ* consults a dozen authorities on Jesus with doctorates from Cambridge, Princeton, Brandeis, and other top-flight institutions to present:

- Historical evidence
- Psychiatric evidence
- Other evidence
- Scientific evidence
- Fingerprint evidence

This colorful, hard-hitting book is no novel. It's a riveting quest for the truth about history's most compelling figure.

"Lee Strobel asks the questions a tough-minded skeptic would ask. Every inquirer should have it."
—*Phillip E. Johnson, law professor,
University of California at Berkeley*

Hardcover 0-310-22646-5
Softcover 0-310-20930-7
Evangelism Pack 0-310-22605-8
Mass Market 6-pack 0-310-22627-9
Audio Pages® Abridged Cassette 0-310-24824-8
Audio Pages® Unabridged Cassette 0-310-21960-4
Audio Pages® Unabridged CD 0-310-24779-9

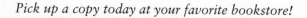

Pick up a copy today at your favorite bookstore!

The Case for Faith

A Journalist Investigates the Toughest Objections to Christianity

In his best-seller *The Case for Christ*, Lee Strobel examined the claims of Christ, reaching the hard-won yet satisfying verdict that Jesus is God's unique son.

But despite the compelling historical evidence that Strobel presented, many grapple with doubts or serious concerns about faith in God. As in a court of law, they want to shout, "Objection!" They say, "If God is love, then what about all of the suffering that festers in our world?" Or, "If Jesus is the door to heaven, then what about the millions who have never heard of him?"

In *The Case for Faith*, Strobel turns his tenacious investigative skills to the most persistent emotional objections to belief, the eight "heart" barriers to faith. *The Case for Faith* is for those who may be feeling attracted toward Jesus, but who are faced with formidable intellectual barriers standing squarely in their path. For Christians, it will deepen their convictions and give them fresh confidence in discussing Christianity with even their most skeptical friends.

Hardcover 0-310-22015-7
Softcover 0-310-23469-7
Evangelism Pack 0-310-23508-1
Mass Market 6-pack 0-310-23509X
Audio Pages® Abridged Cassettes 0-310-23475-1

Pick up a copy today at your favorite bookstore!

ZONDERVAN™

GRAND RAPIDS, MICHIGAN 49530 USA

WWW.ZONDERVAN.COM

The Case for Christ—Student Edition

Lee Strobel with Jane Vogel

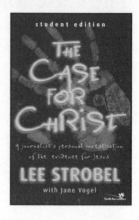

There's little question that he actually lived. But miracles? Rising from the dead? Some of the stories you hear about him sound like just that—stories. A reasonable person would never believe them, let alone the claim that he's the only way to God!

But a reasonable person would also make sure that he or she understood the facts before jumping to conclusions. That's why Lee Strobel—an award-winning legal journalist with a knack for asking tough questions—decided to investigate Jesus for himself. An atheist, Strobel felt certain his findings would bring Christianity's claims about Jesus tumbling down like a house of cards.

He was in for the surprise of his life. Join him as he retraces his journey from skepticism to faith. You'll consult expert testimony as you sift through the truths that history, science, psychiatry, literature, and religion reveal. Like Strobel, you'll be amazed at the evidence—how much there is, how strong it is, and what it says.

The facts are in. What will your verdict be in *The Case for Christ*?

Softcover 0-310-23484-0
Padded Hardcover Edition 0-310-24608-3

Pick up a copy today at your favorite bookstore!

ZONDERVAN™

GRAND RAPIDS, MICHIGAN 49530 USA

WWW.ZONDERVAN.COM

The Case for Faith— Student Edition

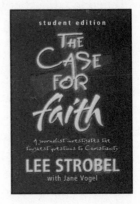

Lee Strobel with Jane Vogel

Despite the compelling historical evidence that Strobel presented in *The Case for Christ—Student Edition*, many people grapple with serious concerns about faith in God. As in a court of law, they want to shout, "Objection!" They say, "If there is a loving God, why is the world so full of suffering and evil?" Or, "If God really created the universe, why are so many scientists convinced that only evolutionary theory explains the origins of life?" Or, "If God really cares about the people he created, how could he consign so many of them to an eternity in hell?"

In *The Case for Faith—Student Edition*, Strobel turns his tenacious investigative skills to the most persistent emotional objections to belief—the eight "heart" barriers to faith. *The Case for Faith—Student Edition* is for those who may be feeling attracted to Jesus but who are faced with intellectual barriers standing squarely in their path. For Christians, it will deepen their convictions and give them fresh confidence in discussing Christianity with even their most skeptical friends.

Softcover 0-310-24188-X

Pick up a copy today at your favorite bookstore!

Surviving a Spiritual Mismatch in Marriage

Lee Strobel and Leslie Strobel

Someone came between Lee and Leslie Strobel, threatening to shipwreck their marriage. No, it wasn't an old flame. It was Jesus Christ.

Leslie's decision to become a follower of Jesus brought heated opposition from her skeptical husband. They began to experience conflict over a variety of issues, from finances to child-rearing. But over time, Leslie learned how to survive a spiritual mismatch. Today they're both Christians—and they want you to know that there is hope if you're a Christian married to a nonbeliever. In their intensely personal and practical book, they reveal:

- Surprising insights into the thinking of non-Christian spouses
- A dozen steps toward making the most of your mismatched marriage
- Eight principles for reaching out to your partner with the gospel
- Advice for raising your children in a spiritually mismatched home
- How to pray for your spouse—plus a thirty-day guide to get you started
- What to do if you're both Christians but one lags behind spiritually
- Advice for single Christians to avoid the pain of a mismatch

Softcover: 0-310-22014-9
Abridged Audio Pages® Cassette: 0-310-22975-8

Pick up a copy today at your favorite bookstore!

GRAND RAPIDS, MICHIGAN 49530 USA

WWW.ZONDERVAN.COM

Inside the Mind of Unchurched Harry and Mary

How to Reach Friends and Family Who Avoid God and the Church

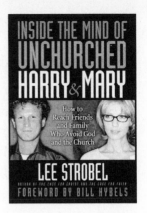

Who are unchurched Harry and Mary? He or she could be the neighbor who is perfectly happy without God. Or the co-worker who scoffs at Christianity. Or the supervisor who uses Jesus' name only as profanity. Or the family member who can't understand why religion is so important.

Inside the Mind of Unchurched Harry and Mary isn't a book of theory. It's an action plan to help Christians relate the message of Christ to the people they work around, live with, and call their friends. Using personal experiences, humor, compelling stories, biblical illustrations, and the latest research, Lee Strobel helps Christians understand unbelievers and what motivates them.

The book includes:

- 15 key insights into why people steer clear of God and the church
- A look at Christianity and its message through the eyes of a former atheist
- Practical, inspirational strategies for building relationships with unbelievers
- Firsthand advice on surviving marriage to an unbelieving spouse.

Softcover 0-310-37561-4

Pick up a copy today at your favorite bookstore!

GRAND RAPIDS, MICHIGAN 49530 USA

WWW.ZONDERVAN.COM

What Jesus Would Say

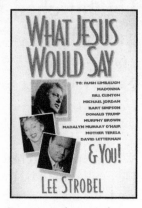

*To: Rush Limbaugh, Madonna,
Bill Clinton, Michael Jordan,
Bart Simpson, Donald Trump,
Murphy Brown, Madalyn Mur-
phy O'Hair, Mother Teresa,
David Letterman, & You!*

In *What Jesus Would Say*, Lee Strobel
helps us to see well-known personalities as Jesus might see them.
Through these people, Strobel introduces us to the God of hope,
the God of the second chance.

What Jesus Would Say takes on topics such as success, sexu-
ality, skepticism, forgiveness, prayer, and leadership with firm,
biblically based concepts. In his often surprising look into the
lives of famous people, Strobel shares encouraging and inspiring
ideas that apply to our own lives as well.

What would Jesus say to today's headline-makers ... and to
you?

Softcover 0-310-48511-8

Pick up a copy today at your favorite bookstore!

ZONDERVAN™

GRAND RAPIDS, MICHIGAN 49530 USA

WWW.ZONDERVAN.COM

WILLOW
Willow Creek Association

Willow Creek Association
Vision, Training, Resources for Prevailing Churches

This resource was created to serve you and to help you in building a local church that prevails
    Since 1992, the Willow Creek Association (WCA) has been linking like-minded, action-oriented churches with each other and with strategic vision, training, and resources. Now a worldwide network of over 6,400 churches from more than ninety denominations, the WCA works to equip Member Churches and others with the tools needed to build prevailing churches. Our desire is to inspire, equip, and encourage Christian leaders to build biblically functioning churches that reach increasing numbers of unchurched people, not just with innovations from Willow Creek Community Church in South Barrington, Illinois, but from any church in the world that has experienced God-given breakthroughs.

WILLOW CREEK CONFERENCES
Each year, thousands of local church leaders, staff and volunteers—from WCA Member Churches and others—attend one of our conferences or training events. Conferences offered on the Willow Creek campus in South Barrington, Illinois, include:

Prevailing Church Conference: Foundational training for staff and volunteers working to build a prevailing local church.

Prevailing Church Workshops: More than fifty strategic, day-long workshops covering seven topic areas that represent key characteristics of a prevailing church; offered twice each year.

Promiseland Conference: Children's ministries; infant through fifth grade.

Student Ministries Conference: Junior and senior high ministries.

Willow Creek Arts Conference: Vision and training for Christian artists using their gifts in the ministries of local churches.

Leadership Summit: Envisioning and equipping Christians with leadership gifts and responsibilities; broadcast live via satellite to eighteen cities across North America.

Contagious Evangelism Conference: Encouragement and training for churches and church leaders who want to be strategic in reaching lost people for Christ.

Small Groups Conference: Exploring how developing a church *of* small groups can play a vital role in developing authentic Christian community that leads to spiritual transformation.

To find out more about WCA conferences, visit our website at www.willowcreek.com.

PREVAILING CHURCH REGIONAL WORKSHOPS
Each year the WCA team leads several, two-day training events in select cities across the United States. Some twenty day-long workshops are offered in topic areas including leadership, next-